The Psychology of Helping and Altruism

Problems and Puzzles

McGraw-Hill Series in Social Psychology

CONSULTING EDITOR

Philip G. Zimbardo

Leonard Berkowitz: *Aggression: Its Causes, Consequences, and Control*

Gary G. Brannigan and Matthew R. Merrens: *The Social Psychologists: Research Adventures*

Sharon S. Brehm: *Intimate Relationships*

Susan T. Fiske and Shelley E. Taylor: *Social Cognition*

Stanley Milgram: *The Individual in a Social World*

David G. Myers: *Exploring Social Psychology*

Ayala Pines and Christina Maslach: *Experiencing Social Psychology: Readings and Projects*

Scott Plous: *The Psychology of Judgment and Decision Making*

Lee Ross and Richard E. Nisbett: *The Person and the Situation: Perspectives of Social Psychology*

Jeffrey Z. Rubin, Dean G. Pruitt, and Sung Hee Kim: *Social Conflict: Escalation, Stalemate, and Settlement*

David A. Schroeder, Louis A. Penner, John F. Dovidio, and Jane A. Piliavin: *The Psychology of Helping and Altruism: Problems and Puzzles*

Harry C. Triandis: *Culture and Social Behavior*

Philip G. Zimbardo and Michael R. Leippe: *The Psychology of Attitude Change and Social Influence*

The Psychology of Helping and Altruism

Problems and Puzzles

❖

David A. Schroeder
University of Arkansas

Louis A. Penner
University of South Florida

John F. Dovidio
Colgate University

Jane A. Piliavin
University of Wisconsin

McGraw-Hill, Inc.

New York   St. Louis   San Francisco   Auckland   Bogotá   Caracas
Lisbon   London   Madrid   Mexico City   Milan   Montreal   New Delhi
San Juan   Singapore   Sydney   Tokyo   Toronto

The Psychology of Helping and Altruism
Problems and Puzzles

 This book is printed on recycled, acid-free paper containing 10% postconsumer waste.

1 2 3 4 5 6 7 8 9 0   DOC   DOC   9 0 9 8 7 6 5 4

ISBN 0-07-055611-3

This book was set in Palatino by Better Graphics, Inc.
The editors were Jane Vaicunas, Laura Lynch, and David Dunham;
the production supervisor was Leroy A. Young.
The cover was designed by Carla Bauer.
R. R. Donnelley & Sons Company was printer and binder.

Cover Painting

Artist:	Diego Rivera
Title:	*The Flower Carrier*, 1936
Medium:	oil and tempera on masonite
Size:	48 × 47 3/4" (121.9 × 121.3 cm)
Credit:	San Francisco Museum of Modern Art
	Albert M. Bender Collection
	Gift of Albert M. Bender in memory of Caroline Walter

Library of Congress Cataloging-in-Publication Data

The psychology of helping and altruism: problems and puzzles / David
   A. Schroeder . . . [et al.].
     p.   cm.
   Includes bibliographical references and indexes.
   ISBN 0-07-055611-3
    1. Altruism.   2. Helping behavior.   I. Schroeder, David A.
BF637.H4P88   1995
158' .3—dc20   94-23437

About the Authors

—————— ❖ ——————

DAVID A. SCHROEDER is Professor of Psychology in the Department of Psychology at the University of Arkansas, where he joined the faculty in 1976; he has served as the Chair of the Department for the past eight years. He received his B.S. in Psychology from Purdue University and his Ph.D. in Social Psychology from Arizona State University. He is the author of numerous professional articles and presentations concerning such diverse topics as attribution processes, social influence techniques, alcoholism, the motivation of helping, and social dilemmas; he is editor of the forthcoming book, *Social Dilemmas: Perspectives on Individuals and Groups*.

LOUIS A. PENNER is Professor of Psychology at the University of South Florida; he was Chair of the Department for seven years. He received his Ph.D. in Social Psychology from Michigan State University. He has served on the editorial boards of the *Journal of Social and Clinical Psychology*, *Contemporary Psychology*, and the *Review of Personality and Social Psychology* and as a member of the Committee on Accreditation of the American Psychological Association. He is the author or coauthor of over fifty scientific publications and seventy-five presentations at professional meetings. He has written or edited five books, the most recent being *The Challenge in Mathematics and Science Education: Psychology's Response* (with G. Batsche, H. Knoff, and D. Nelson).

JOHN F. DOVIDIO is Professor of Psychology at Colgate University. He has been at Colgate since 1977, where he has chaired the Department and served as the Director of Natural Sciences and Mathematics. He received his B.A. from Dartmouth College, and his M.A. and Ph.D. in Psychology from the University of Delaware. He has authored numerous books, chapters, articles, and technical reports on helping and altruism, as well as on contemporary forms of racism. In 1985, he shared the American Psychological Association's Gordon Allport Prize with S. L. Gaertner for their work on aversive racism—racism among the well-intentioned. He is currently serving as Editor of the *Personality and Social Psychology Bulletin*.

JANE A. PILIAVIN is Professor and Chair of the Sociology Department at the University of Wisconsin, Madison. She received her Ph.D. in Psychology from Stanford University in 1962, working with Leon Festinger. Although she has done work on prejudice, attitude change, gender roles, and delinquency, her primary research interest since the late 1960s has been altruism and helping behavior. In addition to many journal articles, she is coauthor of two previous books in this area: *Emergency Intervention* (with J. F. Dovidio, S. L. Gaertner, and R. D. Clark, III) and *Giving Blood: The Development of an Altruistic Identity* (with P. L. Callero). Her current research involves comparisons of different forms of helping (e.g., giving blood, time, and money), cross-cultural comparisons, international helping behavior, and helping and well-being, with a major focus on identities and commitment.

In Memory of—

ARTHUR J. SCHROEDER

ROSE PENNER

JOHN G. DOVIDIO

MARY ELIZABETH ALLYN

HORACE WARREN ALLYN

—who helped teach us how to care about others

Contents

FOREWORD   xi

PREFACE   xv

1   *AN INTRODUCTION TO HELPING AND ALTRUISM*   1

2   *THE CONTEXT: WHEN WILL PEOPLE HELP?*   25

3   *WHY DO PEOPLE HELP? MOTIVES FOR HELPING*   59

4   *THE ORIGINS OF HELPING AND ALTRUISM: ARE WE "COMPASSIONATE BEASTS"?*   91

5   *THE DEVELOPMENT OF ALTRUISM AND HELPING: YOU'RE NOT (ONLY) GETTING OLDER; YOU'RE (ALSO) GETTING BETTER*   126

6   *AND NOW FOR SOMETHING A LITTLE DIFFERENT: WHO HELPS AND WHY?*   157

7   *HELP WANTED? HELP SEEKING: ACTIONS AND REACTIONS*   184

8   *COOPERATION AND COLLECTIVE HELPING*   219

9   *LOOKING BACKWARD, LOOKING AHEAD*   252

BIBLIOGRAPHY   289

INDEXES

   Author Index   323

   Subject Index   331

Foreword

———————— ❖ ————————

The colloquium is about to start. I'm going to get a seat up front because I am already so tired from a long day's teaching that I might fall obviously asleep if I don't sit where I will feel social pressure to stay awake during this lecture. This room is awfully hot and stuffy, with the windows closed and blinds drawn so we can view the overheads and slides. Wow, notice that cool Harris tweed jacket on the speaker, reminds me of Ivy League faculty back in my Yale days, but in this weather it will be more like a furnace around him. Too bad I'm not that interested in the topic, and he is talking so fast, and his overheads are impossible to read even from my front aisle seat. Drifting off, head nodding, I'm trying to stay awake. It is getting near the end, hang on, there will be refreshments in the lounge. Just then a colleague interrupts to pose a difficult question. The speaker is flustered, regains composure, starts out saying, "That's an interesting question, but the data we are now getting do not support your position . . . [I'm feeling sick] . . . but we can discuss it later, if you wish, I have only about five minutes more and I'd like to finish up."

Wow! Wake up call! "Feeling sick?" Did he say that, or did I imagine it? No one else seems to have heard it, or if they did, they are not reacting to it in any way that I can discern. His rapid delivery is slowing down to a normal rpm. Hmm, could that be a sign that I heard him correctly, that his internal monologue slipped past the censor? Total attention now on his every word and gesture. Foolish me, he meant the question is making him feel sick, a metaphor for not liking the taste of it. Good, nothing to worry about, a few minutes more and he is done, get a cold drink and the world is refreshed.

Oh, oh! He seems to be paler. No one is sitting in the first row in front of the small stage. Suppose he fainted? No way, in thirty years of colloquiums, no one has ever fainted, so let's go with the base rate. But just in case, why don't I quietly move up to the front row (trying to be inconspicuous is not easy with my bulky frame). Yes, clearly slowing down—perhaps to emphasize his final points, or is he just running out of steam? Maybe he needs to sit down, get a drink, and then finish his talk. But how

can I tell him that without interrupting his finale, especially if I am reading the situation wrong—and then everyone will think I am a fool? But
suppose I am right and he passes out before finishing, and falls off the
stage? I will know that I could have prevented his accident and did not.
More of his slow words, more of my thoughts about how to solve this
decision dilemma, more words, but no action yet. OK, it's a GO if I get one
more clear signal, then I will intervene—for better or for worse. There it
is, he is perspiring, and look, his pants legs are getting wet from the
sweat! Someone has to help him now no matter what the consequences.
Who should? You should, of course. Yes, go now, take the risk.

I stand up in front of the speaker, put my arms up toward him; he
looks down at me in total confusion. Imagine what my students and colleagues are thinking of this bizarre behavior as I continue to put my arms
around him. The speaker goes limp, unconscious, falls dead weight on
me; we crash back into the first row seats. Guess I was right. Much help
all around, medics called. He comes to, insists upon finishing the final
point in his presentation (that is true dedication to science), staggers back
up on the stage. Stands erect, says he is sorry for the interruption. And
then he collapses once more into my waiting arms.

As he was being taken to the hospital for diagnosis and overnight
observation and care, we all gave him ample applause for having almost
finished under somewhat extraordinary circumstances. It turned out to be
nothing serious, a combination of the onset of flu, being up late taking
care of a sick child, the heat of the room, and anxiety about this critical
audience. He was back in action the next day as if nothing had happened.

Since this experience took place last year at Stanford University, I
have thought much about what had happened to me and about the deep
psychological complexity of bystander intervention. I had never considered the simultaneous equations that must be solved by the bystander,
often riddled with ambiguity and complex cost/benefit analyses that
must be solved in a moment's time. Of course, I am well acquainted with
the pioneering research on bystander intervention by my friends John
Darley and Bibb Latané, but somehow my personal experience had
aspects that were not captured in their model of individual and group
response to emergent demands to act or to internal pressures not to act.
Just then, a proposal appeared for a book in our McGraw-Hill Series in
Social Psychology which would take a new look at the nature of prosocial
behavior. Four active researchers were going to put their heads together
to organize the body of knowledge in the broad field of helping and altruistic behavior, integrate what needed to be made more coherent, analyze
divergent findings and curious results into a systematic framework that
allowed for new theory to be developed and practical answers to be given
to questions about the nature of this vital human activity. Perfect timing,
for me, and now that this labor of love is completed, perfect timing for the
field of social psychology.

My initial skepticism about the likely coherence of a four-authored text was dispelled as soon as this special team began working closely together and generating material that was more than the sum of its parts. Each of these social psychologists brought to the study of prosocial behavior a special vision, a slightly different research style, and an alternate perspective on the theoretical dynamics of helping and altruism. Through openly sharing their communalities and differences, and playing each individual contribution through the ensemble evaluation and refinements of the others, this unique quartet has given us the definitive reading on prosocial behavior.

This gifted team of authors—David Schroeder, Louis Penner, John Dovidio, and Jane Piliavin—has gone well beyond summarizing the available facts and views on the various dimensions of prosocial behavior; they have given us the integrative theoretical score that helps make sense of, and give a new rhythm to, the lyrics. In understanding the nature of prosocial behavior, we come to see the interplay between fundamental themes in psychology, how genetic and personality predispositions are modified by learning and experience, how affect and cognition interact to shape responding potentials, how self-interest and concerns for the well being of others get sorted out in given helping settings. We also become more aware of the differing psychological variables that influence the reciprocal relationship between help seeking and help giving. And finally, in a clear, fluid writing style, the authors provide a theoretical integration that fits together the many pieces of the puzzle of who helps, when, why, and with what effects. In doing so, this author team makes a valuable contribution to psychological knowledge that has significant relevance for the betterment of our daily lives.

The *McGraw-Hill Series in Social Psychology* has been designed as a celebration of the fundamental contributions being made by researchers, theorists, and practitioners of social psychology to our understanding of human nature and to the potential for enriching the quality of our lives through wise applications of their knowledge. It has become a showcase for presenting new theories, original syntheses, analyses, and current methodologies by distinguished scholars and promising young writer-researchers. Our authors reveal a common commitment to sharing their vision with a broad audience—starting with their colleagues, but extending out to graduate students and especially to undergraduates interested in social psychology. Some of our titles, like this one on prosocial behavior, convey ideas that are of sufficient general interest that their messages need to be carried out into the world of practical application for translation into social action and public policy. Although each text in our series is created to stand alone as the best representative of its area of scholarship, taken as a whole they represent the core of social psychology. Some teachers may elect to use any of them as in-depth supplements to a basic, general textbook, but others may choose to organize their course entirely around a set of these monographs. All our authors have been guided by the objective of conveying the essential lessons and principles of their area of expertise in an interesting style that informs without resorting to technical jargon. A related goal has been to write in ways that inspire others to utilize these ideas constructively—for some, to extend them conceptually, for others, to apply them practically.

We are at a critical crossroad in our civilization, a time when the world desperately needs to replace its exploding hostility with helping, its pervasive indifference or insensitivity to violence with altruism. Anarchy and chaos are at the doorsteps of many poorer nations, while crime and violence tear at the fabric of human relationships in our own country. These social evils have multiple causes that need to be understood at many different levels of analysis. But the bottom line of defense against them is the creation of a sense of civility within a caring community. That lofty goal is not easily accomplished when our sons are engaged in "Mortal Kombat" or "Total Carnage" video games and national leaders teach citizens that real war is also an acceptable means for resolving conflicts with the "enemy." It is my hope that *The Psychology of Helping and Altruism* will serve as a beacon of wisdom for those young people who want to make a difference in how their world functions. It is essential that reading its vital messages makes us all the more mindful of why we do not intervene when we could and should, and how we can resist the pressures to act in self-interest or in disinterest. If we can, then we will reach out more readily to those in need of our help, giving it willingly, not as an heroic deed, but simply because that is what the social contract calls for. In doing unto others, we create the interactional context in which they may be more likely to do for us—when that time comes that we need to be helped.

Philip G. Zimbardo
Consulting Editor

Preface

❖

Although we began work on this book in 1991, its true origin can be traced back to the mid-1960s. At that time helping or prosocial behavior was not a particularly hot topic among social psychologists. But a single event changed that. A young woman, Kitty Genovese, was attacked and murdered in New York City while thirty-eight of her neighbors watched from their apartment windows. This horrifying event led some social psychologists (most notably Bibb Latané and John Darley) to examine the causes of the bystanders' inaction. And a few years later, the first articles on bystander intervention in emergencies began to appear. Interest in bystander intervention spread rapidly among social psychologists and social scientists in a number of related areas, and the research floodgates were opened. In the last thirty years, well over 1500 articles on the topic of helping and altruism have appeared in scientific and professional journals.

The 1960s were significant personally as well. Chronologically, philosophically, or professionally, the authors of this book are all in some ways "children of the 60s" and the political activism and idealism that flourished at the time. In the 1960s, Jane Piliavin had already embarked on her academic career. But it was during this time that she began a career-long program of research on prosocial behavior, including long-term prosocial actions such as blood donations. The other authors were students in the 1960s who read the early research on helping and were excited by it. Of course, being independent-minded psychologists, we approached the topic of helping and altruism from different directions. Lou Penner studied prosocial behavior from an individual-difference perspective, asking questions about what personal characteristics differentiate helpers from nonhelpers; Jack Dovidio conducted research on prosocial behavior, at least in part, because it provided a means to study racial and ethnic prejudice; and David Schroeder studied how to make individuals and members of groups more cooperative and helpful even when it might be to their immediate benefit to be selfish. We did not know one another and were literally spread from coast to coast. Despite these differences and distances, all of us shared one very important thing in common. We all saw studying helping and other prosocial actions as a way to combine our social interests and concerns with the research that we conducted. It was this common research interest that eventually brought us together, first as professional acquaintances, then as friends, and now as coauthors of this book.

The book is primarily intended for upper-level undergraduate classes and graduate courses in psychology, sociology, and related disciplines. This is not the only book on helping and altruism that is available to people interested in these topics. There are several edited volumes in which scholars in this area describe their own research work on a particular aspect of prosocial behavior. There are also some excellent books written on specific topics related to prosocial behavior, such as those on the characteristics of the Christians who rescued Jews from the Nazis and on the role of empathy in altruistic actions. The importance of these books to the understanding of prosocial behavior cannot be overstated. Indeed, we cite them extensively in this book. However, these books are often not accessible to students just becoming interested in helping behavior, and their focus may be too narrow for students who want a comprehensive overview of the theories and research concerned with why people offer (or do not offer) to help others. As a result, the sources most readily available to someone interested in learning about the general topic of helping and altruism are usually the brief descriptions that appear in introductory social psychology textbooks. Thus, our goal was to write a book that provides students with a comprehensive review of research literature on helping and altruism and gives the reader a sense of how individual studies fit into the big picture of prosocial behavior. We also hope to stimulate the next generation of students to study the causes and consequences of helping and altruism. We believe this is a very worthwhile goal, because helping and altruism are as important in the 1990s as they were in the 1960s.

It is uncommon for four people to coauthor a book. Indeed, if we had thought about why it is so uncommon before we began this effort, we probably would have never done it. Remarkably, because of the intensity of this endeavor, we are closer friends now than we were when we began writing the book. In addition to theoretical disputes and unprovoked assaults on one another's writing styles, our friendship had to endure the one thing that can turn academics who are close friends into bitter enemies—order of authorship. We resolved this issue with relatively few bruises, but it is important for those who read this book to know that all of the authors contributed roughly equivalent amounts to this project. The most accurate way to represent the authorship of this book would be to create a sign on the cover of the book that would change every three months like a billboard, so that at various times, each of us would be listed as first author. Unfortunately, McGraw-Hill lacks the equipment to do this. But readers should know the following facts: Without the fourth author, Jane, the first author, Dave, would have written a book with two fewer chapters and the remaining seven chapters would have been much poorer in quality; and the reasons why Lou rather than Jack is the second author are: (1) Jack is a nicer person than Lou, and (2) Lou is better at guessing the outcome of coin tosses that Jack.

ACKNOWLEDGMENTS

We have already alluded to the professional debt that we owe Bibb Latané for conducting the research that first made some of us interested in helping behavior. But Bibb has contributed more directly to this project by serving as the organizer and host of the First Nags Head Conference on Altruism and Prosocial Behavior. It was at that conference in 1982 that the four of us met for the first time and began our long personal friendships and professional associations that resulted in the decision to write this book. If we had not met at Nags Head, it is very unlikely that this book would have been written. Bibb has our sincere thanks and gratitude for providing us, and other social psychologists, with the kind of stimulating environment that fosters and promotes the formation of such associations.

In a project of this sort there are always many people who have contributed in a number of different ways. Although it may sound like a cliché, it really is hard to know where to start. We were helped immeasurably by students at each of our universities who did library research, read drafts of our chapters, and stimulated our thinking with their thoughtful and perceptive questions about what we had written. We thank the following students: Neleen Eisenger, Paula Guerra, Adaiah Howard, Stacy Taylor, and Ana Validzic (Colgate University); Linda Matthews, Molly Jensen, Vanessa Nehus-Huber, and Karen Stauffacher (University of Arkansas); and Barbara Fritzsche, Shanker Menon, Tamara Freifeld, and Shelia Rioux (University of South Florida). We are also grateful to Ann Parkhurst, Debra Linneman, and Kim Barnes for their administrative assistance. In addition, we express our appreciation to our friends and other colleagues who helped us locate needed articles, reviewed chapter drafts, and did as much as they could to prevent us from making embarrassing mistakes. (We hope they were successful. If errors do exist, it is probably because we were not paying attention.) Among these people are Peter Callero, Hong-Wen Charng, Jeff Stripling, Doug Behrend, Judith Becker, Eric Knowles, Mike Hoffman, Chris Hill, Rick Condon, and especially the late Roberta Simmons. We want to express our sincere appreciation for the preparation of the test bank by Mark Sibicky from Marietta College and the compilation of the indexes by Sydney Schultz. We are particularly indebted to Michael Cunningham, University of Louisville; Nancy Eisenberg, Arizona State University;

Jeffrey Fisher, University of Connecticut; and C. Daniel Batson, University of Kansas, for their careful reading of the entire manuscript, their insightful and challenging comments, and their constructive suggestions on earlier versions of the chapters. We are also grateful to the extraordinary people at McGraw-Hill who have helped us so much on this project: Chris Rogers, who first brought us to McGraw-Hill; Jane Vaicunas, who picked up the ball and guided this project to completion; Laura Lynch, who skillfully and patiently (very patiently!) assisted us throughout the preparation of the manuscript; Dave Dunham, who was responsible for the final production of the book; and Kim Armstrong, who has handled the marketing efforts.

Resource support for this project came from several sources. The Marie Wilson Howells Fund at the University of Arkansas provided support to Dave Schroeder, while funds from the National Institute of Mental Health (PHS grants #48271-01 and #48721-02) and the Colgate University Research Council assisted Jack Dovidio. The Departments of Psychology at the University of Arkansas and Arizona State University were gracious and generous hosts during Lou Penner's sabbatical. The Wang Foundation provided the funds that brought the authors together for a very valuable week in the summer of 1993 at Colgate University. During that week Linda Dovidio earned our sincere thanks for allowing us to use her home during our discussions about the book, her contributions to these discussions, the wonderful meals she prepared, and for tolerating us in general.

Last but certainly most importantly, we want to thank those closest to us. Our spouses (Susie, Kathy, Linda, and Irv) supported us and tolerated the time we spent away from them to work on the book. Our children (Dave: Lisa and Kevin; Lou: Charlie; Jack: Alison and Michael; and Jane: Allyn and Libby) helped as well; they gave us encouragement and kept us focused on what is really important about life.

David A. Schroeder

Louis A. Penner

John F. Dovidio

Jane A. Piliavin

1

An Introduction to Helping and Altruism

--- ❖ ---

*I*t was about 3 A.M. on a September morning, and the Sunset Limited Amtrak train was speeding through the bayous of rural Alabama on its way from Los Angeles to Miami. As the passengers slept, the train hit an obstruction on a bridge and derailed, plunging several railroad cars into the dark waters of the Big Bayou Canot. It was one of the worst rail disasters in American history. A young lawyer, Michael Dopheide, was one of the people on the train. He was thrown from his seat, and water and smoke began to fill the car in which he rode. Mr. Dopheide was among the first passengers to escape from the train by climbing through a broken window and dropping into the water below the window. He was worried about the diesel fuel in the water around him igniting and about poisonous snakes and alligators that inhabit these bayous. But he did not swim to safety. He returned to the partially submerged railroad car and pulled about thirty passengers out through the broken window. The passengers had to jump 6 feet into the water and swim to a piling about 10 feet away. But some of them could not swim, so Mr. Dopheide remained in the water, placed their arms around his neck, and pulled them to safety. As one passenger who survived this disaster said, "The only thing that kept me going was his calm voice. I just followed his voice to safety" (*The New York Times*, September 26, 1993).

Although you may have never done anything as dramatic as the heroic actions of Michael Dopheide, you certainly have performed numerous helpful acts for others. For example, today you may have done something as simple as opening the door for another student loaded down with books, served as a volunteer for a local service organization, or just listened to a friend who needed to talk to someone about a personal problem. Perhaps in the past week, you came upon an automobile accident and stopped to help in the emergency, helped a

1

Rescuers and salvage workers go through the wreckage of the Amtrak "Sunset Limited" looking for the bodies of victims who were not as fortunate as the passengers who were saved by Michael Dopheide. (AP/Wide World Photos)

classmate with a homework assignment, or participated in a fund-raising drive for some charity. Each of these actions is an example of a helpful behavior.

By the same token, someone probably helped *you* today. You may have asked a friend for change so that you could buy a soft drink. One of your classmates may have explained a difficult concept discussed in one of your classes at school. Perhaps you were feeling down and called on some friends whom you thought would help boost your spirits. In each of these situations, you would have been the recipient of a helpful act.

This is a book about people contributing to the well-being of others—how, when, and why they do it. As the first set of examples suggests, help may be given under many different guises, and one may offer assistance to others for many different reasons. Our goal in this book is to explore the variety of ways that help is given and the many reasons why people help each other. As shown in the second set of examples, helping involves an interaction between a helper and someone being helped, so we must also consider helping from the point of view of the person receiving the help. When will a person ask for help, and what are the psychological consequences of receiving that help? Is being helped always helpful?

At first glance, it may appear that the answers to these questions are quite obvious; it may seem that common sense is all that is needed to understand prosocial behavior. However, common sense does not always provide correct answers to questions about helping and being helped. Consider the following situation. It's early evening and you are on your way home from class; as you round the corner while walking down the street, you twist your ankle on the uneven pavement. You go down in a heap on the empty sidewalk and cannot get up! You are in intense pain; your ankle is badly sprained or even broken. As you lie there, you hear the voices of people in an apartment building across the street. If you hope to be helped, would you rather have a single person or three people know about your plight? It seems so clear that when there are more people available to help there should be a better chance of being helped. After all, conventional wisdom tell us that "there's safety in numbers." Social psychologists, however, often find that such conventional wisdom lets us down. In situations such as this one, help is usually more likely to be given when only a single individual is present than when there are several people available. (More about this in Chapter 2.)

Consider another situation. A new friend of yours is doing very poorly in a course that you are also taking. You are doing extremely well in the course and, because you like your new friend, you decide to offer him (or her) help with the course. You enter your friend's room and announce that you can spend the next few hours tutoring him or her in the course. Will your friend be grateful and appreciate this favor? Research on receiving help suggests the response may surprise you. Your friend may become angry and resent the offer of help! (More about this in Chapter 7.)

Not all the correct answers to questions about prosocial actions are counterintuitive, but we often find that our basic assumptions about prosocial behavior will rarely be correct in all circumstances. By recognizing the limits of common sense and conventional wisdom and the value of empirical research findings, we can understand prosocial behavior more fully.

UNDERSTANDING PROSOCIAL BEHAVIOR: A COMMON CONCERN

Why should we be concerned with prosocial behavior in the first place? Are people interested in this topic? One indirect, but valid way of determining what is important to members of a society or culture is to simply look at what they talk and write about (Goldberg, 1993). Using this approach, there is abundant evidence that people have been interested in trying to understand the nature of prosocial behavior for a long time. Furthermore, this interest has not been restricted to just one culture or to just one period in the history of humanity. The multiple perspectives that have been used by others to understand prosocial behavior may help us recognize some common and enduring themes that can contribute to our understanding of this topic. To gain these insights, we will consider stories illustrating prosocial behavior that come from various cultures, writings from diverse religions, and ideas of major philosophers.

Folktales and Parables about Prosocial Behavior

Folktales, legends, and parables provide insights into the issues that are of common concern to members of a culture and the lessons of life that are considered valuable enough to be passed on from generation to generation. Because prosocial behavior may have an adaptive value that will increase the chances of an individual's, group's, and culture's survival (Campbell, 1975), it is not surprising that the stories and folklore of many cultures stress the value of helping one another. The following stories illustrate the fundamental importance of reciprocal helping and heroism.

One of the most explicit tales of the value of prosocial action comes from African-American culture (see Box 1-1). The story, "Spreading Fingers of Friendship" (Abrahams, 1985), is intended to clearly show the tangible benefits of prosocial action. It provides a vivid contrast between the consequences of selfishness and sharing. This tale of Ba Yua and his wives also reflects the strong sense of communalism and duty to one's social group that pervades African cultures (Boykin, 1983).

Other folktales take a different approach to prosocial behavior. Rather than primarily stressing the personal benefits of ordinary and easy acts of helping, they encourage dramatic selfless behavior by providing members of a culture with stories about heroic acts, some of which may include extreme self-sacrifice. For example, Box 1-2 presents a Native-American legend from the Oneida nation that describes the courage of a warrior maiden, Aliquipiso. This heroine of the Oneidas endures torture and ultimately gives her life to save her people from starvation (Erdoes & Ortiz, 1984). The actions of Aliquipiso serve as a graphic example of the lengths to which some people will go to promote the well-being of others. The fact that the sacrifices of such heroic individuals are widely reported reflect both the distinctiveness of such feats and the great value that people place on such extraordinary actions.

Although the stories of Aliquipiso and the wives of Ba Yua have been passed from generation to generation by oral tradition (until recent years), other tales with similar messages have been maintained in the written mode. The New Testament parable of the Good Samaritan (Luke 10:29–37) serves as an example of this. In this well-known tale, a man who has been beaten and robbed on his way to Jericho received no assistance from two passing men of strong religious convictions, a priest and a Levite. However, a Samaritan, who was considered to be some-

BOX 1.1

Spreading Fingers of Friendship

Ba Yua worked on the plantation. He would bring food from the plantation to his two wives in the city. But when he gave his wives the food, he told them, "When you eat, you must spread your fingers." Now when he said this, the first wife did not understand very well what he meant. He told the second wife the same thing, and she understood what he meant. When he brought them food, they were not to eat alone, they were to share half with others. You must share with people, not keep all for yourself.

Now the first wife, whatever she cooked, she ate. Then she went outside, and spread her fingers to the air, and said, "Ba Yua said when I eat I must spread my fingers." Ba Yua brought her much bacon and salt fish, but she always ate it alone. But when Ba Yua brought the things for the second wife, she shared with other people.

Not long afterward Ba Yua died, and nobody brought anything to the wife who spread her fingers to the air. She sat alone. But to the wife who had shared things with others, many people brought her things. One brought her a cow, one brought her sugar, one brought her coffee.

Now, one day, the first wife went to the second, and she said, "Sister, ever since Ba Yua died, I have been hungry; no one brought me anything. But look how many people have brought provisions for you!" The second wife asked her, "Well, when Ba Yua brought you things, what did you do with them?" She said, "I ate them." Then the second wife said again, "When Ba Yua said to you, 'You must spread your fingers,' what did you do?" She said, "When I ate, I spread my fingers in the air." The second wife laughed and said, "Well, then, the air must bring you things, because you spread your fingers for the air. For myself, the same people to whom I gave food now bring me things in return."

[Adapted from R. D. Abrahams (Ed.). (1985). *Afro-American folktales: Stories from black traditions in the New World* (pp. 124–125). New York: Pantheon.]

thing of a religious outcast, stopped to help the victim, bandaging his wounds and taking him to an inn for further treatment. Jesus indicated that the Samaritan was the "neighbor" of the fallen victim and admonished those listening to this parable to follow the Samaritan's model. Although the Samaritan's action may not have been as dramatic as Aliquipiso's heroic behavior, the message is the same: We need to be concerned about the well-being of others.

Telling these stories with their prosocial themes served and continues to serve as an important means of instruction for successive generations

BOX 1.2

The Warrior Maiden

Long ago, in the days before the white man came to this continent, the Oneida people were beset by their old enemies, the Mingoes. The villages of the Oneida lay deserted, their fields untended, the ruins of their homes blackened. The men had taken the women, the old people, the young boys and girls into the deep forest, hiding them in secret places among rocks, in caves, and on desolate mountains.

Thus, the Oneida people were safe in their inaccessible retreats, but they were also starving. Whatever food they had been able to save was soon eaten up. They could either stay in their hideouts and starve, or leave them in search of food and be discovered by their enemies. The warrior chiefs and sachems met in council but could find no way out.

Then a young girl stepped forward in the council and said that the good spirits had sent her a dream showing how to save the Oneida. Her name was Aliquipiso and she was not afraid to give her life for her people.

Aliquipiso told the council: "We are hiding on top of a high, sheer cliff. Above us the mountain is covered with boulders and heavy sharp rocks. You warriors wait and watch here. I will go to the Mingoes and lead them to the spot at the foot of the cliff where they all can be crushed and destroyed."

During the night the girl went down from the heights into the forest below by way of a secret path. In the morning, Mingoe scouts found her wandering through the woods as if lost. They took her to the burned and abandoned village where she had once lived, for this was now their camp. They brought her before their warrior chief. "Show us the way to the place where your people are hiding," he commanded. "If you do this, we shall adopt you into our tribe. If you refuse, you will be tortured at the stake."

"I will not show you the way," answered Aliquipiso. The Mingoes tied her to a blackened tree stump and tortured her with fire, as was their custom. Even the wild Mingoes were astonished at the courage with which the girl endured it. At last Aliquipiso pretended to weaken under the pain. "Don't hurt me any more," she cried, "I'll show you the way."

As night came again, the Mingoes bound Aliquipiso's hands behind her back and pushed her ahead of them. Soundlessly the mass of Mingoe warriors crept behind her through thickets and rough places, over winding paths and deer trails, until at last they arrived beneath the towering cliff of sheer granite. "Come closer, Mingoe warriors," she said in a low voice, "gather around me. The Oneidas above are sleeping, thinking themselves safe. I'll show you the secret passage that leads upwards." The Mingoes crowded together in a dense mass with the girl in the center. Then Aliquipiso uttered a piercing cry: "Oneidas! The enemies are here! Destroy them!"

The Mingoes scarcely had time to strike her down before huge boulders and rocks rained upon them. There was no escape; it seemed as if the angry mountain itself were falling on them, crushing them, burying them. So many Mingoe warriors died that the other bands of Mingoe invaders stopped pillaging the Oneida country and retired to their own hunting grounds. They never again made war on Aliquipiso's people.

[Abridged from R. Erdoes & A. Ortiz (Eds.). (1984). *American Indian myths and legends* (pp. 252–253). New York: Pantheon Books.]

of a clan, tribe, society, or culture. The message of the need for prosocial behavior is timeless, and the tales are as relevant today as they were when they were first told.

Religion and Prosocial Behavior

The lessons that can be learned from folktales and parables are also represented and have been formalized in the major religions of the world. The tenets of these religions provide abstract ethical principles that the followers of the faith are expected to interpret and follow. In some cases, concrete rules of behavior are specified that leave little room for misinterpretation or confusion. As with the folktales just presented, however, it is easy to identify common themes running through diverse religions.

One common theme is the importance of concern for others. Consider, for example, the Talmud, a collection of commentaries and interpretations written by Jewish scholars concerning the first five books of the Old Testament. According to this important book in Judaism, "benevolence is one of the pillars upon which the world rests" (p. 240). The teachings of the revered Chinese philosopher, Confucius (551–479 B.C.), express a similar sentiment: "Wisdom, *benevolence*, and fortitude, these are the universal virtues" (*Doctrine of the Mean*, 20: 8, emphasis added; cited in Hume, 1959, p. 122). The teachings of Lao-Tze (604–517 B.C.), which serve as the basis for Taoism, also advise that one should deal positively with others. Part of Lao-Tze's description of a good person includes the prescriptions "to help [others] in their straits; to rescue them from their perils" (*Sacred Books of the East*, 40: 237–238; cited in Hume, 1959, p. 142). Within Native-American religions, Fools Crow, one of the most revered medicine men of the Sioux (or Lakota) nations, stated that tribal elders do not let the rest of the tribe forget the teachings of the "wise old ones" who were taught that inner peace and love were the greatest of Wakan Tanka's (Lakota for creator, meaning "great spirit") gifts. According to Fools Crow, "we put the *well-being* of other people and of all nature first. We cling to this like a person clings to a raft on a roaring river" (Mails, 1988, p. 8, emphasis added).

These beliefs of benevolence and love for others are incorporated into a common rule of social behavior found in many of the major religions of the world and often referred to as the golden rule. The Jewish version of the prescription for prosocial action may be found in the Old Testament book of Leviticus: "You should love your neighbor as yourself" (Leviticus 19:18). In Christianity, this rule is presented in the Gospel of Luke: "And as you wish that men would do to you, do so to them" (Luke 6:31, *Revised Standard Version*). Given the close relationship between Judaism and Christianity, this similarity might not be too surprising. However, the same advice can be found in the teachings of Confucius, "What you do not want done to yourself, do not do to others" (*Analects*, 15:23; cited in Hume, 1959, p. 277); Taoism's Lao-Tze, "To those who are good to me, I am good. And to those who are not good to me, I am also good. And thus all get to be good." (*Tao-Teh-King*, 49:2); and Hinduism, "Do naught to others which if done to thee would cause thee pain: this is the sum of duty" (*Mahabharata*, 5:1517; cited in Hume, 1959, p. 277). Although the wording may differ slightly, the sentiment is the same: We should treat others as we would like to be treated. It is clear that this prosocial rule of human behavior is not one that has emerged from a single culture, but rather is a more universal rule for social behavior that appears to play an adaptive function for well-being and perhaps even the survival of the individual and the group.

The notion that human beings *should* be quite concerned with the well-being of other people does seem to be at odds with their natural tendencies to "look out for number one." Therefore, it may not be surprising that the abstract golden rule has been further codified in some religions. For example, one of the five pillars of Islam is *almsgiving*, an annual obligation to contribute a portion of one's assets (zakat) to the community for care of orphans, the indigent, and others in need. Many Christian religions prescribe or at least recommend that their members tithe or give 10 percent of their income to support the activities of the church. The fact that such specific prescriptions for prosocial behavior are needed does suggest that there may be a natural tendency for people to behave selfishly. Laws, whether civil or religious, typically emerge because there are problems that need to be solved or behaviors that need to be changed. We do not, typically, pass laws to reinforce and endorse appropriate behaviors that are already being displayed. When social institutions such as religions find it necessary to establish explicit rules to ensure desirable behaviors, one can reasonably surmise that people are not spontaneously conforming to the highest moral and social standards.

Even differences between kinds of help have drawn the attention of religious writers. Moses Maimonides, a twelfth century talmudic commentator, tried to differentiate among types of helping, no doubt in response to people seeking guidance for their own behaviors. He specified an eight-step hierarchy or "ladder" of prosocial actions (see Box 1-3) in his Golden Ladder of Charity (Ausubel, 1948). The bottom two rungs of the ladder involve help that is given reluctantly or that does not correspond to the need of the sufferer. The middle rungs include help that is not given until it is requested and aid given in such a way that the recipient feels shame. At the higher levels, help is given anonymously, so that the recipient does not know the benefactor and the benefactor does not know the recipient. Finally, at the highest rung of the ladder is charity provided to prevent future need, such as teaching an individual a trade or referring business so that the person can make an honest living and not have to rely on charity. In addition to specifying the types of help that one should give, this classification scheme demonstrates a

BOX 1.3

The Golden Ladder of Charity

There are eight degrees or steps, says Maimonides, in the duty of charity.

The first and lowest degree is to give—but with reluctance or regret. This is the gift of the *hand*, but not of the *heart*.

The second is to give cheerfully, but not proportionately to the distress of the sufferer.

The third is to give cheerfully and proportionately, but not until we are solicited.

The fourth is to give cheerfully, proportionately, and even unsolicited; but to put it in the poor man's hand, thereby exciting in him the painful emotion of shame.

The fifth is to give charity in such a way that the distressed may receive the bounty and know the benefactor, without their being known to him. Such was the conduct of our ancestors, who used to tie up money in the hind-corners of their cloaks, so that the poor might take it unperceived.

The sixth, which rises still higher, is to know the objects of our bounty, but remain unknown to them. Such was the conduct of those of our ancestors who used to convey their charitable gifts to poor people's dwellings, taking care that their own persons and names should remain unknown.

The seventh is still more meritorious, namely, to bestow charity in such a way that the benefactor may not know the relieved person, nor they the name of their benefactor. This was done by our charitable forefathers during the existence of the Temple. For there was in that holy building a place called the *Chamber of Silence or Inostentation*, wherein the good deposited secretly whatever their generous hearts suggested, and from which the most respectable poor families were maintained with equal secrecy.

Lastly, the eighth and most meritorious of all, is to anticipate charity by preventing poverty; namely to assist the reduced brother, either by a considerable gift, or a loan of money, or by teaching him a trade, or by putting him in the way of business, so that he may earn an honest livelihood, and not be forced to the dreadful alternative of holding up his hand for charity. And it is to this Scripture alludes when it says, "And if thy brother be waxen poor and fallen in decay with thee, then thou shalt *support* him: *Yea though he be a stranger or a sojourner*, that he may live with thee."

This is the highest step and the summit of charity's Golden Ladder.

[From N. Ausubel (Ed.). (1948). *A treasury of Jewish folklore*. New York: Crown.]

keen sensitivity to the reactions of the recipient of help, recognizing that receiving help may threaten the person's self-image and possibly lower self-esteem. Maimonides's consideration of the consequences of receiving help anticipated an issue that is of current interest among social psychologists, and we will be returning to this specific issue in Chapter 7.

The religious writings presented above are intended to provide people with strong encouragement to be prosocial in their interactions with others (often with the promise of some "heavenly reward"). Philosophers, social theorists, and others with a more secular perspective have not been concerned with how people *ought* to act; rather these writers attempted to describe how people *do* act. In doing this, they have often reached very different conclusions. As is usual in discussions of philosophy, we begin with the views of the social philosophers of ancient Greece.

Philosophers and Prosocial Behavior

In general, the Greek philosophers were somewhat equivocal about human nature. Socrates (470–399 B.C.) believed that each person pursued that which was "good"—that is, that which was in his or her own best interest. Plato (427–347 B.C.) was a bit more pessimistic about human nature: "Human nature will be always drawing him into avarice and self-ishness, avoiding pain and pursuing pleasure without any reason, and will bring these to the front, obscuring the juster and better" (*Laws*, Book 9, p. 754). However, Plato recognized that there were means by which these base instincts could be curbed: "Mankind must have laws, and con-form to them or their life would be as bad as that of the most savage beast" (*Laws*, Book 9, p. 754). Later, Aristotle (384–322 B.C.) addressed some of the same issues, but he had a more positive view of people, see-ing them as basically noble, generous, and good. He believed humans were quite concerned about their social relationships and, therefore, the well-being of others. Aristotle argued that there is an asymmetry between the reactions of a helper and a person being helped, with the benefactor having a more positive feeling for the recipient than the recipient has for the benefactor.

Almost 2000 years later, other European philosophers also addressed the question of whether people are good or bad by nature. Like the Greek philosophers, they often disagreed in the conclusions they reached. Part of the reason for these disagreements was that often their pronounce-ments on the general character of human nature were, in fact, greatly influenced by the specific time and place in which they lived. For exam-ple, Niccolo Machiavelli (1469–1527) lived in sixteenth-century Florence, Italy, and observed the actions of the members of the famous (or infa-mous) Medici family as they connived, plotted, and even murdered to achieve political power and personal riches. Accordingly, his view of human nature was that it was not particularly friendly or benign. In *The Prince*, he described people as being "ungrateful, fickle, false," and willing to use others to their own end with little or no real concern for those they have used. The notion that people would do something to help others without expecting to receive an even greater benefit for themselves is certainly contrary to Machiavelli's characterization of human nature.

Later Thomas Hobbes (1588–1679), disturbed and frightened by the political and social upheaval he saw in seventeenth-century England, espoused a different, but equally bleak view of human nature. He believed that the natural state of human affairs was of individual versus individual, each doing what was in his or her own best interest. This selfishness might produce helping, but the motivation for such action would certainly be intended to relieve the helper's own distress. In fact, Hobbes felt that the only thing that motivates cooperative actions among humans is fear of some outside agent. In the absence of such a threat to keep "them all in awe," he claimed that people would be in almost continual conflict, with "every man against every man." Hobbes (like Plato) believed that the only solution was for people to establish social contracts in the form of governments (what Hobbes called the Leviathan) that force restrictions on their own inherently selfish desires. The motive that underlies the creation of the Leviathan is not concern for others but only self-concern. Presumably, the best government would be one that provides each of us with protection from the exploitative attempts of others, but imposes only minimal constraints upon *our own* self-serving actions.

There is, of course, another possibility. Maybe it is society that is corrupt and the individual who is good. This was the position of Jean-Jacques Rousseau (1712–1778), a French philosopher who wrote some years after Machiavelli and Hobbes. Like many intellectuals in France at that time, Rousseau believed that people are basically good; he believed humans were "noble savages." In his view, human nature starts out as noble and good—people have an innate sensitivity to others that leads to mutually beneficial relations. If individuals were able to mature in a "natural" state, Rousseau claimed that they would develop a strong moral sense of their obligations to others and live a "virtuous" social existence. As things normally occur, however, this virtue is gradually corrupted by societal institutions, such as the excesses of French society that Rousseau observed and that ultimately led to the French Revolution in the eighteenth century. According to Rousseau, society leads people to derive their satisfaction from "being better" than others rather than from an appreciation of the natural harmony of the inner self, the natural environment, and other people. To eliminate the corrupting influences of society, Rousseau believed that progressive educational programs that addressed the changing needs of a person would promote a genuine concern for the common good and a recognition of the need to live in harmonious relations with others.

Folktales, legends, religious teachings, and moral philosophies provide us with a rich conceptual background for the study of prosocial behavior. But reliance on these sources will not enable us to answer the questions that we might have about helping and altruism. In fact, although some common themes do emerge from these disparate sources, often they reach very different conclusions about how humans should act or do act. In such instances, there is no impartial means to determine which one is correct. Thus, other strategies need to be pursued if we are to finally grasp the full complexities of the domain of prosocial behavior. The strategy we take in this book is to rely on the systematic, scientific study of prosocial behavior.

THE SCIENTIFIC STUDY OF PROSOCIAL BEHAVIOR

Among the scientific disciplines, social psychology has taken the lead in the study of prosocial behavior. William McDougall, author of one of the first social psychology textbooks in 1908, provided an early explanation for prosocial behavior. According to McDougall, social behavior is governed by a set of primary instincts (flight, repulsion, curiosity, pugnacity, self-abasement, self-assertion, and parenting) which are capable of prompting thought and action. These instincts are inextricably linked to corresponding emotions (i.e., fear, disgust, wonder, anger, subjection, elation, and tenderness, respectively). Of particular interest for our purposes is the parental instinct and the associated tender emotion that McDougall posited as being at the root of prosocial behavior. He suggested that a mother's care of her child is the prototype of the parenting instinct, and he argued that it can be more powerful than any of the other instincts. McDougall claimed that the tender emotion is not equivalent to sympathy, but he believed that the prosocial behaviors of "generosity, gratitude, love, pity, true benevolence, and altruistic conduct of every kind" (1936, p. 61) arise from this instinct and emotion.

McDougall's approach to understanding social behavior in general and prosocial behavior in particular sought to identify the underlying processes responsible for this facet of human action. The folktales, religions, and moral philosophies presented above were primarily concerned with the description and prescription of prosocial behavior, focusing on how people *do act* or *should act* rather than trying to understand *why* they act as they do. McDougall's emphasis on questions of why people act as they do represented a major shift in the study of prosocial behavior. Unfortunately, however, the methods of investigation that were available to McDougall in the early 1900s did not lend themselves well to answering the questions he sought to answer. Moreover, the growing influence of behaviorism during this period seriously limited the impact that any instinct-based theory could have on the field of psychology at that time. McDougall had to rely on the same procedures that the early philosophers had used in their attempts to understand helping—a critical conceptual analysis of the phenomenon of interest that ultimately relied on intuition, authority, and rationalism. Although often enlightening, the claims made by those who employed such strategies suffered from a lack of observable, objective kinds of evidence (or data) that would support them. Without objective data, people are forced to rely solely on logical arguments of an authority rather than on direct observations to verify the authority's conclusions.

Perhaps it was for this reason that so little interest was generated in the study of prosocial behavior after McDougall's introduction of the topic. For example, in the first edition of the *Handbook of Social Psychology*, Murchison (1935) provided an outline of the most important topics in social psychology at that time. Virtually no references were made to any type of prosocial behavior, except for brief discussions of cooperation in birds and symbiotic relations among plants! In the second edition of the *Handbook of Social Psychology* (Lindzey, 1954), published almost twenty years later, the only references to helping and altruism concerned food sharing in chimpanzees, the philosophical status of altruism, the development of altruism and cooperation in children, and cooperation as a group problem-solving strategy in laboratory and applied settings. As late as 1969, when the third edition of the *Handbook of Social Psychology* (Lindzey & Aronson, 1969) was published, there were only sixteen entries concerning some aspect of prosocial behavior in over 3500 pages of the five-volume series. There were no specific references to prosocial behavior or helping as topics of research interest for social psychologists in any of the first three editions of the handbook.

This state of affairs changed dramatically in the mid-1960s. The event that is frequently cited as being responsible for this change was the murder of a young woman, known as the Kitty Genovese incident. As Katherine "Kitty" Genovese returned from work to her home in Queens, New York, early one morning, she was attacked and stabbed repeatedly by a lone assailant. Although at least thirty-eight others quietly listened or watched from their apartments, no one came to her assistance. Thirty minutes after the attack had begun, one of the anonymous witnesses finally reported the incident to the police. By then, it was too late to help— Ms. Genovese had been murdered.

Ms. Genovese's death drew the attention of the general public and social scientists alike. The callousness and indifference of people who live in big cities (especially New York) were widely condemned in the popular press. What could possibly have caused such apathy?

Kitty Genovese's murder also attracted the interest of two social psychologists, Bibb Latané and John Darley. But rather than approaching the event from the perspective of philosophy or using a critical conceptual analysis, they applied the contemporary methods and knowledge of social psychology to understanding this unfortunate incident more fully. In particular, Latané and Darley used the experimental method to find answers to many of the questions raised by Ms. Genovese's murder. For example, why did none of her neighbors leave their apartments to give her protection? Why did the one witness who called the police wait so long to make his telephone call, and why did he wish to remain anonymous?

By using the empirical approach that is part of the scientific method, Latané and Darley were able to identify some of the situational factors that can promote or inhibit helping. As we shall see in the next chapter, their research program led to the development of a model of the decision-making processes people use when deciding whether to help someone in distress. In many ways, Latané and Darley opened the floodgates for empirical research on helping and altruism. In the twenty years after Ms. Genovese's murder, over 1000 research articles were published concerning prosocial behavior (Dovidio, 1984). The current edition of the *Handbook of Social Psychology* (Lindzey & Aronson, 1985) recognizes the burgeoning interest in the topic by devoting one-half chapter to helping and altruism. Numerous other entries throughout this edition of the handbook also concern issues related to prosocial behavior. Plans for the fifth edition of the handbook include an entire chapter on helping and altruism. It is this extensive body of research that we will draw upon and review in this book.

We do not want to suggest, however, that the systematic and scientific study of prosocial behavior is the exclusive domain of social psychology. Within psychology, prosocial actions are also of interest to many developmental and personality psychologists. Outside psychology, there are anthropologists, economists, political scientists, and sociologists who study the causes and consequences of positive forms of interpersonal behavior. These approaches complement the social psychological approach to helping and altruism. Psychologists tend to focus on individuals as opposed to collectives (i.e., groups, societies, cultures) and, as a result, they primarily study one-to-one kinds of helping. But to answer some of the important questions about prosocial behavior, we need to also consider the broad social and societal context in which prosocial actions occur. These other social sciences provide this perspective.

Finally, we need to mention that the social and behavioral sciences are not the only disciplines that study prosocial behavior. As we shall see (primarily in Chapter 4), there is considerable interest in altruism and other prosocial actions among ethologists, geneticists, sociobiologists, and other natural scientists.

Defining Our Terms

Thus far, we have been using the words and phrases, altruism, prosocial behavior, and helping in a somewhat loose and informal manner. However, before we can go any further, we need to try to define more precisely these and other terms we will be using throughout this book. However, as we present our definitions of the terms of interest, you will get some sense of the kinds of problems one encounters when one tries to provide precise, scientific definitions of the phenomena of interest. The greatest problem has been the lack of consensus about the definitions of these critical terms. This is reasonable, because as we will stress repeatedly throughout this book, the psychology of helping and altruism involves complex scientific, semantic, and philosophical issues. With this caveat in mind, let us proceed.

We will be trying to understand different kinds of *prosocial* behaviors. Prosocial behavior is the label for a broad category of actions that are "defined by society as generally beneficial to other people and to the ongoing political system" (Piliavin, Dovidio, Gaertner, & Clark, 1981, p. 4). There are several features of this definition that deserve comment. First, as we noted earlier, prosocial behavior is necessarily an interpersonal act: There must be a benefactor and one (or more) recipient of benefits for a prosocial act to occur. Second, the phrase, "defined by society," implies that a given behavior is not inherently or universally prosocial or antisocial. Rather, this is a social judgment that could change dramatically as the result of changes in the circumstances or the historical and political context in which the behavior took place. For instance, normally, taking something from a store without paying for it would be considered an antisocial action; but many people would view taking urgently needed medical supplies from the wreckage of a neighborhood drugstore following Hurricane Andrew as a prosocial action and the person who did this might be viewed as a hero. Conversely, consider the Good Samaritan laws that were enacted in Germany in the 1930s. They required German citizens to help the police round up and imprison criminals and enemies of the state (Piliavin et al., 1981). At first, this may appear to be a prosocial behavior. However, in the 1930s in Germany the police were the SS, or secret police, and the criminals were homosexuals, Gypsies, Jews, and other groups hated by the Nazi government. Many of these people were later killed in concentration camps. Thus, today we see the German citizens' prosocial behavior as antisocial, to say the least.

Although we need to be mindful of the contextual nature of prosocial behavior, it is not this part of the definition that may cause problems for the person who wants to study prosocial behavior. Recall some of the examples presented at the beginning of this chapter: Holding the door for another student, volunteering to help in a service organization, and assisting at the scene of an accident. There would be little disagreement among the vast majority of people in our society that these are all prosocial actions. The problem with the term, prosocial behavior, is that in some instances it is too broad for our purposes. It can be used to describe an extremely wide range of actions. In many instances, the term prosocial behavior does not capture the important differences among the various kinds of prosocial actions in which humans engage. To answer many of the important questions about the phenomena of interest, we must try to distinguish among three subcategories of prosocial behavior: helping, altruism, and cooperation.

Helping. The category of greatest interest to this book is *helping*, which we will define as an action that has the consequences of providing some benefit to or improving the well-being of another person. The definition for helping is not particularly stringent; as long as one person's well-being is improved by the actions of another (e.g., giving a gift, providing resources to accomplish a task), helping has occurred. In some cases, such as donating money to a charitable organization, the benefactor may not even come into direct contact with the recipient of aid.

Literally hundreds of different behaviors have been used in studies of helping. These include simple tasks, such as telling a stranger what time it is or contributing to a service organization, and more difficult tasks that require a significant commitment of time and/or energy (such as chaperoning a group of teenagers to the zoo or helping a heart attack victim). Because Kitty Genovese's murder stimulated much of the work in this area, many researchers have chosen to use similar situations in their investigations. For example, Piliavin and Piliavin (1972) staged "emergencies" in the subways of Philadelphia to determine if the presence of blood would affect bystanders' rate of helping a "victim" (actually a confederate of the experimenters) who had collapsed. Many of these studies have been conducted in laboratory settings, but many others, like the Piliavin and Piliavin study, have been field experiments, conducted in naturalistic situations. Still other studies have used questionnaires, interviews, and naturalistic observations to study helping. There is virtually no limit to the number of the behaviors, kinds of settings, and variety of methods that have been used to study this phenomenon.

In an attempt to provide a clearer picture of what helping really is, Pearce and Amato (1980) proposed a classification scheme (or taxonomy) that categorizes helping situations along three critical dimensions (see Figure 1-1). On the basis of their analysis of helping situations, they suggested that helping situations can be rated according to the extent to which the help is *planned and formal* (e.g., volunteering to serve as a "buddy" for a person with AIDS) versus *spontaneous and informal* helping (e.g., telling someone they had just dropped a package). Helping can also differ according to the *seriousness* of the problem (e.g., the difference between giving change to make a telephone call and giving aid to a heart

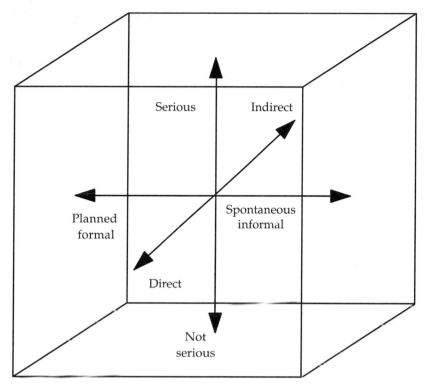

FIGURE 1.1
Pearce and Amato's three-dimensional taxonomy of helping situations.

attack victim). Finally, helping situations can differ in terms of whether the help involves *indirect* giving of assistance, such as making a donation to a favorite charity, or doing something *directly* to help the person in need, such as helping a young child perform a difficult task.

More recently, McGuire (1994) asked college students to list the different kinds of help they had received from and given to friends, casual acquaintances, and strangers. (The most frequent helping behavior reported by the students was helping someone with a homework assignment or schoolwork.) McGuire used the students' answers to generate another classification scheme for different kinds of helping behaviors. According to her, there are four kinds of helping: (1) casual helping—doing some small favor for a casual acquaintance, such as lending the person a pen; (2) substantial personal helping—expending some considerable effort to provide a friend with tangible benefit, such as helping the friend move into an apartment; (3) emotional helping—providing emotional or personal support to a friend, such as listening to a friend's personal problems; and (4) emergency helping—coming to the aid of a stranger with an acute problem, such as helping the victim of an accident.

Although Pearce and Amato's and McGuire's taxonomies differ somewhat, they both lead us to two important conclusions about helping. Namely, not all helping is the same, and the factors that affect helping in one set of circumstances may not have the same impact on helping in other situations. You will find examples of both these conclusions in every chapter of this book.

Altruism. The concept of altruism is very closely related to helping. But if we return to the definition of helping that we just presented, we can begin to see how the two concepts differ. In our definition of helping, the *intent* of the benefactor and whether or not the benefactor also *benefits* from helping were not at issue. This is not the case for altruism. It is often seen as a specific kind of helping with some additional characteristics that concern the helper's intentions and benefits. Among social psychologists, the specific characteristics have been the subject of considerable discussion and sometimes heated debate. In particular, some theorists have reserved the term altruism for cases in which the benefactor provides aid to another *without the anticipation of rewards from external sources for providing assistance* (Macaulay & Berkowitz, 1970). This definition is consistent with a more recent definition of altruism offered by Myers (1993): "Concern and help for others that asks nothing in return" (p. 505).

Other theorists restricted the use of the altruism label even further and imposed the additional condition that helpers must incur some cost for their action (e.g., Krebs, 1982; Wispé, 1978). The addition of this self-sacrifice criterion as a necessary condition for altruism presents some problems, primarily because it shifts the focus of the definition from the beneficial consequences received by the victim to the consequences realized by the helper (Batson, 1991). The self-sacrifice criterion does emphasize, however, the generally accepted notion that a true altruist is not providing assistance in order to gain any personal benefits.

In these definitions of helping and altruism, the major focus is on the *act* of providing assistance and the consequences of the behavior *for the helper*. C. Daniel Batson (1991) proposed an alternative point of view that has been quite influential among social psychologists who study helpful actions. He argued that we should concentrate on the *motivation* of the act rather than its consequences when trying to draw these distinctions. He suggested that the important contrast is between helping that is motivated by egoistic concerns (e.g., If I help that person, it will make me feel good and look good to others) and helping that is motivated by altruistic concerns (e.g., I want to help this victim avoid further suffering). For Batson (1991), altruism refers not to the prosocial act per se but to the underlying reason for the act: "Altruism is a motivational state with the ultimate goal of increasing another's welfare" (p. 6). Of course, as outsiders we cannot directly observe or measure a person's motivational state. As a consequence, it is often very difficult to determine if an act of helping is truly altruistic. For example, the man who rescued the other passengers from the Amtrak train may have been altruistically motivated by his concern for their welfare or he may have been egoistically motivated by feelings of guilt if he left them behind.

According to Batson (1991), the causes of the altruistic motivational state lie in the benefactor's identification with the plight of the victim. He refers to this identification as *empathic concern*. The role of empathy is central to Batson's theory of altruism, serving as the energy source for the beneficial action. Batson's (1991) distinction is not one accepted by all helping researchers. As he points out, there has been a dominant ethos in the social sciences, including psychology, that denies the existence of pure altruism and that embraces an assumption of universal egoism. According to this view, "Everything we do, including everything we do to benefit others, is ultimately done for our own benefit" (Batson, 1991, p. 3). If the hallmark of an altruistic act is selflessness, and if those who claim that all actions are ultimately performed to benefit the self are correct, then a purely altruistic act would be—by definition—an impossibility. Even if no obvious rewards were received, the very fact that the act had taken place would imply that some reward was anticipated, violating the defining condition of altruism.

Batson does not deny the existence of egoistically motivated helping, but he makes a persuasive argument that there are certain instances in which the primary motive for providing help is to improve the state of another. Even if the helper received some social or material reward for providing assistance, as long as the helper's primary intention was to help the other person, Batson argues that the act should be considered altruistic. This is an important issue and we will return to it later in the book.

Other disciplines have still other definitions of altruism. Economists, for example, define it in terms of the value of an act for the recipient and the cost of the action for the donor. Biologists and ethologists view altruism in terms of the contribution that an action makes to the survival of some group's gene pool. More specifically, according to these scientists an altruistic behavior is one that increases the likelihood that an altruist's close genetic relatives will survive and reproduce and, thus, pass their genes on to successive generations (Ridley & Dawkins, 1984). Note that for the biologist, motivational concerns and intentions are essentially irrelevant. Indeed, so-called evolutionary altruism (e.g., a bee sacrificing its life to protect the hive) may occur without any thought or awareness (Sober, 1988, 1992; see Chapter 4).

Given the divergent views of altruistic action and the numerous definitions of altruism, we are not prepared to choose the one correct way of defining it. As a result, there will be some inconsistencies across the chapters in how we use the word altruism. But at a minimum, we are referring to a helpful act that is carried out in the absence of obvious and tangible rewards. Sometimes we will go beyond this rather conservative definition and discuss the motivations, intentions, and consequences for the helper. We recognize that all prosocial acts are not created equal and that the intentions and motives of helpers may be the critical criteria for distinguishing between the various forms of helping we will discuss. But there will be places in the book where we will not be able to make these distinctions, because we will not be completely sure of how to character- ize a particular prosocial action. As we just told you, in something as com- plex and multifaceted as helping, some amount of ambiguity and inconsistency is unavoidable.

Cooperation. Whereas helping and altruism refer primarily to situa- tions in which one person provides aid to another in need, there are times when two or more people come together to work toward a common goal that will be beneficial to all concerned. Raven and Rubin (1983) used the term cooperation to describe this kind of prosocial behavior and empha- sized the mutual dependency of cooperative relationships. For Raven and Rubin, cooperation is "[a] relationship between two or more persons who are positively interdependent with respect to their goals. That is, the movement of one person toward achieving a goal will increase the likeli- hood of the other person reaching his or her goal" (p. 724). Kahn (1986), in his critique of our competitive society, defined cooperation as "an arrangement that is not merely noncompetitive but requires us to work together in order to achieve our goals" (p. 6).

Because cooperators can reasonably expect that they will mutually benefit to some degree from their joint efforts, cooperation is a specific kind of helping. Cooperation differs, however, from the unilateral kinds of helping that we have presented thus far. The primary difference is that, in cooperation, all those involved in the exchange contribute to the group's outcome as more or less equal partners in the group's attempt to achieve some common goal. In other kinds of helping relationships, the two parties are not equal partners. Indeed, in some instances they may be driven apart and have differing goals. For example, as we will discuss in Chapter 7, the benefactor may be perceived as assuming a position of power over the recipient, who may also feel a sense of indebtedness (Nadler, 1991). As a consequence, the recipient's sense of obligation to the helper may strain the relationship. Because of the absence of a power hier- archy and the realization of common rewards, however, greater group cohesiveness and more positive interpersonal relations usually occur in cooperative exchanges.

Just as helping researchers have discovered that there may be both egoistic and altruistic motivations when a person decides to help another, the situations in which cooperation has been studied are often constructed so that different motives of the individuals involved come in conflict with one another. Consider the following situation. The hot water heater in your apartment provides just enough hot water for you and your roommates to each take a quick shower in the morning. You really enjoy letting the hot water beat down on you, but you also realize that your roommates would have to take cold showers if you indulged yourself. What would you do? The answer to this question and the study of cooperative and competitive strategies in this kind of situation is also part of understanding helping and altruism. We discuss this issue in Chapter 8 when we discuss social dilemmas.

SOLVING THE PUZZLE

It is interesting that Latané and Darley's (1970) book reporting the work that sparked so much interest in the area of prosocial behavior was titled with a question—*The Unresponsive Bystander: Why Doesn't He Help*? More recently, Batson (1991) titled his book on this topic *The Altruism Question*. The study of prosocial behavior remains full of unsolved problems and unanswered questions. As researchers working in this field who are trying to understand this phenomenon, we often feel like we are working on a jigsaw puzzle, trying to find just the right pieces to complete the picture, and then putting them together in just the right way. (We also sometimes feel as if all of the pieces are the same color and the box top does not show the right picture!)

There are many questions to be asked and answered about prosocial behavior. For example, although Latané and Darley, and the public at large, were surprised that people appeared reluctant to come to the aid of Ms. Genovese, was there really any reason why we *should* expect someone to provide aid to a perfect stranger? What would make people willing to get involved in an emergency situation or give time or money to some charitable cause from which they will receive little or no benefit? Is there something about a person—some personal characteristics, perhaps—that makes that person more inclined to give help or to cooperate with others? If there is some personal characteristic that is related to a tendency to help, is that tendency due to some inborn, genetic endowment that makes helping a part of the human condition, or has the person simply learned to be helpful in the same way that people learn many other social behaviors? And what about the people who are in need of help? Are there individual differences that make them more or less likely to seek help from others? Are there certain circumstances when people confronted with major problems will try to solve their own problems instead of asking for assistance from someone else?

These kinds of questions illustrate the kinds of broad issues that confront social psychologists and other scientists in their efforts to understand more fully the nature of prosocial behavior. We will use these questions and many others to guide our exploration of this intriguing field of investigation. Each chapter will begin with one or more of these questions about some aspect of prosocial action. Using this question as our starting point, we will then consider the research findings as they pertain to the question. Rather than simply describing a series of research studies, however, we will present the basic concepts and principles that have been identified. That is, we will try to find the pieces of the puzzle. When we believe that all the pieces have been identified and put in their proper place, we will conclude the chapter with a summary and an answer to the introductory question. Below are brief synopses of each of the chapters of the book and the questions asked in each of them.

The focus of interest in Chapter 2 is on how bystanders react when they see a person in distress. More specifically, we are interested in how the context or situation affects a bystander's decision of whether to offer help. We ask a substantially revised version of the question Bibb Latané and John Darley asked twenty-five years ago when they began their research on bystander intervention. Recall that they asked why bystanders do not help. We ask, "When will a bystander help?" and "What conditions lead a bystander to offer help to a person in need?" To answer these questions, we introduce a model of how people make decisions about helping, and we supplement this model with a discussion of the costs and rewards associated with helping someone in distress, and how this cost-reward analysis affects the actions a bystander takes.

Chapter 3 also focuses on bystander intervention, but whereas Chapter 2 asks *when* will people help, Chapter 3 asks the question, "*Why* do bystanders decide to intervene on another person's behalf?" That is, we address the factors that motivate a bystander to offer help. To put the pieces of this puzzle together, we review theories concerned with the roles that learning experiences, emotions and feelings, and social norms play in motivating one person to help another. One very important part of solving the puzzle of why people help is whether helping involves selfish or altruistic motives. Therefore, we spend considerable time on this issue.

The next two chapters approach helping and altruism from a broader perspective. They are concerned with the origins of general and specific forms of prosocial behavior in humans. In Chapter 4, we ask, "Is there a genetic basis for prosocial tendencies in humans?" and, if there is, "What are the processes or mechanisms that are responsible for such tendencies?" To answer these questions, we present concepts from behavioral genetics, evolutionary theory, and sociobiology as they apply to the process of natural selection and the evolution of certain characteristics. We consider the mechanisms that could naturally select for prosocial behavior in humans. Special attention is given to empathy and the role it plays as a possible cause of human helping and altruism.

We discuss the biological mechanisms and social processes that may be responsible for humans' remarkable tendency to empathize with others in need.

Although Chapter 5 is also concerned with the origins of prosocial behaviors in humans, we approach this issue from a much less biological or genetic perspective than we do in the previous chapter. We begin this chapter by noting that as humans grow and mature, there appear to be substantial changes in what motivates them to be helpful. The question around which the chapter is organized is, "What are the processes responsible for these changes?" To answer this question, we turn to general theories of how humans are socialized, such as social-learning theory and cognitive-social development. These theories provide rather specific models and descriptions of how and why humans usually become more prosocial as they mature. As we present these theories, we discuss the specific mechanisms responsible for these changes.

Chapter 6 approaches helping and altruism from a perspective somewhat different from that of the previous five chapters. In the previous chapters, we focus on continuities and similarities among people in terms of when and why they will help. This chapter places greater emphasis on the differences between people in their willingness to help others. We ask, "Are there stable individual differences among people in their propensity to be helpful or altruistic?" and, if the answer to this question is yes, "What are the personal characteristics associated with these differences?" We review the research on specific demographic and personal characteristics that are related to helping, and we then discuss how personal characteristics and contextual or situational factors interact to affect the likelihood that a person will act prosocially.

Chapter 7 represents yet another change in perspective on helping and altruism. We turn our attention from the person who gives help to the person who receives it. We ask two highly interrelated questions: "Why do people with a problem sometimes not ask for help?" and "Why do they sometimes react negatively to the help they receive?" Finding the answers to these questions requires a consideration of the characteristics of the person in need, the nature of the problem that confronts the person, and the characteristics of the potential provider of the help. We discuss each of these and use a general model of reactions to helping to put this puzzle together.

In Chapter 8, we return to the giving of help, but we change our emphasis from individual actions to collective forms of prosocial behavior. We place helping in social and societal context. In such a context, there is interdependence between the actions of individuals of the collective of which they are part. More important, there is often a conflict between the short-term interests of the individual and the long-term interests of the group. This leads us to the very practical question of interest in Chapter 8: "How can we increase an individual's willingness to contribute to the long-term welfare of his or her collective?" To answer this question, we consider theories of interdependent social behavior and the research on the characteristics of those people who are willing to donate their time and effort to the public good.

The final chapter is divided into two distinct sections. In the first, we present a summary of the answers to the questions we asked in each of the chapters and offer two general models that attempt to integrate what we believe we know about helping and altruism. The second section concerns the questions we could not answer and the questions we did not ask. Put differently, the final chapter contains what we know about helping and altruism, and what we do not know but believe we need to learn. We attempt to look into the future and identify important theoretical and applied areas for future research. The exciting prospect for us is that there seem to be so many new areas to study and questions to ask. But let us begin with what we know.

2

The Context: When Will People Help?

———————————— ❖ ————————————

In Chapter 1, we raised a fundamental question, "Are people prosocial by nature?" Then we considered how this question has been addressed across time, cultures, and disciplines. Despite the fables, parables, and the long philosophical debate about helping and altruism, the issue of whether humans are essentially a prosocial species has remained an unsolved mystery. In this chapter, we begin to assemble the pieces of this puzzle; we identify the situations and circumstances that affect people's willingness to offer help.

THE QUESTION

The two incidents described below illustrate the range of responses that bystanders can make when they encounter others in trouble or distress. The first is the assault of Kitty Genovese, mentioned briefly in Chapter 1.

> On Friday night, March 13th, 1964, in New York City Kitty Genovese arrived home late from work. She parked in the lot outside her apartment. As she stepped out of her car, a man emerged from the shadows brandishing a knife. Before she could react, he struck. She cried out for help. Lights went on, and faces appeared in the windows of the apartments overlooking the parking lot; the assailant fled from the scene. But he did not go far, and from across the street he watched what happened. Nobody came to help Kitty Genovese, and the police did not arrive. So, the assailant returned to the parking lot; he stalked and caught his victim again. He stabbed her, and she cried out once more. Lights again went on, faces again appeared, and the attacker again escaped into the darkness. Still, no one came to help. As the wounded woman staggered toward the entrance of her building, the man returned. This time he stabbed her until she died. We know so much about this event, which involved three separate incidents over a 45-minute period, because when the police arrived a short time later, they

Reginald Denny was pulled from his truck and savagely beaten during the riots in South Central Los Angeles in 1992 (left photo). Fortunately for Mr. Denny, four residents of the area who witnessed the beating on television came to his aid and rushed him to the hospital. Unlike the passive bystanders who failed to intervene in the Kitty Genovese case, Reginald Denny's rescuers (right photo, from left, Titus Murphy, Lei Yuille, Terri Barnett, and Bobby Green) chose to risk their own safety to save the life of a stranger in need. (Gamma Liaison)

found that 38 people had witnessed the event from beginning to end. But not one of the 38 witnesses had done anything to stop the attacker or to help Kitty Genovese.

Now consider the assault on Reginald Denny, a more recent incident where a person was in trouble and needed the help of others.

In 1992, "South Central" Los Angeles was ravaged by one of the worst civil disturbances in the history of the United States. On April 29, Reginald O. Denny stopped his sand-and-gravel truck at the intersection of Florence and Normandie Streets. Because of the mobs in the streets, he could not drive his truck any further. Suddenly, the door of his truck opened. Four African-American youths dragged him out and began to beat him mercilessly. They punched him; they kicked him; they hit him with makeshift clubs and bricks. He was close to death from massive head injuries when four strangers—three men and a woman—risked their lives to come to his rescue. Watching this horrifying scene on live television in the relative safety of their homes nearby, they had rushed outside, jumped into their cars, and driven to the scene. Fending off his attackers, they lifted him into the cab of his truck and drove him to the hospital. According to Denny's doctors, had his rescuers brought him to the hospital five minutes later, he would have died. Reginald Denny is White; the four people who saved his life are African-Americans.

The response of the four rescuers in this case seems to reflect the ultimate in caring—the willingness to risk one's own life for the sake of another person. These two cases suggest a paradox of human nature. Are people essentially self*fish* and uncaring by nature? Or, are people self*less* and compassionate? In this chapter, we attempt to unravel this mystery and answer these questions by examining when people *will* help and when they *will not*.

UNDERSTANDING WHEN PEOPLE WILL HELP

As noted in Chapter 1, the Kitty Genovese incident was the primary reason for the explosion of interest in helping in the 1960s and 1970s. Headlines and editorials expressed outrage at the insensitivity of contemporary society. The behavior of the bystanders was obviously morally wrong, and what is wrong is commonly assumed to be abnormal. The question became: Why did these people behave so abnormally? What made them act this way? Was it in their nature, or did things such as the experience of living in a big city cause their actions (or rather, inaction)?

These questions are important and interesting, but we do not want to overlook any important pieces in attempting to solve this puzzle. Therefore, we need to start at the beginning and examine our initial assumptions. Given our social and moral ideals, the behavior of the bystanders in the Kitty Genovese case *seems* immoral and wrong and that of Reginald Denny's rescuers *seems* moral and right. But the first key question we should ask is: Which of these behaviors is more common? Or what is the "normal" behavior in such a situation.

The fact is, there were thirty-eight witnesses to Kitty Genovese's attack, and they all exhibited the *same* behavior—they did not help. There were hundreds of people at the scene of the attack on Reginald Denny and perhaps thousands of others who saw it on live television and could have helped him, but did nothing. To be sure, there are many differences between these two incidents. But, if we look *only* at these two particular situations, and put aside our beliefs about the way the world *ought* to be, then not intervening may be the *normal* behavior. Perhaps those who rescued Reginald Denny are—whatever we may prefer to think—the exception rather than the rule.

This is where we will begin. The first piece of the puzzle is that, given these situations, the behavior of the bystanders who did not help was the more common or normal. What was it about these situations that made nonintervention the *normal* response? In attempting to answer this and other questions of interest in this chapter, we shall rely heavily on the results of laboratory and field experiments conducted by social psychologists interested in the phenomenon of bystander intervention—when a bystander observes a person in distress or need of help, and intervenes (or does not intervene) on that person's behalf. To some people, tightly controlled experiments might seem a strange way to understand the behavior of Kitty Genovese's neighbors, but these investigations have shed a good deal of light on when bystanders will help.

The first systematic attempt to try to explain the Kitty Genovese incident was carried out by two social psychologists, Bibb Latané and John Darley. In the mid-1960s, they began a landmark program of research to find out why normal people might not help another person in distress (Darley & Latané, 1968; Latané & Darley, 1970; also see Chapter 1).

Although the behavior of witnesses during Kitty Genovese's attack seemed cold and uncaring, bystander apathy may *not* have been the cause. Bystanders could have been very concerned for Kitty Genovese's safety but, for a variety of reasons, decided not to intervene.

A Decision Model of Bystander Intervention

Latané and Darley's decision model of bystander intervention proposes that whether or not a person helps depends upon the outcomes of a series of prior decisions. They represent the process as a decision tree (see Figure 2.1). Before a person initiates a helping response, that person goes through five decision-making steps. The bystander must (1) notice that

FIGURE 2.1
Steps in the Latané and Darley decision model of bystander intervention.

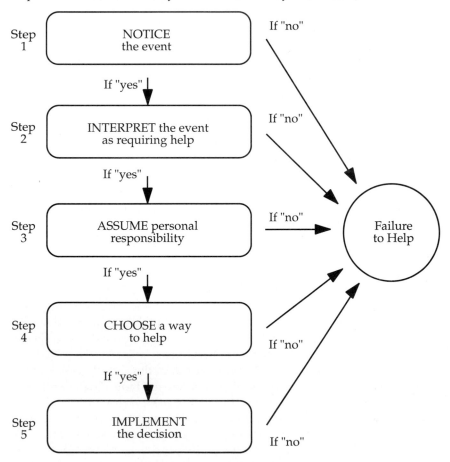

Step 1 — NOTICE the event — If "yes" → If "no"

Step 2 — INTERPRET the event as requiring help — If "yes" → If "no"

Step 3 — ASSUME personal responsibility — If "yes" → If "no"

Step 4 — CHOOSE a way to help — If "yes" → If "no"

Step 5 — IMPLEMENT the decision — If "no"

Failure to Help

something is wrong, (2) define it as an emergency, (3) decide whether to take personal responsibility, (4) decide what kind of help to give, and (5) decide to implement the chosen course of action. The decision made at any one step has important implications for the bystander's ultimate response—a "no" response at *any* step means the victim will not be helped.

At first glance, the steps in the model seem obvious and straightforward. The contribution of this decision tree may seem to simply be that it explicitly identifies the decisions that must be made and organizes them into a logical sequence. However, the apparent simplicity of this model should not obscure more subtle issues and influences. We now consider the evidence for this model. Much of this work was performed during the 1960s and 1970s. While relatively old, this work is not dated. It identifies the key processes involved and provides a foundation for more current work on helping and altruism.

Step 1: noticing that something is wrong. Obviously, a bystander must notice that something is wrong before initiating any action. The critical question is: What is it about a situation that will make people more or less likely to notice that something is potentially wrong? One answer involves that nature of the event: Some events are inherently more attention-getting than others. For example, in one early study (Piliavin, Piliavin, & Broll, 1976), some bystanders saw a vivid scene in which a confederate either stumbled and fell down a flight of stairs or slumped to the floor in a faint. Other bystanders witnessed only the aftermath of the accident or fainting spell (i.e., the confederate rubbing his or her ankle or regaining consciousness). The vividness and action of an entire scenario is presumably more attention getting than only the aftermath of the incident. As would be expected on the basis of the first step of the model, the more noticeable the situation, the more often bystanders helped the victim. They helped 89 percent of the time in the vivid scenario conditions, but they helped only 13 percent of the time in the aftermath conditions. Thus, as outlined in the first step of the Latané and Darley model, people are more likely to help if they notice that something is wrong.

Other aspects of the physical and social context can also make a difference and affect the likelihood that a bystander will help. For example, it is commonly assumed that people are less helpful in urban than in rural environments. Indeed, the research that exists generally supports this conclusion (Steblay, 1987), and the effect is even found in countries other than the United States (Hedge & Yousif, 1992). But as psychologists trying to solve the puzzle of altruism and helping, we must ask additional questions about these kinds of differences: Why do they occur? What causes them? That is, what is it about the experiences of living in large cities that makes the people less likely to help?

One possibility is that people in urban environments are less likely to notice that something is wrong. Cities are busy places, full of noise and activity. To reduce stimulation to a manageable and comfortable level, people may try to restrict their attention to only those aspects of the environment that are most personally important and block out irrelevant stimulation (Milgram 1970). As a consequence, the needs of strangers may go largely unnoticed. Consistent with this *stimulus overload* explanation, Bickman et al. (1973) found that students living in high-rise, high-density dormitories were less likely to return a lost letter than were similar students who lived in less densely populated buildings.

Studies that have directly manipulated environmental stimulation also support the overload hypothesis. In a field experiment, Mathews and Canon (1975) compared helping when there was excessive environmental stimulation (noise from a power lawn mower) and when there was not. The experimenters also manipulated the presence or absence of cues that indicated a need for assistance. In the high-need condition, a confederate wore a wrist-to-shoulder cast; in the low-need condition, the confederate had no apparent disability. The opportunity to help arose when the confederate dropped several boxes of books a few feet in front of a potential helper. When the book dropper was not wearing a cast and apparent need was low, the rate of helping was low (only about 15 percent of the time) regardless of noise level. When the confederate was wearing a cast and apparent need was high, subjects in the low-noise conditions were very responsive. They helped 80 percent of the time. With loud noise, however, the cast appeared not to be noticed; helping remained at 15 percent in both the cast and no-cast conditions. These findings suggest that excessive stimulation can reduce the likelihood that people will notice something is wrong, which according to the Latané and Darley model prevents the bystander from moving on to the next decision step. If people do not notice that something is wrong, they will not help.

Another factor that may influence whether or not people notice something is wrong is their mood. A *mood* is a transitory feeling, such as being happy or being frustrated. There is considerable evidence that when individuals are in a good mood, they are more likely to help (Salovey, Mayer, & Rosenhan, 1991). Could this be due, at least in part, to increased attentiveness to others? Two studies carried out by McMillen, Sanders, and Solomon (1977) suggest that this may be the case. In the first study, the experimenter provided students with positive or negative information about their performance on a task, which produced good or bad moods in them. Then, while a student worked on another task, the experimenters increased the volume of white noise until he or she looked up, indicating that the noise had registered. Students in good moods were more attentive to their environment; they noticed the noise at a significantly lowered decibel level. In the second study, after the same two first steps—the mood manipulation and being assigned to another task—the students saw an overburdened, female confederate, who needed assistance to open a door. The majority of students experiencing good moods noticed her plight and helped, regardless of whether the woman made a noise to attract their attention. Students experiencing bad moods, however, helped her only if she actively tried to attract their attention. Thus, good moods seem to make people generally more sensitive to others' needs.

It is also possible that the way moods affect sensitivity to other people's needs may partially explain some of the urban-rural differences in helping we discussed earlier. In general, the level of environmental stressors (e.g., noise, crowding, air pollution) is higher in urban than in rural areas. Environmental stressors usually have a negative impact on people's moods (Bell, Fisher, Baum, & Greene, 1990). Thus, generally poorer moods among people living in big cities may make them less aware of a person who needs help and, thus, less likely to help.

But even when people do notice that something is out of the ordinary, they will not always help. The next decision within the Latané and Darley model concerns *interpreting* the situation as one in which help is needed.

Step 2: interpreting a need for help. One of the important influences on whether a situation is interpreted as one requiring immediate assistance is the nature of the event. Those that elicit distress cues in the victim are likely to be interpreted as emergencies. One distress cue is screaming, and, not surprisingly, screaming is a particularly effective way of getting a bystander to not only notice an event but also communicate the seriousness of the problem to others. Screams often lead people to interpret an event as an *emergency*; that is, as an unusual event in which the victim's need is serious, deteriorating rapidly, and requires outside assistance (Shotland & Huston, 1979). Figure 2.2 summarizes the results of several experiments that manipulated the presence or absence of screams in potential emergency situations.

Note that there is not only a large difference between helping in emergencies with and without distress cues (such as screams), but also a consistently high level of intervention exhibited by bystanders in situations in which the victim's need is apparent. Victims who make their serious need clear by screaming receive help 75 to 100 percent of the time. Under these circumstances, there appears to be little evidence of bystander apathy. Once subjects interpret the situation as an emergency, they are very likely to help. People who choose to suffer silently or are unable to make their needs known, however, are unfortunately more likely to continue to suffer.

One reason why screams increase the likelihood of helping so much is that they clarify that the situation as one requiring immediate assistance. There are, of course, other ways this could be accomplished, such as presenting the situation to potential helpers as one in which there would be a rapid and serious deterioration of the victim's condition if no one helps. For example, Shotland and Huston (1979) found that people were much more likely to help others who asked for a ride home so they could receive an insulin injection or get back to a roommate who had

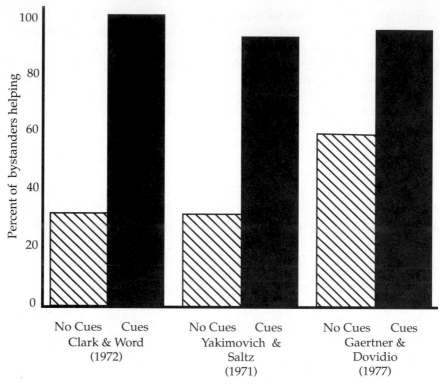

FIGURE 2.2
Clear cues of distress, such as screams, increase the likelihood that the situation will be interpreted as requiring assistance and thereby facilitate helping.

taken too many sleeping pills (an average of 64 percent of the time) than people who needed a ride so they could take allergy medicine or get back to a depressed roommate (an average of 45 percent).

In some circumstances, people may notice that something is amiss but, because the nature of the event is unclear, they cannot readily interpret what is going on. What will these bystanders do then? People have a basic need to understand their environment and, when they are confused, they often look to other people for information and guidance. When objective reality is ambiguous, people will rely on social reality. In such instances, *informational social influence*—using other people's behavior and opinions as information about what is real and what is the correct action to take—becomes important (Deutsch & Gerard, 1955). People in new or unusual surroundings typically look to others in the same situation to learn what they should be feeling, thinking, and doing. Because emergency situations are usually novel and unexpected events, the behavior of others can strongly influence whether an event is interpreted as requiring assistance and consequently can affect the likelihood of intervention.

One of the first experiments by Latané and Darley (1970) illustrates the profound effect that the actions of others can have in emergency situations. Male students were invited to an interview to discuss some of the problems involved in life at a large urban university. As these students were completing a questionnaire, they were exposed to a potentially dangerous situation. Smoke began to pour into the room through a wall vent. The smoke continued until the room was so filled with smoke that a person could barely see the opposite side of the room. Nevertheless, the danger of the situation was somewhat ambiguous, because real smoke was not used. The social context was varied by the presence and actions of other people in the room. The students were either alone, with two equally naïve strangers, or with two confederates who had been instructed only to shrug their shoulders and act as if nothing were wrong. The behavior of the two confederates was designed to lead participants to interpret the situation as one that did not require action. The major question was whether these students would respond in ways that would save *their own* lives (such as leaving the room).

The results supported Latané and Darley's *social influence hypothesis* and showed the tremendous impact of informational social influence. People who were alone were more likely to report the smoke than were those with other bystanders. Whereas 75 percent of the students who were alone reported the smoke, only 10 percent of the students with the two passive confederates responded in ways that ensured their safety. Furthermore, the passive behavior of the confederates led many of the people who did not respond to interpret the situation as something other than critical. These people came to believe that nothing was wrong and therefore no action was necessary. (To make sense out of this unusual situation, some of them even concluded that the smoke was "truth gas"!)

What about the condition with three naïve subjects? Because there were three people involved, you might expect the likelihood that *at least one* of these three people would respond should be higher than 75 percent, the rate of taking action when there was only one person. Actually, only 38 percent of the time did any one of the participants take action in this condition. This is an illustration of a phenomenon known as *pluralistic ignorance*. Each subject, trying to stay "cool" but also trying to understand what was happening, probably looked calm and unconcerned to the other two people. The outward calm of the other two participants then led each person to feel and act more calm, which in turn signaled to the two other participants that nothing was wrong. The group developed a shared illusion that the situation was not critical and that there was no need to take action. Of course, if this emergency had been real, these behaviors could have created an ironic situation in which three people would have died calmly!

Although the presence of others typically inhibits intervention (Latané, Nida, & Wilson, 1981), that outcome is not inevitable. According to the idea of informational social influence, what the other people say and do are critical elements. When other bystanders act calm, they help define ambiguous situations as nonemergencies; when other bystanders act alarmed, the likelihood that the situation will be interpreted as one requiring help will be increased (Wilson, 1976).

Ervin Staub (1974) demonstrated this in another one of the early studies of bystander intervention. Pairs of bystanders heard a crash in an adjoining room, followed by a female victim's cry for help; one of the bystanders was the experimenter's confederate. His behavior was designed to influence how subjects interpreted the situation. In one condition, the confederate emphasized the possible seriousness of the situation by remarking, "That sounds bad. Maybe we should do something," and then prepared to enter the adjacent room. In the other condition, the confederate suggested to the other bystander that the situation really did not require assistance: "That sounds like a tape recording. Maybe they are trying to test us." Those people who heard the confederate reinforce the severity of the situation helped 100 percent of the time. As expected from the social influence hypothesis, those people who heard the confederate minimize the seriousness of the situation helped only 25 percent of the time. By comparison, when two naïve subjects were placed in this situation, help was given 60 percent of the time. Therefore, the presence of others can either facilitate or inhibit helping, depending on whether the action or statements of these others suggest that help is or is not needed.

In this context, let us return to the people who saved Reginald Denny's life. In the trial of the men charged with the attack, one of the rescuers testified that when she and her brother saw the beating on television, her brother looked at her said, "'We are Christians. We've got to go help him out,' and I said 'right.' Then he went and got his keys." (*Newsweek*, September 5, 1993). Without this exchange, Reginald Denny might have died.

We have demonstrated that whether a bystander interprets an event as a situation requiring assistance depends upon both the *clarity* of the situation and the *actions* of other bystanders. How are these factors related? One hypothesis is that when a situation is ambiguous, people's desire to understand it leads them to look to others to define the situation. Conversely, when the event is *un*ambiguous and the need for help is clear, bystanders will have less need to look to others for information and should therefore be less influenced by the reactions of other bystanders. Support for this reasoning comes from a study by Clark and Word (1972).

In this experiment, male college students participated alone or in two-person or five-person groups. While students were filling out questionnaires, they witnessed a university maintenance employee enter an adjacent room carrying a ladder and a set of venetian blinds. After a few minutes, the students heard either an unambiguous or ambiguous emergency. In the unambiguous emergency, there was a loud crash and groans

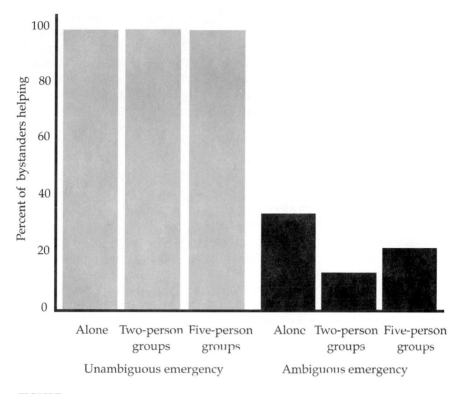

FIGURE 2.3
The impact of informational social influence is greater in ambiguous
than in unambiguous situations. (Adapted from Clark & Word, 1972.)

of pain; in the ambiguous emergency, there was a loud crash but no verbal cues indicating pain or need for assistance.

As illustrated in Figure 2.3, the typical bystander effect (the inhibiting
effect of the presence of others on helping) occurred for groups exposed
to the ambiguous emergency. Students who were in two- and five-person
groups were less likely to intervene than were those who were alone.
When the situation was unambiguous, however, the presence of others
had no effect; helping occurred in every case, regardless of the presence of
others. For these subjects, the emergency was so clear that there could be
only one interpretation for what was happening: The victim was severely
hurt, and assistance was needed immediately. Under these conditions, the
presence of others had little impact on subjects' interpretations and consequently had little effect on bystander response. This may also help to
further explain why the people helped Reginald Denny. The television
pictures provided graphic and vivid information about his very serious
and immediate need, and they responded to it.

In ambiguous situations, however, people will seek social information to gain a better understanding of what is going on. And it is likely that they will be most influenced by those who are perceived to provide the most valid information. Specifically, *social comparison theory* (Festinger, 1954) suggests that people will be most influenced by the behaviors of others who are seen as more similar to them. Similarity may be based on any number of dimensions that are relevant in a given situation: similarity of attitudes, common background or preparation, comparable ability, proximity, or shared fate (Goethals & Darley, 1987). Consistent with social comparison theory, Smith, Smythe, and Lien (1972) found that subjects who were with another bystander (a confederate) generally helped less often than subjects who were alone, *and* the inhibiting effects of this other bystander were much greater when the subjects believed the confederate was similar to them than when they believed the confederate was dissimilar. Bystanders were more likely to accept the no-help-needed definition implied by the confederate's passive behavior when they believed that the confederate was similar to themselves.

The first two steps in the Latané and Darley model (i.e., noticing the event and interpreting it as a situation requiring assistance) are well supported by the research evidence. But, do they explain the behavior of bystanders in the Kitty Genovese incident? Not entirely. The victim's screams brought people to their windows; they noticed the event. Many people also clearly saw the attack; they understood that she needed help. Because most people could not see the reactions of others who were in different apartments, it is unlikely that informational social influence distorted their perception of the victim's need for help. Although noticing the event and defining it as an emergency may increase the likelihood of intervention, there are additional decisions that must be made before people offer assistance. The pieces of this part of the puzzle are not yet in their correct places. The next step in the Latané and Darley model involves the decision to take *personal* responsibility for helping and provides the next piece needed to complete this puzzle.

Step 3: taking personal responsibility. When a person believes that he or she is the only witness to an emergency, the answer to the question, Is it *my* responsibility to help? is fairly obvious. The person bears 100 percent of the responsibility for helping and would bear 100 percent of the guilt and blame for not helping. Not surprisingly, people in these circumstances typically help (see Figure 2.3). However, when a bystander believes that other people are also witnessing the emergency and that these other people are also capable of helping, then the answer to the question concerning accepting personal responsibility is less obvious. If you believe that someone else will take action, then that assumption may relieve you from the responsibility of intervening. But what will happen if everyone believes that someone else will do it? Unfortunately, no one will do it—and that is presumably what occurred in the Kitty Genovese case.

Darley and Latané (1968) devised a laboratory test of the Kitty Genovese incident to examine how the presumed *presence of others* can influence intervention even when no social information about the severity of the situation can possibly be conveyed through their actions or words. College students in separate cubicles discussed problems associated with living in an urban environment over an intercom system that allowed only one person to talk at a time. Participants were led to believe that their discussion group consisted of two people (the subject and the future victim), three people (the subject, future victim, and one other), or six people (the subject, future victim, and four others). A confederate played the role of the victim. Early in the discussion, he casually mentioned that he had epilepsy and that the anxiety and stress resulting from living in a large city made him prone to seizures. Later, he became increasingly loud and incoherent, choking, gasping, and crying out before lapsing into silence. The critical question was whether helping would be affected by the number of bystanders the subjects thought also heard the seizure.

The number of other bystanders believed to be present when the victim had the seizure exerted a strong effect on the way the subjects responded to this emergency. The more bystanders the subjects thought were present, the less likely the subjects were to help. Eighty-five percent of the bystanders who were alone left their cubicles and helped before the end of the seizure (which lasted three minutes), but only 62 percent of the people who believed that one other witness was available and 31 percent of those who thought that four others were present helped during this time period. Within six minutes from the time the seizure began, 100 percent of the bystanders who were alone, 81 percent of the people with one other presumed bystander, and 62 percent of the people with four other presumed bystanders attempted to help.

Because bystanders could not see one another and, therefore, could not be misled by each other's inaction, social influence and pluralistic ignorance cannot account for the failure to intervene. Instead, the key factor seems to be whether bystanders would take personal responsibility. When other bystanders are present, *diffusion of responsibility* occurs. That is, people may feel less personally responsible for helping because they come to believe that others will intervene. This process seems to be the best explanation for the lack of action by the witnesses to the Kitty Genovese incident; the witnesses saw the lights in their neighbors' apartments and assumed that one of the other witnesses would call the police or go to Kitty Genovese's rescue.

It is important to emphasize that the inhibiting effect of the presence of others through diffusion of responsibility is not bystander apathy. People may be truly concerned about the welfare of the victim, but they sincerely believe that someone else will help (see Latané et al., 1981). Holding this belief, they do not have to assume personal responsibility and, therefore, do not help (Otten, Penner, & Waugh, 1988). One implication of this reasoning is that bystanders may diffuse responsibility when there are other witnesses who are capable of helping but not when there are people who are incapable of helping (Korte, 1969).

Leonard Bickman (1971) conducted a direct test of this hypothesis. Subjects, who believed that they either were the only bystander or were one of two bystanders, heard an emergency over an intercom system. Subjects who believed that the other person was as close to a victim as they were (in the same building) and equally capable of helping diffused responsibility: They were much less likely to help than were subjects who believed that they were alone. However, when bystanders believed that the other person was in another building and was unable to intervene, they helped as frequently as those who were alone. Therefore, people who diffuse responsibility are not necessarily uncaring; they may simply believe that others are more likely or perhaps better qualified to help.

One way of preventing diffusion of responsibility from occurring, besides making it clear that others are not as capable of helping, is to focus responsibility onto one person. Although others are present, the responsibility for helping belongs to the person in charge. For instance, have you ever asked a stranger to watch your possessions while you were gone for a short time? Did you ever wonder whether this was *really* effective, or did it just make you *feel* more secure? An experiment provides an answer (Moriarty, 1975). Confederates either asked sunbathers on a beach to watch their possessions while they went for a walk or, in a control condition, asked them for a match as they left for their walk. Soon after, a second confederate wandered by, snatched a radio from the unoccupied blanket, and ran down the beach. For people who had agreed to accept responsibility, the response was impressive. Ninety-four percent intervened, often in dramatic and physical fashion. By contrast, only 20 percent of the bystanders who were not explicitly made responsible tried to prevent the theft. Thus, once people assume positions of leadership in a group, agree to accept responsibility, or publicly state their intention to help, they are likely to intervene, even though other potential helpers are available (Baumeister, Chesner, Sanders, & Tice, 1988; Schwartz, 1977).

Social norms and rules. Besides diffusion of responsibility, the decision concerning whether or not to accept personal responsibility for helping may depend on social norms. Social norms are unwritten standards about how people should behave in a given situation. Urban-rural differences in helping, which were discussed earlier, may be attributed to norms concerning the acceptance of personal responsibility for helping, as well as differences in noticing that something is wrong (the stimulus overload hypothesis). Specifically, small towns and large cities are generally believed to have different norms concerning helping. At least in terms of stereotypes, residents of small communities are expected to be helpful and socially supportive, whereas urban dwellers are expected to be unhelpful and insensitive to the needs of others (Krupat & Guild, 1980).

We have already noted that people who live in large cities are less likely to notice other people in need. But, if these different norms actually exist and also influence helping, then urban-rural differences in helping should be observed even when a person cannot avoid noticing the event. Consistent with the normative explanation, in situations in which potential helpers were stopped and specifically asked for assistance, people were still less helpful in urban than in rural environments (Steblay, 1987). Similarly, Foss (1983) found that proportionately more blood was donated on smaller college campuses. Thus, urban and larger social environments lead to decreased helping, relative to rural and smaller environments, not only as a consequence of coping with stimulus overload (i.e., not noticing events) but also because people seem less concerned about the needs of others once these needs are recognized. (See Chapter 8 for a further discussion of rural-urban differences in helping.)

Bystanders seem to be sensitive not only to general social norms but also to specific social rules. In a 1971 study, Staub established social rules by telling seventh-grade students that they either were permitted to enter an adjacent room to take a break from the questionnaires they were completing or that they were expressly prohibited from entering the room because they might influence each other's answers on the questionnaires. Later, the students heard an apparent emergency, an accident involving a person in the next room. Would seventh graders let the rule prohibiting them from entering that room prevent them from intervening? It would seem that the potential consequences to the victim for not being helped should outweigh personal consequences to the bystander for violating the rule. (In fact, because the reason for not entering the room—sharing answers with the person in the room—would no longer be relevant if an emergency were in progress, the prohibition was actually meaningless.) Nevertheless, social rules still exerted a substantial effect. Whereas 91 percent of those who were given prior permission to enter the room offered help, only 45 percent of the seventh graders who were previously prohibited from entering the room offered help.

Would adults act in the same way? In a second study, Staub (1971) showed that they do. Adults (ages 18 to 28) who were previously prohibited from entering the room (so that the person working on a timed task would not be disturbed) were less likely to help than were subjects permitted to enter the room to get a cup of coffee (61 percent versus 89 percent). Once again, the social context strongly influenced a bystander's decision to take personal responsibility for intervention, the third step in the Latané and Darley model.

Steps 4 and 5: deciding what kind of help to give and implementing the decision. The fourth and fifth decision steps involve deciding *what* to do and *implementing* the chosen course of action. Whereas the first three steps in the Latané and Darley model have received careful empirical scrutiny and support, these last two steps have not been the focus of much research. That is, most of the studies of bystanders' responses in emergencies have examined whether or not people will do *something* but not what that something is. The research that does exist, however, supports these parts of the model.

A large proportion of college students are trained in first-aid procedures. Shotland and Heinold (1985) considered the question of whether this knowledge would actually make people more effective helpers. In the

Help is more likely to be received from bystanders who have previous experience or some special training that prepares them to provide effective assistance. While the emergency depicted may not arise often, the victim is fortunate that a bystander who knows what to do is present. (The Far Side cartoon by Gary Larson is reprinted by permission of Chronicle Features, San Francisco, Ca. All rights reserved.)

"Calm down, everyone! I've had experience
with this sort of thing before . . . Does someone
have a hammer?"

context of the Latané and Darley model, will bystanders with first-aid training be better able to decide what to do (step 4) and then act effectively on that decision (step 5)? In Shotland and Heinold's experiment, bystanders who did or did not have previous first-aid training encountered an emergency in which the victim had profuse arterial bleeding. Consistent with the first two steps of the model, the clearer the emergency was at its onset, the more likely it was that a bystander would do *something*. In addition, bystanders without first-aid training were just as likely to do something as were bystanders with this background. First-aid training, however, had a significant impact on *what* these bystanders did. Consistent with the fourth and fifth steps, people with first-aid training offered help with greater medical effectiveness than did those without training. In fact, the assistance given by people without training was often medically harmful to the victim.

Ineffective assistance can also be harmful to the helper. Clark and Word (1974) found that people who had little experience with electricity would sometimes inadvertently jeopardize their own lives while attempting to help a victim who had been severely shocked. These subjects ran over and impulsively touched the victim who was still holding a "live" electrical wire. If the situation had been real, this action would have been both ineffective for the victim and deadly for the bystander. Thus, the last two steps of the Latané and Darley model are critical. Bystanders must decide what to do and know how to do it before intervention is truly helpful.

Summary

The decision-tree model of bystander intervention proposes that before a bystander actually intervenes on behalf of a victim, he or she makes a set of sequential decisions: Is something wrong? Is it an emergency? Is it my responsibility to offer help? What kind of help should I give? and How should I give it? These decisions are influenced by the situation in which the emergency occurs, the nature of the emergency, the presence of other bystanders and their reactions, and social norms and rules. Overall, the Latané and Darley decision model of intervention provides a valuable framework for understanding when bystanders will or will not help others in need. Although the model was initially developed to understand how people respond in emergencies that require immediate assistance, aspects of the model have been successfully applied to many other situations, ranging from preventing someone from driving drunk to making a decision about whether to donate a kidney to a relative (Borgida, Conner, & Manteufel, 1992; Rabow, Newcomb, Monto, & Hernandez, 1990).

The model does not present a complete picture, however. There are situations in which bystanders will not intervene even though the need of a victim is apparent and the personal focus of responsibility is clear. Some of these are fairly obvious. For example, the greater the personal cost to the helper, the less likely people are to help (Omoto & Snyder, 1990; Snyder & Omoto, 1992a, 1992b). To account for these additional factors influencing helping, frameworks such as the *cost-reward analysis* have been developed. The basic assumption of this perspective on helping is that when bystanders decide on what actions to take, they try to minimize costs and maximize rewards. The cost-reward analysis, which is covered in the next section, in some ways serves to "fine-tune" some of the processes outlined by Latané and Darley. That is, a cost-reward analysis allows a more fine-grained analysis of how the nature of the situation and characteristics of the victim influence helping. The puzzle pieces are getting smaller, but even small pieces are needed to complete the picture.

FILLING IN THE GAPS: A COST-REWARD ANALYSIS

A cost-reward analysis of helping assumes an economic view of human behavior—people are motivated to maximize rewards and minimize their costs (Dovidio, Piliavin, Gaertner, Schroeder, & Clark, 1991). From this perspective, people are relatively rational and mainly concerned about their self-interest. In a potential helping situation, a person analyzes the circumstances, weighs the probable costs and rewards of alternative courses of action, and then arrives at a decision that will result in the best personal outcome. This is one form of universal egoism discussed briefly in the first chapter. There are two categories of costs and rewards: those for helping, and those for *not* helping. Costs for helping can involve lost time, effort, danger, embarrassment, and disruption of ongoing activities. But helping can also be rewarding. Rewards for helping may include money, fame, self-praise, avoidance of guilt, thanks from the victim, and the intrinsic pleasure derived from having helped. Helping is more likely to occur when the rewards for helping outweigh the costs. Anything that lowers the costs or increases the rewards for helping enhances a person's inclination to help. Costs for *not* helping may involve feelings of guilt and the cognitive and emotional discomfort associated with knowing another person is suffering. Helping is more likely as these costs increase. One advantage of the cost-reward approach is that once potential costs and rewards have been identified, the effects of this combination of factors can be readily predicted. In the next section, we examine a variety of situational dimensions that influence costs and rewards and thus helping, typically in circumstances in which the need for help is clear.

Costs and Rewards for Helping

The negative value associated with the costs for helping and the positive value associated with rewards for helping are subjective ones. They are based on the perceptions of the bystander, not on objective assessments of uninvolved outsiders. Therefore, to address this issue, most researchers have attempted to set up situations in which most people's perceptions of costs and rewards are similar. Researchers have identified several situational factors that yield similar cost estimates from different people. Table 2.1 summarizes these and how they influence helping.

Effort and time. Earlier in this chapter, we reviewed several experiments in which people witnessed emergencies where the victims' screams made it appear that they were seriously injured (see Figure 2.2). Subjects in these experiments were near the victim, and it was relatively easy to help. These are situations in which the personal costs for helping in terms of time and effort are outweighed by the combination of rewards for helping (praise and potential fame) and costs for *not* helping (the victim dying). As you recall, helping is very likely under these circumstances.

In other situations, however, bystanders' own concerns and time pressures may prevail over the needs of another person. Bystanders weigh the needs of the victim and their own needs and goals, and then decide whether helping is too costly in that circumstance (Dovidio et al., 1991; Piliavin et al., 1981). This decision is based on a relatively rational assessment of the situation, and a person who fails to help is not necessarily a "bad" person. For example, Darley and Batson (1973) conducted a study in which seminary students (presumably "good" people) were asked to make a presentation on some topic. The talk was to be given in another building, and time pressure was manipulated by leading the participants to believe that they were either early, on time, or late for their presentations. On their way to give the speech, the seminarians passed a person who was slumped in a doorway. The seminarians who were early for their presentations were the most likely to help, and late subjects were least likely to help. Those seminarians who thought that they were late not only hurried past the victim, but even stepped over him. The costs of helping associated with time pressure made these otherwise "good" people less responsive to the needs of others. (This study is discussed further in Chapter 6.)

Possible physical harm. As suggested earlier, helping is sometimes dangerous, and in many real-life emergencies, fear of being harmed may be a major deterrent to intervention. In the Kitty Genovese incident, for instance, it is possible that many of the bystanders hesitated to help because rushing to her aid might have meant putting their own lives on the line. The impact of these kinds of fears is clearly illustrated in a field experiment conducted in the New York subway (Allen, 1970). In this experiment, one confederate asked a subway rider (the subject) for directions. Another confederate interrupted and gave obviously incorrect information. The behavior of interest was whether people would help the person asking for directions by providing the correct information. Fear of

TABLE 2.1 EXAMPLES OF COSTS AND REWARDS ASSOCIATED WITH HELPING AND NOT HELPING

COSTS FOR HELPING

Type of Cost	Example
Psychological aversion	Situations involving someone (e.g., a drunk) or something (e.g., blood) that people find unpleasant
Possible physical harm	High likelihood that direct intervention may be dangerous (e.g., possible personal attack) or painful (e.g., possible electric shock) to the helper
Effort and time	Helping that involves the interruption or postponement of important or desired activity (e.g., missing a scheduled appointment)
Money expended or foregone	Helping that is perceived as being more financially costly (e.g., $25 vs. $1)
Social disapproval	Intervention that requires breaking a social rule (e.g., going someplace that is prohibited; violating group norms to help)

REWARDS FOR HELPING

Type of Reward	Example
Monetary compensation	Promise of higher financial reward (i.e., expectations of more money)
Social reward	Expectation that there will be social benefits to the helper (e.g., fame, gratitude, reciprocity)

COSTS FOR THE VICTIM RECEIVING NO HELP

Types of Costs Relating to Concern for the Victim	Example
Victim deservingness	Victim seen as innocent or not responsible for the problem
Victim need	The situation involves the serious need of the victim (e.g., severe injury or psychological problem)
Clarity of victim's need	The need of the victim is unambiguous and is unlikely to be misinterpreted (e.g., situation involving screams for help)

TABLE 2.1 continued

Types of Costs Relating to Personal Concerns	Example
Guilt or blame	Anticipated negative outcomes for not helping (e.g., the possibility of being publicly identified as someone who failed to help a person in need)
Potential irresponsibility	Bystander has clear responsibility (e.g., personally identified as responsible; in position of responsibility, such as group leader)
Unpleasant arousal	Feelings of upset and distress associated with witnessing another person suffer

harm was manipulated by varying the behavior of the confederate who gave the incorrect information. Some subjects saw him physically intimidate another person (still another confederate) who had apparently tripped over him; others heard him shout verbal abuse without physical threats; and in a control condition, the tripping incident passed with no response from him.

As you might expect, even though it was easy to help in this situation, the potential costs associated with contradicting the possibly abusive confederate strongly influenced people's behavior. Only 16 percent of the people who witnessed threats of physical violence helped and 28 percent of those who heard the verbal abuse helped. By contrast, 50 percent of the people in the control condition helped and gave the correct directions. Obviously, self-interest in avoiding harm influenced whether these people behaved in a helpful manner. In addition, research has shown that less life-threatening but potentially painful risks (e.g., receiving electric shocks) can make people reluctant to help. Not surprisingly, people are less likely to help another person when helping means that they will suffer some discomfort themselves (Batson, O'Quin, Fultz, Vanderplas, & Isen, 1983; McGovern, 1976).

Unpleasant emotional consequences. Helping someone may sound like a very desirable activity, but it can often involve unpleasant experiences. Helping opportunities are often unusual and unexpected events, and when we encounter them, we may experience a range of insecurities. If we are asked to do something unfamiliar, we typically feel some self-doubt, potential embarrassment, and concern about failing others. These are all potential costs for helping, and the stronger these feelings the less likely people are to offer assistance (Edelmann, Childs, Harvey, Kellock, & Strain-Clark, 1984; Glick, DeMorest, & Hotze, 1988; Midlarsky & Hannah, 1985).

In emergencies, victims are often physically injured or disfigured. Intervention may require that the bystander come in contact with blood and other bodily fluids. Clearly, this cost could make even the most well-intentioned bystander reticent to become involved. Experiments have directly examined this possibility. The setting of one study was in a train on the Philadelphia subway (Piliavin & Piliavin, 1972). The victim, a confederate of the experimenter, staggered forward across the car, collapsed to the floor, and stared at the ceiling. For half the trials, the victim fell, and a trickle of blood ran down his chin; for the other half, there was no blood. Because many people have an aversion to blood, the researchers reasoned that the presence of blood would increase the unpleasantness (i.e., costs) associated with providing help. As expected, bystanders were not only slower to help the bloody than the nonbloody victim, but they also directly helped the bloody victim less often overall (65 percent versus 95 percent). Personal costs for helping in the form of anticipated negative experiences can readily outweigh even the serious need of a victim. This study was conducted over twenty years ago; it is very likely that visible bleeding would have an even stronger impact on helping today. The fact that the human immunodeficiency virus (HIV) can be transmitted through contact with blood would dramatically increase the potential costs for helping. Indeed, in some recent instances, even emergency medical personnel have refused to help seriously injured and bleeding people because they fear these people may be HIV positive.

Rewards for helping. According to the cost-reward framework, rewards should increase helping. Although a considerable amount of research has focused on the effects of costs for helping, relatively few studies have examined the effects of rewards. As those who have received allowances from their parents would suspect, monetary rewards increase helping (Wilson & Kahn, 1975). Social rewards are also very important (Deutsch & Lamberti, 1986). People are more likely to donate their time and money to charity if they believe it will increase their popularity (Reddy, 1980). Even a simple thank you can be effective. In an experiment by McGovern, Ditzian, and Taylor (1975), a female confederate asked male subjects to take an electrical shock for her. If the subjects agreed, she responded with thank you in a reinforcement condition, but she said nothing in a control condition. After the initial shock trial, subjects who had been reinforced continued to be more helpful throughout the experiment than did the nonreinforced subjects. Reinforcement from the person being helped can also come indirectly. For example, the helper may experience personal gratification when she or he sees the situation improve for the person in need. This also increases helping. People are more helpful when they can perceive that their help is actually improving the other person's condition (Smith, Keating, & Stotland, 1989; Warren & Walker, 1991). In general, then, rewards do increase helpfulness.

Rewarding moods. When we discussed factors affecting whether or not one notices an event, we noted that being in a good mood seems to make one more attentive, leading to a greater likelihood of helping. Being in a good mood may also lead to more helping through at least two other routes related to costs and rewards.

First, being in a good mood appears to make one think more about good things (such as rewards) than about bad things (such as punishments). Alice Isen and her colleagues have found that individuals who were in a good mood because they had unexpectedly received cookies from a stranger or found change in a pay telephone at a mall were more likely to think about positive things, to retrieve from memory more positive thoughts, to have a more positive outlook on life, and to offer help to others (Isen, 1970; Isen, Clark, & Schwartz, 1976; Isen & Levin, 1972; Isen, Shalker, Clark, & Karp, 1978). Thus, people in good moods may think more about the rewards for helping and think less about the costs. Second, when people are in good moods, they may compare their own circumstances to those of people around them (Isen, 1993). If they feel an imbalance between their own good fortune and the situation of less fortunate others, they will be motivated to correct this inequity, and one way of doing this is by helping others. The reward for helping is in restoring a sense of fairness and balance.

Not all good moods will increase helping, however. Rosenhan, Salovey, and Hargis (1981) had students imagine either themselves on a vacation in Hawaii or a close friend on the same wonderful vacation. Both conditions led to good moods. However, only the first condition led to more helping than a neutral mood (control) condition. Salovey (1992) speculates that this is because focusing on other people's good fortune may evoke envy and a feeling of unfairness that increase the costs of helping.

Thus far we have only examined those pieces of the puzzle that concern the situational context in which a bystander is asked to help. But, as we noted in Chapter 1, helping is an interpersonal act, and often there are implicit costs and rewards associated with helping different kinds of people. Therefore, in the next section, we consider how the bystander's relationship to the person in need can affect costs and rewards and, thus, helping.

Taking Care of Your Own: Relationships to People in Need

The nature of the relationship between a potential helper and the person in need can significantly alter the balance between costs and rewards. We consider three aspects of the relationship between persons in need and potential helpers: attraction, similarity, and racial characteristics.

Attraction. Positive feelings about the person in need, or interpersonal attraction, also increase helping. This effect occurs whether the attraction is based on physical appearance, friendly behavior, or personal qualities (Dovidio & Gaertner, 1983; Kelley & Byrne, 1976; Mallozzi, McDermott, & Kayson, 1990). Even just being associated with a popular person can increase the amount of help that someone receives. For example, Penner and Fritzsche (1993) found that Magic Johnson's announcement that he was HIV positive produced a dramatic increase in college students' willingness to help someone they also thought was HIV positive.

The cost-reward analysis can explain these results. For instance, one reason why physical attractiveness may promote helping, particularly by members of the other sex, is because it may increase potential rewards. For example, helping may provide an opportunity to initiate a relationship.

Although this explanation fits with common sense and experience, it cannot completely account for these findings. Suppose you found a job application that was left accidentally in a phone booth, and needed to be mailed. The application included a picture of either a physically attractive or unattractive woman. Would that person's attractiveness make a difference, even though helping (that is, mailing the application) would be anonymous, and it would be highly improbable that you would ever meet the applicant? For a substantial number of people, the answer is yes (Benson, Karabenick, & Lerner, 1976). People helped the attractive person about half the time, but they helped the unattractive person only about a third of the time. Interpersonal attraction can thus increase helping even when the rewards are not tangible.

Similarity. We have all heard the saying, "Birds of a feather flock together." Our concern is Will these birds be helpful? Does similarity between a potential helper and a person in need influence the probability of helping? Several experiments have examined this issue. Similarity has been manipulated in various ways, including dress style, nationality, personality, and attitudes. The results are consistent: People are more likely to help others who are similar to themselves than they are to help those who are dissimilar (see Dovidio, 1984). One reason for this is that perceived similarity leads to interpersonal attraction (Byrne, 1971).

Similarity may also provide another explanation of why good moods increase helping. People in good moods tend to see other people as closer and more similar when they are feeling good (Isen, 1993). Did you ever notice that when you are feeling very happy, everyone seems like your friend? Seeing people as more similar to you may then make you more likely to help them (Holloway, Tucker, & Hornstein, 1977).

The similarity-helping relationship is also a cross-cultural phenomenon. For example, Feldman (1968) found that residents of Athens, Paris, and Boston were more likely to help a person from their own country than from another country. Although this general tendency to help members of your own group more than members of other groups occurs cross-culturally, the effect is stronger in some societies than in others. In some cultures, such as in Japan and China, people are socialized to place higher value on group achievement than on individual success. In these collectivist cultures, the interests of the individual are often subjugated to the needs of the group. In other cultures, such as in the United States, the emphasis is on individual achievement. These are considered individualist cultures. The similarity-helping effect is stronger in collectivist cultures. Kwok Leung (1988), for instance, found that Chinese and Japanese subjects helped members of their own groups more than did subjects from the United States. In contrast, American subjects helped people from other groups more than did Chinese and Japanese subjects. Thus, socialization plays an important role in how people respond to similar and dissimilar others.

Why does similarity lead to more helping? We have already noted that it leads to attraction, and we are likely to help people to whom we are attracted. Additionally, being with others who share our values, interests, and beliefs is much more pleasant than being with those who do not. People who are seen as dissimilar are typically perceived as unpredictable, holding different beliefs and values, and threatening. From a cost-reward perspective, therefore, the costs of simply being with similar others are lower, and the benefits are higher. Also, there may be special costs associated with not helping a person who is similar, such as greater shame or guilt. For example, the more similar the victim is to the bystander, the greater the guilt (cost) for *not* helping, the less apprehension (cost) about how the other person will react, and perhaps the greater the anticipated appreciation (reward) for helping. (In Chapter 4, we will also discuss the possible biological basis for the similarity-helping relationship.) Based on cost-reward factors such as these, it is not surprising that people are eager to help others who are more similar to themselves.

As we saw with respect to cross-cultural differences, helping can be an inter*group* as well as an interpersonal act. Consequently, the relationship of others to a person's social group (e.g., race or ethnicity), even within the same culture, can also influence helping. We focus on race in the next section to illustrate the impact of a specific type of social attitude—racial attitudes.

Racial characteristics. The prediction concerning how racial characteristics (i.e., racial similarities and differences between the bystanders and the person in need) would affect helping seems straightforward. Feelings of similarity tend to increase helping, but racial dissimilarity often leads to the assumption of belief dissimilarity (Rokeach & Mezei,

1966; Stein, Hardyck, & Smith, 1965). Therefore, bystanders should be less likely to help someone of a different race than someone of their own race. Also racial prejudice stigmatizes the target of the prejudice, and stigmatized persons are less likely to receive help than nonstigmatized persons, which should lead to lower cross-racial helping (Edelmann, Evans, Pegg, & Tremain, 1983; Walton et al., 1988).

The relationship between helping and racial differences is not this simple, however. Recall from the incident presented in the beginning of this chapter, it was four African-American people who heroically rescued the white victim, Reginald Denny. Research findings also suggest that racial effects in helping are quite complicated. Some experimenters have found that subjects help people they believe belong to another racial group *less* often than people they believe belong to their own racial group (Benson et al., 1976; West, Whitney, & Schnedler, 1975; Wegner & Crano, 1975). Other researchers have found no differences associated with the victim's race on the amount of help that white (Bickman & Kamzan, 1973; Wispé & Freshley, 1971) and African-American (Gaertner & Bickman, 1971) bystander offer. Still other investigators have found that whites are more likely to help African Americans than whites (Dovidio & Gaertner, 1981; Dutton & Lake, 1973). Another puzzle?

Aversive racism. When will whites discriminate against African Americans in their helping behavior? Samuel Gaertner and one of the authors of this book (Gaertner & Dovidio, 1986) have used research on helping and on race prejudice to develop a broad model of interracial behaviors. It uses the concept of *aversive racism* to understand whites' racial attitudes and behavior. Aversive racism represents a modern, subtle form of racial bias. According to this perspective, many whites who may truly believe they are not prejudiced still harbor *unconscious* negative feelings toward African Americans. As a consequence of possessing both conscious, nonprejudiced convictions and unconscious, negative feelings, aversive racists discriminate against African Americans in some situations but not in others.

What kinds of situations are these? Gaertner and Dovidio (1986) propose that in situations in which the social norms for appropriate behavior are clear and unambiguous, aversive racists will *not* discriminate against African Americans or other targets of prejudice and discrimination. Wrongdoing would be obvious under these circumstances and would threaten their self-belief that they are nonprejudiced. That is, there are significant costs associated with discriminating against an African American under these conditions. However, aversive racists' negative feelings will be expressed and discrimination *will* occur when social norms are weak or ambiguous, or when a person can justify a negative response on the basis of some factor other than race (e.g., the person caused this problem by not working hard enough; Frey & Gaertner, 1986). For example, whites may express support for programs like affirmative action *in principle*, but they may seize on excuses (e.g., concerns about maintaining traditional standards) to oppose implementing these programs *in practice* (see Dovidio, Mann & Gaertner, 1989).

How important is aversive racism in helping situations? One study by Gaertner and Dovidio (1977) suggests that it is a critical determining factor even when an African-American victim has suffered a life-threatening injury. White college students overheard a very serious accident involving the person who was attempting to send them messages from a nearby cubicle. The experimenters varied two important aspects of this situation. First, some of the students believed that they were the only witness to the emergency, whereas others believed that there were two other (white) bystanders who also heard the accident. The presumed presence of others allowed participants to diffuse responsibility—if they were so inclined. Second, the experimenters led some participants to believe that the victim was white and others to believe that the victim was African American.

As the researchers expected, when white bystanders believed that they were the only witness to an emergency—when appropriate behavior was clearly defined—they did not discriminate against the African-American victim. In fact, they helped African-American victims slightly more often than they helped white victims (94 percent versus 81 percent). However, when they believed that there were other people present, they helped African-American victims about half as often as they helped white victims (38 percent versus 75 percent). The opportunity to diffuse responsibility offered a non-race-related excuse for bystanders to treat victims differently but in a way that allowed them to avoid recognizing racial bias as a factor. It was not due to a decision to intentionally let the African-American victim suffer—that would be obviously racist. Instead, it was a decision to let someone *else* help. Nevertheless, in an emergency situation this serious, the consequences can be just as deadly.

The aversive racism framework identifies additional cost-reward considerations that make the effects of race on helping more complicated than the effects of similarity or attraction might suggest. In particular, there are special costs for aversive racists associated with discriminating against African Americans. It would threaten a very important aspect of their self-image. Thus, when discrimination would be obvious (as in not helping an African-American victim when you are the only witness), these cost considerations outweigh the influence of similarity. In fact, because it may be rewarding for aversive racists to reaffirm their nonprejudiced self-images (Dutton & Lennox, 1974), they are often more likely to help African Americans than whites under these conditions. However, when aversive racists can rationalize not helping on the basis of some factor *other* than race (as in the belief that someone else will help), their self-image is no longer threatened and these special costs do not apply. These whites are then less likely to help African Americans than whites, as the research on similarity and attraction suggests.

Summary

We have seen that costs and rewards have relatively straightforward effects on helping. As costs for helping increase, helping decreases; as rewards for helping increase, intervention increases. These costs and rewards may be directly related to the helping opportunity or may be associated with the potential benefactor's relationship to the person in need. As we noted earlier, this type of cost-benefit analysis fine-tunes the steps in the Latané and Darley decision model. Once people notice the event, interpret the situation as one requiring assistance, and recognize their personal responsibility, the costs and rewards associated with helping determine the level of intervention. The research on the race of the person in need, however, suggests the potential complexities of the cost-reward approach that allows predictions to go well beyond the scope of Latané and Darley's five steps. Costs and rewards come in various forms, such as threats to your self-image or opportunities to meet an attractive person. These considerations can influence how likely a bystander is to assume *personal* responsibility for helping. Thus, costs and rewards affect not only what happens *within* each step of the model but also influence how people proceed *through* these steps.

PUTTING MORE PIECES TOGETHER: COMBINING COSTS AND REWARDS

How do people move through the decision-making process that may ultimately lead to helping? More specifically, how do they combine the costs and rewards associated with the alternative courses of action available to determine how they should act? Over the past twenty-five years, one of the authors of this book, Jane Piliavin, and her colleagues have developed the *arousal: cost-reward model* that considers more fully the nature of costs of helping, the effects of different combinations of costs, and their effects on the *type* of response bystanders will make (Piliavin, Rodin, & Piliavin, 1969; Piliavin et al., 1981; Dovidio et al., 1991). Because of the complexity of this model, we will divide our consideration into two parts. We will devote the remaining pages of this chapter to the cost-reward component of the model and how these considerations affect the kind of help that is given. We will reserve our presentation of the arousal component, which considers the motivation of helping, for the next chapter.

The Arousal: Cost-Reward Model

In the arousal: cost-reward model, there are two basic categories of potential costs and rewards for a bystander. One category is *personal costs for
helping*. These costs involve negative outcomes directly imposed on the
helper for making a direct helping response. Injury, effort, and embarrassment are examples of potential costs for helping, as we discussed in
earlier sections of this chapter. The other category is *costs for the victim not
receiving help*. It contains two subcategories. First, there are personal costs
for not helping, which are direct negative outcomes to the bystander for
failing to aid the victim. These include guilt, shame, and criticism; we
alluded to these costs previously as well. Second, there are empathic costs
for the victim receiving no help, which are based primarily on the
bystander's awareness of the victim's continued distress. In particular,
these empathic costs involve internalizing the victim's need and distress
as well as more sympathetic and concerned feelings for the victim.

The arousal: cost-reward model makes predictions not only about
whether a bystander will make a response but also *what* the response will
be. The response is a function of both the costs for helping and the costs
for the victim not receiving help. As can be seen in the upper left-hand cell
of Figure 2.4, when the costs for no help to the victim are high (e.g., the

FIGURE 2.4
Costs for direct help and costs for no help to the victim combine to determine
how people will respond. (Adapted from Piliavin et al., 1981.)

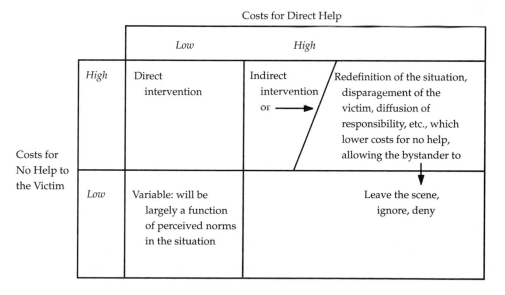

Costs for Direct Help

		Low	High	
Costs for No Help to the Victim	High	Direct intervention	Indirect intervention or →	Redefinition of the situation, disparagement of the victim, diffusion of responsibility, etc., which lower costs for no help, allowing the bystander to ↓
	Low	Variable: will be largely a function of perceived norms in the situation		Leave the scene, ignore, deny

person is seriously injured) and when costs for direct help are low (e.g., helping is not dangerous), direct help (e.g., rushing to the aid of the victim) is most likely. However, direct helping becomes less likely as the costs for helping increase. The literature on the effects of costs on helping, which we covered earlier in this chapter, strongly supports this hypothesis.

What happens when the costs for helping and costs for not helping are both high? (See the upper right-hand cell of Figure 2.4.) This is when the bystander is between the proverbial rock and hard place. The Kitty Genovese incident, to which we have referred several times, fits this description. The bystander has a strong desire to do something. The costs to Ms. Genovese for not being helped are high—her death. But, the high cost of direct intervention (i.e., the possibility of the bystander being killed) deters the bystander from becoming directly involved. The bystander, therefore, experiences a very strong conflict between the need to help and the fear, distaste, or, in some cases, the physical impossibility of helping. The arousal: cost-reward model's prediction is that bystanders can resolve this conflict either by *indirect help*, such as seeking an institutional helper (doctor, police officer, etc.), or by *cognitively reinterpreting* the situation. That is, bystanders psychologically alter the perceived costs to the victim for not helping. They can do this by cognitively altering the perceived costs of not helping by redefining the situation as not an emergency, by concluding that someone else will intervene (i.e., diffusing responsibility), or by convincing themselves that the person is not deserving of help (e.g., in the case of Kitty Genovese, bystanders may have asked, "What kind of person would be out at this time of night?"). These rationalizations lower the perceived costs for not helping (e.g., "Even if I do not help, someone else will") and allow bystanders to leave the scene or return to their interrupted activity.

Research supports these predictions and suggests that some responses may be more common than others. In serious emergencies (high cost for not helping situations), indirect helping becomes more likely as costs for helping increase (Piliavin et al., 1981). Overall, however, indirect helping is relatively infrequent, perhaps because it is difficult for bystanders to pull themselves away from such involving situations to seek others who can help better than they can. Cognitive reinterpretation seems to be the most common and possibly the most efficient way of resolving the high cost for helping/high cost for not helping dilemma. For instance, bystanders are more likely to diffuse responsibility when the person in need is physically disfigured (creating a relatively high cost for helping) than when the person is not (Piliavin, Piliavin, & Rodin, 1975; Walton et al., 1988). Although the reinterpretation process occurs quickly and probably without conscious awareness, it is as if the bystander initially recognizes the need for assistance, becomes hesitant because of the costs for helping, and then searches for a reasonably justifiable excuse for not helping (Gaertner & Dovidio, 1977; Schwartz & Howard, 1982). As we have indicated before, this is not the same as apathy. People do care; ironically, it is the fact that they are very sensitive to the other person's need that initially places them in the dilemma.

Now consider the bottom right-hand cell of Figure 2.4. In it, the costs for no help to the victim are low and the costs for direct help are high. Imagine that you see a dangerous-looking hitchhiker while you are driving down the highway. Will you stop and offer assistance? The cost to the hitchhiker for no help seems low (he is not in any jeopardy); the potential cost to you for helping (possible attack) seems high. Under these circumstances, people are most likely to leave the scene (e.g., drive by) or deny the legitimate need of the hitchhiker for help.

The response of bystanders in situations in which both costs for help and costs for no help are low (the bottom left-hand box of Figure 2-4) is most difficult to predict. For instance, suppose you see someone drop his or her books in the hallway. In such a situation, social norms, personality differences, and relationships to the person in need are presumed to have their strongest impact (Piliavin et al., 1981; see Chapter 6). Small changes in the situation will also have noticeable effects. Helping will increase as the costs (both personal and empathic) for the victim *not* receiving help begin to increase. Among these are making it more difficult for the bystander to escape the situation unnoticed or without guilt, increasing the need of the victim, having the victim make stronger and more immediate appeals for help, or making the person in need seem more deserving of help (see Dovidio et al., 1991). These changes tend to move the situation from the bottom left-hand cell to the top left-hand cell of Figure 2.4. In summary, the arousal: cost-reward model extends earlier work by identifying various kinds of costs and illustrating how different combinations of costs lead to different types of actions.

THE ANSWER: SUMMARY AND IMPLICATIONS

We began the chapter with the broad question, "When will people help?" Stimulated by the Kitty Genovese incident, in which thirty-eight people witnessed an assault and murder but did not help, Latané and Darley (1970) developed a decision-tree model of bystander intervention. The five steps in this model are important pieces to the puzzle. The evidence in support of the model is strong: The more likely bystanders are to notice an event, interpret it as a situation requiring help, and assume personal responsibility, the more likely they are to help. In addition, people who are more knowledgeable about what to do and better trained to deliver assistance are more likely to help effectively.

Additional pieces of the puzzle were added when we considered the situational factors and psychological processes that determine whether bystanders will notice the event, how the event will be interpreted, and whether people assume responsibility. These influences, which are presented in Table 2.2, are not confined to helping situations; they are general principles of group and individual behavior that are relevant to a broad range of social functioning.

The cost-reward analysis also relates to general principles of human behavior and extends the Latané and Darley model in three ways. First, among bystanders who recognize the need for helping and accept personal responsibility, assessment of costs and rewards accounts for some of the differences in helping because of aspects of the situation (e.g., danger) and characteristics of the person in need (e.g., attractiveness). Second, a cost-reward analysis (e.g., the arousal: cost-reward model) illustrates the dynamic and cyclical nature of the decision to help. When help is badly

TABLE 2.2 SUMMARY OF SITUATIONAL FACTORS AND PSYCHOLOGICAL PROCESSES THAT DETERMINE WHETHER A PERSON WILL BE HELPED

Decision Steps	Possible Influences	Impact
1. Notice the event	Clarity and vividness	Clearer and more vivid events are more likely to be noticed
	Stimulus overload	Excess environmental stimulation reduces the likelihood that an event will be noticed
2. Interpret the event as requiring help	Perceptual cues	Events that involve more cues of another person's need are more likely to be interpreted as situations requiring help
	Informational social influence	Particularly in perceptually unclear (ambiguous) situations, the behavior of others will define whether help is required
	Relationship to the person in need	People are more likely to recognize the need of others with whom they are closer
	High costs for helping	People may resolve the high cost for helping– high cost for no help dilemma by reinterpreting the situation as one not requiring assistance

TABLE 2.2 continued

Decision Steps	Possible Influences	Impact
3. Assume personal responsibility	Immediate and general norms	Norms affect whether people will feel that they *should* help
	Presence of others	The opportunity to come to believe that other people can help allows a person to diffuse responsibility
	Focusing responsibility	Persons who are in positions of explicit responsibility
	Relationship to the person in need	People are more likely to accept personal responsibility for helping others with whom they are closer
	High costs for helping	People may resolve the high cost for helping– high cost for no help dilemma by diffusing personal responsibility for helping
4. Choose a way to help	Knowledge and training	People who are more knowledgeable about the situation can better evaluate alternative courses of action
5. Implement the decision	Training and experience	Bystanders who are well trained are more likely to help safely and effectively

needed but is very costly to give, bystanders in this high-high dilemma may actively reinterpret the situation in ways that alter perceived costs (e.g., by becoming more likely to diffuse responsibility). Third, this framework explicitly considers not only whether a bystander will do something but also what that something is: direct help, indirect help, reinterpretation, or leaving the scene.

As we gradually assembled the pieces of this puzzle in this chapter, one theme became clear. Whereas many people who hear about the Kitty Genovese incident attribute the lack of help to widespread bystander apathy and "bad" or "abnormal" people, the research findings suggest a very different picture. When the need of the victim and the responsibility of the bystander are clear and the cost-reward considerations are favorable, people will help—very frequently and very dramatically, as was the case in the rescue of Reginald Denny. People are far from apathetic. In fact, it is remarkable that people will be so helpful to strangers. Why *do* people help others, anyway? That is the question we consider in the next chapter.

3
Why Do People Help? Motives for Helping

------------- ❖ -------------

Helping is an everyday behavior that occurs frequently and spontaneously among people of all ages, from the very young to the elderly (Midlarsky, 1991). In addition to the kinds of spontaneous helping discussed in the previous chapter, people also help by donating substantial sums of money and volunteering an impressive amount of time to benefit schools, religious organizations, and other charities. Donations to charity represent the most common form of prosocial action in the United States. In 1989, for example, charitable donations by individuals amounted to nearly $123 billion (United States Bureau of the Census, 1992). The three most popular areas for financial contribution are religion, education, and health (Reddy, 1980).

People are also willing to give freely of their time. According to the United States Department of Labor (1990), almost 40 million people worked at least a few hours each week as volunteers for some charitable organization in 1989. Based on these figures, it is estimated that each year in the United States there are over 9 billion volunteer hours worked, representing at least $45 billion of free labor. People are even willing to give of themselves—literally. About 14 million units of blood are donated by nearly 10 million people in the United States each year (see Piliavin, 1990; Piliavin & Callero, 1991).

THE QUESTION

The central question of this chapter is *why* do these people help. At one level, there is a very simple answer: People help to benefit other people. But at another level, the answer is not so simple. We are really interested in understanding why someone would want to help another person. This issue returns us to the old debate among philosophers (see Chapter 1): Are people altruistic or egoistic, selfless or selfish? It is easy to demonstrate that people can be motivated by self-interest. A critical question for psychologists, however, is whether people are *ever* motivated primarily by concern for others? These are the pieces to the puzzle that we search for in this chapter.

What motivates the impressive level of donating and volunteering we just discussed? If you simply ask people, they will often tell you that their motives are selfless and altruistic. For example, in a survey by Reddy (1980), almost half the people interviewed stated that they first became volunteers because of their fundamental concern for others: They "wanted to do something useful," "help others," or "do good deeds for others." Similarly, the most frequent reasons cited for donating blood are humanitarian or altruistic concerns (Piliavin & Callero, 1991). The typical reason that people give for *not* donating money, giving blood, or volunteering is that they simply were not asked (e.g., Drake, Finkelstein, & Sopolsky, 1982; Marcus, 1973).

People's true motives are often more complex, however, and self-interest may be involved. People may donate money to achieve recognition, to get ahead in their careers, to gain the respect of others, or even for personal gain (Reddy, 1980). In fact, Reddy found that "the most powerful single variable" in determining whether people make charitable contributions is whether the donation would reduce their taxes.

Motives for volunteering time may also involve personal benefits. One-third of volunteers surveyed by Reddy said that they donated their time because they "had an interest in the activity," "thought [they] would enjoy doing the work," or wanted to "feel needed" (Reddy, 1980). More recently, Snyder (1992a) found similar kinds of motivations among volunteers who help people with AIDS. Two in-depth studies of volunteerism conducted over thirty years apart (Daniels, 1988; Sills, 1957) both found that humanitarianism was mixed with personal interest, a feeling of power, feelings of obligation, identification with the goals of the organization, the desire for social contact, and other self-centered motives (see also Chambre, 1987; Pearce, 1983). Thus, although people often report "altruistic" reasons for helping, personal needs and goals also appear to be very important.

Psychologists recognize that people do not always fully understand what motivates them (Ross & Nisbett, 1991). What people say and even what they honestly believe may not always accurately represent the actual causes of their behavior. Simply asking people where the pieces of this particular part of the altruism and helping puzzle go (i.e., asking them why they help) may not enable us to complete it.

Within psychology, attempts to understand what motivates people to help have focused on three possible processes or explanations: (1) learning, (2) arousal and emotion (affect), and (3) social and personal stan-

Funky Winkerbean

Although the reasons that people give when asked to explain why they have donated blood or given to charities usually imply altruistic motives for their actions, self-interest and anticipated rewards may often be the true reasons for these acts.

dards. The *learning* explanation applies general principles from learning theories to the acquisition of helping skills and beliefs about why these skills should be used to benefit others. Whereas the learning explanation tends to focus on what people *think and do*, explanations based on the *arousal and affect* approach emphasize what people *feel* in potential helping situations. But many of the arousal and affect theories do share a guiding principle with learning theory: People are motivated to behave in ways that bring them some kind of reward—in this case, feeling *better*. However, there are some theorists who argue that under some very special circumstances people may be motivated by the primary goal of making *another person* feel better, by true altruism. Finally, there is the *social and personal standards* approach, which considers how people's personal values can motivate helping by affecting both cognitive (what people think) and affective (what people feel) processes.

LEARNED HELPFULNESS

As we observed in the first chapter, philosophers have long debated whether people are inherently good or bad. Nevertheless, philosophers who were on opposites sides of this issue have agreed on one thing: Society needs its members to be concerned about the welfare of others and to be helpful toward them. Psychologists have focused on how such values can be taught to the members of society.

A basic principle of learning theory has been Thorndike's *law of effect*. This principle is quite simple, but very important—people will be more likely to engage in actions that are rewarded and less likely to engage in actions that are punished. Building on Thorndike's law of effect, learning theorists have identified certain fundamental learning processes. One of these, *operant conditioning*, concerns the extent to which the occurrence of a behavior can be modified by the positive or negative consequences of the action. Research on operant conditioning shows that people are motivated to help others because they have been reinforced for helping in the past. Reinforcement may occur through the presentation of positive outcomes (e.g., praise) or the relief of negative circumstances (e.g., terminating electric shock). Conversely, people may learn *not* to help others because helping has led to negative consequences (i.e., the costs of helping discussed in Chapter 2 that may have to be borne by the helper; see also Grusec, 1991b; Staub, 1981).

Positive or negative outcomes for helping can have virtually immediate impact. For example, in an experiment by Moss and Page (1972), individuals were approached by a confederate on a busy street. The confederate asked for directions to a local department store, one for which most residents knew the location. In most cases, the person complied with the request. The consequences of helping were systematically varied. In the positive reinforcement condition, the confederate smiled and said, "Thank you very much. I really appreciate this." In the negative consequence (punishment) condition, the confederate rudely interrupted the person and remarked, "I can't understand what you're saying. Never mind, I'll ask someone else."

These consequences had a dramatic effect on subsequent helping. A short time later, participants encountered another person who had "accidentally" dropped a small bag. More than 93 percent of the positively reinforced participants subsequently helped this person, whereas only 40 percent of those who had been punished offered assistance. People in a control condition, who were neither previously rewarded or punished, exhibited an intermediate level of helpfulness, about 85 percent. Thus, being punished for being helpful made the people much less likely to help.

One limitation of the effect of punishment should be noted. Whereas punishment *for* helping reduces subsequent helping, it is not the case that punishment for *not* helping will increase prosocial behavior. In the short run, punishment arouses negative feelings, such as anger, that are incompatible with a prosocial orientation; hostile people tend not to be helpful. In the long run, these negative feelings may interfere with the socialization of concern for others and intrinsic motivations for helping (Grusec, 1991b; Hoffman, 1994). Teaching a child to be helpful is, in itself, a helping opportunity. Consequently, if parents punish their child for not helping, they may be sending a mixed message. Punishment in this context may therefore be particularly confusing and may inadvertently teach the child to also respond to others' needs with coldness and rejection (see Chapter 5).

Besides direct experience, people can also learn to expect certain consequences for helping or not helping through information from other people—*social learning* (also see Chapter 5). This information can come through specific instructions or by watching how other people behave. As Albert Bandura (1977, p. 22) has noted, "Learning would be exceedingly laborious, not to mention hazardous, if people had to rely solely on the effects of their own actions to inform them what to do." For example, trial and error would not be a good way to learn skydiving.

Social learning commonly occurs by observing others' behavior and the consequences it produces for them. In an experiment that illustrates the effects of social learning on helping, people walking down a street saw a person (really a confederate) return a lost wallet (Hornstein, 1970). This person either appeared pleased to be able to help or displeased at the bother of having to help. Later, in the experiment, the subjects also came across a "lost" wallet. People who had previously seen the person who was pleased to help helped much more than people who had observed the unpleasant consequences for helping.

In summary, both direct reinforcement and modeling can affect an individual's desire to be helpful in a given situation. People *learn* to be helpful—in much the same way they can learn to be selfish or aggressive. There is, of course, much more to the process of learning to be helpful. These are discussed in more detail in Chapter 5 when we consider the mechanisms by which children learn helpfulness. So, now we will turn to the other processes that may explain why people help.

FEELINGS AND HELPFULNESS

People are aroused by the distress of others (see Eisenberg & Fabes, 1991). This reaction appears even among very young children and occurs across cultures. In fact, this phenomenon is so strong and universal some

researchers have proposed that *empathic arousal*, arousal generated vicariously by another person's distress, has a biological and evolutionary basis
(Cunningham, 1985/1986; Hoffman, 1990; see Chapter 4). People may be
inherently empathic. The role of empathic emotions in prosocial motivation is the focus of several arousal and affect models of helping.

   Although many researchers agree that empathic arousal is important
and fundamental (see Dovidio, 1984), there is much less agreement about
how it feels to be empathic and how this emotion actually motivates people to help. In general, the emotions that people feel are at least partially
determined by how they interpret arousal that they are experiencing.
People may interpret unexplained arousal as fear if they are around
frightened people; this same arousal may be experienced as anger if they
are around angry people (Schachter & Singer, 1962). Depending on the situation, arousal may sometimes be interpreted as one emotion, sometimes
as a somewhat different emotion. Recall the last time you came home late
and your parents were waiting up for you. How quickly did their arousal,
which they had been interpreting as worry, become reinterpreted as
anger?

   Similarly, empathic arousal may produce different emotions. In
severe emergency situations, bystanders may become upset and distressed; in less critical, less intense problem situations, observers may feel
sad (Cialdini et al., 1987), tense (Hornstein, 1982), or concerned and compassionate (Batson, 1991). How arousal is interpreted can shape the
nature of prosocial motivation.

Emotions and Helping

What determines the specific emotion that a person experiences in
response to another's problem? Bernard Weiner (1980, 1986) suggests that
another's need for help stimulates a search for causes by the observer.
People seek to understand *why* the person needs assistance. They consider
whether the person needs help because of an internal and controllable
cause (e.g., the person's lack of effort on a task) or an external and uncontrollable cause (e.g., the difficulty of the task). These explanations, or attributions, in turn, create an emotional experience that may motivate action.
Weiner suggests, for example, that attributing a person's problem to
uncontrollable causes (e.g., bad luck) produces sympathy that motivates
helping. Attributing the same problem to controllable causes (e.g., lack of
effort, bad judgment) may generate anger, which may inhibit helping.

   Imagine this situation. You are walking across campus one afternoon
when a male student, whom you do not know, stops you. He says that
you are both in the same class, and he asks you to lend him your class
notes from last week. Would you do it? Schmidt and Weiner (1988) presented students with this scenario and asked them that question. To test

their hypotheses about the role of attributions, they varied why the person was asking for the notes. For some students the person's need was presented as beyond his control. In this condition, the person asking for the notes was wearing an eyepatch and dark glasses and explained that he needed the notes because eye treatments prevented him from taking his own. For other students, the problem was the person's own fault: He needed the notes because he had gone to the beach instead of going to class.

Not surprisingly, students were more likely to help the person who had eye trouble—the person whose problem was due to factors beyond his control. Of particular interest, however, is *why* these differences occurred. The nature of people's emotional reactions was critical. The more the requestor could be blamed for his problem, the more anger students reported; the less responsible the requestor was held for his problem, the more sympathy was elicited. And it was the nature of these emotions that directly determined the helping decision: The more sympathy and the less anger people reported they would feel in the situation that was described, the more they said they would help. Thus, as Weiner (1980) has proposed, "Attributions guide our feelings, but emotional reactions provide the motor and direction for behavior" (p. 186).

Negative Moods

Although Weiner's model suggests that some negative emotions, such as anger and disgust, make people less likely to help, other unpleasant emotions can actually increase helping. Guilt for causing harm to another person is a powerful motivator. People are more likely to help others when they feel they have harmed these individuals in some way (Salovey et al., 1991).

People who feel guilty are not only more likely to help the person they have harmed, they are also more likely to help *anyone* else who needs assistance. In one field experiment (Regan, Williams, & Sparling, 1972), a confederate stopped women at a shopping center and asked them to use his camera to take a picture of him. As a woman would attempt to take his picture, the camera would break. In the guilt condition of the experiment, women were led to believe that they were responsible for breaking the camera; in the control condition, they were told that it was not their fault. Soon after this incident, the participants in this experiment had an opportunity to help a woman whose groceries were falling from her shopping bag. The results were clear: 55 percent of the participants who were made to feel guilty helped, whereas only 15 percent of those in the control condition helped. This effect has been found across a wide range of situations. People help more when they have previously transgressed than when they have not.

Although, as we saw in Chapter 2, positive moods can also increase helping, the processes responsible for the effects of positive and negative moods on helping do not appear to be the same. Michael Cunningham and his colleagues (Cunningham, Steinberg, & Grev, 1980) argued that, because there are neurologically distinct areas for reward and punishment, it is likely that the motivations aroused by negative moods are different than those produced by positive moods (e.g., increased attentiveness to others, more prosocial thoughts, feeling closer to others).

To demonstrate this point, Cunningham et al. combined the procedures other researchers had developed to create positive moods and negative moods. His subjects were shoppers in a mall. Half found a coin in the return of a telephone in the mall (positive mood), and half did not (neutral mood). Shortly thereafter, these people were asked to take a person's picture with a camera that malfunctioned. Some were led to believe that they were responsible (guilt condition); others were told it was not their fault (no guilt condition). All the shoppers were later given the chance to help another person who had dropped a file folder containing papers. Cunningham and his colleagues reasoned that if the same motivational processes were involved in positive and negative moods, the greatest amount of helping should be found when the people experienced *both* positive mood and guilt. However, if different motivational processes are activated by positive and negative moods, Cunningham et al. suggested that the combination of positive and negative mood inductions could result in a "subtractive interaction." According to this explanation, the two processes would cancel each other out, resulting in *less* help being given. This is exactly what happened: A smaller percentage of people who were first induced to be in a good mood and then experienced a guilt-producing event helped (33 percent) than did people who experienced only a positive mood (80 percent) or only a negative mood (also 80 percent). Thus, these data clearly imply that different motivational processes are responsible for the increases in helping found among people in positive versus negative moods.

If negative moods such as guilt increase helping through different processes than do positive moods, what are these mechanisms? When people feel guilty, why do they help? One explanation is that when people feel that they have unfairly harmed others, their self-esteem suffers. Therefore, they try to make amends. This *image-reparation hypothesis* suggests that by making a positive social response, people's self-esteem is restored, their self-image is repaired, and they can again appear to be "decent" people. The notion that people are motivated to repair their self-images seems to explain why people who cause harm are more helpful, but it does not totally explain this phenomenon. For instance, it cannot explain why people who simply *witness* a transgression against someone else also become more helpful. Robert Cialdini and his colleagues have proposed a broader model, the *negative-state relief model* (Cialdini, Kenrick, & Baumann, 1982; Cialdini et al., 1987) to explain such reactions.

Negative-State Relief Model

According to this explanation for why negative moods may promote helping, *harming* another person or *witnessing* another person being harmed can produce negative feelings such as guilt or sadness. People who experience these negative states are then motivated to reduce them. Through socialization and experience, people learn that helping can serve as a secondary reinforcer (Williamson & Clark, 1989; Yinon & Landau, 1987; also see Chapter 5); the good feelings derived from helping may therefore relieve their negative mood. Thus, negative moods such as guilt and sadness may motivate people to help, because of the processes of operant conditioning. That is, helping produces the reward of making them feel better. In contrast to the image-reparation hypothesis, the negative-state relief model proposes that people are motivated primarily to *feel* good rather than to *look* good. In both theories, however, the motivation for helping is essentially egoistic. That is, the primary motive for helping another person is that helping improves the helper's own situation.

There are three fundamental assumptions in the negative-state relief model. First, the negative state that motivates a person to help can originate from a variety of sources. It may be guilt from having personally harmed a person or sadness from simply observing another person's unfortunate situation; alternatively, it could come from feelings of guilt from a transgression against an unrelated person or sadness associated with a different person's problem. All these emotions, because they are negative experiences, can motivate helping (Cialdini, Darby, & Vincent, 1973).

A second assumption is that other events besides helping may just as effectively make a person feel better. Helping is just one way that the negative feelings can be eliminated. According to the negative-state relief model, if some other event that improves the potential helper's mood precedes the opportunity to help, the potential helper would no longer be particularly motivated to provide assistance. In one of the initial tests of this model, Cialdini et al. (1973) created feelings of guilt by having participants accidentally ruin a graduate student's master's thesis data or feelings of sadness by having them witness another person ruin the data. Some of these participants later experienced a positive event (i.e., received praise for their performance on a maze-tracing task). This presumably relieved their negative state before the helping opportunity occurred. Other participants did not have such a positive experience. As illustrated in Figure 3.1, guilt and sadness increased helping compared to a neutral-

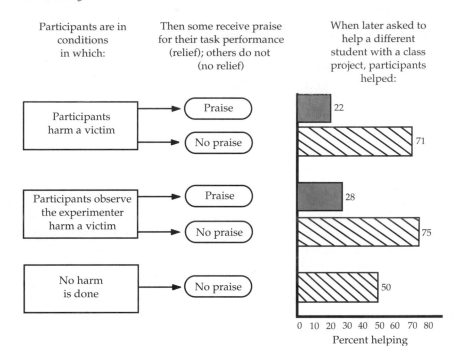

FIGURE 3.1
The negative-state relief model: People who cause or witness harm are more helpful, except when a positive event, such as praise, relieves these negative feelings before the helping opportunity. (From Cialdini, Darby, & Vincent, 1973.)

mood control group, except when subjects first experienced the positive event (praise). Once these subjects' negative moods were relieved by receiving praise, they were no longer highly motivated to help others. Perhaps for similar reasons, people are more helpful as they enter a Catholic church for confession (when presumably they are feeling guilty) than after they leave confession (and are presumably absolved of their sins; Harris, Benson, & Hall, 1975).

Furthermore, simply the anticipation that one's mood will be improved is enough to reduce the motivation for helping. If people believe that their mood will improve without having to do anything, why should they go through the effort of helping someone else to improve their mood? A study by Schaller and Cialdini (1988) demonstrated this point. They found that people who were feeling sad helped less when they expected that they would soon be listening to a comedy tape than when they thought the tape would not be funny. Because the comedy tape would lift their spirits, there was no longer any personal benefit for helping another person.

A third assumption of this model is that negative moods motivate helping only if people believe that their moods can be improved by helping. Negative feelings will *not* promote helping if people believe that these feelings cannot be relieved. Remember, according to the negative-state relief model, people are acting out of self-interest.

In one study illustrating this point (Manucia, Baumann, & Cialdini, 1984), participants were administered a substance, Mnemoxine (actually a placebo), which they were told was a fast-acting memory drug. The experimenters informed some people that the substance had an unusual side effect. It would "take whatever mood is present and prolong it artificially. So . . . [if] you are feeling sad when it takes effect, you will continue to be sad for the next 30 minutes or so, no matter what." The researchers told other people that Mnemoxine had no effects on mood. To create a sad mood, some participants were then asked to reminisce about sad experiences. Two key findings supported the negative-state relief model. First, as in previous studies, participants who felt sad helped more than did participants who were in normal, neutral moods when they thought the substance had no side effects (that is, when they believed that helping could improve their mood). The second, new finding was that when people believed that Mnemoxine had "frozen" their moods, and therefore that helping could not improve their mood, feeling sad did not motivate people to help. According to the negative-state relief model, there was no reason to help in the "frozen mood" condition because it would not make them feel better.

Although a number of studies support the negative-state relief model, there is some disagreement and controversy surrounding the negative-state relief model (see Carlson & Miller, 1987; Cialdini & Fultz, 1990; Miller & Carlson, 1990; Salovey et al., 1991). Some people question whether a mood-management explanation really accounts for why people help. For example, Carlson and Miller (1987) conducted a comprehensive review of the literature, and they concluded that there was little support for the negative-state relief explanation per se, suggesting instead that "features that are structurally and necessarily intertwined with the experience of negative mood, such as degree to which one focuses attention on the problems of oneself or another, are the underlying variables that account for the relation between negative mood and helpfulness" (p. 104).

However, as might be suspected, Cialdini and Fultz (1990) and Salovey et al. (1991) have taken issue with Miller and Carlson's conclusion. In particular, Salovey et al. suggested that whereas helping may not always improve people's moods in the short run, it may have this effect in the long run. This would provide a powerful incentive to help, even when the immediate impact of helping might be quite negative. As we saw at the beginning of this chapter, many people say they volunteer because it makes them feel good. In further support of this argument, Salovey and his colleagues observed that although people who rescued the Jews from the Nazis during the Second World War often paid a heavy price for helping, they later felt a very central sense of self-satisfaction because of what they had done (Oliner & Oliner, 1988). Despite this controversy, the negative-state relief model continues to be generally accepted as a viable motivational framework for helping.

Arousal: Cost-Reward Model

Arousal is a central motivational concept in the Piliavin et al. (1981) arousal: cost-reward model, which we introduced in Chapter 2 (see also Dovidio et al., 1991). Arousal motivates a bystander to take action, and the cost-reward analysis shapes the direction that this action will take. Specifically, this model proposes that *empathic arousal* is generated by witnessing the distress of another person. When the bystander's empathic arousal is attributed to the other person's distress, it is emotionally experienced by the observer as unpleasant, and the bystander is therefore motivated to reduce it. One normally efficient way of reducing this arousal is by helping to relieve the other's distress. The key elements of this model are summarized in Table 3.1. We will discuss the first three, which primarily concern arousal and helping.

Proposition one: becoming aroused. There is substantial evidence for the first proposition that people are fundamentally responsive to the distress of others (see Fabes, Eisenberg, & Eisenbud, 1993). Adults and children not only report feeling empathy, but they also become physiologically aroused by the pain and suffering of others. In a study by

TABLE 3.1 THE FIVE BASIC PROPOSITIONS OF THE AROUSAL: COST-REWARD MODEL

1. Observation of another's problem or crisis arouses bystanders. The degree of arousal is directly related to the clarity, severity, and duration of need and to bystanders' psychological and physical closeness to the person in need.
2. In general, arousal occasioned by observation of a problem or crisis and attributed to that event becomes more unpleasant as it increases, and bystanders have greater motivation to reduce it.
3. Bystanders will choose responses that most rapidly and completely reduce the arousal and incur as few net costs (costs minus rewards) as possible.
4. There will be (a) special circumstances that give rise to, and (b) specific personality types who engage in, rapid, impulsive, noncalculative, "irrational" helping or escape behavior following observation of an emergency.
5. On termination of contact with the situation, arousal will decrease with time, whether or not the victim is helped.

Katherine Vaughan and John Lanzetta (1980), for instance, subjects saw a person show strong facial distress in response to repeated, apparently painful electric shocks. These subjects reacted with physiological arousal and with facial expressions that were similar to those of the person being shocked. Observers, then, did not just feel bad *about* the person being in pain; they seemed to be experiencing what the other person was feeling. Preschool children also spontaneously show signs of facial concern and physiological arousal at the distress of others (Fabes et al., 1993), and there is evidence that even 1- and 2-day-old infants will respond with crying to the distress of another infant (Sagi & Hoffman, 1976).

Proposition two: the attribution of arousal. The evidence also supports the second proposition of the arousal: cost-reward model (see Table 3.1), that empathic arousal attributed to the other person's situation motivates helping. Gaertner and Dovidio (1977), for example, measured heart rates while people were deciding whether to help in an emergency. As the arousal: cost-reward model predicted, people who were more aroused at the time of an emergency were more helpful. This relationship between empathic arousal and helping is now well established (Dovidio, 1984), although recent work by Eisenberg and her associates (e.g., Eisenberg & Fabes, 1990; Fabes et al., 1993) suggests that extreme *empathic overarousal* may actually begin to reduce helpfulness. Facial, gestural, and vocal indications of empathy, as well as self-reports, are consistently positively related to helping (see Dovidio et al., 1991; Eisenberg & Miller, 1987).

Of course, people will differ in how much arousal is experienced and how that arousal is interpreted. The model recognizes this and identifies some of the characteristics of the bystander (e.g., his or her social sensitivity toward others), of the victim (e.g., attractiveness), and of the helper-victim relationship (i.e., a sense of we-ness), as well as characteristics of the situation (e.g., severity) that may influence the amount of arousal generated. A simplified view of this part of the model is illustrated in Figure 3.2. In general, arousal is greater the more empathic the bystander, the more socially attractive the victim, the closer the bystander-victim relationship, and the more serious the emergency situation (see Piliavin et al., 1981).

The importance of the association of arousal with the other person's distress is demonstrated by studies that manipulate how people attribute and interpret their arousal. If the arousal: cost-reward model is correct, then the primary determinant of helping is not the absolute amount of arousal experienced, but rather the amount of arousal that the potential helper *believes* is due to the other person's situation. If you are initially aroused by another person's problem, but you later come to believe that something else is the cause, then the arousal would not be expected to motivate intervention. Helping would not be perceived as relieving the cause of the arousal.

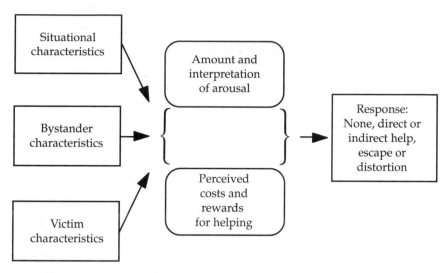

FIGURE 3.2
Simplified version of the arousal: cost-reward model.

Gaertner and Dovidio (1977) demonstrated this using a misattribu-tion paradigm in another experiment on helping. The objective in a mis-attribution paradigm is to lead two groups of people who are initially aroused by the same event to *believe* that the causes of arousal are differ-ent. One way of doing this is by giving different participants different possible explanations for their arousal before they experience it. Gaertner and Dovidio informed participants that their study examined the effects of a pill (actually a placebo) on their ability to receive ESP messages. Some people were told that the pill would soon arouse them, thus potentially confusing them about the source of any subsequent arousal. To minimize the potential for confusion for people in another group, they were informed that the pill would *not* arouse them. Later people in both groups heard an ambiguous emergency, a possible accident involving another participant in the experiment (really a confederate). The results supported the model. People who could attribute their arousal to the placebo pill helped less often (55 percent versus 85 percent) and responded more slowly than did participants who could not readily attribute their arousal to the pill. Because the placebo pill in fact did not arouse people, the key element here was what people *believed* had aroused them, not differences in their overall level of arousal.

Misattribution can also make people *more* helpful. Sometimes, people may experience arousal for one reason and then attribute it to a very dif-ferent source. Arousal due to one source (e.g., fear or suspense) can become associated with another source (e.g., a member of the other sex).

Once this misattribution is made, people respond more intensely than they normally would (Dutton & Aron, 1989; Zillman, 1983).

Applying this process to helping behavior, bystanders should be more helpful than normal if prior arousal becomes associated with another person's problem. This is what occurs. Arousal from such diverse sources as exercise (Sterling & Gaertner, 1984), erotic films (Mueller & Donnerstein, 1981), and aggressive films (Mueller, Donnerstein, & Hallam, 1983) increases helpfulness when it is attributed to the immediate need of another person. Consistent with the second proposition of the arousal: cost-reward model, these findings represent powerful evidence that arousal attributed to another person's need motivates helping.

Proposition 3: assessing the situation. The arousal: cost-reward model suggests not only that arousal motivates action, but also that it can affect how people perceive costs and rewards for various potential actions. One effect of increased arousal is that it narrows a person's focus of attention toward important aspects of a situation and draws attention away from less central aspects (Easterbrook, 1959; Eysenck, 1977). High levels of arousal may thus alter how people perceive and weigh information in assessing potential costs and rewards (see Chapter 2). Because a victim and his or her need may capture the attention of a highly aroused bystander, the bystander may not consider potential dangers associated with intervention. The costs associated with not helping the victim (e.g., that the victim might die) dominate the bystander's evaluations of the potential costs for helping by the bystander. As a consequence, highly aroused bystanders may help apparently *impulsively* and possibly heroically—responding very rapidly and apparently without regard to personal costs.

However, it is possible for bystanders to help too quickly and in ways that are dangerous. As we previously discussed in Chapter 2, Clark and Word (1974) found that all their subjects very rapidly helped a victim who was apparently being electrocuted by a "live" wire. A large proportion of these subjects directly intervened and touched the victim, an action that would have electrocuted them had the situation been real. Many of these subjects later realized the consequences of their action but reported, like many actual "heros," that they "just didn't think." According to proposition 3, perhaps they did think, but not about all those possible costs associated with intervention.

Thus, there is considerable support for the major propositions of the arousal: cost-reward model that empathic arousal motivates helping. But the nature of this motivation, however, is essentially egoistic. Another's distress may generate empathic arousal, but the bystander's primary goal in helping is to reduce his or her *own* unpleasant state. Helping may typically be perceived as an efficient way to reduce this arousal, but other ways (such as leaving the scene; see Figure 3.2) are possible, sometimes even more attractive, alternatives.

Comparing the Negative-State Relief and the Arousal: Cost-Reward Models

Although these two egoistic models of what motivates people to help may appear similar, there are at least two important differences between them. First, the attribution of arousal plays a central role in the arousal: cost-reward model; only arousal *attributed to the plight of the other person* will motivate helping. In contrast, the negative-state relief model posits that, *regardless of their attributed source*, negative states (particularly guilt and sadness, see Cialdini et al., 1987) can motivate helping. The second major distinction between the two models concerns the goal of the help that is given. The arousal: cost-reward model is a tension-reduction model which assumes that the victim's need produces an arousal state in the potential benefactor and that the goal of the benefactor's intervention is to alleviate his or her own aversive state by eliminating the distress of the victim. According to the negative-state relief model, however, people in negative moods are looking for ways to eliminate or neutralize their negative mood. Obtaining the affective rewards that come with helping is one way, but any other event that might improve the emotional state of the observer, including events that have nothing whatsoever to do with benefiting the person in distress, may serve this purpose equally well.

Thus far, the motivations for helping that we have considered all represent some form of egoism. Although helping obviously benefits the recipient, the *primary reason* that people help others is to benefit themselves. Learning theory suggests that people are motivated to obtain rewards from others (e.g., praise) or from oneself (e.g., pride) and to avoid punishments (e.g., blame or shame). This principle also applies to the arousal and affect theories. The common theme is that people help others mainly to make themselves feel better. The primary motivation for helping is a hedonistic one. What is your reaction to this? Is selfishness your only motivation for helping? Is it even possible for altruistic helping to occur? Or to use our recurring puzzle analogy: Are all the pieces of the helping puzzle selfish ones? In the next section, we consider a different viewpoint. Namely, that there is such a thing as truly altruistic helping. This disagreement has dominated research on helping for many years. The important controversy between the egoists and the altruists provides an excellent illustration of how psychologists try to solve a puzzle such as what motivates people to help.

The Empathy-Altruism Hypothesis

In contrast to the egoistic models of helping, C. Daniel Batson and his colleagues (see Batson, 1991) present the empathy-altruism model of helping. Batson acknowledges that egoistically motivated helping occurs. In fact, he recognizes that *most* helping may be egoistically motivated. But, he also argues that true altruism may exist as well. As we told you in Chapter 1, Batson (1991, p. 6) defines altruism as "a motivational state with the ultimate goal of increasing another's welfare."

Of course, just believing that altruism can motivate helping is not enough. Empirical evidence that shows the existence of altruistically motivated helping must be found. Most of this evidence comes from the carefully controlled confines of the laboratory. That is where Batson and his colleagues began their search for altruism.

The primary mechanism in Batson's empathy model is the emotional reaction to another person's problem. As we have already seen in this chapter, witnessing another person in need can produce sadness or personal distress (e.g., upset, worry, alarm). Batson suggests that under some circumstances it elicits a different emotion, *empathy* or *empathic concern*, which he defines as, "an other-oriented emotional response (e.g., sympathy, compassion) congruent with the . . . welfare of another person" (Batson & Oleson, 1991, p. 63). Whereas sadness and personal distress generate an egoistic desire to reduce *one's own* distress, Batson (1987, 1991) proposes that empathic concern produces an altruistic motivation to reduce the *other person's* distress. Feelings representing empathic concern, personal distress, and sadness are presented in Table 3.2 (Fultz, Schaller, & Cialdini, 1988).

To explain how his model of motivation for helping differs from the ones we have previously discussed, Batson (1991) identified three different "paths" to helping. A simplified version of Batson's presentation of these paths is depicted in Figure 3.3. The first two paths are egoistic. Path 1 is based on social learning and reinforcement; it corresponds to the processes proposed in the negative-state relief model. Path 2 involves ten-

TABLE 3.2 ITEMS REFLECTING EMPATHIC CONCERN, PERSONAL DISTRESS, AND SADNESS

Empathic Concern	Personal Distress	Sadness
Moved	Upset	Sad
Warm	Worried	Dejected
Softhearted	Alarmed	Sorrowful
Tender	Grieved	Low-spirited
Compassionate	Disturbed	Downhearted
Sympathetic	Distressed	Downcast
Touched	Uneasy	Heavy-hearted
Concerned	Troubled	Feeling low

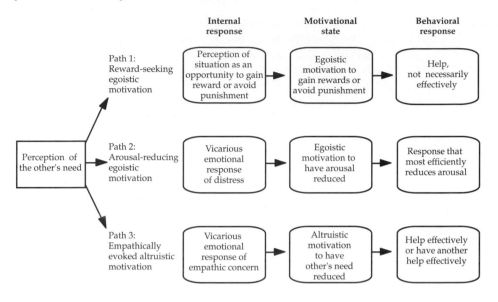

FIGURE 3.3
Key elements in Batson's three motivational paths to helping.

sion reduction and concerns the mechanisms described in the arousal: cost-reward model.

Path 3 represents altruism. In this path, perception of another person's need in conjunction with a special bond to that person (e.g., because of similarity to the person or a deliberate attempt to take that person's perspective) generates empathic concern. Empathic concern, in turn, evokes altruistic motivation. The altruistically motivated person will then help if (1) helping is possible, (2) helping is perceived to be ultimately beneficial to the person in need, and (3) helping will personally provide greater benefit to the person in need than will assistance from another person able to offer it. Thus, empathic concern is hypothesized to produce greater concern for the welfare of the other person.

How can we test whether people are altruistically motivated? Because motives are not directly observable, you could ask them. But as we saw in the interviews of volunteers that began this chapter, even if someone said they were motivated by altruistic concerns, that would not necessarily be strong evidence. The person could simply be saying something that sounds good to you and is flattering. On the other hand, you could systematically vary the helping situation to rule out alternative explanations. For instance, you could ask a person to help you with a class assignment. If the person said yes, then you might say, "You know, right after I finish this assignment, I'm leaving this city forever." If the person still helped you, you could be reasonably sure that he or she was not helping you now in order to get a different type of help back from you later. This strategy is the one that Batson and his colleagues adopted in their experiments on why people help.

Batson and his colleagues began with the hypothesis that empathic concern generates an altruistic motivation for helping. They then tried to rule out alternative explanations that would explain their results. The puzzle of the existence of altruistic motivation has therefore been approached in a series of steps. It has been like a mystery story in which the detective eliminates one suspect after another until only one is left. In particular, Batson and his colleagues have tried to sequentially rule out egoistic explanations and, by implication, to find support for the existence of altruistic motivation. If it is not egoism, then Batson would argue that it must be altruism.

Consider the egoistic explanation that when people experience more empathic arousal they are more helpful because helping is seen as an efficient way to reduce the arousal. How can you demonstrate that under certain circumstances, people are instead primarily altruistically motivated to increase the welfare of another person? One way would be to make it easy for people to reduce their arousal by leaving the scene. According to Batson, when escaping from the situation would be easy, egoistically motivated people concerned mainly about their own welfare should choose to leave the scene rather than help; escaping is the less costly option. Altruistically motivated people, in contrast, would help because that is the only way to improve the *other* person's welfare. That is, altruistically motivated people will do what is best for the other person even if it is not the most efficient way to reduce their *own* arousal.

Leaving or helping? There are two ways to make helping less costly than leaving the scene, and thus a less desirable way of reducing arousal. One is to make it difficult to help, whereas the other is to make it very easy to escape the situation without helping. Batson and his colleagues have typically chosen the latter strategy in their experiments. For instance, in one of the early studies on altruistically motivated helping (Toi & Batson, 1982), college students listened to a radio broadcast tape of another student, "Carol Marcy," who had broken both her legs in a car accident. She needed help with her class notes to complete her psychology course so she could graduate on time. In terms of time and effort (several hours of tutoring), helping was moderately costly. The costs for helping relative to the costs for leaving the scene were manipulated by varying whether or not subjects expected that they would see Carol in the future. Toi and Batson reasoned that if students were likely to meet Carol again in the future, guilt, shame, and anticipated blame would make leaving the scene *more costly* than helping. But when it was unlikely that students would see Carol again, escape from the situation would be easy and thus *less costly* than helping.

The central prediction was that egoistically motivated people would do whatever was personally less costly—leave the scene when escape was easy and help when escape was more difficult. In contrast, because altruistically motivated people are concerned primarily about the other's welfare, they were predicted to help even when helping was more costly. To elicit empathic concern, which is assumed to produce altruistic motivation, some students were instructed to imagine how the person in the interview felt. As Toi and Batson predicted, these empathically concerned students helped at equivalently high levels regardless of whether it was relatively easy or difficult to leave the scene without helping (71 percent versus 81 percent). That is, these students seemed altruistically motivated by the desire to improve the other person's welfare, because they chose to help even when it was more personally costly to help than to leave without helping. Only helping—not leaving the scene—will relieve the other person's problem. In contrast, students who were not experiencing a high degree of empathic concern showed the egoistic pattern of helping. They helped very frequently (76 percent) when it was easier (i.e., less costly) to help than to leave. When it was easier to leave than to help, however, these students typically left; only 33 percent helped. They seemed to do whatever was best for themselves.

These results present a fundamental challenge to the assumption that altruistically motivated help cannot occur. Empathically concerned people helped even when it was easier not to. Batson and his colleagues have found these effects in a large number of additional experiments (see Batson, 1991; and Batson & Oleson, 1991, for full reviews). Thus, although people may be egoistically motivated to reduce their arousal under some conditions, as the arousal: cost-reward model suggests, this explanation does not seem to account for how empathic concern motivated people in these studies.

Psychology is dominated by principles of egoism and hedonism, however, and a persuasive demonstration of truly altruistic motivation must withstand the challenge of *all* alternative interpretations based on egoistic motivation. As long as other researchers can identify other plausible "suspects," the case for the existence of altruistic helping is not totally convincing. What other explanations for these results are possible? Several researchers have proposed alternative explanations that challenge Batson's contention that helping may be altruistically motivated.

Punishment for not helping: empathy-specific punishment. What kind of people would say that they are concerned and sympathetic—that is, empathically concerned—and then turn their backs on a person in need? No decent person would do that, would they? Thus, feeling empathic concern may generate additional costs for not helping that make these people likely to help even when helping requires moderate effort. From this perspective, the motivation that Batson and his colleagues described as altruistic may represent a subtle form of egoism. A demonstration of altruism requires that this option be ruled out. Actually, there are two versions of this option. One deals with concerns about what *other* people might think—such as the concern that others will think that someone who expresses concern but does not help is a bad person. This egoistic explanation focuses on anticipated *social punishments* for not helping (Archer, 1984; Archer, Diaz-Loving, Gollwitzer, Davis, & Foushee, 1981). If this explanation were true, empathic concern should motivate high levels of helping *only* when potential helpers believe that others will learn of their behavior. There is evidence that suggests we can eliminate this explanation, however. In two studies, Fultz, Batson, Fortenbach, McCarthy, and Varney (1986) found the altruistic pattern of helping that Batson finds will occur regardless of whether this kind of social evaluation is possible. The other version of the empathy-specific punishment explanation relates to our *self-image*. People are not only interested in what others think of them, but they are also concerned about how they think of themselves. Even if others do not notice, people normally feel bad when they know that they have behaved poorly. Thus, the reason that empathically concerned people may help is to avoid negative self-evaluations (Schaller & Cialdini, 1988).

This explanation may seem almost impossible to rule out, because we normally know how we are doing. We do not, however, always know *why*. People are often very good at deceiving themselves and rationalizing their behavior (Lockard & Paulhus, 1988). The phrase, "all work and no play makes Jack a dull boy" provides many students license to attend any party at any time in college. Thus, tempting people with good excuses is one way of finding out what their true motives are. One way of finding out what people's true motives are is to tempt them with good excuses for acting (or not acting) in a certain way.

Applying this idea to helping, Batson reasoned that if people are egoistically motivated, they would readily accept reasonable justifications for not helping. Why help if you do not have to? However, if people are altruistically motivated, they would be expected to help even when they could rationalize not helping. They are *not* looking for an excuse. Batson's experiments again supported the empathy-altruism hypothesis. Empathically concerned students remained very helpful even when they were explicitly told that most people did not help the person in need under the same circumstances (Batson et al., 1988, studies 2 and 3). Students who had low levels of empathic concern (and presumably were *not* altruistically motivated), in contrast, accepted these potential excuses for not helping and intervened less in these situations. Thus, it seems as if this alternative can be ruled out as well.

It may seem as if eliminating anticipated punishments might end the debate over the existence of altruism. However, social psychologists are an imaginative and skeptical group. Some new possibilities have emerged. Whereas arousal-reduction approaches (such as the arousal: cost-reward model) suggest that social and self-punishments account for what Batson and his colleagues call altruism, social learning and reinforcement approaches suggest that anticipated *rewards* for helping provide yet another egoistic explanation for apparently altruistic behavior. That is, because people have learned that helping leads to rewards such as praise and pride, when they feel empathy they think about these rewards and are motivated to attain them by an egoistic desire. Like a hotly contested case in a court of law, the weight of the evidence on this issue moves back and forth, for and against the existence of altruism.

Rewards for helping: empathy-specific reward. One version of this empathy-specific reward interpretation is essentially the flip side of the punishment explanations. It proposes that people help others because they expect a reward from the recipient, from others who observe the act, or from themselves. Several specific versions of this alternative egoistic explanation have been proposed and tested. One involves the desire to share in the other's joy—empathic joy. Another concerns the helper's reactions to the relief of the other person's need.

What do empathically concerned people think about in a potential helping situation? Perhaps the thoughts about the rewards are subtle; they may involve anticipated shared rewards or empathic joy. The egoistic empathic joy interpretation suggests that, because the reward involves *sharing* in the other person's relief and joy, empathy should promote helping when people believe they will learn about the positive consequences of their acts, but not when they are unable to know the positive consequences of their actions, or to share the joy. However, what would you expect if people were altruistically motivated? The empathy-altruism hypothesis predicts, again based on the assumption that the primary concern of an altruist is the welfare of the other person, that learning about the consequences of one's actions will be irrelevant. The altruistic goal is to *do good* for the other person rather than to *feel good* about doing it.

The evidence with respect to empathic joy is mixed. In support of the egoistic perspective, Smith, Keating, and Stotland (1989) found that subjects who were high in empathy helped more when they believed they would learn of the consequences for helping than when they believed they would not. But a subsequent study by Batson and his colleagues that also varied the likelihood of learning about the consequences of helping produced support for the empathy-altruism hypothesis (Batson et al., 1991). Thus, this version of the empathy-specific reward explanation, although still possible, does not definitely disprove the existence of altruism.

The other explanation concerns how people respond to the person in need being helped. If empathically concerned people are primarily motivated by a personal desire for reward, they should feel better if *they* help (and earn the reward) the person in need than if *someone else* does it. In contrast, if people are altruistically motivated, they should feel better just knowing that the person in need is helped, regardless of who the helper is. When you care primarily about another person's welfare, what matters is that this person is better off. Empathically concerned people seem to care for others in this way. Their moods improve when they learn that the other person's need has been relieved, regardless of the source of relief (Batson et al., 1988).

In a variation on this theme, recent work by Sibicky, Schroeder, and Dovidio (in press) suggests that empathically concerned subjects may take a long-term perspective concerning the welfare of a person in need, and as a consequence, may actually be *less helpful* in some circumstances. Suppose providing too much assistance to a person might make it more likely that the person would experience even greater harm in the future. From a helper's point of view, what response would be of greater benefit to the person in need —to provide immediate help that may leave the person at risk in the future or to refrain from intervening to protect the individual from later harm? In such situations, egoistically motivated helpers appear to be very self-focused, worrying primarily about their immediate plight and intervening with little or no regard for the long-term consequences of their actions for another person. Empathically motivated individuals, however, offer more measured responses, engaging in what Batson (1991) calls a "hedonic calculus" that balances the possible short- and long-term costs of the person in need. Somewhat paradoxically (but consistent with the empathy-altruism hypothesis), the altruistic response is to give less immediate help! In general, then, the weight of the evidence is on the side of the empathy-altruism hypothesis. The behavior that Batson and his colleagues identify as altruistic cannot fully be explained by a desire to obtain personal rewards.

Relieving sadness. Although it appears that research on the empathy-altruism hypothesis has successfully addressed virtually all the egoistic explanations, the most controversial challenge is still being contested. Cialdini and his colleagues (Cialdini et al., 1987; Schaller & Cialdini, 1988) have argued that empathic people may have a greater motivation to help because empathy has aroused a specific egoistic need. What is that need? We return to the negative-state relief model, which proposes that it is the personal need to feel better (see path 1 of Figure 3.3). Essentially, the argument is that sadness may accompany empathic concern, and it is the egoistic need to relieve this sadness that is really motivating helping.

The weight of evidence has swayed back and forth. A series of studies by Cialdini and his colleagues provided initial support for this challenge to altruism. They found that empathy produced high levels of sadness as well as empathic concern (Cialdini et al., 1987, study 1). Furthermore, this sadness operated in the way predicted by the egoistic motivation portrayed by the negative-state relief model. Empathy increased helping except when another positive event (payment or praise) that presumably relieved the negative mood occurred first (Cialdini et al., 1987, study 1). Furthermore, as we discussed earlier concerning sadness generated by recalling past events, empathically concerned people showed high levels of helpfulness *only* when they believed that their mood could be improved by helping (Cialdini et al., 1987, study 2). Thus, Cialdini and his colleagues concluded that increased helping by empathic people is not based on altruistic motivation, as Batson (1991) contends, but rather on "an entirely egoistic reason: person mood management" (Cialdini et al., 1987, p. 750).

More recent research suggests that this conclusion may be premature. In two subsequent studies, Batson et al. (1989) led some empathically concerned students to believe they would soon see a videotape that would improve their moods. Others were not led to expect this convenient mood-enhancing opportunity. Contrary to what Cialdini and his colleagues concluded, Batson et al. found that anticipating a mood-enhancing event did *not* lead people high in empathic concern to be less helpful. Apparently, these individuals' primary goal was not to make themselves feel better; regardless of whether their own moods would soon be improved, they were highly motivated to help the other person.

Two other studies also support the existence of altruism. One experiment was very similar to that of Cialdini et al. (1987, study 2) and manipulated whether subjects believed that their moods could be altered, and thus managed (Schroeder, Dovidio, Sibicky, Matthews, & Allen, 1988). One important difference between these studies was that Cialdini et al. may have inadvertently distracted participants' attention away from the person in need when the unusual side-effect of their memory drug that would "freeze" the participants' mood was described (Batson & Oleson, 1991). This focus on the other person's need may be a key element in altruistic motivation. In contrast, Schroeder et al. explained this side effect to participants at the beginning of the study and thus allowed them to maintain their focus on the person in need later. Contrary to the negative-state relief interpretation and consistent with the view that empathic people are motivated by the other person's welfare, they found that people experiencing high levels of empathic concern demonstrated high levels of helpfulness even when they believed that their own moods were unalterable.

The second experiment examined whether empathic concern operates like other negative states (Dovidio, Allen, & Schroeder, 1990). Recall from earlier in this chapter, guilt increases helping directed not only toward rectifying the harm (e.g., helping the person on the experiment that was ruined) but also in unrelated areas (e.g., helping someone pick up dropped groceries). Do the prosocial effects of empathic concern also generalize to other situations? The answer is no. In particular, Dovidio et al. (1990) demonstrated, in support of the empathy-altruism hypothesis, that empathically aroused subjects helped a person in need more when helping relieved the person's main problem, but not when the help was for an unrelated problem. Inconsistent with the negative-state relief model, *any* type of helping would not do—only helping that would alleviate the problem that produced the empathic concern. Eliminating another problem or finding another way to feel better would not alleviate the other person's main problem. These results, taken together with findings of Batson et al. (1989) and Schroeder et al. (1988), provide compelling evidence that truly altruistic motivation may exist—all helping is not necessarily egoistically motivated. Although this issue remains controversial, there is a very real possibility that people can be linked to one another—even virtual strangers in a laboratory—in genuinely selfless ways.

The State of the Altruism Question

Psychologists who use the mechanisms of arousal and affect to explain why people help are agreed that a potential helper's feelings play a critical role in motivating him or her to action. The critical question that divides these researchers, however, is the nature of these feelings. Are helpers always motivated by the selfish, egoistic desire to make *themselves* feel better, as the negative-state relief and arousal: cost-reward models propose? Or are helpers motivated (at least occasionally) by the selfless, other-oriented, and altruistic desire to make *another person* feel better, as the empathy-altruism model proposes? This is the issue of whether altruism actually exists. The research suggests that it is sometimes possible for people to act out of purely altruistic motives, but usually helpers are motivated by egoistic concerns. Helping others can reduce the helper's arousal and make the helper feel better. *But* when the helper feels empathic concern, she or he is likely to help, even when helping produces neither of these effects.

Demonstrations that purely altruistic helping can take place—even those that occur in the somewhat sterile environment of a laboratory—have significant implications both within psychology and beyond. Within psychology, the existence of altruism challenges the assumption that people are inherently motivated *only* by self-interest. This hedonistic view of human nature has been a fundamental principle underlying approaches as disparate as Sigmund Freud's psychoanalytic theory (e.g., the pleasure principle) and B. F. Skinner's behavioristic perspective (e.g., the law of effect).

The implications beyond psychological theorizing may be even more profound. If altruistic helping really exists and we can understand the causes of altruism, then perhaps we can make human behavior more humane. The selfish motivations that drive interpersonal, intergroup, and even international conflict may be transformed—at least to some extent— to more cooperative and constructive relations.

Although the context may be sterile and the distinctions may seem too fine, this laboratory activity is critical. Just as researchers attempt to understand the causes of disease such as cancer and AIDS with microscopes and test tubes, behavioral researchers are attempting to understand the essence of why people help others. Although these techniques might seem microscopic, the implications and potential applications are profound. And like many areas of medical research, we have not yet identified all the pieces to this part of our puzzle. There is certainly evidence that altruism *may* exist, but the case is not yet closed. In the next section, we leave the details of the egoism-altruism debate and examine how social and personal expectations influence helping.

SOCIAL AND PERSONAL NORMS

The third motivational perspective involves social and personal norms. As we noted in Chapter 2, social norms are rules for accepted and expected behavior. Personal norms are an individual's expression of feelings of obligation to behave in a particular manner in a particular type of situation (Schwartz, 1977). They are more specific than social norms, which are assumed to apply to most people most of the time.

Although the specific mechanisms by which norms motivate helping are rarely identified in experiments, both affective and cognitive (learning) factors are probably involved. Personal and social norms provide standards of appropriate behavior, something to strive for. Thus, meeting these normative standards may be rewarding. Norms also define what people *ought* to do. Failure to satisfy these obligations may make people feel bad or generate criticism from others. Norms may therefore provide both the proverbial carrot and the stick, leading people to strive for personal and social rewards and to avoid personal negative feelings and social punishments.

Social Norms

Normative theories of helping emphasize that people help others because they have expectations based on previous social learning or because the current behavior of others suggests that helping is the socially appropriate response. One of the most common reasons people give for becoming involved in volunteer work is to satisfy others' expectations of them (Reddy, 1980). Researchers have identified two classes of social norms involving helping. One class relates to feelings of fairness and involves perceptions of reciprocity (Gouldner, 1960), equity (Walster, Walster, & Berscheid, 1978), and justice (Lerner, 1980). The other class of norms relates to very general norms of aiding, such as the social responsibility norm that people should help a person who is dependent upon them (Berkowitz, 1972).

The norm of reciprocity. People learn through socialization how to coordinate their actions with others' behaviors. For example, taking turns in games and other activities is a critical social skill for children to develop (e.g., Garvey, 1990). Think back when you were a small child and remember your reaction to the playmate who would not take turns? Or, more recently, to the person who cut in line in front of you at the store? The strength of these reactions indicates how basic this unwritten rule of social behavior is in our society. The norm of reciprocity refers to a type of turn taking with regard to helping. According to this norm, people should help those who have helped them, and they should not help those who have denied them help for no legitimate reason (Gouldner, 1960).

This principle implies that people attempt to maintain stable, reciprocal relationships with others. An imbalance is uncomfortable and motivates a person to reciprocate. For example, visits are often traded back and forth between families to keep the social ledger in balance. To illustrate this principle, consider this intriguing finding from a field study. Two researchers sent out Christmas greeting cards to total strangers. A surprising number of these strangers (about 20 percent) responded with holiday greetings of their own—even though they did not know who these people were or why they sent the cards in the first place (Kunz & Woolcott, 1976)!

Does this kind of social ledger exist for informal helping relationships as well? It appears so. People normally reciprocate assistance to others who have helped them. This is particularly true when the person expects to see the helper again (Carnevale, Pruitt, & Carrington, 1982), although it can also occur when there is no expectation of future interaction (Goranson & Berkowitz, 1966). Also, the more assistance a person receives, the more help he or she subsequently gives (Kahn & Tice, 1973). The need to reciprocate may also influence our behavior more generally. Suppose someone does you a favor but is not around to provide you an opportunity to reciprocate. Will you be more likely to do someone *else* a favor? Apparently so. In one experiment (Berkowitz & Daniels, 1964), some participants received favors, whereas others did not. Although the helper was no longer involved, students who had received favors were more likely to offer assistance to another person in need than were students who had not previously been helped.

Reciprocity is such a fundamental principle that, as we will see in the next chapter, some researchers have proposed that it even has a biological basis. Perhaps because this motive is so strong, it can also be manipulated to exploit us. Salespeople often begin their pitch with a free gift. The strategy is, people who receive something will want to give something back—possibly enough to make a significant purchase. It often works. In one study (Regan, 1971), students who were participating on a task with a confederate, were given a brief rest period. During the break, the confederate performed an unexpected favor for half the students: He returned from the break carrying two soft drinks and said, "I bought one for you, too." In another condition, the confederate returned from the break empty-handed.

Now, according to the norm of reciprocity, the students who received the drink should feel obligated to do something nice for the confederate who brought back the soda. As the confederate and the students were about to leave the room, the confederate asked them to do *him* a favor. He explained that if he sold the most tickets for a raffle, he would win a $50 prize himself. He then asked the students to buy some tickets, and "the more the better." Students who had received the unexpected favor were eager to satisfy their feelings of obligation; they bought twice as many tickets than those who had not received a favor. If this sounds fair, it is because we are familiar with and endorse the norm of reciprocity. What makes this situation exploitative, however, is that soft drinks cost only 10 cents at the time, but the raffle tickets cost 25 cents each. In their attempt to repay the favor, these students bought an average of two tickets each. The "free" drink they received was not free after all—it cost them almost five times as much as if they bought the soda themselves!

Equity. The principles of fairness and balance that underlie the reciprocity norm are related to two other social needs. One is the need for equity. Equity exists when people in a relationship believe there is a balance or fairness between what they contribute to the relationship and what they receive from it (Walster et al., 1978). When people perceive an imbalance, they are motivated to restore equity. There is considerable evidence showing equity motives in helping. People who have unfairly received benefits—for example, those who receive too much reward based on their contribution to a group activity—often freely choose to give up some of their reward (e.g., Schmitt & Marwell, 1972). The key element here is that people *perceive* that they have been unfairly overcompensated. This does not always happen. Because people tend to overestimate the value of their contributions, they typically believe they have earned and deserved what they have received. On the other hand, if people feel they have been undercompensated, they will contribute less. George (1991) found, for example, that workers who felt they had been treated unfairly were less helpful.

The need to see the world as fair and just is also central to Melvin Lerner's just-world hypothesis (Lerner, 1980). Like equity theory, the just-world hypothesis suggests that people will be motivated to help others who have been treated unfairly—to make the world fair and just again.

There are a variety of other responses to another's misfortune that can make the world *appear* just. Besides compensating the victim, one can punish the perpetrator or come to believe that the victim got what he or she deserved. In fact, Lerner and his colleagues have shown that people will often devalue an innocent victim, because they are motivated to see the world as just. If helping is a possibility, most people will choose to help. However, if a person cannot be helped, the just-world hypothesis suggests that people will disparage the victim, thus making the world right again. Innocent people do not suffer unfairly; they are simply getting what they deserve. This tendency to blame the victim may explain why innocent victims of crimes (e.g., victims of rape) are sometimes accused of being responsible for their victimization. Ironically, the need to see the world as just can lead people to make unfair judgments about what people deserve based on what they have received.

The norm of social responsibility. According to this social norm, people are expected to help others who are dependent upon them. Much of the classic work in this area was conducted by Leonard Berkowitz. In a series of experiments, students assembled paper envelopes under the supervision of another student. They were told that their work was actually a test of the other person's supervisory skill. Berkowitz and his colleagues varied how much the students believed the evaluation of the supervisor would depend on their performance. In general, the participants in this study were socially responsible. Even when there was no possible gain for themselves, students were more motivated to work when the consequences for the supervisor were greater (e.g., Berkowitz & Daniels, 1963). The norm of social responsibility also explains why, as we saw in Chapter 2, people are very likely to help others who are physically handicapped and who are seen as having a significant need (Clark, 1976).

People's willingness to help others who are dependent upon them has its limits, however. There are several exceptions to this rule. One involves *why* people are dependent. As we saw earlier in Weiner's attributional model, people have different reactions when a problem is caused by the person (e.g., needing notes because of going to the beach) than when it is caused by forces beyond the person's control (e.g., for medical reasons). For example, people who believe that African Americans' disadvantaged economic status is due more to lack of effort rather than to social barriers are less likely to support social welfare programs designed to help them. More recently, students have been found to be less sympathetic and less likely to help a person who developed AIDS through sexual contact than through a blood transfusion (Weiner, Perry, & Magnusson, 1988). Similarly, people are less likely to help others whose own behavior caused their dependency (Frey & Gaertner, 1986).

There are also many differences across groups and cultures that influence reactions to dependency. Some cultures are more individualistic, oriented toward individual gain; others are more collectivistic, directed toward the group welfare. The Americans and British tend to be individualistic, whereas the Chinese and Japanese tend to be collectivistic. As one consequence, people in these cultures may respond differently to others' dependency. Chinese psychologist Hing-Keung Ma (1985) asked people in London and in Hong Kong their reactions to a range of other people's problems. Hong Kong residents appeared more responsive to the needs of others. There have also been traditional gender differences within the United States. Women are generally more sensitive to the dependency of others than are men (see Chapter 6). In fact, men often respond to people who are very dependent on them by providing *less* rather than more help (Enzle & Harvey, 1979). Thus, the norm of social responsibility is only a *general* rule; it does not apply equally in all situations or to all people.

Personal Norms and Standards

Whereas general norms of social responsibility may provide only vague guides for behavior in concrete situations, the use of personal norms and standards is valuable for predicting how a particular person will behave in a specific situation. According to Schwartz and Howard (1982, 1984), *personal norms* are "feelings of moral obligation to perform or refrain from specific action" (1984, p. 234). Personal norms are generated in a specific situation by a person considering what the possible choices are and the implications of such actions for personal norms and values. The more central these personal standards are, the stronger will be the emotional arousal associated with acting or not acting in a certain way.

Personal norms do predict actual helping. For example, personal norms have been found to correlate significantly with such prosocial behaviors as giving blood or bone marrow, tutoring blind children, working with elderly welfare recipients (Schwartz & Howard, 1982), and participation in community recycling programs (Hopper, 1991). The average correlation, however, is usually quite low (around .3). The influence of personal norms on helping behavior is greatly increased, however, if dispositional tendencies such as awareness of consequences (i.e., the extent to which people notice others' needs spontaneously) and denial of responsibility (i.e., the extent to which individuals accept excuses for inaction under circumstances that arouse personal normative standards) are also considered. For individuals who are high on awareness and low on denial, the correlations between personal norms and actions are often close to .50. The most striking finding of this kind involved asking Israeli students about their willingness to tutor blind children and then observing their actual behavior. For students high on denial, the correlation was −.03; essentially no relationship was found between their words and deeds. But among those low in denial of responsibility, there was a correlation of .72 between their personal norms and actions. These people put their money (in this case their time) where there mouths were (Schwartz & Howard, 1981).

The impact of personal norms also depends upon how much people think about the normative standards. If you hold a personal norm that you should help in a particular situation, focusing on that norm should increase helping. Focusing your attention inward produces a state called *objective self-awareness*, in which you are likely to compare yourself to some important standard or ideal behavior (Wicklund, 1975; Gibbons, 1990). If these standards involve helping, you will be more likely to help (Hoover, Wood, & Knowles, 1983).

The research on personal norms and standards converges to paint a relatively clear picture. People who possess standards of helping in specific areas will be inclined to help. Whether they ultimately help, however, depends upon whether they attend to these norms and accept personal responsibility for helping. This topic also introduces a critical issue that we will consider in detail in Chapters 5 and 6. There are important individual differences in helping. Nevertheless, even though people may have different standards and norms, the nature of the motivation to help—to meet those standards and satisfy feelings of moral obligation—may be fundamentally similar.

THE ANSWER: SUMMARY AND IMPLICATIONS

In conclusion, the puzzle concerning why people help has pieces that concern both thoughts and feelings (i.e., cognitions and emotions). With regard to cognitions, people can learn through their direct experience or from observing others that helping is a positively valued social behavior. The other important kind of cognitions involve social and personal norms. Norms that establish standards for when people should help may also lead people to expect certain social and personal rewards and punishments. Personal norms, for example, motivate helping because people have developed ideals about how they should act in certain situations and also experience feelings of personal responsibility and obligations to help.

Turning to feelings, the way people interpret empathic arousal shapes their motivation to help. These pieces of the puzzle come in many shapes. If the emotion is anger or disgust, people are motivated *not* to help. If the emotion is personal distress, sadness, guilt, or tension, they are egoistically motivated to improve their own welfare by helping others. If, however, there is a special bond to the person in need that leads people to interpret their arousal as empathic concern, they may be altruistically motivated to help. That is, their primary goal is to reduce the other person's distress. Although researchers continue to debate whether this motivation is truly altruistic, and this part of the puzzle is not yet complete, the picture is becoming clearer: There are both egoistic *and* altruistic motivations to help.

The use of terms such as egoistic or even selfish to describe why people sometimes help may make us lose sight of an important point: Even egoistic motivations to help others are essentially *prosocial*. If I am motivated to help you because I am distressed or saddened by your situation, I am still motivated to help you. In fact, it is quite remarkable how the fates of people who have never met can be so intertwined and complementary. Your benefit is mine; mine is yours. Furthermore, the possibility remains that on top of this mutually beneficial interdependence, true altruism exists.

But the part of the puzzle concerned with why people help cannot be completed yet. In the next chapter, we look more closely at another possible cause of helping and altruism in humans. Specifically, we consider possible biological foundations and examine how children develop prosocial motivations.

4

The Origins of Helping and Altruism: Are We "Compassionate Beasts"?

———— ❖ ————

In Chapter 3, we examined cognitive and emotional forces that motivate people to be helpful to others and, possibly, to be truly altruistic. The basic issue addressed in the present chapter concerns whether or not humans are genetically predisposed to be altruistic and helpful; whether we have inherited such tendencies from our recent, distant, and very, very distant ancestors. This issue is of interest to both scientists and nonscientists alike, and opinions on it are divided.

Two best-selling books, Desmond Morris's *The Naked Ape* (1967) and Lionel Tiger and Robin Fox's *The Imperial Animal* (1971), argued that humans are the most aggressive of all animal species and that altruism is not a natural human tendency. There is certainly evidence that aggressiveness is a basic human characteristic. Aggression is present in almost every culture and society in the world and has been throughout history. Most theories of how animals (including humans) survive and evolve argue that aggression is vital to the evolutionary success of these organisms. But does this mean that humans cannot also be altruistic? Or is it possible that humans are *both* innately aggressive and innately altruistic? Some people believe so. In 1990 in another popular book, *The Compassionate Beast*, Morton Hunt argued quite persuasively that humans are inherently altruistic.

THE QUESTION

Like aggression, helpfulness has been found in all known cultures (Fiske, 1991). The basic question in this chapter concerns the reasons for the pervasiveness of this kind of behavior. Are humans prosocial and altruistic by nature? If so, where do these tendencies come from and how are they passed on from generation to generation? Of course, we are not the first to ask these kinds of questions about human nature. As we noted in the first chapter, the issue of whether the essence of human nature is basically "good" and altruistic or fundamentally "bad" and selfish is a very old one. As social scientists, however, we attempt to approach it from a scientific rather than a philosophical or religious perspective. We believe this approach may help us solve some more pieces of the puzzle of human nature.

The question of whether there is a genetic basis to altruism and helping is a simple one to ask but a difficult one to answer. We begin this chapter with a consideration of some of these difficulties. In the second section we ask how altruism could contribute to the survival of a species. Following this, we discuss whether genetic and environmental influences jointly affect altruism among humans. That is, if humans are naturally inclined toward altruism, do these tendencies operate independently of a person's environment, or are they moderated and modified by events such as early learning experiences and parents' child-rearing practices? Finally, we attempt to reconcile the genetic and biological perspective on altruism, presented in this chapter with the social psychological perspective of the previous two chapters. By solving these interrelated puzzles, we can arrive at an answer to the general question about altruism and human nature.

SIMPLE QUESTIONS WITH COMPLEX ANSWERS

In the twentieth century, behavioral geneticists, biologists, psychologists, and other social scientists have attempted to answer the kinds of questions we examine in this chapter. One problem confronted by these researchers is agreeing on a definition of the term *altruism*. In Chapters 1 and 3, altruism was defined in terms of people's intentions and motivations when they offered help to another person. The question was whether the goal was primarily to improve the other person's welfare. This represents a social psychological perspective. This chapter is on genetic influences, and thus we will adopt this perspective and the terminology that accompanies it. According to geneticists and sociobiologists, altruism is any action that involves some costs for the helper, but increases the likelihood that the altruist's close genetic relatives will survive, reproduce, and, thus, pass their genes on to successive generations. So, for the sociobiologist, the beneficiary of altruism is not a particular individual but a particular gene pool. The issue of motivation is not part of this definition because it is not particularly productive for biologists, who study organisms such as bees, to focus on what insects intend or wish to do.

Much of the research on this kind of altruism has focused on genes and their relationship to behavior. There have been some remarkable advances in our knowledge of genes and how they directly and indirectly influence complex social behaviors. For example, medical researchers have identified specific genes associated with several diseases, such as Parkinson's disease and Alzheimer's disease. In addition, the ambitious Human Genome project, which attempts to map the entire human genetic structure, opens up the possibility that eventually we will know all the genes for all the physical and behavioral characteristics that are genetically determined.

However, it would be a mistake to assume that the essence of human nature can be easily discovered. Even if some behavior is primarily due to biological or genetic factors, this does *not* mean that it is immune to environmental, social, and cultural influences or that the behavior will be carried out in a rigid, inflexible, and robotlike manner (DeKay & Buss, 1992). Instead, contemporary behavioral genetics recognizes that a person's environment, learning experiences, and culture will play an important role in determining if and how genetically based predispositions would be expressed in actual behaviors.

No responsible scientist would claim that he or she is able to prove that altruistic inclinations are (or are not) inborn in humans in general or in any individual in particular. Altruistic tendencies are not directly observable, as are physical characteristics such as eye color. Furthermore, altruism is a complex process. Thus, like most human traits and behaviors that have genetic determinants, altruism is likely to be affected by a large number of genes. For example, general intelligence is thought to be influenced by over thirty different genes, as well as by environmental events (Plomin, DeFries, & McClearn, 1990).

Thus, it will be a long and difficult task for science to answer our basic question: Is there a biological or genetic basis for altruism? What follows is what researchers in the biological, social, and behavioral sciences have learned. As you will see, the questions may be simple, but finding correct answers to these questions is often quite problematic.

Asking Questions about Genetics and Altruism

How can we determine whether a characteristic is inherited or is genetically based? For physical traits, such as eye color, that question may not seem difficult. Your parents have the same eye color, and you were that way from birth. From that evidence, you might readily conclude that eye color is genetically determined. But now consider a behavioral trait such as extraversion. Imagine that both you and your parents are extraverted and outgoing people. You may have inherited this aspect of your personality from your parents. Or the similarity may be the consequence of two gregarious and outgoing people teaching you to be extraverted.

The research on innate differences in temperament provides another illustration of this point. According to Bates (1989), the term *temperament* refers to general patterns of behavior such as how active a person is or how responsive the person is to the people and things around him or her. Developmental psychologists who study the behaviors of neonates (newborns) report individual differences in their temperaments from almost the moment of birth. For example, some babies are "hard" (i.e., fussy, cranky, prone to cry); others are "easy" (i.e., calm, quiet) (Sroufe, Cooper, & DeHart, 1992). Most researchers believe that these kinds of differences in newborns' temperaments are due to genetic or biological factors (Bates, 1989). However, the question of whether such differences are stable and persist over an extended period of time is still unanswered. At this time, it appears that individual differences in temperament may not become reliable or stable until children are about 1 year old (Sroufe et al. 1992). And of course by then infants have been exposed to a vast array of learning experiences that could affect their temperament.

Thus, with humans, separating genetic and learning influences is particularly problematic; they are capable of learning an incredible number of things very quickly and very early in their lives. Therefore, once children have reached a certain age, it is often very difficult to say what is innate and what is learned.

Despite these kinds of problems, there are several techniques that can be used to discover whether or not behaviors are part of our species' genetic heritage. Several of these strategies look for similarities in these behaviors across organisms, cultures, and individuals who are genetically close but who have had very different learning experiences. If common outcomes and processes can be identified despite vast differences in socialization, then an inherited biological capacity is likely to be involved. Cross-species, cross-cultural, and behavioral genetics studies are techniques that represent this approach.

In cross-cultural studies, researchers investigate whether certain social behaviors or personal characteristics are found in a large number of different and apparently unrelated societies. If they are, this would suggest that the common behaviors or characteristics are critical to human survival and, thus, have some genetic basis. In cross-species comparative research, demonstrating that the same pattern of behavior found in humans is also consistently present in other animals (particularly in gorillas and chimpanzees, with whom we share 98 percent of our DNA sequences) would provide a clue that it may be a natural part of us. Behavioral genetics techniques consider genetic relationships between individuals (such as family members or twins) that might produce similar talents or predispositions (Segal, 1993). Have you ever noticed behaviors that seem to "run in families"? For example, almost all of Johann Sebastian Bach's family had musical talents. A large percentage of outstanding athletes have parents who also excelled at sports.

Other researchers use the neonate (newborn baby) studies mentioned previously. Infants' behavior is examined in situations in which the influences of socialization and learning experiences are minimized. As was suggested earlier, these studies do find evidence of some innate social behaviors in humans. For example, babies less than a day old are able to imitate the facial expressions of adults (Meltzoff, 1985). This finding, along with evidence that other primates also imitate adults at an early age, strongly suggests that the tendency to imitate is innate.

As another example of apparently innate behaviors, consider this finding. Babies who are born deaf will produce all the same speech sounds as do hearing babies, and babies born blind show recognizable facial expressions for joy, anger, fear, and surprise (Eibl-Eibesfeldt, 1989). This indicates that the ability to produce these sounds and expressions exists independently of learning experiences.

Finally, there are other techniques that directly investigate the impact of genetic processes on behavior. For instance, hormones influence several forms of behavior (e.g., aggression, sexual behavior, maternal behavior). Experiments conducted with animals (e.g., varying levels of testosterone) and studies of hormonal or genetic abnormalities in humans (e.g., a male possessing two Y chromosomes instead of the normal one) provide evidence of genetic causes of social behaviors. Thus, there are several methods that enable us to ask whether some human behaviors are innate.

Of course, there are also significant limitations to these approaches. Each approach is fallible in its own way. For example, cross-cultural similarities could be the result of similar necessities of life that produced the development of similar cultural solutions all around the world. Cross-species generalizations should also be made cautiously because humans clearly are very special animals, in the sense of how much our behavior is affected by socialization and how much we have been able to alter our natural environments. Thus, methodologically, only a convergence of conclusions across these different techniques should be taken as strong evidence of a genetic basis of altruism or any other complex human behavior.

Someone who wishes to study possible genetic or biological causes of human behaviors must also be aware of the history of such investigations and the political and social controversies that accompanied some of them. Among contemporary social scientists, it has often been considered inappropriate to propose that there may be genetic bases for human behavior. One major reason for this feeling is that, in the past, such genetic explanations were often linked with conservative, reactionary, and even Fascist political ideologies. The social Darwinism (the survival of the fittest) of the late nineteenth century was used to justify colonialism and the exploitation of people of color in Africa. Racist ideologies based on claims of genetic superiority have provided the bases for the Nazi holocaust, apartheid in South Africa, and, most recently, the genocidal civil war in the former Yugoslavia.

Because of this historical association between biologically based theories of human behavior and racist, bigoted ideologies, many social scientists have, quite reasonably, found repugnant the suggestion that genetic factors can be responsible for differences among individuals in any aspect of personality, skills, or behavior. Even today, the desire of sociobiologists to map the human biogram in regard to behaviors is sometimes greeted with suspicion as possibly a veiled attempt to justify inequalities between people of different genders, ethnic backgrounds, and racial ancestry, and to defend ethnocentrism and bigotry as being natural processes.

Heritability Reconsidered

We share our colleagues' sensitivities about racism and bigotry masquerading as scientific theories, and we are aware of the tragedies that have occurred when such "theories" have been used to justify prejudice, discrimination, and even genocide. However, we believe that there should be open and thoughtful inquiry into how genes affect human personality, behavior, and abilities. Part of the reason for the distrust of these kinds of explanations of human behavior lies in a frequent misunderstanding of what is meant by the term *heritability*. Many people believe that it concerns *how much* of some behavior is determined by heredity; this is incorrect.

Heritability concerns the percentage of the *differences* among people that is inherited or may be due to heredity. If a characteristic has 50 percent heritability, this means that half the variation or differences among people in that trait can be traced to differences in heredity. Even if a trait is inherited, if there is very little difference among people on it, heritability is really not of much value in understanding that trait. For instance, even though the size and shape of earlobes are certainly inherited characteristics, there is not enough variation in earlobes for this to be a socially significant characteristic. Also, heritability enables us to make predictions at an aggregate or population level, but not at an individual level. For example, we can predict that individuals with two alcoholic parents will have a much greater chance of becoming alcoholic adults than will individuals with no alcoholic parents—whether they are raised by those natural parents or not. This does not tell us, however, which of those children of alcoholics will, indeed, become an alcoholic.

Does prosocial behavior such as the nurturing of this
baby orangutan by its mother suggest that there may
be a biological basis for helping and altruism in
humans? While social and cultural influences may
affect prosocial behavior, there is evidence that
genetic factors may predispose people to help others.
(Liaison International)

One other limitation of only using inherited characteristics to explain
a person's or group of people's behavior is that no gene—not even those
for height or eye color—ever works independently of the environment.
Thus, environmental forces can increase or decrease the impact of genetic
predispositions. For example, Asian Americans who are third, fourth, or
fifth generation in this country are much taller than their parents and
grandparents. Nutritional and behavioral environments in which people

are reared can therefore overshadow what appear to be genetic factors. Sex differences that are often assumed to be determined by genetics can also be modified by the social environment. For instance, the greater tendency of girls and women to participate in athletics today may be leading to the decreasing difference in height between men and women in the United States (Osborne, personal communication; see also Tanner, 1966).

Thus, we need to be clear about what the phrase "a gene for altruism" does and does not mean. Most biologists do not believe that a single gene, operating independently from other genes and environmental factors, irrevocably and irreversibly determines whether a person will or will not engage in a complex behavior such as altruism (Ridley & Dawkins, 1984). A gene *for* something merely creates a tendency to do or be something. Environmental influences and other genes also shape the eventual outcome. Therefore, although genetic tendencies may favor some behavioral characteristics, these tendencies do not necessarily unequivocally determine our destiny. Thus, we believe that it is appropriate for social scientists to study the genetic bases of behavior, but the question still remains whether this approach will actually provide evidence of a genetic basis for altruism in humans. We now turn our attention to the main issue.

ALTRUISM AND "SURVIVAL OF THE FITTEST": AN OXYMORON?

As we discussed in Chapter 3, until quite recently most social scientists believed that true altruism could not exist. Whether one spoke to a psychologist, psychiatrist, sociologist, or political scientist, the answer was the same: Any behavior that appears to be solely motivated by a concern for someone else's needs will, under closer scrutiny, prove to be due to ulterior, selfish motives. This traditional view was very skeptical about the existence of true altruism. For example:

> The economy of nature is competitive from beginning to end. . . . The impulses that lead one animal to sacrifice himself for another turn out to have their ultimate rationale in gaining advantage over a third. . . . Where it is in his own interest, every organism may reasonably be expected to aid his fellows. . . . Yet given a full chance to act in his own interest, nothing but expediency will restrain him from brutalizing, from maiming, from murdering—his brother, his mate, his parent, or his child. Scratch an "altruist," and watch a "hypocrite" bleed. (Gheselin, 1974, p. 247; cited in Ridley & Dawkins, 1984.)

Given this viewpoint, it is not surprising to learn that in some psychiatric theories, true altruism in humans was simply dismissed as an unusual and pathological pattern of behavior.

To a certain extent, these arguments about the existence of true altruism are more applicable to altruism as it was defined in the previous chapter (i.e., a person's purely other-oriented motivation for helping) than to altruism as it is being defined here. But for a long time, scientists also doubted that there could be an innate tendency to sacrifice one's own welfare for the good of others. The pendulum has now begun to swing the other way. In the next section, we consider some of the reasons.

Altruism in Nonhuman Species

Do we find evidence of altruism, as it has been defined here, in most species? If so, it would be difficult to imagine that humans are the exception. Indeed, one major argument presented by those who believe that humans may be inherently altruistic is that altruism exists across such a wide range of other animals.

We begin with a personal example. One of the authors of this book is a gardener. There is a beehive under the boards of her house near her garden. Every time she tries to weed the section of the garden near the hive, a few guard bees come out and buzz her. Usually she retreats. A few years ago, she did not, and her nose was sore for days from the suicidal attack of one of those guards! The guard bee made the supreme sacrifice in the act of protecting the hive; stinging someone is fatal to a bee. When it embedded its stinger in the victim's nose and then withdrew, the bee died. But bees are not nature's only altruists. Many kinds of birds and animals place themselves at great danger—to the benefit of others—by making warning calls when they see a predator.

Turning to primates, when a baboon troop is threatened by a predator such as a leopard, the females and young flee, while the older males form a group and fight the cat. Although adult male baboons are equipped with strong teeth, they are no match for a full-grown leopard; it is common for at least one of them to be wounded or killed. There are also undocumented sea tales that sailors have been rescued by dolphins supporting them in the water after they have fallen overboard or been shipwrecked. Whether or not such stories are true, dolphins do this for each other (Sienbenaler & Caldwell, 1956). Other anecdotal evidence also demonstrates that animals engage in cross-species altruism. For example, Batson (1983) describes an incident in which a family's pet dog dove into a burning car and pulled his owners' daughter to safety.

These stories notwithstanding, there is still a basic problem in accepting the notion that altruism is an innate human characteristic. If altruism is inborn, then it must be a characteristic that has been passed from generation to generation through our genes. But for this to occur, altruism must also be a characteristic that has survival value. This creates one of the major puzzles in this book.

Altruism and Evolution: Survival of the Nicest?

At the very core of the Darwinian theory of evolution is the concept of the "survival of the fittest." According to Darwin, "nature is red in tooth and claw"; it is "the struggle of all against all." If this is true, how could a tendency for self-sacrifice have evolved? Consider the bee that dies to protect the hive, the prairie dog that calls out a predator warning, the baboon that challenges the leopard, or people who risked their lives in the stories that began Chapters 1 and 2. These individuals are unlikely to survive, either personally or genetically. Members of a species that sacrifice their lives for others will, on the average, have fewer offspring than those that save themselves. Thus, in Darwin's terms, these individuals cannot be the "fittest." This logically leads to the conclusion that evolutionary forces should select against the genetic transmission of altruistic tendencies.

Nevertheless, more current evolutionary perspectives suggest mechanisms that might allow for the development of innate altruistic tendencies. In the next section, we consider three processes that could produce genetic bases for altruism in humans. Following that section, we examine environmental and social conditions that might foster the evolution of altruistic behavior.

Evolutionary mechanisms: genes, not people. How can altruistic tendencies evolve when altruists, by definition, should be less likely to survive? To answer this, we must reconsider how evolution takes place. Whereas the Darwinian view was that natural selection takes place at the level of the individual—that the fittest people will survive—a prevalent view today is that evolution takes place at the level of genes (Settle, 1993; Wilson, 1992). According to Ridley and Dawkins (1984), "the animal can be regarded as a machine designed to preserve copies of the genes inside it" (p. 32). It is therefore not the survival of the organism that is critical in the process of natural selection but rather it is the survival of the gene. Thus, genes for altruism can be "selected for" (i.e., have a higher probability of being passed on to future generations), even if individual altruists—the carriers of these genes—perish at a higher rate than their more selfish contemporaries. Hamilton (1964) coined the term, *inclusive fitness*, to describe the successful transmission of individual's genes to a subsequent gene pool. There are three possible ways by which altruistic genes might survive and be passed on: group selection, kin selection, and reciprocity.

Group selection. The group selection approach proposes that groups with altruistic members are less likely to become extinct than are groups comprised entirely of selfish individuals. Although this is intuitively reasonable, there is a critical problem in the logic of group selection: Group selection works too slowly (Krebs & Miller, 1985). It takes a very long time for an entire group to become extinct. Meanwhile, in the short run, selfish members have a competitive edge over selfless members. (More about this in Chapter 8.) Thus, the forces guiding the behavior of individuals are incompatible with the evolution of a group with altruistic members. The altruistic members will all die out long before the group does. Because of this problem with the notion of group selection, most attention has focused on the two other mechanisms by which altruism may evolve.

Kin selection. A common sentiment among most, if not all, parents is that whatever their children do, they will still love and care for them. This is, of course, what good parents are *supposed* to say. But genetic theories of the origins of altruism suggest that this sentiment may be more than just a self-serving refrain. Specifically, kin selection theory focuses on the actions of people who are genetically related. It proposes that the chil-

Kin selection may explain the mother bear's reaction to protect her cub and thereby increase the chances that her genes will be passed on to future generations. (One can only wonder what Mrs. Anderson's reactions will be.) (The Far Side cartoon by Gary Larson is reprinted by permission of Chronicle Features, San Francisco, Ca. All rights reserved.)

THE FAR SIDE   By GARY LARSON

11-2 Larson © Chronicle Features. 1983

And no one ever heard from the Anderson brothers again.

dren of a parent who is totally indifferent to their needs are unlikely to survive; thus a "neglectful parent gene," which might have been passed on to these unfortunate offspring, is unlikely to survive. Thus, it is quite reasonable to propose that the vast majority of parents are genetically inclined to be altruistic to their children. Note that we have momentarily returned to the social psychological definition of altruism: It is help that is primarily intended to benefit another person. (Unfortunately, of course, there are dramatic and tragic exceptions to these general tendencies. Pathologically abusive and uncaring parents are, however, very much the exception rather than the rule. And there is evidence that this behavior is environmentally caused.)

Some of the most dramatic examples of altruism among other animals involve self-sacrifice by parents to benefit their offspring. Many ground-nesting birds, such as the killdeer, attempt to distract predators who threaten their young. As the predator approaches, the parent leaves the nest to attract attention to itself, limping as if its wing were injured. The

---

BOX 4.1

The Genetic Benefits of Altruism

From a genetic perspective, the survival of a group of related individuals depends upon the survival of its gene pool. Altruism is any self-sacrificing action that contributes to this goal. Geneticists also believe that altruists' genes can be maintained in a gene pool even if their actions result in their death before they have offspring. To explain this paradoxical statement, we must introduce the concept of relatedness. *Relatedness* represents the probability that a selected gene from one individual will be represented in a relative. For example, the probability that a parent and child will share a gene is .50, the same probability that siblings (brothers and sisters) will share a particular gene. The probability that aunts and uncles will share a selected gene with nieces and nephews is .25. If altruistic

actions increase the *reproductive success* (i.e., the probability that an individual will have offspring) of genetic relatives of the altruist, this can also increase the *genetic success* (i.e., the likelihood that a specific gene will be passed on to subsequent generations) of the altruist's genes.

To illustrate this concept, we present three hypothetical cases in which a person must choose between an altruistic and a selfish action. To simplify the matter, in all three cases the reproductive success of the individuals involved is assumed to be the same—they all would have one offspring.

Case 1: Choosing between saving one's own life or the lives of three siblings. Which choice is more likely to preserve the actor's genes in the group's gene pool?

predator, spying easy prey, is lured away from the nest to stalk the "injured" parent. At the last possible moment, the bird abandons all pretense and takes to the air, leaving the predator confused and hungry. The animal that threatened the nest is now distracted and some distance away; it is unlikely that it will be able to find the nest and the helpless young birds in it. In this way, the young are saved, but only at great risk to the parent.

Why does parental self-sacrifice make evolutionary sense? Remember from an evolutionary perspective, the sole purpose of reproduction is to increase the incidence of one's genes in subsequent generations (Alcock, 1989). A parent passes on 50 percent of its genes to each offspring. Thus, if an altruistic parent gives his or her life to ensure the survival of at least two of its offspring and they are fertile, there is no net loss of their genes in the family.

Box 4.1 explains this in more detail. It shows that even altruism that benefits relatives who are not the offspring of the altruist increases the

---

BOX 4.1   (continued)

Answer: Saving the three siblings.
Explanation: The genetic benefit of saving oneself would be .5, assuming one offspring in the future. This is outweighed by the genetic benefit of saving three brothers or sisters, who each have a .5 probability of sharing a gene with the altruist. Thus, the probable genetic benefit to the altruist would be 1.5 (3 persons × .5 = 1.5). The *net* benefit is therefore +1.0 (1.5 − .5).

Case 2: Choosing between saving one's own life or the lives of three nieces or nephews. Which choice is more likely to preserve the actor's genes in the group's gene pool?
Answer: Saving the three nieces and nephews.
Explanation: Again the genetic benefit of saving oneself is .5 (1 person × .5). This benefit is less than the genetic benefit of saving the three nieces and nephews. The probability of each of

them sharing a gene in common with the altruist is .25. Thus, the probable genetic benefit of this action is .75 (3 × .25 = .75). The *net* benefit is +.25.

Case 3: Choosing between saving one's own or the lives of three unrelated strangers? Which choice is more likely to preserve the actor's genes in the group's gene pool?
Answer: Saving oneself.
Explanation: The genetic benefit of saving oneself is (again) .5. However, because the relatedness between these three people and the potential altruist is 0 (they are not relatives), there is no direct genetic benefit to saving them (3 persons × 0 = 0). The *net* benefit is +.5.

Thus, in many (but not all) instances, altruistic actions can produce long-term genetic benefits that outweigh the immediate personal benefits of selfishness.

[Based on Alcock (1989).]

likelihood of the altruist's genes surviving and being passed on to successive generations. The examples presented in this box show how altruists who give their lives to save the lives of siblings or even siblings' children do more to pass on their genes—to increase their inclusive fitness—than do nonaltruists who save their own lives at the expense of their relative's lives.

As long as relatives live near each other or can be recognized as relatives so that altruistic actions can usually be directed toward kin, an altruistic gene will survive and, in fact, outcompete a selfish gene.

Although the issue of how well kin selection theory applies to humans remains controversial (Caporael & Brewer, 1991), there are strong arguments in favor of the theory (Rushton, 1989). In addition, this theory has been used to explain why people are more likely to help others who are more similar to them (see Chapter 2); people may unwittingly associate similarity with genetic closeness (Krebs, 1987). Nevertheless, there are limitations. Even though kin selection might be able to explain altruism among family members and similar others, it does not address how altruism might exist more generally among members of larger and unrelated groups, such as societies. Other evolutionary processes might relate to this more general altruistic orientation.

Reciprocal altruism. In Chapter 3, we discussed the norm of reciprocity, which seems to be a universal norm across cultures. The norm dictates that people should help others who have helped them. As we noted at the beginning of this chapter, cross-cultural similarities in behavior suggest that genetic influences may be involved. Robert Trivers (1971) first used the term *reciprocal altruism* to refer to a genetic tendency for mutual helping. Reciprocal altruism easily explains cooperation when mutual benefits are simultaneously received by all participants. For example, emperor penguins conserve heat by huddling together. By huddling together, each penguin benefits by exposing less body area to the winter cold. Reciprocal altruism also explains why people tend to help others who have previously helped them. In essence, it is the genetic version of the golden rule: Do good unto others under the assumption that, when they have the chance, they will reciprocate and do good unto you. Reciprocity selection works because cooperative behavior may, on the average, increase the fitness (i.e., likelihood of survival) of the cooperating individuals. Reciprocity selection favors genes that influence cooperation between individuals who are not necessarily related.

A critical problem for the evolution of reciprocal altruism is that it is hard to see how a new gene for it could become established. If very few people carry the gene, those who do will not be likely to meet others who carry it and will give away their benefits to people who will never reciprocate. Rothstein and Pierotti (1988) propose that other easier forms of cooperation (such as the cooperative huddling of emperor penguins) may have evolved first and formed a basis for the development of more complex types or reciprocal helping across time. Because sharing, helping, and cooperation are behaviorally similar, they may be emotionally interconnected (Moore, 1984). In this way, genetic selection for sharing could lead to positive emotions associated with all forms of helping, and the norm or ethic that favors them should be reciprocated.

As we noted earlier in this chapter, genetic processes by themselves are unlikely to determine altruistic behavior. Environmental circumstances are also critical factors. In the next section we identify environmental and social influences that can foster the evolution of altruism.

Fostering the Evolution of Altruism

The preceding material makes a reasonable argument that the growth and maintenance of altruistic genes may be of benefit to the survival of a species. However, it is also probably true that, in contrast to characteristics such as strength or intelligence that would likely be selected for under any circumstances, altruism is more fragile and needs special circumstances if it is to be passed on across generations. What kinds of circumstances will best foster the development of innate altruistic tendencies? In general, conditions are needed that will increase the likelihood of mutual altruistic tendencies among individuals and decrease the likelihood of exploitation. There are three environmental or social factors that seem to facilitate the process: isolation, the ability to recognize other altruists, and the ability to detect cheating.

Isolation. An altruistic gene will have a better chance to develop if groups are somewhat isolated from each other. This isolation increases the probability that altruists will eventually benefit from others' altruistic behavior. This factor is particularly relevant to human evolution. Early humans lived in rather small bands of related individuals, somewhat isolated from other groups. In addition, the requirements of the hunting and gathering lifestyle should have selected positively for a number of cooperative and altruistic behaviors, given that people were mating within the group.

Obviously, evolutionary theories cannot be tested in experiments using real people. However, there are alternative methods. For instance, computer programs can be written that simulate different evolutionary circumstances. The output from these simulation programs can tell us what conditions were most likely to produce altruistic tendencies in a species. Morgan (1985) used such a computer simulation to study the conditions that might best foster the emergence of altruism in a group. According to this simulation, when groups remained isolated from one another, reciprocal altruism fostered the development of an altruistic gene. When groups split up, but individuals favored interactions with members of their own kind, an altruistic gene evolved whether altruists helped reciprocally, helped only others who were related to them, or helped any other individual.

From an evolutionary perspective, altruistic behavior appears to have long-term benefits that offset the potential costs to the individual. Indeed, these computer simulations of evolutionary processes also showed that in groups that included both altruists and nonaltruists, individual altruists had lower inclusive fitness—that is, they left fewer descendants—than did nonaltruists. However, the more altruists there were in the group, the better off the group members were, on average. This provides evidence of the importance of physical and social isolation for the evolution of altruism.

Recognition. It is important to remember that evolutionary benefits of altruism are not necessarily limited to members of the altruist's immediate family, who would be well-known and easily recognizable to her or him. Conceivably, help that is given to any genetic relative (e.g., a cousin) could affect the incidence of the altruist's genes in subsequent generations. Thus, for kin altruism to be evolutionarily successful, potential altruists must be able to recognize (consciously or unconsciously) who are their kin and who are not. If altruism is directed too often at nonkin, the selection mechanism presented in Box 4.1 will not work. Nevertheless, it is not always easy to identify more distant kin from nonkin. Recall the last time you attended a large gathering, such as a wedding, that included many close and distant relatives and nonrelatives. How many times did you need to be reintroduced to your genetic kin? How then can altruists spontaneously recognize their kin?

One possibility is that there may be biological cues. J. Phillipe Rushton and his associates (e.g., Rushton, Russell, & Wells, 1984) proposed that there is an innate basis for the ability to recognize that another individual is genetically similar, and this underlies both kin and reciprocity selection. In support of the existence of this ability, they presented data showing that a wide variety of animals reared apart can recognize their relatives and that animals (including humans) mate with those genetically similar to them. In addition, many animals can specifically recognize genetically related individuals using smell, appearance, or some other observable characteristics.

It appears that humans may also have this ability (Porter, 1987). For example, new mothers can pick out pictures of their own infants from a set of pictures within a few hours after birth, even though there had been very little contact with the infant (Porter, Cernoch, & Balogh, 1984). Unrelated individuals presented with pictures of mothers and infants could also match them with above-chance accuracy, indicating that there is a detectable resemblance between mothers and their babies as early as the second day of life (Porter, 1987). Odors, such as those on T-shirts just worn by an infant, are also reliable cues for humans (Porter, Cernoch, & McLaughlin, 1983; Porter, Cernoch, & Balogh, 1985).

Social cues may also be involved. Because animals usually live with their relatives, simple proximity and familiarity often serve this purpose well (Sherman, 1985). Animals typically help those with whom they live and interact most often. Social cues may also be important for reciprocal altruism. For reciprocal altruism to work, it is important that individuals bearing the reciprocity gene be matched with each other. Humans and other animals must therefore be equipped with strategies and abilities for recognizing other altruists when they meet them. Similarity may provide the cue. That is, individuals may infer that others who are similar to them in appearance or personality may also be similar to them genetically (Glassman, Packel, & Brown, 1986; Segal, 1993). Thus, altruists should be more inclined to help others who are similar to them.

As we saw in Chapter 2, strangers regularly exhibit this tendency. Furthermore, even within families, helping is more common among members who are more similar in personality (Leek & Smith, 1989, 1991). Thus, there may be a genetic basis for the finding that people prefer to help similar others. Carrying this a step further, Box 4.2 presents the intriguing, but untested, notion that perhaps there is even a genetic basis for things such as ethnocentrism (favoring members of one's in-group and disliking members of out-groups) and patriotism.

The ability to detect cheating. It is said that cheaters never prosper. But can they? If one considers the situation coldly and rationally, the best survival tactic for anyone would be to appear to be an altruist while in fact being quite selfish. Such a person would receive help without having to experience the costs or the risks for helping others. Because being a nonaltruist among altruists is the best possible survival strategy, as long as one is not caught, the ability to deceive others is adaptive. As the noted sociologist Erving Goffman (1959) has noted, the best way to deceive others is to appear to be completely sincere. Recent research suggests that this is true. For example, when someone uses both verbal and nonverbal cues to convey a false impression to us, we are usually not very successful at detecting that we are being deceived (DePaulo, 1992). But we must quickly add another finding from studies of deception. When people attempt to manipulate the impressions that others have of them, they often come to believe these impressions themselves (e.g., Schlenker, Dlugolecki, & Doherty, 1994). Findings such as these have led some theorists to speculate that the capacity for self-deception might even have developed in connection with reciprocal altruism (Vine, 1983; Lopreato, 1981; Badcock, 1986).

For reciprocal altruism to survive selectively, there must be a willingness to punish those who do cheat or ways of socializing people so that

BOX 4.2

Is There a Genetic Basis for Ethnocentrism and Patriotism?

Johnson (1986) uses the ideas of kin selection and similarity detection to try to explain ethnocentrism and patriotism. He first discusses the question of how kin recognition probably takes place. During the hunting and gathering phase of our evolution, humans were nomadic, so location cues would have been useless. However, most of our associates were very likely to be kin, and kin share some family resemblance. So it was fairly easy to determine who was friend and who was foe.

Johnson proposes that altruism should be most likely directed toward close associates and toward those perceived as similar to the helper. In support of this argument, he cites research that found that altruistic suicide—falling on a hand grenade—was more likely in highly cohesive than in less cohesive combat units (Blake, 1978). He also suggests that people may use physical similarity as a basis for deciding whom to help:

> On these grounds, one would predict . . . that when other things are equal humans will discriminate behaviorally on the basis of race. Within races one should find discrimination on the basis of racial subtype. And within racial subtypes one should find discrimination based upon even finer differences in physical appearance. The prevalence of these forms of discrimination in the contemporary world requires no comment. (p. 133)

He also predicts that social class, ideology, religion, and so on, are bases for extending altruism to other members of the in-group and denying it to members of the out-group. We will feel kinship, then, toward those defined as similar (by nationality, race, country) or toward those we think of as our associates. Finally, Johnson concludes that

> patriotism in large-scale societies is a brand of manipulated altruism. . . . A genetically based capacity for altruism has been produced by the operation of kin selection on our forebears. The elicitation of altruism depends upon the presence of kin recognition cues. The cues capable of eliciting altruism in humans are probably association and phenotypic [outward appearance] matching. Large-scale human societies . . . have evolved processes of socialization which exploit these cues by which altruism originally came to be elicited. . . . Among the altruistic dispositions these socialization processes produce is patriotism. (p. 135)

This raises the possibility that the same genetic mechanisms may underlie both aggression and altruism. Just as we learn to direct altruism to those defined as part of the in-group, we learn to direct aggression to those in the out-group.

Of course, even if Johnson's proposal has some validity, this does *not* mean that prejudice and discrimination toward people different from ourselves is natural, unavoidable, or should be accepted by society. Rather, the proposal only suggests that humans may be somewhat predisposed to be biased against people who are different from themselves.

they refrain from cheating. Sociobiologists have considered this matter. Some have proposed that reciprocity selection will tend to favor the evolution of strong emotions that will motivate swift and severe punishments for cheating, which will serve to ensure that cheaters do not prosper. According to Trivers, "tendencies . . . to detect and punish cheaters with 'moralistic aggression' should tend to be selected for, as should guilt at failure to reciprocate" (cited by Vine, 1983, p. 4). There is very good reason to believe that such tendencies exist in humans.

Recall, for example, your reactions the last time you felt cheated by someone. The feelings were probably automatic, intense, and, of course, very negative. In addition, as we saw in Chapter 3, feelings of guilt for unfairly harming another person can motivate helping. Cross-cultural studies of helping indicate that specific beliefs and custom about helping vary considerably from country to country. However, in every society that has been studied it has been found that people value fairness in their dealings with others, and believe that, under normal circumstances, if someone helps them, they have an obligation to reciprocate the favor in some way—and vice versa. Violations of these expectations and beliefs usually produce distress and anger (see Chapters 3, 5, and 7). These findings suggest that perhaps negative reactions to cheaters might be innate.

Kinship, Reciprocity, and Helping

If there is validity to the notion that the mechanisms of kin selection and reciprocal altruism played important roles in the evolution of altruism, then we should find some evidence of their existence today. That is, there should be differences in willingness of individuals to help others as a function of (1) their relatedness and (2) beliefs about their likelihood of reciprocating. In addition, if there is a genetic basis to these processes, we would expect convergence in the results of studies that use a wide variety of approaches.

Studies of animals indicate a preference for helping relatives and other members of the social group over nonrelatives and strangers. For example, Curry (1988) observed that mockingbirds were more likely to feed hungry, closely related nestlings (other than their own) than they were to feed unrelated nestlings; Sherman (1985) found that when threatened by predators such as coyotes and weasels, ground squirrels were much more likely to warn genetically related squirrels and squirrels with whom they lived than unrelated squirrels or those from other areas. Figure 4.1 presents the results of another study on kinship and helping in animals (Sherman, 1981). In this study, Sherman recorded the percentage of female squirrels that helped another squirrel chase away animals that entered the first squirrel's territory. The figure shows that the greatest number of cooperative chases occurred among mothers and daughters

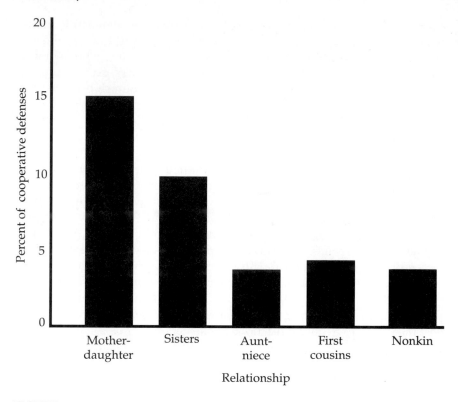

FIGURE 4.1
More closely related squirrels are more cooperative in the defense of space.
(Adapted from Sherman, 1981.)

and among sisters. Note that the more closely related the animals were, the more cooperation there was between them.

Social psychological research with humans is also consistent with both kin selection and reciprocal altruism mechanisms. Michael Cunningham (1985/1986) reviewed the research that has specifically tried to test these kinds of predictions derived from sociobiological theory. A number of studies have used a role-playing methodology in which people are asked to imagine themselves in a certain situation and to respond as they think they would if the situation were real (e.g., Cunningham, 1983). Overall, these studies have found that the closer the kinship relation, the greater the expectations that help would be given, resentment if help were withheld, and willingness to provide aid to distressed person. Interestingly, participants in these studies also indicated that the closer the relationship, the more they expected that the help given would be reciprocated. People report similar patterns of help in their own lives. For example, in one study 300 women were asked to recall the times when they received help with finances, emotional support, everyday living, illness, and housing (Essock-Vitale & McGuire, 1985). Exchanges with blood relatives (both giving and receiving) were the most common. The more valuable the help, the more likely it was to have come from kin. Thus, these findings provide support for both kin and reciprocity processes.

The cross-cultural evidence is also supportive. Data from thirteen anthropological studies across a wide variety of cultures revealed that relatives were given more help overall than nonrelatives, with close kin receiving the most help (Essock-Vitale & McGuire, 1985). In addition, large gifts and long-term loans were most likely to come from kin. Also, reciprocal helping occurs cross-culturally, and, consistent with mechanisms to prevent cheating, people across a broad range of cultures experience guilt and other negative emotions when they are unable to reciprocate assistance (Moghaddam, Taylor, & Wright, 1993).

Finally, behavioral genetics research provides additional convergent results. The more closely people are related genetically, the more helpful they are to one another. This helping may often involve significant sacrifices. For example, would you be willing to give one of your kidneys to another person? If so, to whom? In a study of living kidney donors, Borgida, Conner, and Manteufel (1992) found that donors were about three times as likely to do this for a relative as for a nonrelative (73 percent versus 27 percent). Another study specifically investigated the degree of relatedness between the kidney donor and the recipient (Simmons, Marine, & Simmons, 1977). The closer the relationship, the more likely people were to help: 86 percent of parents, 76 percent of children, and 47 percent of siblings of the person who needed the kidney agreed to donate it to their relative. The high proportion of parents who were willing to help is consistent with the kin selection argument, particularly because most parents would be past reproductive age. Helping a child survive would be the best way to ensure that their genes would be passed on. However, there is one unanswered problem with the kin selection explanation. It does not explain why the rate was lower among siblings than among children of the kidney recipients; the genetic relationship among siblings and children is equivalent. Other social factors, such as the motivation of children to reciprocate parental altruism, are probably involved.

Comparisons between fraternal and identical twins represent a particularly powerful behavioral technique that also points to a genetic basis for altruism (Segal, 1993). Identical twins have the same genetic makeup, whereas fraternal twins share 50 percent of their genes on the average— the same as other siblings. Assuming that both fraternal and identical twins share common family and environmental influences, any systematic differences between them that are observed are likely to be genetically based. Indeed, in an experimental study Nancy Segal (1984) found striking evidence for greater cooperation between identical than between same-sex fraternal twins. The two kinds of twins were carefully matched on overall IQ levels and on IQ similarity within a pair. Nevertheless, 94 percent of the identical twins, but only 46 percent of the fraternal twins cooperated on a puzzle task. On a second task in which twins worked once for their own benefit and once for their co-twin's benefit, identical twins worked significantly harder for their co-twins than did fraternal twins. Identical twins are also more cooperative than fraternal twins on tasks in which participants make choices to compete for their personal gain or to cooperate and trust the other person and cooperate for their mutual benefit (Segal, 1991).

Summary

Animal, social psychological, cross-cultural, and behavioral genetics research provide convergent evidence for a genetic or inherited basis for altruism. In our society and cross-culturally, reciprocity is the norm. When people are unable to reciprocate, they experience negative emotions that minimize the likelihood of cheating. Furthermore, people are more likely to offer help to others with whom they are more closely related. Consistent with the old adage, with respect to altruism, "blood is thicker than water." Also, depending on the degree of the relationship, some blood is thicker than others.

A portion of the puzzle considered in this chapter has been solved. Although selfishness certainly has survival value, so does altruism; there are mechanisms for the genetic transmission of altruistic tendencies from one generation to another. The coexistence of both tendencies in our genetic heritage is not a logical or natural contradiction. Sometimes competition and selfishness are needed; other times cooperation and altruism are more beneficial. Now we can move to another part of this puzzle: Through what mechanisms do our genes affect altruistic actions?

FROM GENES TO ACTION

Unlike other animals, humans engage in few (if any) rigidly controlled, highly stereotyped behaviors that can be directly tied to their genetic heritage. Behaviors like alarm calls in birds or the suicidal altruistic responses of worker bees when their hive is threatened are simply not found in humans. So how would such a gene *for* altruism operate? How can genetic tendencies be translated into action?

Genes probably influence behavior in an indirect manner. They may affect some part of the nervous system and predispose people to be especially sensitive to certain aspects of their environment (e.g., loud, unexpected cries) or to experience certain emotions. The parts of the human brain that govern emotions are evolutionarily quite old and basic. Thus, emotion might provide a mechanism through which genes can produce altruistic actions. As we saw in the previous chapter, a range of emotions (such as guilt, sadness, distress, and concern) can motivate helping and altruism in humans. The capacity to experience empathy in response to another person's problem or distress might therefore be the key element linking genetic predisposition to immediate action (Cunningham, 1985/1986; Hoffman, 1981; MacDonald 1984). Recall from Chapter 3 that affective empathy represents "the vicarious experiencing of an emotion which is congruent with, but not necessarily identical to, the emotion another person is experiencing" (Barnett, 1987, p. 146).

Empathy

There are three major reasons why empathy has attracted so much interest as a possible link between genes and altruistic actions. The first and most important of these is that there is a substantial relationship between the ability to experience empathy and willingness to engage in prosocial behaviors. For example, Nancy Eisenberg and her associates (e.g., Eisenberg & Miller, 1987; Eisenberg & Fabes, 1990) reported that the more empathic children were, the more likely they were to act prosocially. As you read in the previous chapter, a similar relationship is found among adults: Empathy plays a critical role in adults' decisions to offer or not to offer help (e.g., Batson & Oleson, 1991; Davis, 1994). One accepted measure of empathy is vicariously induced physiological arousal (e.g., changes in heart rate in response to another person's distress). Several studies have found that changes in heart rate predict how likely it is that people will help and the speed with which they help (Dovidio et al., 1991; Eisenberg et al., 1990). Thus, across a wide range of people and situations, empathy is a critical element in helping

Although there does appear to be a consistent relationship between empathy and helping, this relationship, in and of itself, does not prove that biological factors are responsible for altruism. As we will discuss below (and in the next chapter as well), people's learning experiences as they grow up can and do dramatically affect how likely they are to experience empathy when another person is in trouble. Therefore, additional convergent evidence is needed to place empathy in a biological context. The second and third reasons for interest in empathy among advocates of a genetic basis for altruism provide some of this evidence.

The work of neuroscientists who have studied the human brain and how it operates provides a second reason why empathy has so much attention among researchers interested in the genetic basis of altruism. There appears to be a specific part of the brain that gives humans the physiological or neurological capacity to empathize with other people. The portion of the brain that appears to enable a person to be emotionally involved with other people is called the *limbic system*. This brain structure was present very early in human evolutionary history (Maclean, 1973, 1985). Indeed, it may have been present among the earliest mammals, over 180 million years ago. Therefore, even our most primitive ancestors may have had the capacity for empathy.

Empathic responses can lead to altruistic actions and, as discussed earlier, altruistic actions may have considerable value in the survival of some gene pools or kinship groups over others. Therefore, empathy could have increased the likelihood that certain kinds of humans survived "and continued to evolve into increasing complex forms as their brain developed and grew" (Hoffman, 1975, p. 610). We should also mention that the limbic system appears to have evolved independently from those structures associated with aggression and hedonism (Hoffman, 1975). Thus, biologically, it appears possible for humans to be both altruistic and selfish.

The third reason is that empathy-like reactions have been observed in humans at very early ages. Recall that one of the major criteria for concluding that a behavior is innate rather than learned is that it occurs so early in a person's life that it is not likely to be influenced by learning or conditioning. Over sixty years ago, researchers found that 4-month-old babies would cry when they heard other children cry (Arlitt, 1930; Humphrey, 1923). This suggests an innate capacity, although one could quite reasonably argue that 4-month-old infants could have already learned to associate distress in others with distressful circumstances for themselves. However, as mentioned in Chapter 2, more recent research has found vicarious crying in infants as young as 1 day old (Martin & Clark, 1982; Sagi & Hoffman, 1976; Simner, 1971). For example, Martin and Clark exposed 1-day-old infants to tape recordings of three different sounds: another newborn crying, an 11-month-old child crying, and the child's own crying. The tape that elicited the most crying in babies was the one that contained the sound of another newborn crying. In fact, it produced more crying than the sound of the child's own crying!

Of course, these studies of newborns' crying do not conclusively prove empathy is an innate emotion. Even children this young are capable of learning simple associations, and they may have already learned to associate distress in others with unpleasant consequences for themselves (Hoffman, 1978). Infants also could simply be reproducing a sound they have heard (Thompson, 1987). But one must still be impressed with the fact that humans show at least the precursors of true empathy within a day or two after birth. This seems to suggest that, at a minimum, humans are predisposed to be empathic. We now consider how this predisposition might develop in humans.

The development of empathy in humans. Martin Hoffman is one of the foremost proponents of the idea that there is a genetic basis for human empathy in response to distress in others, which in turn can lead to attempts to help them. However, Hoffman (1978, 1984, 1990) does not believe that true empathy emerges until an infant has passed through several developmental stages. The first and most primitive stage is global empathy. Hoffman uses this term to describe the crying responses in newborns that were discussed earlier. He argues that during the first year of life, human infants do not have a sense of themselves as unique individuals separate and distinct from others; they are unable to differentiate themselves from other people. What happens to others, in essence, is happening to them. Hoffman (1990) provided a clear example of how children respond at this stage of their development. An 11-month-old girl saw another child fall and cry. The girl looked as if she were going to cry herself and "put her thumb in her mouth and buried her head in her mother's lap as she does when she herself is hurt" (Hoffman, 1990, p. 155). The child's feelings represented some degree of empathy; she understood the other child's pain. Nevertheless, Hoffman argues that this kind of self-centered emotional response (i.e., feeling personally distressed) is not likely to lead to helpful actions toward the other child.

By the time children reach about 1 year of age, they are beginning to become aware that they are physically distinct from others, and they have developed a rather rudimentary awareness that other people can be in distress or pain while they are not. But their empathy is still rather self-oriented. That is, they assume that someone in distress feels exactly the same way they would feel if they were distressed, and they also respond accordingly. A typical response for 1- or 2-year-old children who see another child in distress might be to give their own favorite toy or their "security blanket" to the other child. For example, one child brought his *own* mother to comfort a distressed playmate, despite the fact that the playmate's mother was nearby (Hoffman, 1978).

By the time children reach the age of 2 or 3, their empathic skills are more fully developed. They now understand that different things can distress different people and that different actions are needed to alleviate this distress. Furthermore, because they now have the tool of language at their disposal, they can understand rather complex feelings in others, such as disappointment, sadness over something lost, and even feeling bad about oneself (i.e., low self-esteem). The final stage in Hoffman's model of the development of empathy occurs in late childhood. At this age, children can experience empathy in response to another person's life conditions rather than just that person's immediate circumstances. Their vicarious reactions can be produced by events that happened to the person before they met or will happen after the two part company. The ability to experience such feelings may even cause children to help or comfort someone whom they do not know well.

Although Hoffman's model is widely accepted, it is based more on general theories of child development than on systematic observations of how infants actually behave. One of the more comprehensive attempts to directly examine empathy and prosocial behavior in infants and toddlers has been carried out by Marion Radke-Yarrow and Carolyn Zahn-Waxler. Their work is important for two reasons. First, it provides some empirical tests of Hoffman's ideas, and second, it permits us to examine the interplay between inherited predispositions to be empathic and prosocial and the effects of parental behaviors and other learning experiences.

Naturalistic observations of infants and toddlers. Radke-Yarrow, Zahn-Waxler, and their associates (e.g., Radke-Yarrow & Zahn-Waxler, 1984; Zahn-Waxler, Radke-Yarrow, Wagner, & Chapman, 1992a) have studied empathy and prosocial behavior in children as they interact in their natural environment with their parents, playmates, and others. In contrast to the typical laboratory experiment, the children were observed in their own homes. To do this, these researchers enlisted the aid of the children's mothers, who were trained to systematically observe and tape-record their children's reactions to distress in other people. Sometimes the distress the children saw was real; sometimes the mothers simulated certain emotions. Within the real situations, the researchers examined those in which the children were merely innocent bystanders and those in which they themselves were responsible for the other person's distress.

Zahn-Waxler et al. (1992a) studied a group of children at three different ages: 13 to 15 months, 18 to 20 months, and 23 to 25 months. The major question was whether the children's reactions to distress in others changed as they grew older. Although the researchers studied many reactions, we will only discuss empathy (which they defined as "emotional arousal that appears to reflect sympathic concern for the [distressed person]") and prosocial behavior (e.g., offering physical or verbal comfort, providing direct help, or sharing something of value). As Figure 4.2 shows, there were substantial changes in both empathy and prosocial behavior as the children matured.

When the children were 13 to 15 months old, distress in others was unlikely to produce an empathic response; less than 10 percent of the children showed empathy for a distressed person (even their mothers). Prosocial actions toward someone in distress were equally unlikely. However, by the time the children were 2 years old, about a quarter of them showed empathy for a distressed person, and almost half acted prosocially toward the person in distress (e.g., they hugged the distressed person or verbally comforted him or her). This increase in empathy and prosocial behavior occurred even when it was the child who had caused the other person's distress. We see a steady increase in empathy and helpfulness as children mature.

Zahn-Waxler and Radke-Yarrow have found this pattern of changes in several different studies, but they are quick to point out that within these developmental patterns there were substantial differences among

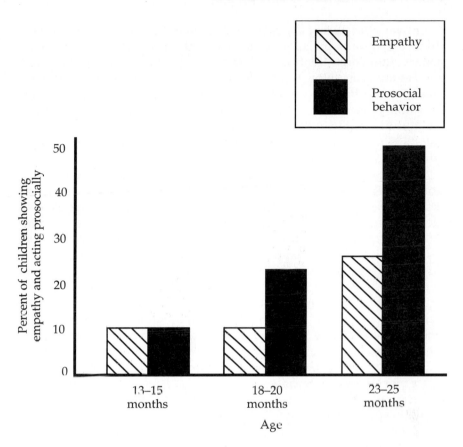

FIGURE 4.2
Developmental trends in empathy and prosocial behavior: both increase with age. (Adapted from Zahn-Waxler et al., 1992a.)

the children they studied. Some children were much more empathic and prosocial than others. How can these individual differences be explained? Are they due to inherited differences among the children or to differences in their environments? As is true with any nature-nurture questions, the answer is probably both.

The heritability of empathy. One common method for studying the heritability of empathy is the twin study. If identical twins (who have the same genes) are more alike on some characteristic than fraternal twins (who, on the average, share only half their genes) even though they share the same environment, this is evidence of heritability. As explained earlier in this chapter, heritability is the percentage of *differences* that exist among people (or variability) on some characteristic that may be due to heredity.

In one study using the twin methodology, 71 percent of the variability in empathy in response to others' distress was found to be due to genetic influences (Matthews, Batson, Horn, & Rosenman, 1981). In another study, Rushton et al. (1986) administered a self-report measure of empathy to about 600 adult identical and 800 adult fraternal twins (Rushton, Fulker, Neale, Nias, & Eysenck, 1986). They estimated the heritability of empathy in their subjects to be about 50 percent; that is, about half the differences between the empathic tendencies of their subjects was attributable to genetic effects.

More recent research (e.g., Davis, Luce, & Kraus, 1994; Zahn-Waxler, Robinson, & Emde, 1992b) produces similar but less dramatic estimates of the heritability of empathic tendencies. Davis and his colleagues gave 509 identical and 330 fraternal twins questions that measured positive affective empathy (feelings of compassion and concern for unfortunate others), negative affective empathy (feelings of personal discomfort and distress in response to distress in others), and cognitive empathy (the ability to see things from another person's perspective). For both kinds of affective empathy, Davis et al. found larger correlations between the scores of the identical twins than the fraternal twins. Thus, again we see evidence that heredity plays a role in affective empathy. However, Davis et al.'s estimates of the heritability of affective empathy were lower than those obtained in the earlier studies. Furthermore, on the measure of cognitive empathy (or perspective taking), the differences between identical and fraternal twins were not significant, suggesting that genetic factors are not responsible for individual differences in this kind of empathy.

Zahn-Waxler and her associates (1992b) observed and recorded displays of positive and negative affective empathy in 14-month-old identical and fraternal twins, observed them again when the twins were 20 months old. The researchers concluded that at 14 months about 30 percent of the differences in the children's empathic tendencies were inherited. However, they found that the heritability of empathy had declined somewhat by the time the children were 20 months old. In fact, the heritability estimate for negative empathy was no longer significant.

These findings underscore something we noted earlier in this chapter; the fact that a behavior has a genetic component does not necessarily diminish the importance of environmental and social influences. We must assume that socialization also plays a critical role in the development of empathic and prosocial orientations. Maternal sensitivity, reasoning with the child, and emphasizing the child's responsibility for the welfare of others all relate to how empathic and prosocial 2- to 3-year-old and young school-age children are (Eisenberg, Fabes, Schaller, Carlo, & Miller, 1991; Zahn-Waxler, Rodke-Yarrow, & King, 1979). For example, children whose parents teach them how to cope with their problems and who attempt to restrict their inappropriate, hurtful emotional displays are more empathic in response to other people's distress relative to children whose parents do not do these things. More generally, empathic, sympathetic parents have children who tend to be empathic and sympathetic when they see others in distress (Fabes, Eisenberg, & Miller, 1990; Fabes, Eisenberg, & Eisenbud, 1993). These findings suggest that learning plays a very important role in the development of empathy in children. We now turn to the kinds of things that children may learn from their parents and other adults.

Regulating emotions. Nancy Eisenberg and her colleagues (e.g., Eisenberg et al., 1991, Fabes et al., 1994) believe that individual differences in empathy may, in part, be due to inherited differences in children's temperaments—some children may be inherently more emotional and sensitive to the world around them than others. These inherited differences predispose some children to react more emotionally when they see others in distress. However, the way in which parents respond to, and deal with, these innate emotional responses plays a critical role in the development of empathy and results in some children being more empathic than others. More specifically, these researchers believe that when more empathic children are very young, their mothers may reinforce their natural inclinations to experience strong emotions when they see someone else in distress. However, as the children get older, the mothers also teach them how to regulate their emotions and keep them under some control. Thus, the children's emotions do not become so strong that they become more concerned with their own feelings than with the feelings of the person in distress. As a result, these children are predisposed to be empathic and helpful when they see someone in distress.

Learning to be empathic. Certain specific kinds of learning experiences may also be important in the development of empathy. In Chapter 3, we briefly discussed the roles of operant and observational learning as they relate to prosocial behavior. (They are discussed at greater length in Chapter 5.) Another learning process, classical conditioning, may also be important in the socialization of empathy (Aronfreed, 1970). The common example of classical conditioning is Pavlov's dogs learning to salivate at the sound of a bell that had been repeatedly associated with food. Aronfreed and Paskal (1965) attempted to classically condition specific empathic responses and helping 6- to 8-year-old girls.

In the first phase of this experiment, the girls watched an adult operate a machine with two levers on it; pulling one lever illuminated a red light; pulling the other dispensed candy to the person working the machine. The candy provided an incentive for the child to select that lever later. The experimenters systematically varied the actions of the model associated with the red light, that is, when she pulled the lever that did not produce the candy. In one condition of the experiment, the adult expressed pleasure when the red light went on; in another condition, she said nothing but hugged the child seated next to her. In the third condition, she both expressed pleasure and hugged the child. The children were then asked to work the machine. The question was, When would the children choose to illuminate the light and please the adult instead of obtaining candy for themselves? The answer was, When the children had experienced the pairing of the adult's pleasure with the hugs. The repeated pairing of the adult's pleasure with direct affection for the children produced empathy and a willingness to benefit the adult at the cost of candy for themselves.

These findings about direct learning, plus those concerned with maternal responses to emotional displays in children, suggest that learning is a key element in the development of empathy and prosocial action. However as we said earlier, the issue is quite complex and subject to alternative interpretations. For example, the relation between parental actions and empathy in their offspring could be explained by the fact that the parents and the children share a common genetic heritage. It is possible that both the parental tendency to teach a child to act responsibly and the tendency in the child to respond empathically are due to genetic characteristics the family members share in common.

Also, although the intent of Aronfreed and Paskal's work was to demonstrate that empathy was entirely learned, they may have shown how an environment-expectant emotional system works. They had no controls for nonaltruistic learning in the same situation, which might have been much harder to teach. There is evidence from studies using both nonhuman and human species which show that it is easier to condition some responses than others. For example, it is easier to condition monkeys to fear pictures of snakes than pictures of flowers (Cook & Mineka, 1989, 1990). Ohmman and Dimberg (1978) used human subjects and found it was easier to condition a physiological response to angry faces than to happy faces. Thus, there seems to be a genetically based readiness to learn to fear specific stimuli. Perhaps children are also genetically more "ready" to learn helpful than nonhelpful behaviors in response to rewards. Nevertheless, even if genetic predispositions can combine with learning and socialization, environmental experiences still play an important role in the development of altruism.

Spontaneous Communication

In another approach to the link between genes and behavior, Ross Buck and Benson Ginsburg (1991) proposed that it is not a tendency toward empathy or altruism that is genetically determined, but rather it is a system of affective communication. They proposed that most, if not all, organisms have the capacity for spontaneous communication, which they define as "nonintentional, nonpropositional, affective communication about feelings and desires or emotions and motives" (1991, p. 156). There are biological structures for sending and receiving these signals. Of course, these structures will vary across different organisms. In some animals, it might be odors they secrete or calls they make; in humans, these structures probably consist mainly of facial and vocal expressions of emotions. The function of this communication is social coordination, and it evolved because it was adaptive for the species to transmit this emotional information. The fact that even infants are highly susceptible to emotional communications such as cries and facial expressions provides some support for this idea.

According to Buck and Ginsburg, humans are not preprogrammed to be altruistic; rather, they are preprogrammed to communicate. They will communicate most often and, thus, most effectively with their kin and people with whom they must have positive reciprocal relations. Humans, then, learn to respond with empathy and altruism to those with whom they communicate affectively. In other words, Buck and Ginsburg are proposing that it only appears that there is kin and reciprocity selection for altruism when, in fact, it is the potential for spontaneous affective communication that is activated in kinship and reciprocal relationships. Better emotional communication, in turn, makes experiencing empathy possible—and likely.

We believe that Buck and Ginsburg's novel approach to the origins of empathy in humans is interesting and merits further exploration. However, as Michael Cunningham has pointed out (personal communication, December 1993), their model does not directly deal with the issue of why humans are inclined to *respond* to the messages they receive from others. That is, what motivates us to react to distress in others? To answer this question, researchers may need to go beyond the basic mechanisms proposed by Buck and Ginsburg and examine the role of empathy in this communication process.

We must also remember that learning experiences may influence the processes of interest to Buck and Ginsburg. People are more likely to feel empathy (and thus act prosocially) toward others with whom they have had more frequent emotional interaction and communication. As Aronfreed and Paskal's research suggests, children can readily learn about communicating affectively with others.

Summary

We have discussed two mechanisms that may provide the link between genetic tendencies and actual human behavior. The first of these was empathy, or the ability to have an emotional response to what happens to someone else. The evidence supporting empathy as a link between genes and prosocial behavior is substantial: It is likely that the earliest humans had the ability to empathize; empathic responses appear in humans almost as soon as they are born, and there is considerable evidence that at least some portion of empathic tendencies is inherited. But we must also remember that some of the pieces of this puzzle involve environmental factors as well. Individual differences among adults reflect both their genetic heritage and significant learning experiences they have had as they matured.

The other mechanism was spontaneous communication—the well-developed human ability to communicate emotions to one another. This human capacity is also part of our genetic heritage and can be traced to structures that have been present in the human brain from our earliest beginnings. The distinction between the spontaneous communication approach and the genetically based empathy perspective is subtle but important. It concerns the specific mechanisms that link genes and behavior. The two explanations agree that, in humans, genes do not directly cause altruistic actions; rather, genes affect certain structures and mechanisms, which in turn influence behavior. However, spontaneous communication is more general; it establishes the communicative foundation that would lead to the emergence of empathy and altruism among members of a culture. So several large and important pieces can be placed in the puzzle. There are mechanisms whereby genes can affect altruism, but it appears that the processes are indirect rather than direct.

This brings us to the end of our discussion of the genetic and biological bases of altruism—almost. Before concluding this chapter there is one more issue that merits some attention. It involves an attempt to integrate the concept of altruism as it was considered in the earlier chapters (involving the motivation to benefit others) with the genetic view of altruism (involving benefiting others with some personal cost) used in the present chapter.

TYPES OF ALTRUISM

Up to this point in this chapter, we have been almost exclusively concerned with a geneticist's definition of altruism as behavior that increases the chances of another's survival at some cost to the helper. Unlike the altruism discussed in earlier chapters, conscious motivation has nothing to do with this kind of altruism. We can see this when we consider the actions of animals such as ants, bees, and birds. They display behaviors that are "hardwired" into the organism and performed without any apparent hesitation or thought. The ground squirrel sees a hawk and gives the alarm; the ant smells the intruder and attacks. Sober (1988, 1992) calls this *evolutionary altruism*. However, with higher mammals, and in particular primates, this is not the way things usually work. There is thought and deliberation before an altruistic act occurs and, of course, sometimes it may not occur. Sober calls this *vernacular altruism*—a conscious action specifically intended to benefit another person at some cost to the actor, taken with an understanding of what is to be gained and lost. Vernacular altruism is relatively rare in nonhuman species. But what about humans? Do they display both kinds of altruism? If so, could there be two different mechanisms affecting human's altruistic behavior, both involving innate components?

The case for vernacular altruism is an easy one to make for humans. It is based on conscious, rational decision making and involves intentions to benefit another person. Chapter 3 discussed in detail the processes influencing such deliberative types of helping. Because intentions are involved, the social psychological distinction between altruism (with the goal of improving another person's welfare) and helping (with the goal of improving one's own welfare) is relevant. The capacities for empathy and emotional communication are two mechanisms that can contribute to the processes involved in this type of helping. But do humans also currently display evidence of evolutionary altruism? This more primitive form might be triggered under very specific conditions and would lead to rapid, perhaps unthinking, altruistic action. Evolutionary altruism would be less subject to environmental variables and higher-order mental processes than would the more sophisticated vernacular altruism.

Although humans are more rational and reflective than other animals, we still share our heritage with many other species. As a consequence, many vestiges of our evolutionary past—including evolutionary altruism—remain. We briefly noted in Chapter 3 that under highly arousing emergency conditions people may engage in very rapid, almost reflexive helping. Piliavin et al. (1981) reviewed a large number of experiments involving apparently real emergencies and found considerable evidence of *impulsive* helping. This type of helping resembles evolutionary altruism in other species—it is rapid and is generally unaffected by the social context (e.g., as the opportunity to diffuse responsibility onto others) and potential costs for intervening (e.g., personal danger). Also, it occurs under very specific circumstances: When the emergency is clear, the study is conducted outside a laboratory setting, and there has been prior contact between the victim and the bystander.

Piliavin et al. proposed that clear, realistic situations involving friends or acquaintances produce high levels of arousal and focus attention on the victim's plight. As a consequence, the bystander is most concerned with

> the costs for the victim receiving no help. Personal costs of helping (to the bystander) become peripheral and are not attended to. Therefore, the impulsive helping behavior that may appear irrational to an uninvolved observer . . . may be a quite "rational" response for a bystander attending primarily to the costs for the victim receiving no help (1981, p. 174).

This description comes very close to Sober's definition of evolutionary altruism. The response is rapid, relatively unthinking, and without consideration of concerns for personal safety. Piliavin et al. pointed out that, "one of the factors that seems to be predictive of impulsive helping is prior acquaintance between the observer and the victim" (p. 174). In the case of a strong friendship or a love relationship, it is even more likely that impulsive helping will occur, because of increased arousal as well as greater sensitivity to the other's problem (Clark, Mills, & Corcoran, 1989). Note that this proposal and Buck and Ginsburg's (1991) communicative gene hypotheses are also consistent. The closer two people are, the better the affective communication between them and the stronger the response of one to the other's distress. Thus, both sophisticated reasoning and more primitive, noncognitive biological mechanisms may permit humans to perform a range of altruistic behaviors well beyond those of other organisms. We may indeed be a uniquely compassionate and altruistic beast.

THE ANSWER: SUMMARY AND IMPLICATIONS

This chapter has been primarily concerned with a genetic and biological approach to human nature. More specifically, we examined whether there may be an inborn tendency in human beings—as there is in other animals—to care about what happens to others and a desire to do something to help them. We cannot say that we have proved such a tendency exists, but the evidence seems to suggest that it does. This evidence involves the convergence of findings from cross-cultural, cross-species, behavioral genetic, biological, and newborn infant research. At the genetic level, altruism may be essential to the survival of all animals (including humans), and it can coexist with other tendencies toward selfishness and aggression. We have also seen that there are mechanisms by which a tendency toward altruistic actions could have evolved during the time in which humans existed in small nomadic bands of hunters and gatherers. Consistent with models of these mechanisms, altruistic tendencies are directed toward those defined as in-group members and may be strongest toward those who are closest genetically to the altruist.

It does not appear likely that genes directly cause specific altruistic behaviors. Rather genetic influences operate indirectly by giving people the capacity to respond empathically and/or the ability to effectively communicate with other people. These tendencies to respond to the emotional displays of others make it much more likely that altruistic behaviors will occur. The natural propensity to empathize and help is clearly moderated by learning experiences. Thus, the essence of human nature may be both good and bad; altruism may be both a behavior that has evolved because it is vital to the survival of humanity and a behavior that is learned and reinforced by most societies because it is vital to the survival of their culture.

The observant reader may have noted (perhaps with some irritation) that the puzzle of where prosocial tendencies in humans come from is not yet completely solved. Although this chapter has dealt extensively with the origins of evolutionary altruism, the origins and development of vernacular altruism and other acquired kinds of human prosocial behaviors received almost no mention. The next chapter concerns the search for the pieces to this part of the altruism puzzle.

5

The Development of Altruism and Helping: You're Not (Only) Getting Older; You're (Also) Getting Better

❖

T he previous chapter addressed the question of whether or not there is a genetic basis for altruism. As part of the discussion of this question, we presented studies that examined the behavior of infants and toddlers. These studies provided impressive evidence that at least the antecedents of altruistic behaviors are present at a very early stage of life. For example, 1-day-old infants respond empathically to other infants' cries of distress, and children who are 1 or 2 years old clearly display empathic reactions to others who are in distress. As we discussed in Chapter 3, empathy plays a very important role in helping. But do infants, children, and adults experience empathy in the same way? There may be very basic and substantial differences between what motivates infants and toddlers to help another person and what motivates adults. Among very young children, helping is usually under the control of external and tangible rewards, such as a smile or praise from a parent. This is not necessarily the case among adults; adults are much more likely to help because of internal and intangible influences, such as their feelings, standards about the importance of helping, or concern about the welfare of another person. This fact brings us to the part of the helping puzzle that is the major focus of this chapter.

Several developmental processes may help us to understand the help that this child is giving to his friend. Whether expecting rewards in the form of praise and smiles from the adults who observe him or simply imitating his parent's behaviors, this little boy has already learned some of the basics of being prosocial. (AP/Wide World Photos)

THE QUESTION

The central questions in this chapter are (1) How do helping and other aspects of prosocial behavior change as humans mature? and (2) What processes are responsible for developmental changes in helping and altruistic behaviors? To answer the first question, psychologists conduct cross-sectional studies, which look at the responses of different people of different ages and longitudinal studies, which look at the responses of the same people at different ages. They use these two strategies to identify age-related changes in the things that motivate people to help, the way people think about helping, and helpful and altruistic behaviors.

Turning to the second question, most researchers who study the developmental changes in prosocial behavior believe that there are two interrelated processes responsible for these changes. One of these involves maturational changes in certain cognitive skills and abilities. Researchers who study these kinds of changes focus on the ways people think about themselves and the people around them. As children mature, there are substantial changes in the manner in which they think about helping; these appear to be part of broader developmental changes in cognitive skills and abilities. Just as people's physical characteristics (e.g., height, weight) change as they mature, changes also occur in the way they think about the causes of their own and other people's behavior, in their feelings of responsibilities for others, and in their beliefs about what is right and what is wrong. These changes play important roles in the development of helpful and altruistic behaviors.

The other explanation of the changes in prosocial thoughts and actions involves learning processes. Speaking very broadly, this approach to developmental changes argues that as people mature, their own experiences and the things they learn from others teach them to value being prosocial and enjoy doing things that benefit others.

Of course, changes in cognitive processes and learning experiences do not occur independently of one another. In fact, they typically combine to produce many of the changes in helping and altruism that are the focus of this chapter. Therefore, wherever possible, we will discuss how the two processes jointly affect the development of helping and altruism.

In the first section of the chapter, we describe developmental changes in human's prosocial thoughts and actions. We examine how people change with regard to what motivates them to help and how they make decisions about when and why they should help. In the next section we examine the processes that are believed to be responsible for developmental changes in helping. Specifically, we discuss the kinds of cognitive development and learning experiences that may be responsible for these changes. Finally, although most of the chapter focuses on developmental changes in children, we conclude with a brief consideration of life-span developmental changes in the behavior of adults.

DEVELOPMENTAL CHANGES IN PROSOCIAL THOUGHTS AND ACTIONS

It is generally agreed that as children grow up, the things that motivate them to help others change. There are several models that describe these changes in children's motivations to help. Two of the more widely accepted ones are Robert Cialdini's socialization model (Cialdini & Kenrick, 1976; Cialdini, Kenrick, & Baumann, 1982) and Daniel Bar-Tal's (1982) cognitive-learning model.

Cialdini's Socialization Model

According to Cialdini et al. (1982), as children mature, they go through three stages related to helping. In the *presocialization* stage, children are not aware that other people value and reinforce helping; they will help if asked or ordered to do so, but helping itself has no positive consequences for them. In the second stage, called *awareness*, children learn that the society in which they live desires and values helpfulness from its members. They become aware of and sensitive to social norms about prosocial behaviors. Children in this stage may initiate acts of helping, but such acts are motivated primarily by desires to please the adults who are present or attempts to comply with the norms about helping. Cialdini et al. (1982) estimated that the transition from the first stage to the second stage typically occurs when a child is 10 to 12 years old. By the time most children are 15 or 16 years old, they will have moved into the third and final stage of the socialization of helping, *internalization*. In this stage, helping is intrinsically satisfying and can actually make a person feel good. The external norms that motivated helping during the awareness stage have been internalized.

These developmental changes are illustrated in a study by Froming, Allen, and Jensen (1985). These researchers looked at how children who were in the presocialization stage and children who were in the awareness stage reacted to the presence of an adult who could evaluate them. They found that among children in the presocialization stage, the presence of the evaluative adult had no influence on how much they donated to a charity, but the adult's presence significantly increased the donations among children in the awareness stage. Froming et al. explained these results by proposing that because the younger children had not yet learned that most adults value helping and expect them to engage in it, there was no reason for them to increase how much they helped in the presence of an adult. However, the older children had learned about the social norms for helping and how adults feel about being helpful. Thus, the adult's presence motivated these children to be more helpful in the awareness stage.

In another experiment concerned with motives for helping, Cialdini and Kenrick (1976) used the concept of negative-state relief (see Chapter 3) to test their socialization model. Recall that the theory of negative-state relief proposes that people who are sad are more likely to help if they believe that the reward of helping will alleviate their negative mood. Relating this to developmental changes in motivations for helping, Cialdini and Kenrick investigated whether sadness would have this effect on helping among young children who had not yet learned that helping is rewarding.

The participants in this study were children, 6 to 8 years old, and adolescents in their midteens to late teens (15 to 18 years old). In each group of subjects, half the participants were asked to think about something sad from their past (e.g., the loss of a favorite pet), whereas the other half were told to think about a neutral past experience. This manipulation produced a negative or sad mood in the former group of subjects, but not in the latter group. Both groups of subjects were then presented with an opportunity to help other students anonymously by giving them some coupons (redeemable for prizes) they had won in a game. The number of coupons that each subject donated was discreetly measured by the researchers.

Cialdini and Kenrick reasoned that most of the younger children would be in the presocialization stage, and it was unlikely that any of them would *intrinsically* value helping or believe that helping would make them feel better. Thus, young children in the sad mood condition would not be more motivated to help than those in the neutral condition. In fact, giving away something they had won would probably make them feel even worse. As a result, children in the sad condition were expected to help less than those in the neutral condition. In contrast, most of the 15- to 18-year olds would have presumably reached the internalization stage; they would value helping and recognize the reinforcing effects that could be realized by helping someone else. Adolescents in the sad mood condition could thus use helping to reduce their negative mood. Therefore, they were expected to help more than those in the neutral condition.

These predictions were confirmed. Among the young children in the presocialization stage, those in the sad mood condition donated less than half as many coupons as those in the neutral mood condition. But, among the late adolescents, those in the sad condition donated *over four times* as many coupons as did those in the neutral condition. It is important to note that Cialdini and Kenrick believed that these developmental changes were due to learning or socialization experiences rather than some kind of biologically based, maturational process. Not all children will go through the stages at the same time; the rate at which children move through the stages depends on children's learning experiences and their culture (Fiske, 1991). Indeed, some people may never reach the third stage.

Bar-Tal's Cognitive-Learning Model

Social and developmental psychologists are sometimes criticized because they seem to use only one method—experiments—to study what they are interested in and because they often restrict their research subjects to people from the United States (or at least North America). Critics argue that one cannot be sure whether the same kind of results would be obtained if different methods of collecting data were employed or if different groups of people were studied. Fortunately, this is not the case for developmental models of changes in helping. Other researchers, using other methods and subjects from other countries, have reached very similar conclusions about how children change as they mature.

We see this in the developmental model proposed by Daniel Bar-Tal, an Israeli psychologist. Bar-Tal based his model on observations of how children of different ages responded to different kinds of requests to help another child. The procedures used by Bar-Tal and his colleagues can be illustrated by one of the studies they conducted on helping among school children in Israel (Bar-Tal, Raviv, & Leiser, 1980).

In this study, pairs of $4\frac{1}{2}$- to $9\frac{1}{2}$-year old children played a game. On a random basis, one of the children was designated as the winner and received several pieces of candy as a prize. The adult who had given out the prize then left the two children alone, with no instructions about sharing the candy. Unknown to the children, they were observed for the next few minutes. If, during this time, the winner had not shared some of the candy, the experimenter returned, read a story about sharing, and left the room again. Three minutes later, children who had still not shared the candy were told that their teacher would probably give an important part in a school play to a child who shared his or her candy. The child was given another chance to share, but if this did not happen, the child with the candy was explicitly told to share it with the other child. If the child still did not comply, the experimenter repeated the request and offered the child a big additional prize for sharing. Note that over time the consequences for sharing became more external and tangible. The question Bar-Tal and his colleagues asked was whether children of different ages would react differently to the requests. They did. In general, the older the children, the less external and tangible an inducement was needed to get them to share. For example, 38 percent of the oldest children had shared by the second phase of the study (hearing a story about helping), but only 7 percent of the youngest children had shared by then. Findings such as these led Bar-Tal (1982) to propose a stage model of helping much like that of Cialdini and his associates.

Bar-Tal's model proposes that as children mature, the things that motivate them to help others change. He argued that among very young children helping is usually motivated by the promise of a specific reward or the threat of a specific punishment. Without such rewards, there will be no helping. Like Cialdini, Bar-Tal believed that later in childhood, helping may also be motivated by a desire to receive the approval and praise of others. As children move into adolescence, these egocentric motivations for helping begin to be replaced by the final kind of motivation in Bar-Tal's model, altruism. In this stage, the person helps "out of a moral conviction in justice, . . . [and may experience] self-satisfaction or raised self-esteem" (1982, p. 110).

Table 5.1 presents the major stages in Cialdini's and Bar-Tal's models of the developmental changes in the motivation to help. We present these models side by side to provide a clear illustration that, despite the differences in their methods and the countries in which their studies were conducted, they arrived at a very similar view of the developmental changes in prosocial behavior. They both propose that as children mature, helping

TABLE 5.1 BAR-TAL AND CIALDINI'S MODELS OF THE DEVELOPMENT OF PROSOCIAL BEHAVIOR

Cialdini	Bar-Tal
Stage 1. Presocialization: Individuals are unsocialized about helping and rarely act altruistically because it involves a loss of resources.	**Phase 1. Compliance—concrete:** Individuals help because they have been ordered to do so, with explicit threat of punishment. **Phase 2. Compliance:** Individuals help if an authority requests them to do so. The threat of actual punishment is no longer needed.
Stage 2. Awareness of norms: Individuals help because they have learned that people expect them to help and may punish them if they do not. They are concerned about social approval.	**Phase 3. Internal initiative—concrete:** Individuals help because they expect a tangible reward. **Phase 4. Normative behavior:** Individuals help because they know social norms about helping and are concerned about social approval. **Phase 5. Generalized reciprocity:** Individuals help because they believe that the recipient would and should reciprocate.
Stage 3. Internalization: Individuals help because it makes them feel better.	**Phase 6. Altruistic behavior:** Individuals help because they want to benefit the other person. Helping increases their self-esteem and satisfaction.

Adapted from Bar-Tal, D., & Raviv, A. (1982). A cognitive-learning model of helping behavior development: Possible implications and applications; and Cialdini, R. B., Kendrick, D. T., & Baumann, D. J. (1982). Effects of mood on prosocial behavior in children and adults. Both in N. Eisenberg (Ed.), *The development of prosocial behavior.* New York: Academic Press.

changes from an action that occurs because it produces some external, concrete benefit for the helper to an action taken because it makes the helper feel better or because it benefits another person.

Moral Reasoning

Developmental psychologists have long been interested in how children reason or think about themselves and the world around them. Although they may disagree in their theories of specific reasoning processes, almost all developmental psychologists agree on this point: Children reason differently from adults, and as they grow up, the way they reason changes. One area of children's reasoning that has attracted considerable interest and attention from psychologists is how they reach decisions about what is the right way to act and what is the wrong way. The study of moral reasoning concerns the principles people use when they make such a decision. Most developmental psychologists believe that children also pass through several levels or stages of moral reasoning as they mature. At each level, the principles or criteria on which they base their moral judgments are qualitatively different. The best known model of the development of general moral reasoning is the one proposed by Lawrence Kohlberg (1985; Colby & Kohlberg, 1987).

Kohlberg's model. As part of the development of his model, Kohlberg presented people with what he called *moral dilemmas* and recorded the ways in which they resolved them. Here is an example of the kind of dilemmas people had to consider. A man's wife will die unless she receives an expensive drug. He has scraped together much of the money needed to buy the drug, but he does not have enough, and the pharmacist refuses to give him the drug. In desperation, the man later breaks into the pharmacy and steals the drug. Is the man's action right or wrong? Why?

People's responses to these dilemmas led Kohlberg to propose that there are three separate levels of moral development, and within each level there are distinct, sequential stages. Each successive level and stage represents more mature and sophisticated kinds of moral reasoning. The first level, which Kohlberg called *preconventional morality*, contains two stages or orientations toward whether an action is moral or immoral. In the first stage, people's judgments about the morality of their actions are based on fear of punishment. In the second stage of this level, people decide if something is moral on the basis of whether it provides them with some kind of reward.

Kohlberg and his associates used cross-sectional and longitudinal studies to investigate developmental changes in moral reasoning. Up until the age of 7, most children use this preconventional level of moral reasoning, making their moral decisions almost exclusively in terms of avoiding punishment and gaining rewards from others (i.e., stages 1 and 2). As children mature, there are changes in the extent to which they reason in this way. After age 7, the incidence of preconventional moral reasoning begins to decline and by midadolescence, many people's judgments about what is moral and immoral have progressed to the next level of moral reasoning (Kohlberg, 1963; Colby, Kohlberg, Gibbs & Lieberman, 1983).

Kohlberg called this level, *conventional morality*, and in the first stage (stage 3) judgments of right and wrong are based on whether the person's actions would win the approval or disapproval of others; in the later stage (stage 4), these judgments are based on whether an action conforms to society's formal and informal rules and laws. People have an obligation to obey legitimate authority. The majority of people do not reach stage 3 before their early teens (Colby et al., 1983); few people display stage 4 moral reasoning before they are adults; and some people simply never reach stage 4 in their moral reasoning.

The highest level of moral reasoning, *postconventional morality*, involves internalized and personal moral standards. In the first stage at this level (stage 5), moral decisions are based on concerns about the rights and well-being of others; an action that achieves these goals may be moral even if it challenges certain laws. In stage 6, moral decisions are made on the basis of the person's own ethical principles or conscience and reflect a concern for universal justice even if this contradicts social norms and laws. Kohlberg considers this highest level a reflection of the standards of moral leaders such as Mahatma Gandhi and Dr. Martin Luther King, Jr. Colby et al.'s longitudinal study of moral development indicated that few people (less than 10 percent of the people studied) ever reach stage 5, and almost no one reaches stage 6. Similar (but not identical) patterns of moral development were found in Turkey and Israel (Colby & Kohlberg, 1987).

Although many people have used Kohlberg's general model of moral reasoning to explain developmental changes in altruism and helping, Nancy Eisenberg (1982, 1986) has suggested that if one is interested in such changes, it may be more appropriate to examine developmental changes in reasoning specifically concerned with prosocial actions. She noted that Kohlberg's model was generated from people's responses to situations in which there was a conflict between some law or rule and the person's own sense of right and wrong; the person had to decide whether he or she should follow or break some rule. If we want to understand developmental changes in helping, we may need to examine children's reasoning when there is a conflict between their own needs and wants and the needs and desires of others. Eisenberg and her associates have developed a model which describes such changes. As we present this model, you may notice how closely related it is to Cialdini's and Bar-Tal's models of the things that motivate children to help. This is not a coincidence; Eisenberg believes that a child's prosocial moral reasoning reflects, in part, the child's motives when his or her own needs are in conflict with the needs of others.

Prosocial moral reasoning. Eisenberg wanted her model of moral reasoning to specifically address developmental changes in what children think are good and bad reasons to act prosocially. So, to study this process, Eisenberg (previously Eisenberg-Berg) and her colleagues (e.g., Eisenberg-Berg 1979; Eisenberg-Berg & Neal, 1981; Eisenberg-Berg & Roth, 1980) presented children with prosocial moral dilemmas and asked them what they would do. An example of one such dilemma follows:

A girl named Mary was going to a friend's birthday party. On her way, she saw a girl who had fallen down and hurt her leg. The girl asked Mary to go to her house and get her parents so the parents could take her to the doctor. But if Mary did run and get the child's parents, she would be late for the birthday party and miss the ice cream, cake, and all the games. What should Mary do? Why? (From Eisenberg, 1982, p. 231)

The responses from children of different ages to this and other similar stories led Eisenberg to propose the developmental model of prosocial moral reasoning presented in Table 5.2. At the lower developmental stages of her model, judgments about what is right and what is wrong are based on self-centered, pragmatic, and hedonistic concerns. For example, children say that if they help someone, it would be because the recipient might help them later or because they were afraid they would be punished by an adult if they did not help. But as children mature, their judgments become more pragmatic and less hedonistic. They begin to consider the feelings of those in need and the way other people react to helping. For instance, in dilemmas like the one described above, children say that they would help because it would make the other child happy or because their parents would be proud of them. In the final stages of the model, prosocial moral reasoning is based largely on the person's sense of obligation to others and concern for their welfare. In these stages, the individuals help because it makes them feel good about themselves; they would not think well of themselves if they did not offer aid.

In recent years, Eisenberg and her colleagues have conducted longitudinal studies of whether or not the model accurately describes developmental changes in prosocial moral reasoning (Eisenberg et al., 1987; Eisenberg, Miller, Shell, McNalley, & Shea, 1991). It appears that it does. Preschool children engage in a good deal of hedonistic and self-centered moral reasoning, but by the late grade-school years, these kinds of reasoning decline and more sophisticated and other-oriented kinds of reasoning increase. When boys reach early adolescence, they may regress to more hedonistic kinds of reasoning, but in late adolescence both boys and girls began to display higher-level kinds of moral reasoning (i.e., stages 4 and 5). Thus, moral reasoning seems to develop pretty much in the manner that Eisenberg originally proposed.

A second and equally important question is whether these changes in moral reasoning are, in fact, related to changes in helping. The relationship is not perfect, but Eisenberg and others have found that as children move toward more mature and sophisticated forms of reasoning about prosocial dilemmas, their propensity to display sympathy and empathy and to spontaneously help others also increases (Eisenberg et al., 1987; 1991; Raviv, Bar-Tal, & Lewis-Levin, 1980).

With the exception of Bar-Tal's work, most of the studies we have presented in this section were conducted in the United States. Would the

TABLE 5.2 STAGES OF PROSOCIAL MORAL REASONING

Stage 1: Hedonistic, pragmatic orientation. The individual is concerned with self-ish, pragmatic consequences rather than moral considerations. "Right" behavior is that which is instrumental in satisfying the actor's own needs or wants. Reasons for assisting or not assisting another include consideration of direct gain to the self, future reciprocity, and concern for others whom the individual needs and/or likes.

Stage 2: Needs of others orientation. The individual expresses concern for the physical, material, and psychological needs of others even though the other's needs conflict with one's own needs. This concern is expressed in the simplest terms, without clear evidence of role taking, verbal expressions of sympathy, or reference to internalized affect such as guilt ("He's hungry" or "She needs it").

Stage 3: Approval and interpersonal orientation and/or stereotyped orientation. Stereotyped images of good and bad persons and behavior and/or considerations of others' approval and acceptance are used in justifying prosocial or nonhelping behaviors. For example, one helps another because "It's nice to help" or "He'd like him more if he helped."

Stage 4a: Empathic orientation. The individual's judgments include evidence of sympathetic responding, role taking, concern with the other's humanness, and/or guilt or positive affect related to the consequences of one's actions. Examples include, "He knows how he feels," "She cares about people," and "I'd feel bad if I didn't help because he'd be in pain."

Stage 4b: Transitional stage. Justifications for helping or not helping involve internalized values, norms, duties, or responsibilities, or refer to the necessity of protecting the rights and dignity of other persons; these ideas, however, are not clearly and strongly stated. References to internalized affect, self-respect, and living up to one's own values are considered indicative of this stage if they are weakly stated. Examples include, "It's just something I've learned and feel."

Stage 5: Strongly internalized stage. Justifications for helping or not helping are based on internalized values, norms, or responsibilities, the desire to maintain individual and societal contractual obligations, and the belief in the dignity, rights, and equality of all individuals. Positive or negative affects related to the maintenance of self-respect and living up to one's own values and accepted norms also characterize this stage. Examples of stage 5 reasoning include, "She'd feel a responsibility to help other people in need" or "I would feel bad if I didn't help because I'd know that I didn't live up to my values."

From Eisenberg, N. (1982). The development of reasoning regarding prosocial behavior. In N. Eisenberg (Ed.), *The development of prosocial behavior* (p. 234). New York: Academic Press.

same patterns of development be found elsewhere in the world? Studies of moral reasoning in different countries suggest that the *content* of prosocial moral reasoning (i.e., the specific kinds of actions that are judged as good or as bad) is probably affected by the culture in which one lives (Miller, in press). However, the basic *patterns* of changes in what motivates helping and in moral reasoning described in the models can be found around the world.

For example, Eisenberg (1992) reports that similar changes in moral reasoning occur in most Western countries, and other research suggests that these developmental patterns do not appear to be confined to children raised in Western cultures. Studies of Japanese children (Munekata & Ninomiya, 1985) and children of a tribe in New Guinea (Tietjan, 1986) find quite similar developmental patterns. After reviewing such research findings, Radke-Yarrow, Zahn-Waxler, and Chapman (1983) concluded that across all cultures that have been studied, as children mature, their thoughts and actions tend to become less egocentric and more other-oriented.

We must be careful, however, in how we interpret this relationship. We cannot say with certainty that changes in the things that motivate helping and in moral reasoning *cause* people to be more helpful. It is also possible that engaging in more spontaneous prosocial action causes changes in the way people think about their prosocial actions. It does seem safe to conclude, however, that as children mature, the way they reason about what are good and bad prosocial actions changes, and that there are concomitant changes in the factors that motivate helping. As the title of this chapter notes, as children get older they also tend to become better—at least in terms of their prosocial orientation.

Summary

As children mature, there are substantial changes related to helping and altruism. One of the major changes is in what motivates a child to help. We saw that young children do not derive much intrinsic pleasure from helping others and, as a result, they are not terribly inclined to help spontaneously. Rather, they help either because they are directly asked to do so or because they believe that helping will produce some tangible benefit for them. However, as children get older different things motivate them to help. By the time they are adolescents, some are motivated to help because this will earn them social approval; and by the time they reach adulthood, many people help because it is intrinsically rewarding and makes them feel good.

Closely paralleling these motivational changes are developmental changes in children's moral reasoning. As they get older, children's general moral reasoning usually becomes less egocentric and rule-bound and more other-oriented and sophisticated. Moral reasoning about prosocial behaviors develops in a similar fashion. When asked to make decisions in situations that pit their own needs against the needs of others, small children resolve these dilemmas in self-serving and egocentric ways. As they mature, they become more sensitive to the rights and needs of others. By the time they are adults, most (but not all) people believe they have a personal, moral obligation to further the welfare of others. Violating this personal norm has a negative effect on their self-image and self-esteem.

Thus, we have the pieces of the first puzzle in place. The completed puzzle provides a fairly clear answer to the question about the developmental changes in helpful and altruistic thoughts and actions. Now, we turn to the second and more difficult question—What processes are responsible for these changes? That is, in the pages that follow, we turn our attention from how people change to why these changes occur.

SOCIAL/COGNITIVE DEVELOPMENT

The first general explanation of the developmental changes related to helping and altruism is based on the following premise: As humans mature, their cognitive skills, abilities, and capacities also mature and change. These changes affect the way humans think about the physical world around them and their social world. This results in changes in the things that motivate people to help, the reasons why they help, the ways they think about helping. For example, Leahy (1979) presented first graders, fifth graders, and adults with descriptions of situations in which one child gave his lunch to another child. The rewards and punishments used to induce this behavior were systematically manipulated. After reading a scenario, the subjects indicated how kind they thought the helper in the story was. Among the young children, the act of giving the lunch to someone else was seen as kinder when it was rewarded than when it was not rewarded. Apparently, they focused on the *consequences* of the action. Fifth graders and adults responded in just the opposite way; they saw the unrewarded actions as kinder than those that were rewarded. They seemed to pay much more attention to the helper's *intentions.* Thus, younger and older people tend to see helping in very different terms.

Such differences are the result of natural maturational changes in human cognitive processes. When these changes involve cognitive processes related to social thoughts (or cognition) and social behavior, the process is called *social-cognitive development.* To understand this kind of development, we must begin with a consideration of general-cognitive development.

Cognitive Development

Jean Piaget (1932/1965), whom many consider to be the "father" of research on cognitive development in children, believed that the differences between the thinking processes of children and adults reflected more than the simple fact that adults have accumulated more knowledge about the world around them. Piaget argued that children think about themselves and the world around them in ways that are fundamentally different from adults.

Developmental theorists (e.g., Flavell, 1985) propose that cognitive development proceeds in stages, with the thought processes in each successive stage being more sophisticated and complex than the preceding one. Although people may differ with respect to how rapidly they move through these stages, all people within the normal range of intellectual abilities will pass through the stages in the same order. These changes are as natural a part of the maturational process as growing taller or heavier. The particular cognitive stage that individuals are in will largely determine how they think about helping others. More specifically, social-cognitive theorists believe that two cognitive abilities are critical to the development of spontaneous, internally motivated helping. The first of these is the ability to see things from the other person's perspective. This may be called role taking, perspective taking, or cognitive empathy. The second is the tendency to make personal or internal attributions about the causes of one's own behavior and the behavior of others.

Cognitive empathy. In the discussion of empathy in the previous chapter, we distinguished between *affective empathy* (emotional responses to another person's circumstances) and *cognitive empathy* (the ability to understand the thoughts and take the perspective of another person) (Davis, 1994). As we saw in the previous chapter, the work of Carolyn Zahn-Waxler and her colleagues (e.g., Zahn-Waxler, Radke-Yarrow, Wagner & Chapman, 1992a) strongly suggests that by the time children are 2 years old, they are quite capable of experiencing affective empathy. The discussion of affective empathy in Chapter 4 and in the previous two chapters makes it clear that this kind of empathic response plays a critical role in helping and altruism among children and adults.

Cognitive empathy is also quite important in the development and maintenance of prosocial behavior. However, the capacity for cognitive empathy, or perspective taking, appears to take somewhat longer to develop than does affective empathy. Piaget believed that when children are quite young (under 5 or 6 years of age), they have great difficulty taking the perspective of others, regardless of whether the task involves visual or social stimuli. For example, Piaget and Inhelder (1971) showed young children a papier-mâché model of some mountains and asked them how the mountains would look from the perspective of someone standing on the other side of the model. The children found this task extremely difficult. This led Piaget and Inhelder to conclude that before the age of 5 or 6 children were unable to adopt the perspective of others. However, more recent research suggests that children as young as 3 years of age may be quite able to take the perspective of another person (Chandler, Fritz, & Hala, 1989). Nonetheless, it is true, as Piaget proposed, that before the age of 5 or 6, children have an extremely egocentric view of the physical world and are not particularly likely to see it from other people's perspective.

Similarly, at this age children are *interpersonally* quite egocentric. They are unable or unwilling to take another person's perspective and usually see interpersonal situations only from their own point of view. Thus, they often have difficulty understanding how other people feel or what they want. By the time children are 8 or 9 years old, they are capable of true cognitive empathy; they are able to take the perspective of another person. However, they still have great difficulty considering their own perspective and the perspective of another person at the same time (Selman, 1980). It is probably not until around the time of puberty that children are fully capable of the kinds of cognitive empathy that are displayed by adults.

According to Bar-Tal and Raviv (1982) and others (e.g., Eisenberg & Fabes, 1991), an understanding of the perspective of others is critical to helping and altruistic behaviors. Small children will help others in need or distress if the source of the distress also directly affects them or involves something they have also experienced (e.g., missing one's mother). Otherwise, children have great difficulty understanding what the other person is feeling. As a result, they will be unlikely to spontaneously come to the person's aid—not because of a lack of caring, but because of a lack of understanding. Note what is being suggested here: Very young children are *not* selfish; they are just egocentric. They fail to help others only because they lack the ability to understand the other's needs. As children mature, they develop the cognitive abilities to see physical events and social stimuli from another person's perspective, and as their ability to take the roles of others increases, so does their propensity to help others (Eisenberg & Fabes, 1991; Eisenberg & Miller, 1987).

Internal attributions. The second cognitive process involved in the development of helpfulness concerns the manner in which children make attributions about the causes of their own actions as well as the actions of others. A behavior can be explained by internal, personal causes or by external, situational causes. According to Diane Ruble and her associates (e.g., Feldman & Ruble, 1981; Ruble & Rholes, 1983), before the age of 7 or 8, children react to information about other people quite differently than do adults. In general, younger children react only to a person's concrete, external characteristics (e.g., "She has red hair,"), immediate actions (e.g., "He took my truck,"), or the consequences of actions (e.g., "She received a prize."). They do not focus on unobservable aspects of other people (e.g., their personality traits or intentions). They are unable or unwilling to use traits to explain a person's behaviors or to make inferences about other people's underlying personality disposition (e.g., "He did that because he is selfish; he is a selfish person."). The attributions offered by young children typically involve external rather than internal causes. By the time children are 9 or 10, they begin to make abstract inferences about other people and tend to make attributions much as adults do—mainly to internal or personal causes.

The relationship between attributional tendencies and helping may not be as obvious as the relationship between cognitive empathy and helping, so perhaps a little more explanation is needed. As we will discuss in more detail later, self-attributions play an important role in how children learn to be helpful. If children look at an instance in which they are helpful and infer that they did this because they are helpful persons (i.e., an internal attribution), it is likely that they will help more on subsequent occasions. However, before a certain age, children may be unable to fully comprehend internal attributions about their helpful actions. This is illustrated in the results of a study by Grusec and Redler (1980). When adults made internal attributions about 8-year-old children's helpful behavior ("You are a helpful person."), this increased their subsequent prosocial behavior. However, the same statement had little effect on the actions of 5-year-olds. Therefore, for social labeling of helpfulness to be fully effective, the child must have reached a certain stage of social-cognitive development. The age-related shift in how children make attributions about behavior plays an important role in their likelihood of spontaneously offering help to others.

These developmental changes in cognitive processes are quite consistent across diverse groups of people. And as we have already noted, in many different cultures there is an underlying similarity in how prosocial thoughts and actions change as children mature. These facts might lead you to conclude that there is a basic biological process at work here. That is, just as a genetic code directs humans' physical growth as they mature, a similar genetic code may directly and indirectly affect the development of helpful and altruistic tendencies. We do not dismiss this possibility, but we do not believe that genetically based maturational changes alone are able to adequately explain the kinds of changes in helping that we have been discussing. This part of the puzzle cannot be solved that easily.

Cultural diversity. Although there are many cross-cultural similarities in prosocial development, there are also many differences. For example, Miller (in press) attempted to apply Western models of moral development to moral development in India. She argues that Kohlberg's and other Western models [e.g., Carol Gilligan's (1982) gender-based model] are probably not applicable in India and other non-Western cultures in which individualism is not strongly stressed or valued. Other studies have found great differences in the absolute levels of helpfulness and cooperation in different cultures. For example, Whiting and Whiting (1975) compared the helpfulness of children from six countries (India, Kenya, Japan, Mexico, the Philippines, and the United States) on a scale of altruistic behaviors. Whereas all the Kenyan children were rated above the median (i.e., the fiftieth percentile) altruism score for the entire sample of children, only 8 percent of the children in the United States were above this international norm. Thus, there are vast differences among cultures in how helpful their members are. The next section discusses the processes that are the most likely cause of these differences.

LEARNING EXPERIENCES: LEARNING TO BE A HELPER

We cannot totally discount the possibility that biological factors are responsible for some of these cultural differences, but we think it is much more likely that they are due to differences in specific learning experiences across the cultures (Fiske, 1991; Moore & Eisenberg, 1984); that is, because different societies have somewhat different customs, values, and norms, they teach their children different things about helping and other kinds of prosocial behavior.

Social Learning

Despite this variety and diversity in the characteristics and customs of the different human cultures and societies, children in all cultures share one very basic experience in common: *socialization.* Socialization is a complex, multifaceted process that has two basic goals: (1) to teach children the norms and values of the society in which they live, and (2) to get them to accept and internalize these norms and values (Grusec, 1991a, 1991b). Joan Grusec (1982) noted that in the case of altruism and helping, the specific goal of the socialization process is to encourage children to "to show concern for others 'for its own sake'" (p. 142). The process that most people believe is responsible for this kind of socialization is social learning (see Chapter 3). According to social-learning theorists, the socialization of helpfulness and altruism involves three basic kinds of social learning: experiencing direct reinforcement for behavior, observing models in the environment, and being told things about helping (Rushton, 1982).

Direct reinforcement. In the previous chapter, we briefly discussed the role of classical conditioning in the acquisition of empathic reactions (Aronfreed, 1970). In Chapter 3, we considered another kind of conditioning, called *operant* or *instrumental* conditioning. The basic principle in operant conditioning is that behaviors that produce positive consequences are more likely to occur in the future, and those that are associated with negative consequences are less likely to occur again. If rewards regularly follow some behavior, that behavior will be learned, and it will subsequently be performed more frequently when the conditions are appropriate. If punishments follow a behavior, the connection will also be learned, but the behavior will be performed less frequently. Some examples of research on the effects of rewards and punishments on helping are presented below.

Interest in the effects of *rewards* on helping is based on the simple premise that if you reward a child for being helpful, the child will learn this behavior. Rewards can be very tangible. For example, giving children even a few pennies every time they help increases their helpfulness in the future (Smith, Gelfand, Hartmann, & Partlow, 1979). But how long-lasting and generalizable are the effects of rewards? The effects of social rewards appear resistant to extinction. In a study by Rushton and Teachman (1978), for instance, an adult subtly induced children to donate tokens they had won to a charity. Some of the children were praised for their actions, others were criticized, and still others experienced no consequences for their generosity. Two weeks later, the children's generosity was measured again. The effects of the praise on the children's generosity were still evident. Children in the praise group were the most generous, and the children in the criticism group were the least generous.

In fact, social rewards, such as praise, seem to be even more effective reinforcers for helping than material rewards, such as money (Gelfand & Hartmann, 1982; Grusec, 1991a; Rushton, 1982). For example, in the previous paragraph we described a study in which some children received pennies as reinforcers for helping (Smith et al., 1979). Other children in that study received praise rather than money when they helped. Later, both groups of children were asked *why* they had helped. The children who received the pennies said they helped to get the money, but the children who received the social reward said they helped because they were concerned about the welfare of the child whom they had helped.

Not only are material reinforcers relatively ineffective in eliciting prosocial behavior from children, in some instances they may actually reduce the probability that a child will spontaneously act prosocially. A study by Richard Fabes and his associates illustrates this (Fabes, Fultz, Eisenberg, May-Plumlee, & Christopher, 1989). Fabes et al. examined the behavior of grade-school children whose mothers had said they often used rewards to get their children to act prosocially. These children were placed in a situation where they had two opportunities to help "sick and poor children in the hospital" (by making games for them). Some of the children received a material reward (a toy) the first time they helped; others did not. Then all the children were given a second chance to help.

Fabes et al. found that whereas less than half (44 percent) of those who received the toy for helping were willing to help the second time, all the children in the no-toy condition spontaneously helped the second time. How can this be explained? The researchers speculated that the reward may have decreased spontaneous helping because it undermined intrinsic motivations for helping (Lepper, 1981); that is, giving the children the toy may have caused them to believe that they were helping because of this toy rather than because they wanted to help the people in the hospital. When there was no longer any extrinsic motivation for helping (i.e., no toy), the children saw no reason to be helpful. Thus, material reinforcers may be relatively ineffective in motivating spontaneous helping because they provide children with an external or extrinsic explanation of why they have helped. Children who continuously receive material reinforcers for helping may come to believe that they are not "helpful" people, but rather they may believe they helped because of the rewards for doing so. As will be discussed shortly, such self-perceptions can have a strong influence on how people react to requests for help.

Parents appear to understand intuitively the short- and long-term effectiveness of social reinforcers on helping. Grusec (1982, 1991b) trained the mothers of 4- to 7-year-olds to record how they reacted to their children when the children were prosocial or helpful. Parents almost always responded to such actions in some manner, usually with social reinforcements, such as thanking the children, smiling at them, or praising them. They almost never rewarded their children's prosocial behaviors with a material reward. This finding suggests that parents already know that giving material rewards is not the most effective way to teach their children to be helpful.

There is, of course, another side of the consequences "coin." It is the use of punishment, discipline, or negative reinforcers to teach a child to be helpful. This is not the first time we have discussed the costs of not helping. Recall from Chapter 2 that Piliavin et al. (1981) included such costs in the arousal:cost-reward model, which explained when bystanders will or will not intervene in an emergency. However, that model has focused mainly on helping by adults, and most of the costs considered are internal and self-generated. Here we will be focusing more on externally administered costs for failing to help.

To train prosocial behavior, punishment could be administered by an adult if a child either failed to be helpful or acted selfishly. Whereas there is consensus about the effects of rewards on helping, the picture with regard to punishment is more complex. Martin Hoffman (1970, 1994) has argued that there are different techniques of discipline, and some may be more effective than others in promoting prosocial actions.

One kind of discipline involves the use of power and threats and is based on the fact that adults are larger and stronger than children and can, if they desire, physically punish or withhold rewards from a child; Hoffman called this kind of discipline *power assertion*. Another kind of discipline is *love withdrawal*, in which parents attempt to control or modify children's actions by ignoring them or withholding their approval or attention.

The final kind of discipline identified by Hoffman does not involve punishing children, but rather reasoning with them. He called this *induction* (or other-oriented induction) discipline. In it, parents explain why a behavior was wrong, point out the effects of the child's behavior on another person, and suggest ways in which the child might right the wrong that he or she has committed. Hoffman (1994) argues that children disciplined with induction are more likely to display mature moral reasoning, compassion, and sympathy than are children who are disciplined with either power assertion or love withdrawal. There have been several studies that have attempted to test Hoffman's ideas about discipline. The results of these studies are complex. One reason for this is that in the real world parents rarely use a single kind of discipline. Rather, when parents discipline a child, they often say things that contain elements of all three discipline techniques (Grusec & Lytton, 1988). However, the results of these studies generally suggest that induction-based discipline is more likely to result in prosocial thoughts and actions than discipline that primarily involves either power assertion or love withdrawal (Brody & Shaffer, 1982; Crockenberg & Litman, 1990).

Why is discipline based on power assertion and love withdrawal less effective than induction in promoting prosocial thoughts and behaviors? One reason is that power assertion and love withdrawal often involve threat and perhaps actual punishment, and this may produce considerable arousal in a child. High levels of arousal will probably cause children to focus on themselves and react in a self-centered or egoistic way (Fabes, Eisenberg, & Eisenbud, 1993). Discipline that causes considerable arousal may also interfere with children's ability to remember *why* they are being disciplined or the content of what their parents are saying to them (Hoffman 1990). Finally, Grusec and Goodnow (1994) proposed that if discipline threatens a child's independence and autonomy (as would almost certainly be the case in power assertion), this may actually increase the child's motivation *not* to comply with these wishes.

In contrast, there are several reasons why inductive discipline should be effective. It provides children with standards against which they can evaluate their actions in the future (Hoffman, 1977). Induction also enables parents to discuss emotions that would lead to concern for others such as guilt and shame, teaches children how to empathize with people in distress, and provides children with information about how they *should* behave toward others (Eisenberg, 1992; Grusec & Goodnow, 1994; Hoffman, 1994). Thus, induction does more than control children's behavior; it also serves to teach them how to act prosocially. As a result, it may increase a child's tendencies to spontaneously act in a prosocial manner.

Observing helpful and altruistic models. The second process that is involved in learning to be helpful is called *observational learning* or *model-*

ing. This concept was introduced briefly in Chapter 3. According to social-learning theorists, such as Albert Bandura (1977, 1986) much of what children learn about helping (and other social behaviors) is the result of observing the actions of models in their environment.

Modeling can affect the development of helping in at least two ways. First, it can teach children helpful behaviors that they did not know. Second, it can show children what will happen when they engage in certain helpful (or selfish) behaviors that they already know. For both of these reasons, it is important that models behave consistently (Lipscomb, McAllister, & Bregman, 1985). Thus, both what models say and what models do are important. But which is *more* important?

In one study (Rushton, 1975), half the children saw an adult model act generously; the other half saw a model behave selfishly. Within each of these two groups, half the children heard the model preach generosity, and half heard the model preach selfishness. The children in each of these four conditions were then given a chance to donate money to Bobby, a poster boy in a charity campaign. The immediate effects of the models' actions and words on the children's behavior are presented in Figure 5.1. Children were only minimally influenced by what the model said—children exposed to the model who preached selfishness donated slightly less than did children who heard the model preach generosity; the immediate effects of the model's *actions* were much more powerful. Regardless of what the model said, the children donated more when the model acted generously than when the model acted selfishly. When the children were tested again, two months later, the impact of the model's actions were still present, but now the model's words affected the children as well. Those exposed to a model who preached generosity donated more than did those exposed to a model who preached selfishness. So while in the short run "actions speak louder than words," in the long run both what a model does and what a model says affect children's prosocial actions.

Models do not have to be "live" and physically present to make an impression on children. The models that children see on television are also important. Children between the ages of 4 and 6 typically spend between 2.5 and 4 hours per day watching television, and in many homes, they may spend more time watching television than interacting with their parents (Liebert & Sprafkin, 1988). Most people are aware of the possibility that watching violent models on television might have some impact on aggression in children. Can televised models also have some impact on how helpful children are?

Several field studies have examined whether television shows with prosocial characters or themes have a long-term influence on the behavior of children who watch them. In a study conducted in Australia, Ahammer and Murray (1979) found that exposing children to prosocial television shows for a half hour per day for five days produced increases in the children's cooperativeness and willingness to help others. Furthermore, exposure to prosocial television programs combined with

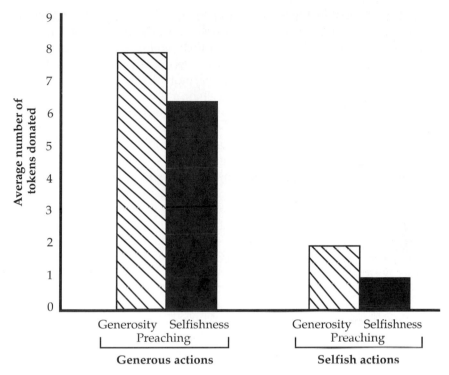

FIGURE 5.1
A model's actions are more influential than words for promoting prosocial
behavior. (Adapted from Rushton, 1975.)

training in prosocial behavior has a consistent and powerful effect on
children's cooperativeness, helpfulness, and generosity (Friedrich-Cofer,
Huston-Stein, Kipnis, Susman, & Clewett, 1979; Friedrich & Stein, 1975).
Hearold (1986) conducted a comprehensive review of the research on how
television programs with prosocial themes or messages affected the children who watched them. She concluded that these programs had a strong
positive impact on children—much stronger, in fact, than the negative
impact of programs with aggressive or antisocial themes.

Studies of the effects of real-life models have identified some of the
factors that make one model more effective than another. In general, models who are seen by a child as powerful and those who have a warm, nurturant relationship with the child produce the strongest modeling effects
(Grusec, 1982; Moore & Eisenberg, 1984). Perhaps because of these qualities, parents are the most important models for children.

Some parents, however, are more effective prosocial models for their
children than are others. Why? One explanation is based on *attachment
theory* (Ainsworth, 1973; Bowlby, 1969). Attachment theory deals with the
quality of the relationship between parents and their children, and there

is a powerful relationship between attachment and helping. First, helping can increase attachment between parents and children. Helpful parents tend to have closer relationships with their children. Then, because of these close relationships, those parents become increasingly effective models. As a result, these children are more likely to internalize the behavior and values of their parents than are children without strong attachments. One of the consequences of this internalization is that the children come to see themselves as people who are concerned about other people and also to see other people as worthy of such concern. This, in turn, makes them more likely to help others.

This process begins quite early and appears to have fairly long-term effects. For example, several researchers have recorded the quality of parental attachments of infants and correlated this with prosocial reactions a few years later when the children are in preschool. The general finding is that the stronger and more secure the early relation with the parent, the more empathic and prosocial these children are when they interact with their preschool classmates a few years later (Grusec, 1991a; Kestenbaum, Farber, & Sroufe, 1989; Main & Weston, 1981).

The impact of prosocial parents can be seen throughout a child's lifetime. For example, in a study presented in the previous chapter, Fabes et al. (1990) found that primary school girls who were sympathetic to children in distress had mothers who also were sympathetic in such situations, suggesting that the children were, in part, modeling their mothers' reactions. There is also evidence that prosocial parental models may exert a strong influence on the behavior of their children even after they have reached adulthood. For instance, whites who actively participated in the civil rights movement in the early 1960s had parents who regularly displayed prosocial behaviors (Rosenhan, 1969). Many of the people who risked their lives to rescue Jews in Europe during World War II had parents who displayed strong commitments to prosocial moral actions (London, 1970; Oliner & Oliner, 1988); we will address this relationship in more detail in Chapter 6. The effect is also evident in more day-to-day types of helping. Piliavin and Callero (1991) reported that almost 60 percent of a sample of first-time blood donors said that someone in their family gave blood. Given the fact that no more than 10 percent of those eligible to give blood in the United States actually donate blood, it would appear that modeling the actions of family members may be a strong factor in a person's initial decision to donate blood. Parental modeling of giving time and money also relates to willingness to help in these ways (Piliavin, Lee, & Call, 1992). Thus, the prosocial behavior of parents has a profound impact on children throughout their lifetimes.

Parental influences can also help explain cross-cultural differences in helping. For example, as noted earlier, there are considerable differences in the levels of prosocial behavior and helping in different countries. For example, children from Kenya, Mexico, and the Philippines were much more helpful than children from the United States (Whiting & Edwards,

1988; Whiting & Whiting, 1975). Some of these differences may be explained by different kinds of family socialization. Helping was more frequent in those areas where children were expected to cooperate with other family members when performing chores and to share in the care and raising of other children. Helping was less frequent when children were not expected to assume family and household responsibilities and were encouraged to compete with others.

The adults in a child's environment do more than provide models; they are also teachers. They directly and indirectly instruct children about what is good and what is bad—what they should and should not do. This kind of social learning is considered next.

Talking about helping and altruism. Although actions often speak louder than words in modeling prosocial behavior, words are still important. Most of us can recall more than one instance when we acted selfishly and our parents gave us a lecture about being helpful, cooperative, considerate of others, or concerned about the welfare of someone else. Two of the male coauthors of this book can vividly recall the lectures on the rights of others they received when they refused to share toys with their quite deserving, but younger (and, not coincidentally, smaller) sisters. What kinds of words and approaches are most effective with children? Three kinds of verbal communication will be considered here: direct instruction, preaching, and how parents explain why their child has acted prosocially.

Direct instruction is the most specific type of verbal communication. It involves telling the child explicitly what to do. For example, Grusec, Kuczynski, Rushton, and Simutis (1978) simply told children that they were to share half the prizes they won in a game with poor children. Not surprisingly, this induced a high level of donating immediately after the children received the instruction. But, can specific instructions produce long-term and generalized increases in helping? In fact, direct instructions have been found to affect helping as long as four weeks after the children receive them (Israel, 1978; Israel & Brown, 1979), and these instructions can cause an increase in subsequent prosocial behaviors that were not specifically mentioned in the instructions (Barton & Osborne, 1978; Staub, 1992). Apparently, once children understand what should be done, they are willing and able to generalize these ideas to new situations.

Preaching (also called *moral exhortation*) is a rather common way by which parents try to induce altruism in their children; it involves teaching children the *value* of helping. For example, Grusec (1982) trained mothers to record their own responses to altruistic and selfish behaviors by their children. Preaching to the child about the virtues of helping others was the most common response when a child failed to comply with a specific request to be helpful.

Moral exhortations can be quite effective in producing prosocial behaviors in children (Grusec, 1982; Moore & Eisenberg, 1984). The effects appear to persist for some time and to generalize beyond the specific situation in which the "sermon" was delivered. However, it also appears that some forms of preaching about behaving prosocially are more effective than others. For instance, Grusec, Saas-Kortsaak, and Simutis (1978) presented children with two kinds of exhortations. One was relatively specific in its message, discussing one particular kind of helping and the reason for it; the other discussed the importance of being helpful to others in general terms. Initially, the two kinds of messages were equally effective in promoting prosocial behavior, but a month later, when the children were asked to help an adult they had never seen before, the children who heard the general message were much more generous than those that heard the specific message. Thus, although children respond to both methods, teaching children that it is generally good to be helpful is more effective than teaching children that helping is appropriate in specific situations.

The final, and most indirect, kind of verbal communication that appears to affect helping relates to the *explanations* that are made about the child's helpful actions. In social psychology, these are called *attributions*. Attributions were discussed briefly earlier; now we will consider their effects on helping in more detail. Attribution theory (e.g., Heider, 1958; Kelley, 1967, 1973) suggests that if we believe that we have taken an action on our own, without external coercion or expectation of a large reward, we are likely to give a personal or internal explanation of our behavior. We will attribute our behavior to an enduring characteristic or disposition that we possess (e.g., I am the kind of person who helps others in need). Once we believe that we are the kinds of persons who do helpful things, we will be more likely to act in ways consistent with that self-perception in the future.

Attributions offered by others may also be accepted, internalized, and serve as guides for future behavior. Imagine, for example, that one of us had actually shared a toy with his younger sister. Our fathers could have said, "What a generous boy you are!" and made an internal attribution about his son's behavior. Alternatively, he could have remarked, "You knew it would make me happy that you shared with your sister" and made an external attribution about his son's behavior. Which would be more effective? Among children 8 years old or older, internal attributions typically produce more generalized helping than do external attributions (Grusec et al., 1978).

Grusec and Redler (1980) directly compared the short-term and long-term effects of social reinforcers and internal attributions. Children were induced to share some tokens they had won in a game with poor children. The experimenter then either verbally praised the child ("It was good that you gave your tokens to those poor children . . . that was a nice and helpful thing to do") or made an internal attribution about the child's behavior ("I guess you're the kind of person who likes to help others whenever

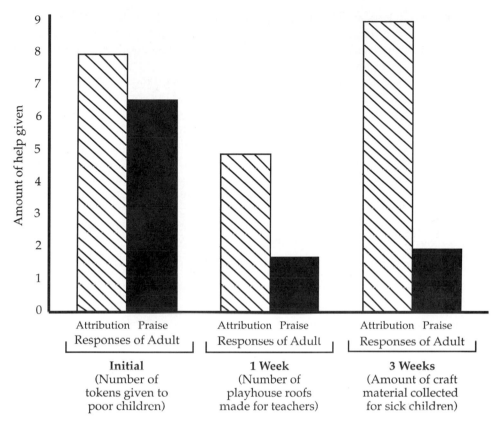

FIGURE 5.2
Attributions of helpfulness can have more enduring effects on prosocial behavior than
social reinforcers such as praise. (Adapted from Grusec & Redler, 1980.)

you can. . . . You are a . . . helpful person"). The researchers recorded how
helpful the two groups were immediately after the attribution or praise.
They also assessed helpfulness one week and three weeks later. The
results of this study are presented in Figure 5.2. Initially, there were no differences in how helpful the children were, but when they were observed
on the two later occasions, the children who received the internal attributions were much more helpful than those who received the social reinforcers.

In summary, it is clear that social learning or the socialization process
plays an important role in developmental changes in altruism and helping. However, to understand this process fully and find the right place for
these pieces in the puzzle, we must ask *why* these learning processes are
so effective. The social learning theorists would argue that children learn
to self-regulate prosocial behaviors as the product of these learning expe-

riences. Repeated learning experiences teach children the benefits of help-ing and altruistic actions. Having once learned this lesson, children act prosocially without the aid of external reinforcers, models, or instructions from their parents.

A second possibility, proposed by Grusec (1991a) and others (e.g., Moore & Eisenberg, 1984), is based on some of the cognitive processes dis-cussed in the previous section. These authors give special attention to self-attributional processes. They propose that if children repeatedly act prosocially, they will come to believe that they are doing so because they are prosocial people. They make internal, personal attributions about their behavior and, as a consequence, they are more likely to help even when there are no external reinforcers, models, or exhortations to be help-ful. Of course, these theorists add a very important qualifier to this expla-nation. Before a certain age, children are not capable of engaging in such cognitive processes. Thus, the effectiveness of learning processes depends on a child's cognitive and social development. As we noted at the begin-ning of this chapter, one needs both the cognitive and learning ap-proaches to understand developmental changes in helping.

ADULT SOCIALIZATION OF HELPING (IT AIN'T OVER 'TIL IT'S OVER)

Philip Costanzo, a social and developmental psychologist, says that many social-psychological theories of adult social behaviors, including those related to helping and altruism, are like a book that begins at Chapter 4—they ignore the important developmental events that preceded the behav-ior (personal communication, October 25, 1992). We believe that these last two chapters have spared us from this criticism, but we do not want to err in the other direction either. We do not want to suggest that the processes involved in the socialization of helping and altruism cease to operate when a person reaches some specific age. Even among adults, there are events and experiences that can exert long-term influences on how much people help and the reasons why they do so. We now consider some of these adult socialization experiences.

Modeling

Just as models influence the helping behavior of children, they influence adults as well. As we noted in Chapter 3, many studies have shown that there are increases in donations and other forms of helping with the pres-ence of models who display prosocial behavior (Hornstein, 1970; Macaulay, 1970). For example, Rushton and Campbell (1977) demon-strated the impact of modeling on blood donation decisions among adults. Students walking with a confederate were either asked to give blood or observed the confederate's positive response to a request to donate blood. When the student was asked first, only 25 percent agreed, and none actually showed up for the appointment. Among those exposed to the complying model, however, 67 percent also agreed to give blood, and 33 percent actually donated. Thus, the principles of observational learning and modeling apply as much to adults as to children.

Self-Attributions and Roles

Earlier in this chapter, we told you that if children make internal attributions about why they help, this will often lead to long-term increases in helpfulness. The same process appears to operate with adults. Adults consider the consequences of their helping to determine *why* they helped. If adults are offered money to help, are subjected to external solid pressure to offer help, or help a person who has previously helped them (arousing the reciprocity norm), they *perceive* themselves to have acted less altruistically than if they helped without such external inducements (Batson, Fultz, Schoenrade, & Paduano, 1987; Thomas & Batson, 1981; Thomas, Batson, & Coke, 1980). Thus, inducing helping with obvious external and tangible incentives may make adults *less* helpful in the future.

Alternatively, when adults identify themselves as helpful people, they may become even more helpful. How can adults be led to label themselves this way? The most direct way is by telling them that they are! Because helping is valued in our society, most people will quite willingly adopt the label of a helpful person. For example, in one study by Swinyard and Ray (1979), experimenters conducted door-to-door interviews. At the conclusion of the interview, the interviewer told half the respondents that they were the type of person who was "interested in their fellow man." Some time later, all the people who were interviewed received mailings asking them to volunteer for Red Cross activities. Although the assignment to conditions was done randomly, those people who had been told that they were concerned about others were significantly more likely to volunteer than those who had not received such an attribution.

There are also more subtle techniques for influencing people's self-images. One of these is called the *foot-in-the-door* technique (Freedman & Fraser, 1966). The foot-in-the-door technique involves an initial request for a small favor, which is then followed by a request for a much larger favor. The technique gets its name from the actions of door-to-door salespeople; these salespeople believed that getting potential customers to agree to watch a brief demonstration or to accept a small gift would greatly increase their likelihood of making a sale. To keep customers engaged, they would literally put their foot between the door and the door jamb, so that the customer could not shut the door and lock them out. Freedman and Fraser demonstrated the effectiveness of this technique. In one study, they were able to get a large number of people to place a very large and ugly sign in the middle of their front yard (a large commitment) by first getting them to agree to place a small, inconspicuous sign in a window of their house or in their car (a small commitment—the foot in the door). One explanation of this effect is that after individuals comply with the initial request, they begin to define or see themselves as helping people and will continue to comply in order to maintain that self-perception. In general, the foot-in-the-door technique produces small, but consistent increases in compliance with requests for favors (Beaman, Cole, Preston, Klentz, & Steblay, 1983).

The "foot" in the foot-in-the-door technique may also be one's own. That is, if a person repeatedly engages in a behavior, this can change the person's self-image and perceptions about why she or he is engaging in the activity. Think about an activity that you regularly engage in. Why, for example, do you jog every day, even when the weather is rainy or cold? Perhaps it is because running has become part of your identity: Runners run, and to not run would be inconsistent with your self-image and, thus, would be distressing. This process also applies to helping. For instance, college students who donate blood regularly develop strong *personal* feelings of moral obligation to donate in the future. They become intrinsically motivated to give blood and, as attribution theory suggests, these effects are even stronger among donors who have no external justifications (e.g., a blood drive) for their most recent donation (Piliavin & Callero, 1991). Thus, the donors' own behaviors can change their self-image and perceptions of the causes of their behavior. One might say they are able to socialize themselves to be blood donors.

Regular and public commitments to helping, such as donating blood or volunteering for charities, can lead to the development of social roles for helping. A *role* is defined as the set of expectations for the behavior or performance of a person who occupies some position. Whereas self-attributions may lead to a person's *own* identity as a helper, a role involves *others'* expectations as well. For example, we have expectations about how a police officer, a school teacher, or even a drug dealer should behave. We also acknowledge and share others' expectations about our own roles (e.g., student, parent, faculty member). Although roles have not received much attention in studies of children, researchers interested in changes in adult social behavior place great importance on the concept of roles. They believe that part of the socialization process of adults involves people identifying themselves with certain long-term roles—establishing a *role identity*. Such an identity becomes an important aspect of the person's self-schema or self-image and may subsequently influence the individual's behavior.

Some theorists have suggested that simply committing to some behaviors can lead to the development of a role identity consistent with those behaviors (McCall & Simmons, 1978; Stryker, 1980; Turner, 1978). For example, not only are one's own feelings of moral obligation and personal identity important in deciding whether to donate blood, but also the perceived expectations of significant others (e.g., friends, family) are critical. Students who believe that others expect them to continue giving blood express stronger intentions to give blood in the future and, as a consequence, they *are* more likely to donate blood (Callero, 1985/1986; Charng, Piliavin, & Callero, 1988; Piliavin & Callero, 1991). Thus, one's self-identity, which can itself motivate people to donate blood, can become more publicly formalized in terms of social roles and others' expectations. Similarly, people may perform volunteer work in hospitals or for charity because it has become a part of their own identity and what others expect of them. These influences continue to develop across an entire lifetime. Older volunteers who help others, for example, report that they are motivated to fulfill a "meaningful role" (Bengtson, 1985; Midlarsky & Hannah, 1989).

In summary, developmental changes in helping do not stop at a certain age. People grow and change in this respect throughout their entire lives. Although there are certainly many differences between the processes affecting changes in children and those influencing changes in adults (e.g., biological maturation), there are many similar influences (e.g., modeling, self-perceptions). Through social learning and direct reinforcement, people can learn new ways to benefit others. Through self-attributions and regular activities, they can also develop new roles and identities. Among the elderly, for instance, these helping identities and roles contribute to the maintenance of high self-esteem and a positive outlook on life (Midlarsky, 1991). Thus, the development of prosocial behavior is a lifelong process.

THE ANSWER: SUMMARY AND IMPLICATIONS

This chapter sought to answer two more important questions about helping and altruism. First, as people mature, how do they change with regard to the things that motivate them to help and the way they think about helping and altruism? In general, there is an increase in the extent to which helping is motivated by internal and intangible things. Accompanying this change is an increase in the extent to which people consider the rights and well-being of others when they have to make a decision about helping. As a result, adults are more likely to spontaneously help than are small children.

This led us to the second question: What processes or mechanisms are responsible for these developmental changes? The research suggests that two general processes are responsible. One involves developmental changes in how children think about helpful and altruistic behaviors. It appears that as children mature, there are quantitative and qualitative changes in the ways they think and reason about the physical and social world around them. These affect children's thoughts and actions related to helping. For example, whereas the very young child (3 to 5 years of age) sees the world primarily from an egocentric perspective, the young adult is able to see the world through the eyes of other people. As a result, young adults are more likely to understand that other people have needs and more likely to help them satisfy these needs.

The other process involves social learning and socialization. As the result of social learning mechanisms such as direct reinforcement, modeling, and verbal communications, long-term and generalized changes in children's prosocial behavior take place. These changes occur initially because children come to learn that society values prosocial actions, and they eventually internalize these values. At the same time, engaging in helpful actions produces changes in children's perceptions of themselves and the explanations they offer for their own behavior. Among older children and adults of all ages, repeatedly engaging in prosocial actions may shape their personal identities and social roles. These, in turn, can motivate future helpful behaviors.

Although the two processes were presented separately, they are highly interdependent. Children cannot learn from certain experiences until they are cognitively ready. Similarly, many of the changes in the way children reason and make moral decisions are the product of the learning experiences they have.

This chapter and the one that precedes it allow us to put several more large pieces of the puzzle in their correct places. There is surely a genetic basis for helping and altruism among humans, and maturational processes play an important role as well. However, we cannot explain and understand many of the helpful actions that we observe in humans unless we also consider the culture in which they live and the learning experiences they have had.

The picture of when and why people will help is becoming clearer, but large parts of it are still missing. In the first five chapters of this book, we have focused on the *similarities* in how people react to certain situations, the *common* genetic heritage of humans, and the *shared* experiences that socialize human beings. In this chapter, we have concentrated on the variables that would lead all people to react the same way to requests for help; we have almost completely ignored differences among people in their willingness to offer help. However, there is considerable evidence that such differences do exist, and if we are to fully understand helping and altruism, we must examine these differences as well. Therefore, we turn our attention to individual differences in helping in the next chapter.

6

And Now for Something a Little Different: Who Helps and Why?

❖

The material presented in the previous chapters might lead you to conclude that helping is a behavior which is pretty much a part of human nature and that everyone is equally helpful. Chapter 2 described such situations in which most people will help most of the time. Of course, there are instances, such as the murder of Kitty Genovese, where people did not help. But even then, everybody acted in the same way. In Chapter 3, you may recall learning that there is an impressive range of explanations why people are likely to help others and donate their time, money and energy to charitable organizations. Chapter 4 suggested that prosocial tendencies are probably part of everyone's biological heritage. And Chapter 5 showed that much of the effort adults invest in socializing their children is directed toward making them helpful and prosocial. Therefore, it would seem that given the right conditions, anyone who sees a need for help should provide it.

This conclusion, while quite reasonable, is also quite wrong. There is considerable variability in how humans respond to someone in need of help. For example, whereas many people do respond to appeals for contributions to charity, a substantial number do not. Even the psychologists who propose models concerning why people are motivated to help (see Chapter 3) acknowledge that it is quite likely there will be substantial differences in people's reactions when they see someone who needs their help (e.g., Dovidio et al., 1991). Some potential helpers may become quite aroused, but some may not; some may empathize a great deal with the victim, but others may not. Some may empathize and help, while others may empathize but still not help.

This observation may not come as a great surprise to you. In fact, it is probably consistent with your own experiences. There often appear to be more differences in people's social behavior than similarities. Think about your friends. Certainly there are some who are consistently helpful, who are always willing to share their notes with their classmates or devote some free time to a local charity. And there are others who are not at all helpful. These individual differences in prosocial tendencies are the subject of this chapter.

THE QUESTION

The basic question to be addressed in this chapter is, what personal characteristics are associated with being helpful and prosocial? In other words, what personal characteristics distinguish generally helpful people from generally nonhelpful people? The questions in the previous chapters were primarily about the *similarities* in people's willingness to offer help, but the questions in this chapter are about the *differences*. However, correctly answering questions about the differences in prosocial tendencies among people depends a great deal on the research discussed in the previous chapters. One cannot solve the puzzle of consistent individual differences in helping without an understanding of the context in which that act of helping occurs. Similarly, the models of people's motives for helping may explain why a certain personal characteristic is associated with helping, and people's biological and social backgrounds may help us to better understand why one person is more (or less) helpful than another. So, although we have said this chapter is about something different, in fact, there is continuity and complementarity between it and the preceding ones. The puzzle in helping and altruism can only be solved if we identify all the relevant pieces and how they fit together.

This chapter is divided into two major sections. The question we address in the first section is whether people with different demographic characteristics differ in how and when they help. A *demographic characteristic* (or variable) is some aspect of a person's background or personal characteristics that concerns their physical or social status, such as their sex, race, age, religion, or socioeconomic class. The demographic variable on which we will focus in this chapter will be a person's sex. The specific questions of interest are, do men and women differ in terms of how helpful they are, and, if so, what are some of the reasons for these differences? These are simple and straightforward questions, but as you have learned by now, the answers to questions about altruism and helping are rarely simple and straightforward.

The question in the second section of this chapter concerns how personality characteristics (or traits) and other individual differences affect altruism and helping. A *personality characteristic* is a relatively enduring aspect of a person's psychological makeup that influences his or her thoughts and actions. We will discuss whether personality characteristics actually influence people's willingness to help and examine some of the specific personality traits that are believed to be associated with altruistic and helpful actions.

MALE-FEMALE DIFFERENCES IN HELPING

Although, as mentioned above, biological sex is not the only demographic characteristic that helping researchers have studied, in recent years it is the one that has received the most attention. Note the phrase, *in recent years*. Male-female differences in helping were largely ignored until the 1970s, partially because helping researchers focused so intently on how the situation affected most people's decisions to intervene in emergencies. It is also true that at that time many social psychologists did not believe that differences in the social behaviors of men and women were of particular theoretical or practical importance. The growth of the women's movement in the 1970s played a major role in making social psychologists aware that if they were to fully understand *human* social behavior, they had to consider the similarities and differences between the sexes in their research. This is certainly true with regard to helping and altruism. By the 1980s, researchers were asking many more questions about how a person's sex might affect his or her willingness to offer help.

Sex Differences in Helping: Myth or Reality?

Do men and women differ in their willingness to help? Yes. And no. And it depends. The "yes" refers to the fact that two comprehensive reviews of the existing research on the helping behavior of men and women (Eagly & Crowley, 1986; Piliavin & Unger, 1985) have found that in the majority of the studies men were more likely to help than women. More recently, Johnson et al. (1989) conducted a cross-cultural comparison of helping in six countries (Australia, Egypt, Korea, China, the United States, and the former Yugoslavia). According to their self-reports of helping, men were more likely to give help than were women. The "no" reflects the fact that this difference did not hold in all situations; there are a substantial number of studies that reveal no sex differences in helping (Eagly & Crowley, 1986; Piliavin & Unger, 1985). The "it depends" relates to the finding that the relationship between a person's biological sex and helping may depend upon the characteristics of the situation in which helping is studied. In some situations, men help more than women; in other situations, women help more than men; and in still other situations, there are no sex differences.

Why does this simple question about the relationship between sex and helping have no simple answer? One reason, which we will discuss in more detail later in this chapter, is that personal characteristics and situational characteristics usually *jointly* influence a person's actions. This also probably does not surprise you. Even that helpful friend you thought of earlier is not helpful in every single instance. Thus, it is difficult to make predictions about her (or his) behavior that will be correct every time.

A second reason why the puzzle of sex-related differences in helping defies an easy solution is that (obviously) psychologists cannot manipulate a person's biological sex in the same way they manipulate independent variables in an experiment. In a true experiment, researchers randomly assign people to different conditions of the study and carefully control other features of the situation to ensure that the only thing that could cause differences among people in different conditions is the variable they are studying. However, when the variable of interest is a person's biological sex, you cannot be sure that the *only* difference between male and female subjects is their biological characteristics. Sex differences are systematically associated with other differences. As a result, even if a study finds sex-related differences in helping, the researcher may not be able to specify the exact cause of sex-different behaviors (Piliavin & Unger, 1985). They may be due to (1) biological differences between men and women, (2) enduring personality differences associated with the way men and women are raised and socialized in our society, or (3) differences in what is viewed as socially appropriate or acceptable behavior for men and for women in a particular situation. Thus, like other demographic variables, sex is a "carrier variable," reflecting a range of other physical, social, and personal differences.

In summary, the answer to the straightforward question about who is more helpful, women or men, may not be straightforward. The first few pieces of this puzzle did not fit together well. Nevertheless, by considering other pieces, they might. These other pieces relate to the costs of helping.

The Costs of Helping

At the time of the Eagly and Crowley (1986) and Piliavin and Unger (1985) literature reviews, most of the studies that had been conducted had examined just one kind of helping—bystander intervention in emergencies. There is a good reason for this. As you may recall from Chapters 1 and 2, it was the failure of bystanders to intervene in the stabbing of Kitty Genovese that caused the explosion of interest in helping in the 1960s. Is there something about helping in emergencies that might lead men to intervene more than women?

There is evidence from real life to indicate that men are more likely to engage in heroic actions than are women. Since 1904, the Carnegie Hero

Commission has given ordinary citizens who are not professional helpers (e.g., emergency medical personnel, fire fighters, police officers) awards for acts of heroism. These acts involve helping that is clearly both heroic and chivalrous—such as rescuing small children from fires or saving people who are drowning. Between 1904 and 1986, almost 7000 heroes have been recognized by the commission, and less than 9 percent of them have been women. Another example of the same kind of sex-related difference comes from a study by Huston, Ruggiero, Conner, and Geis (1981). They interviewed people who had recently been publicly recognized as heroes by the state of California—they had intervened to protect someone during a dangerous criminal act (e.g., mugging, a bank robbery). Only one of the thirty-three people that had been so honored was a women.

The concept of costs of helping might explain the overrepresentation of men among the people recognized as heroes. As you may remember, the arousal: cost-reward model proposes that once they are aroused, potential helpers consider the costs of helping (and not helping) before they make a final decision about intervening. As the costs for helping increase, the likelihood that a bystander will help usually decreases.

Piliavin and Unger suggested that women may help less in these dangerous situations not because they are less helpful people than men, but because it would cost them more to be heroic than men. For example, the fact that men, on average, are physically larger and stronger than women might make the cost of intervention less for men than for women.

But how can one show that it is the costs of helping rather than the helpers' biological sex that is responsible for these differences? If costs are playing a role in sex-related differences in these kinds of helping, then we should find them operating even among members of the same sex. And this is what Huston et al. found in their study of the California heroes. They compared the male heroes to a comparison group of other men who had not intervened to save or rescue someone. They found that their heroes were taller, heavier, and had more police and medical training than did the members of the comparison group. Huston et al. believed that the heroes were more likely to intervene, at least in part, because it cost them less to do so.

Physical differences between men and women cannot, however, completely account for sex-related differences in helping. Another important part of understanding when and why such differences might occur are the concepts of gender and gender role.

Sex and Gender

Although many people use the terms *sex* and *gender* interchangeably, most social psychologists make a distinction between them. Eccles (1991) proposed that the term *sex* be used to refer to a person's "personal and reproductive status (solely) on the basis of genitalia." In contrast, *gender* should refer to "one's personal, social, and legal status as male and female, or mixed, on the basis of somatic and behavioral criteria" (p. 164). To social psychologists, a person's gender is *at least* as important a cause of social behavior as is the person's biological sex, because gender involves a person's socialization experiences, the way he or she sees and reacts to the world, and how other people see and react to the person.

A very important aspect of a person's gender status is his or her gender role. A *role* is a pattern of behavior expected of a person who occupies a certain position or status; associated with a role are social norms or standards. Compliance with these norms may bring positive social consequences; failure to comply with them may bring negative social consequences. Social norms are usually shared by the person who occupies the position and those who come into contact with the person. Most people simultaneously occupy many roles. For example, consider some of the many positions that you might presently occupy: sister or brother, student, employee, and, of course, being a woman or a man. The last role is associated with your sex status and called your *gender role*, which Eagly and Crowley (1986) define as a set of norms about how people should behave based on their presumed biological sex.

Although gender-role differences would not automatically lead to differences in *how much* people help, they could lead to differences in *when* people help and in the *kinds* of help they offer (Eagly & Crowley, 1986). For example, the female gender role encourages women to be caring and nurturant, especially to their friends and family. In addition, even though they may not experience empathy physiologically more strongly than men, traditional gender roles may lead women be more likely to interpret this arousal as empathic emotion (see Chapter 3) or to express these feelings as empathy on self-report measures (Eisenberg & Lennon, 1983). In accord with this expectation, women are much more likely than men to provide their friends with personal favors, emotional support, and informal counseling about personal or psychological problems (Eagly & Crowley, 1986; Eisenberg & Fabes, 1991). Gender of the recipient is also important. Women provide more help to female friends and to platonic male friends than to male romantic partners (Barbee et al., 1993). Although there are a number of reasons for a person's career choice, it is important to note that females have traditionally been greatly overrepresented in "helping" professions such as nursing and social work.

The male gender role promotes a different kind of helping. Whereas women are more likely to provide emotional assistance, men may be more likely to provide physical aid. Because of the norms associated with the male gender role, men are expected to engage in two related kinds of helping: *heroic*, in which they risk their own well-being in order to help others, even strangers; and *chivalrous*, in which they protect individuals who are less able and powerful than they are. As discussed earlier, men do seem more likely than women to engage in these kinds of helping.

Further, because chivalrous helping is much more consistent with the male gender role than the female role, men should help women more than they should help other men. But women, who are not likely to be chivalrous helpers, should not favor one group over the other. This pattern has been found rather consistently in studies of helping (Eagly & Crowley, 1986).

These kinds of data are informative and suggestive, but they cannot directly test the validity of a gender-role explanation of male-female differences in helping. A more precise approach would be to conduct a systematic review of the results of studies that found sex-related differences in helping, and this is what Eagly and Crowley (1986) and Piliavin and Unger (1985) did.

Gender roles and helping. One consistent finding from the studies reviewed by these authors was that people tend to offer the kinds of help that are most consistent with and appropriate for their gender roles. For example, men are more likely than women to help someone whose automobile has broken down but are less likely than women to help someone who has a personal or emotional problem (Johnson & Aries, 1983; Penner, Dertke, & Achenback, 1973; Otten, Penner, & Waugh 1988; Pomazal & Clore, 1973). As another example of this, Dovidio (1993) had male and female college students ask male and female customers in a laundromat to help them by either carrying their laundry or folding their laundry. More men than women were willing to carry the laundry; more women than men were willing to fold it.

Mikolay, Dovidio, Ellyson, Maggiano, and Keating (1989) showed that even among people of the same sex, gender role can influence helping. Some individuals are *sex typed*—they almost always engage in behaviors that are expected of people of their biological sex. For example, a man who almost always acts in an aggressive manner shows little sensitivity to the feelings of others, and uses his leisure time to play baseball or basketball would be displaying very traditional male gender-role behaviors. Likewise, a woman who is always docile and dependent, never assertive in her dealings with others, and has no hobbies other than needlepoint would be displaying very traditional female gender-role behaviors. There are, however, people who engage in behaviors that are appropriate for people of both sexes (e.g., men and women who are both assertive and sensitive to the feelings of others; men and women who enjoy playing basketball and doing needlepoint); such people are called *androgynous*. Mikolay et al. (1989) found that on traditionally feminine helping tasks, sex-typed women were more likely to help than were androgynous women. The pattern was reversed on less traditionally feminine tasks.

It was also found that the presence of other people usually exacerbates these kinds of gender-related differences in helping. Eagly and Crowley (1986) reasoned that this was because the presence of others makes the norms associated with gender roles more salient and, thus, increases people's tendencies to act in ways that are consistent with their gender role. The arousal: cost-reward explanation of this effect would be that the salience of these norms makes it more costly for a person not to conform to their gender role. Thus, there is a greater cost for not helping.

Other findings suggested that the extent to which people adhere to or believe in traditional gender roles affects their helping behavior. For example, Latané and Dabbs (1975) found a greater bias in favor of males helping females in the southern United States than in the midwest or the northeast. This appears to be due to the fact that, historically, traditional gender roles have been the strongest in the south.

Receiving help. Another difference predicted by both the gender-role explanation and the arousal: cost-reward model is that women should receive help more than men. According to the first explanation, occupants of the female gender role are seen as more dependent and in greater need of help than are occupants of the male gender role. The arousal: cost-reward model would propose that such perceptions would lead to perceived higher costs (e.g., more guilt or shame) for not helping a woman. Both explanations of sex-related differences in receiving help would also predict that the less a woman conformed to the female gender role, the less help she would receive. This prediction has been supported. For example, women who are identified as feminists, who dress in a non-feminine manner, or who are somewhat unattractive (and thus are seen as less traditionally feminine) are less likely to receive help (Harris & Bays, 1973; Piliavin & Unger, 1985; Unger & Crawford, 1992).

Before leaving the topic of sex-related differences in helping, we want to briefly discuss some additional research on women receiving help. As noted, women are usually more likely to receive help than men. There are, however, certain circumstances in which some women may not be helped, and one of these is when they are being attacked or assaulted.

Violence against women. Please place yourself in the following situation. You are asked to watch a psychodrama in which two other students are supposed to play the roles of people who had a conflict. Sometimes the parties to the conflict are the same sex, sometimes they are of different sexes. Unbeknown to you, the participants in the psychodrama are really professional actors. The conflict gets out of hand, and one actor begins to physically assault the other one—slapping, punching, and kicking. The assault is very realistic. It looks as though the person on the receiving end could really get hurt. In the different-sex pairs, sometimes the aggressor is a man, and sometimes the aggressor is a woman. Would you intervene? Which victim would you be most likely to help?

Borofsky, Stollack, and Messé (1971) created this situation and measured how many bystanders intervened and how quickly they did so. In all conditions of this study, except one, the subjects moved quickly to break up the (staged) fight. Remarkably, the one exception was when male bystanders watched a man assaulting a woman. (Recall that Kitty Genovese's attacker was male.)

The problem of violence against women is a serious one. As one example, consider sexual assaults. It is estimated that at least 15 percent of all women in the United States have been the victim of some sort of sexual assault during their lifetime (White & Sorenson, 1992), and 20 percent of all married women have been the victim of a physical assault by their husbands (Strauss, Gelles, & Steinmetz, 1980). Women are far more likely to be assaulted by men they know well than by strangers. Thus, whereas Borofsky et al.'s findings are quite startling, the level of nonintervention in *domestic* violence might be even more disturbing. One reason why people may not intervene in domestic violence is that they do not want to interfere in another family's business. Are people even less likely to rescue women who are victims of spouse abuse than those abused by a stranger? In an experiment by Shotland and Straw (1976), subjects were individuals waiting for an elevator. When the elevator arrived and the door opened, they saw a man fighting with a woman. In one condition of the experiment, the subjects heard the woman say, "Get away from me! I don't know you." In another condition, she said, "Get away from me! I don't know why I married you." Figure 6.1 shows the differences in how the subjects reacted to the fight between the "strangers" and the "married couple." Only about one-third as many people helped when the woman was being attacked by her "husband" as when the woman was being attacked by the "stranger."

Why were people reluctant to help the victims of domestic violence? Subjects offered a variety of explanations that appear to relate to cost considerations. Shotland and Straw (1976) found that subjects believed that (1) the woman being attacked by her husband was in less danger than the woman being attacked by the stranger (lower costs for not helping); (2) the husband was more likely to attack them if they intervened than was the stranger (higher costs for helping); and (3) they had less responsibility to help the woman being attacked by her husband (lower costs for not helping). Thus, when the victim was supposedly the wife of the assailant, the perceived costs of helping were higher and the perceived costs of not helping were lower than when the assailant was a stranger. As a consequence, helping was lower.

A more recent student on definitions of rape (Freetly, 1991) provides another possible explanation for a greater likelihood of dismissing violence perpetrated by intimates than by strangers. College students were given seven vignettes involving a man and a woman; in all of them the woman turned down the man's sexual advances, but eventually intercourse occurred. The relationship of the man to the woman was varied from stranger, to work acquaintance, neighbor, date, fiance, former hus-

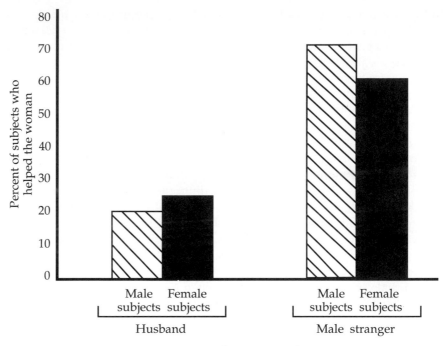

FIGURE 6.1
Bystanders are less likely to help a woman being attacked by her husband than
by a male stranger. (Adapted from Shotland & Straw, 1976.)

band, husband. The students were asked to answer whether the man's
behavior was acceptable and whether what he did could be considered a
crime. There was unanimity that forced sex by a stranger was completely
unacceptable and was certainly a crime. But, as the degree of acquaintance became closer, fewer and fewer respondents were willing to say that
the behavior was completely unacceptable. Women consistently saw the
behavior as less acceptable, at all levels of intimacy above mere acquaintance, than did men. Disturbingly, less than half the college men saw rape
by a fiance or husband as a clearly unacceptable action. One wonders
whether the same kind of perceptions might make bystanders less likely
to help the alarming number of women who are the victims of date rape
and other kinds of physical assaults by their boyfriends and husbands
(Shotland, 1992). Marital rape is still not acknowledged by a large proportion of the states.

Summary

Men and women do differ in how and when they help. Only part of the
reason for these differences is the biological differences between men and

women. Men and women may be genetically predisposed to engage in different kinds of helping, and the physical differences between them may make certain kinds of helping more appropriate for men than women. But biology cannot explain the majority of the male-female differences in helping. Social variables play a very important role. Specifically, gender roles influence how men and women will react to someone in need of help, whether they will help, and in what types of situations they will come to the aid of others. In general, people are more likely to help if the prosocial action is consistent with their gender role than if it is inconsistent, and requests from people who do not conform to their gender roles are less likely to produce helping. We will now turn to the question of whether the personality traits and characteristics of the helper represent an important piece in the puzzle of why people help.

PERSONALITY AND HELPING

Do people differ in how helpful they are because of their personalities? Although many people outside psychology would quickly answer yes to this question, there has been considerable disagreement among psychologists about the relative importance of personality characteristics as causes of social behaviors.

   This debate goes back many years. Kurt Lewin, who was one of the most influential people in the history of social psychology, said that behavior is a function of both the person and the environment, or in Lewin's (1936) shorthand formula, $B = f(P,E)$. Lewin believed that in order to understand completely a person's social behavior, one must know about the characteristics of the person (P) and the characteristics of the situation in which the behavior occurs (E). However, Lewin's students, who dominated social psychology for many years, focused on the "E" in his formula. They believed that situational characteristics were the key to understanding social behavior, and they more or less ignored the role of individual difference variables in their theories and experiments. A much smaller number of psychologists focused on the "P" in Lewin's equation. For many years, proponents of these two positions engaged in what has been called the "person versus situation" debate. They argued about which was more important—personality or social situations? We consider the positions of each side in this debate before we turn to the specific question of personality differences in helping. We begin with the personality point of view.

Personality and Behavior

Most contemporary personality theorists take a *trait approach* to personality: our personalities are comprised of traits. What exactly is a trait? Traits are characteristics of individuals. Some traits are physical, observable characteristics, such as a person's height, eye color, and the like; other traits are not directly observable, but must be inferred from observable behaviors. Among these are intelligence and, of primary interest here, personality traits. Like other traits (e.g., height, intelligence), personality traits are usually normally distributed throughout the entire population, and people differ widely with respect to where they fall on this distribution. That is, just as some people you know are much taller than others, some people you know possess more of a given personality trait (e.g., extraversion) than others.

Personality theorists believe that differences in personality traits can produce differences in people's behavior. But how do we really know that a trait is causing a particular behavior? Because personality traits are not directly observable, their existence must be inferred from people's actions or, more commonly, from their responses to questions about their personal characteristics (i.e., responses to personality questionnaires or rating scales). If the scores on a scale predict behaviors related to that characteristic, this is taken as evidence that a personality trait has caused the behavior. For example, evidence of the trait of extraversion would be reflected in the finding that your ratings on a scale designed to measure this characteristic uniquely predicted how sociable and outgoing you are when you meet new people.

So a *personality trait* is an enduring aspect of a person's character that manifests itself in thoughts and actions that are related to the trait. Personality theorists acknowledge that these thoughts and actions are influenced by the situations people confront, but they also believe that much of the consistency in people's actions and thoughts across time and across situations is due to personality traits. With regard to helping, these researchers believe that some people do consistently exhibit prosocial tendencies across time and across situations, and some of the differences among people in their willingness to help are due to differences among them in their personality traits (Rushton, 1984).

How important is personality? The personality point of view is sharply challenged by many social psychologists who believe that most social behavior is due to the characteristics of the situation in which the behavior occurs. This argument is based on the findings from many studies that suggest if you change the situation a person is in, the person's behavior will also change. Furthermore, there was little evidence of consistency in people's behavior across different situations. To quote Richard Nisbett (1980), a major proponent of situational explanations of social behavior, "The trait approach to the determination of social behavior . . . is largely wrong" (p. 110).

We can use the results from an early study of helping as an example of the kind of findings that convinced Nisbett and other situationists they were correct. Recall from Chapter 2 the Darley and Batson (1973) study in which seminarians were supposed to give a presentation in another building. Some of the subjects believed they were late for this appointment, and some believed they were going to be early. While the subjects were on their way to the appointment, they came across a man slumped in a doorway, groaning.

A short time before the experiment was conducted, Darley and Batson gave the subjects a questionnaire that measured their religious beliefs, a factor that may affect orientation to others (see Chapter 8). Based on their responses to this questionnaire, subjects were divided into two groups: those whose religious beliefs should lead them to be concerned about the welfare of others and to be helpful; and those whose beliefs were also religious but should not display such prosocial tendencies.

The critical question for this chapter on individual differences is whether the two groups of subjects, who differed in this personality characteristic, would also differ in their reactions to the man in need of help. As we reported before, subjects who believed that they were late for the appointment were much less likely to help than were subjects who believed that they had ample time. In contrast, there was absolutely no difference in helping between the subjects with the helpful and the non-helpful religious beliefs. In other words, this personality characteristic had almost no impact on the subjects' behavior, whereas the situational variable (being late for an appointment) strongly influenced whether the seminarians helped the man.

Do these results surprise you? That is, did you expect that the personality variable would be much more important than it was? If you did, you are not alone. Pietromonaco and Nisbett (1982) asked subjects to predict the effects of the same situational and personality variables in circumstances that were almost identical to the one in the original study by Darley and Batson.

Look at Figure 6.2. On the left side of the figure are the actual results of the original study; on the right are the subjects' predictions. The left side shows what we have just noted; the situational manipulation had a large influence on the subjects' willingness to help, the personality difference had none. Now look at the right side of the figure. The most obvious difference between the two sides of the figure is that the subjects dramatically overestimated how much people would help under these conditions. But of more importance is that the subjects predicted that the situational variable would have no effect on helping, but that the personality differences would produce rather large differences in helping!

According to Ross and Nisbett (1991), someone who incorrectly believes that the personal characteristics would influence helping more than characteristics of the situation would be committing the *fundamental attribution error*—overestimating the importance of personal characteristics as causes of human behavior. The fact that people often commit such

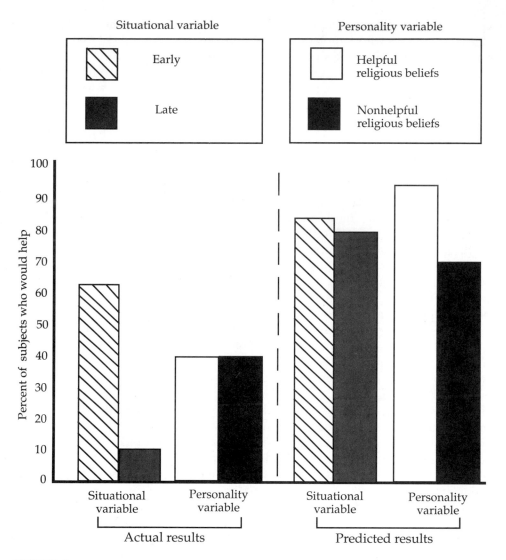

FIGURE 6.2
People tend to overestimate the influence of others' personality on their actual behavior.
[Adapted from Darley & Batson (1973) and Pietromonaco & Nisbett (1982).]

perceptual errors led Nisbett and others to conclude that the importance of personality traits as causes of social behavior has been dramatically overestimated.

Humans are often poor judges of the actual causes of their own behavior and the behavior of other people (Ross & Nisbett, 1991). The belief in the importance of personality traits as important causes of social behavior might, in part, be illusory. But even if humans were perfectly accurate in their social judgments, there was also the problem (for personality theorists) that in studies of helping conducted at that time, individual differences in helping usually produced rather weak and inconsistent results (Gergen, Gergen, & Meter, 1972). The status of personality variables as explanations of why people help was succinctly summarized by Piliavin et al (1981), "The search for the 'generalized helping personality' has been futile" (p. 184).

However, the situation has changed rather dramatically in recent years. Personality variables are no longer seen as irrelevant to the puzzle of altruism and helping. Most contemporary social psychologists, while acknowledging that people do make attributional errors and that situational factors do play major roles in social behavior, are coming to believe that personality traits can help us understand why people do (or do not) offer help. Indeed, in 1991, the same authors who had described the search for the altruistic personality as "futile" ten years before wrote that "despite the pessimism of earlier reviews of this area, . . . a growing body of literature suggests the importance of individual differences in helping" (Dovidio et al., 1991, p. 101). The research presented below played a major role in this dramatic change in perspective.

The Prosocial Personality

The prosocial (or altruistic) personality can be conceived of as a set of traits that predispose a person toward helpful and prosocial thoughts and actions. Many researchers interested in helping believe that the prosocial personality plays a very important role in helping, especially long-term and planned helping (Graziano & Eisenberg, in press). One kind of evidence that supports this position comes from studies that find consistencies in people's prosocial tendencies across a wide variety of situations and across long periods of time (e.g., Oliner & Oliner 1988; Savin-Williams, 1987).

To illustrate the cross-situational consistency of helping behaviors, we can return to the people, discussed at the beginning of Chapter 3, who are volunteers or donors to charities. These individuals certainly appear to be consistently prosocial. Several studies have consistently shown that those who belong to one voluntary organization are likely to belong to several others as well. Such individuals give time and money not only to organizations with which they are directly associated but also to other charitable organizations (Reddy, 1980). Savin-Williams and his colleagues also found substantial consistency in the prosocial actions of adolescents attending summer camps across a variety of different situations (Savin-Williams, Small, & Zeldin, 1981).

There is evidence of consistency in prosocial behavior across extended periods of time. For example, forty years after World War II ended, people who had risked their lives to save Jews from the Nazis were still more helpful than people who had not rescued Jews (Oliner & Oliner, 1988). Marwell and his associates (e.g., Marwell, Aiken, & Demerath, 1987) conducted a long-term study of some of the white college students who had actively worked for civil rights for African Americans in the 1960s. Twenty years later, these people were compared to people of the same age who had not engaged in these prosocial actions as college students in the 1960s. The former civil rights activists were much more likely than members of the comparison group to be involved in prosocial activities, such as fund-raising, donating money, and volunteering for charities.

We can now answer the central question presented in this section. Personality is important. It does appear that some people are consistently more prosocial than others, and there is such a thing as the prosocial or altruistic personality. Our task now is to identify the specific traits that make up this personality; this is a challenging puzzle in its own right. There have been two general approaches to solving it. One strategy is to find small groups of people who have already been identified as altruists—individuals who have engaged in exceptional acts of altruism. After locating these people, the researcher conducts in-depth examinations of them, focusing on their personal backgrounds and personalities. The goal is to find out what makes the altruists different from ordinary people. The other approach is to study large groups of people drawn more or less at random from the population and identify the personality characteristics that make some of them consistently more helpful than others. The results from studies that have used each approach are presented in the following sections.

Uncommon People: The Traits of Altruists

There may be no episode in history more horrible than the attempt by Adolf Hitler and his subordinates to systematically annihilate all people of Jewish ancestry. Hitler's campaign to exterminate all Jews formally began on November 9, 1938, in Germany, on a night that has come to be called *kristallnacht*—literally, the night of broken glass. Jewish synagogues were destroyed, Jewish-owned businesses were set afire, the mobs of Hitler's followers drove Jews from their homes, took their property, and beat them. Shortly thereafter, the Nazi leadership decided that the "final solution" to the so-called "Jewish problem" was to kill them all. As Germany conquered other countries in Europe, the scope of the genocide against the Jews increased. In a few countries, large numbers of people actively resisted the Germans' attempt to slaughter the Jews who lived there. For example, when all the Jews in Denmark were ordered to wear an arm band with the Star of David on it, the King of Denmark, a Christian, appeared wearing such an arm band. In one night, Danish citi-

Oskar Schindler (center) was welcomed as he arrived in Jerusalem for
Remembrance Day ceremonies in 1962 by hundreds of the Jews whom he saved
from Nazi concentration camps during World War II. His heroic efforts were the
subject of *Schindler's List*, the book and movie. (AP/Wide World Photos)

zens helped over 7000 Jews escape from the Nazis to neutral Sweden
(Arnold, 1967). But in most countries, the citizens aided the Nazis in the
mass extermination of the Jews. The actual number of Jews killed in
Hitler's concentration camps will never be known, but most experts agree
that at least 6 million Jews died in the Holocaust. The Nazis also extermi-
nated members of other ethnic minorities (e.g., Gypsies), homosexuals,
and people with physical and mental disabilities.

There were, however, a few individuals in even the most cooperative
countries who refused to go along with the extermination of the Jews.
They were people, like the now well-known Oskar Schindler, who risked
their own lives to save the lives of Jews. There have been several studies
of these rescuers; one of the more notable of these was conducted by
Samuel and Pearl Oliner (1988). Samuel Oliner himself was a survivor of
the Holocaust. Although the rest of his family died in a concentration

camp, he was rescued by a Christian family who were friends of his parents (Hunt, 1990). Many years later, he and his wife, Pearl, began a systematic study of the characteristics of people who, like the family who had rescued him, had attempted to save Jews from the Nazis. The Oliners were able to locate 231 such individuals. These rescuers were compared to a sample of 126 individuals with essentially the same demographic characteristics as the rescuers (i.e., their age, sex, education, the place where they had lived during the war), but who had not helped any Jews escape from the Nazis. The specific question that the Oliners asked was, "What characteristics differentiated the two groups of people?"

Some of the differences between the rescuers and nonrescuers did not seem to have much to do with an altruistic personality. For example, compared to nonrescuers, the rescuers reported greater actual and perceived similarity between themselves and people of Jewish ancestry. This finding has also been obtained in other studies of different rescuers (e.g., London, 1970; Midlarsky, 1985/1986), and it is consistent with the general finding that perceived similarity leads to helping (see Chapter 2). The rescuers were also more likely than the nonrescuers to have been directly asked to help a Jew escape the Nazis. Again, as you have already read, a direct request for help usually produces results. These findings indicate that situational differences may have produced at least some of the differences among the people the Oliners studied.

But there were other differences between the rescuers and the nonrescuers that appear to be related to socialization and to personality differences. One of the socialization differences involved how they had been disciplined by their parents. The parents of the rescuers were more caring individuals who were much less likely to use physical punishment to control the behavior of their children. Instead, the rescuers' parents reasoned with their children and explained what the children had done wrong and what kinds of behaviors were expected of them. As you may recall from Chapter 5, Martin Hoffman (1970) called this induction, or other-oriented discipline, and proposed that it will produce helpful, prosocial children.

Another difference involving the parents was that rescuers were much more likely to identify strongly with a parent who was very moral and provided a model of moral conduct. This relationship was also found by London (1970) in his study of other rescuers and is consistent with the results of studies of other groups of altruists. For example, David Rosenhan (1970) reported that white Americans who made great sacrifices to help African Americans in their struggle for civil rights in the 1960s also had such parents who provided models of moral conduct.

The remaining differences between the rescuers and nonrescuers involved personality traits. Two of these relate directly to the motivational and situational characteristics that we discussed earlier in the book. One was the tendency to empathize with other people's feelings (see Chapter 3). The rescuers were generally inclined to be much more *empathic* individuals than the nonrescuers. A second personality characteristic that distinguished the two groups was the *willingness to accept responsibility* for one's own actions and, more important, for the well-being of other people (see Chapter 2).

Other personality traits that differentiated rescuers and nonrescuers were more complex. One of these was labeled *extensivity*. Extensivity involves the combination of empathy, a sense of responsibility, and the capacity to feel concern for and attachment to other people. In particular, people high on extensivity are distinguished by unusually high levels of empathy and feelings of social responsibility toward members of groups other than their own. Whereas most people would reserve these feelings primarily for someone who is similar to them and part of their own group, the rescuers also feel this for dissimilar people who are members of other groups. Thus, whereas most of the nonrescuers were biased in favor of members of their group (i.e., other Christians), most of the rescuers had the same feelings for members of other groups (e.g., Jews) as they had for members of their own group. They felt that "justice is not just for yourself and your own kind, but for others beyond your group" (Oliner, quoted in Hunt, 1990, p. 204). It is fairly unusual for people to feel this way (Dovidio & Gaertner, 1993) and makes the rescuers different from most people.

Finally, the rescuers were people who "felt that they could control events and shape their own destinies and . . . perceived themselves as actors capable of making and implementing plans and willing to accept the consequences" (Oliner & Oliner, 1988, p. 177). Such people are often described as having a sense of *self-efficacy* (Bandura, 1986); they believe they will succeed in the things they attempt to do. This characteristic has also been found in other studies of altruists. For example, Colby and Damon (1992) conducted in-depth interviews with twenty-three exceptional individuals who had made significant, long-term contributions to the betterment of other people. According to Colby and Damon, one of these people's most salient traits was that they almost welcomed the challenges to achieving their goals and were unlikely to be discouraged by the obstacles that stood in the way of helping others.

Although the Oliners' study is very impressive, it is not without its critics. For example, Piliavin and Charng (1990) noted that given all the personality traits the Oliners examined, there were relatively few that differentiated the two groups. There is another more subtle, but potentially more serious problem with studies that use this approach to learn about the personality characteristics of altruistic individuals. Long before they were interviewed, the rescuers had already been publicly identified (and honored) as heroes or "true altruists." This may have resulted in their answering the personality questions in the way they *thought* an altruist should. Thus, their earlier actions may have been a cause of the personality differences that were found rather than their personalities having caused their prosocial behavior. The potential problem with this approach to defining the altruistic personality means that we must continue a little further before we can draw any firm conclusions about the personality traits that are part of it.

Common People: Altruistic Traits

Whereas the previous approach focused on the personality characteristics of a relatively small number of exceptional people, the approach to be considered now focuses on a few traits that may exist in any person. In this approach to personality research, people fill out scales that measure how much of a certain trait they possess, and the prosocial behaviors of people who possess a great deal and very little of a trait are then compared. If the two groups differ in their behavior, then we can reasonably conclude the trait is part of the prosocial personality. We will examine the answers that this method provides to the same question asked above: What personality traits are part of an altruistic personality? Of special interest is whether the traits identified by this approach are the same as those identified by the Oliners. To anticipate the results of this comparison, it would appear that they are.

Empathy. There have been several studies that have examined the relationship between empathy and helping. To distinguish empathy as it is being used here from the transitory kind of empathy discussed in Chapter 3, we will call it *dispositional empathy*—a consistent tendency to respond emotionally to other people's emotional experiences and to understand their point of view. Mark Davis (1980) developed the Interpersonal Reactivity Index (IRI) to measure empathy. Some of the items from Davis's scale are presented in Table 6.1.

There are several studies which have found that empathy is related to prosocial actions, particularly those that require some planning and thought (Eisenberg & Miller, 1987). For example, Davis (1983) administered the IRI to students who had watched the annual Jerry Lewis Muscular Dystrophy Telethon and obtained self-reports of how much money they had donated to this charity. Davis found a significant corre-

TABLE 6.1 SAMPLE ITEMS FROM DAVIS'S IRI REFLECTING INDIVIDUAL DIFFERENCES IN EMPATHIC CONCERN

1. I often have tender, concerned feelings for people less fortunate than me.
2. When I see someone being taken advantage of, I feel kind of protective toward them.
3. I would describe myself as a pretty soft-hearted person.
4. I am often quite touched by things that I see happen.

lation between empathy and how much students donated to the telethon. Rushton (1984) reported that people who volunteer for community charities are more empathic than those who do not. Otten, Penner, and Altabe (1991) found professional helpers (psychotherapists) who scored high on Davis's measure of empathy were more likely to help a person with a work assignment (writing an article about psychotherapy) than were therapists who had scored low. The trait of empathy also relates to long-term commitments to help; community mental health volunteers tend to be unusually high on this dimension (Allen & Rushton, 1983). Thus, like the research on situational motivators and the Oliners' work, people who are dispositionally more empathic are generally more helpful.

A sense of responsibility. A number of studies have found, as the Oliners did and as we saw for situational determinants of helping, that a sense of responsibility for the welfare of others is associated with prosocial behavior. For example, Staub (1974) found that subjects who accepted social responsibility and engaged in other-oriented moral reasoning were likely to come to the aid of a person who was feeling ill. Berkowitz and Daniels (1964) found that people who scored high on their measure of social responsibility were, relative to people who scored low, more likely to help someone who was dependent on them for help.

Other-oriented empathy. Recently, Penner and his associates found that the traits of empathy, a sense of responsibility, and the concern about the welfare of others are all highly related to one another. Therefore, they combined questions which measured these characteristics into a single composite personality scale. They called the characteristic measured by the scale *other-oriented empathy*, and it appears to be very similar to what the Oliners called *extensivity*. Even among ordinary people, other-oriented empathy appears to be related to a number of prosocial feelings and behaviors.

For example, people who score high on this scale estimate the cost of helping others as lower, report more sympathy and concern for someone who is in trouble, and are more likely to help a friend with a personal problem. Behaviorally, other-oriented empathy also distinguishes between volunteers and nonvolunteers at a shelter for homeless families. Moreover, the longer people had worked as volunteers, the higher they scored on this measure (Penner & Craiger, 1991; Penner, Fritzsche, Craiger, & Freifeld, in press; Penner & Fritzsche, 1993). This combination of characteristics also relates to spontaneous helping.

Of course, these are planned and nonspontaneous forms of helping. How does this personality characteristic correlate with more spontaneous kinds of helping, such as bystander interventions to help a distressed person? We would expect the relationship to be somewhat weaker because, as we will discuss in more detail shortly, strong situational cues usually reduce the influence of personality on behavior. Bystander intervention situations usually involve strong cues about how people should behave. Nonetheless, personality traits like extensivity appear to be correlated with the willingness of bystanders to intervene. Bierhoff, Klein, and Kramp (1991) found that witnesses who intervened to help victims of traffic accidents were more empathic and had a stronger sense of social responsibility than bystanders who did not intervene. Carlo, Eisenberg, Troyer, Switzer, and Speer (1991) further demonstrated the importance of the nature of the situation. Carlo et al. (1991) developed a composite personality scale very similar to the one just described. They gave their scale to a group of college students several weeks before the students participated in a laboratory experiment. Subjects in the experiment watched a person working on an unpleasant task. The person (really a confederate) became quite distressed by the task and asked the subject to take her place. For some subjects, the situational demand for helping was strong; if they refused, they would have to stay and watch the distressed person continue to work on the task. For other subjects, the situational demands were weaker; if they refused to take her place, they would be allowed to leave the experiment shortly and not have to watch her suffer.

Carlo et al. predicted that personality characteristics would correlate more strongly with the decision to help when the situational demands were weaker. When the situational demands are strong, as we noted at the beginning of this chapter, most people respond in the same way—they help. When the situational demands are weaker, there is more latitude in behavior, and people rely more on their personal inclinations to guide their actions. This prediction was confirmed. Most people (78 percent) helped when the situational demand was strong; about half the subjects (49 percent) helped when demand was weaker. Furthermore, as expected, subjects in the weak demand condition who scored high on their measure of prosocial personality traits were more likely to take the confederate's place than were those who scored low. In the strong demand situation, this effect was less pronounced. Thus, both personality and situations are important.

Self-efficacy. The final characteristic that distinguished the Oliners' rescuers from the nonrescuers was a sense of self or personal efficacy; the rescuers were self-confident individuals who believed they could successfully meet the challenges that confronted them. It needs to be reemphasized, however, that these people described themselves in this way almost forty years after they had actually demonstrated that they were capable of overcoming some incredible challenges. Thus, their previous acts of heroism may have made them feel self-efficacious. Is there any evidence that this personality characteristic *causes* people to act prosocially? In younger age groups, children who are assertive are more likely to initiate prosocial acts than those who are not assertive (Graziano &

Eisenberg, in press). Rushton (1984) found that people who were volunteers at a community mental health center were independent individuals who were particularly likely to believe that they controlled what happened to them. More recently, Penner and Fritzsche (1993) found that helpful people are also self-assured and confident of their abilities.

Subsequent research (Penner et al., in press) may explain why this sense of self-efficacy is related to helping. They gave a group of college students the other-oriented empathy scale described above and a personality scale that measured self-efficacy. About a month later, the students were given a list of twenty helpful acts, and they reported how often they had done each of them during the past month. The scores on the self-efficacy scale were not correlated with helping. But respondents who scored high on other-oriented empathy *and* believed in their self-efficacy engaged in significantly more helping than did those who were other-oriented but did not believe in their self-efficacy. That is, the most helpful people were those who had the prosocial personality traits and who believed their prosocial actions would be effective. Graziano and Eisenberg (in press) noted, "altruism involves not only an other-orientation but also the ability to enact helping actions, [therefore] it is reasonable to expect [positive] correlations between altruism indices and [measures of] individual competence and control" (p. 59). Thus, people not only need to possess the inclination to act prosocially but also to believe that they are capable of helping others.

We now have a pretty good picture of traits that make up the prosocial personality: empathy, a sense of responsibility, concern for the welfare of others, and a sense of self-efficacy. However, before we can conclude this discussion, one last issue remains.

But is it altruism? Daniel Batson, who has made major contributions to the evidence for altruism, does not believe that the existence of an altruistic personality has been conclusively demonstrated. Batson (1991) does not question that personality traits play a role in prosocial behavior; he readily acknowledges that they do. His argument is a more subtle one and involves what motivates a person to help. Recall from Chapter 3 that Batson says an act can only be considered altruistic if the primary motivation for it is the desire to benefit another person or increase another person's well-being. Batson (personal communication, April 9, 1993) questions whether it has been demonstrated that altruistic motives (as he defines them) are responsible for the actions of the prosocial people we have just described. Batson and his associates (e.g., Batson, Bolen, Cross, & Neuringer-Benefiel, 1986; Dyck, Batson, Oden, & Weeks, 1989) have found that personality characteristics, such as empathy and a sense of responsibility, do correlate with helping, but only when the helping is egoistically motivated; they have been unable to find individual differences in helping under the conditions that Batson believes lead to altruistically motivated helping. Rather, Batson believes that empathic or socially responsible people help because this makes them feel better. For example, helping may reduce an empathic individual's distress at the sight of another person in trouble; helping may enable the socially responsible individual to avoid the personal costs of not living up to her or his self-image. Thus, although researchers have identified many of the personality pieces of the puzzle, the picture is not yet clear. In the next section, we consider some additional pieces.

Personality and *Situations*

Batson's argument about whether the altruistic personality represents egoistic or altruistic motives brings us back to the question with which we began this chapter. We asked, Which is more important, personality or the situation? Before we close this chapter, we return to this debate. We need to do this because much of the material in the last few pages might cause you to believe incorrectly that personality traits alone are the key to understanding the puzzle. We did not say much about situational variables, because we wanted to present a clear picture of the personality characteristics that have been found to be associated with helping. But these personality traits do not operate independently of the situation in which the helping occurs; a purely trait-based explanation of helping would be as incorrect or incomplete as one that only included situational variables. So let us try to put the record straight. In our view, Kurt Lewin was right almost sixty years ago when he said that *both* the person and the environment affect social behavior [i.e., B = f(P, E)]. In contemporary psychology this position is called *interactionism.*

Strong and weak situations. The person × situation framework is often described as the *interactionist* approach. As the multiplication sign between the person and situation suggests, behavior is the *product* of the person and the situation. Interactionists believe that it is the strength of the situational demands that determines how influential personality differences will be (e.g., Romer, Gruder, & Lizzardo, 1986). They propose that in circumstances in which there are strong and unambiguous cues of how a person should behave, personality traits will not be important causes of behavior. But in circumstances in which these cues are weak and ambiguous, personality traits will be important causes of behavior (Monson, Hesley, & Chernick, 1982; Snyder, 1992a). For example, if an elderly person carrying a cane falls down, cries out in pain, and directly asks you and another person for help, there will probably be few differences in how the two of you respond. Both of you will probably offer assistance. If, on the other hand, a young, apparently able person falls, makes no sound, and says nothing about needing help, there may be great individual differences in how the two of you respond to the problem. The strength of the situational cues affects the strength of personality influences on behavior.

For example, recall that in the study of helping by psychotherapists (Otten et al., 1991), dispositional empathy was related to the therapists' willingness to provide a person with nonprofessional help. In this study, the therapists were also asked if they were willing to see the person in therapy to provide professional help. Dispositional empathy was unrelated to the therapists' willingness to provide professional help. Why? Probably because among therapists there is a strong expectation (situational demand) that if a person needs therapy, they are obligated to provide it. No such demand exists for informal, nonprofessional helping and, thus, individual differences in helping are more likely to emerge in the latter kind of helping.

Seeing situations differently. Although situations may affect how strong the impact of personality is, personality characteristics can also affect how people interpret the objective characteristics of the situation. Some personality characteristics will lead people to be more attuned to certain aspects of potential helping situations. For example, the personality dimensions that have important influences in emergencies are those related to arousal, emotionality, and willingness to take personal risks (Huston, Geis, & Wright, 1976; Wilson, 1976). These are prominent elements of emergencies. In contrast, in nonemergency situations, cost-reward considerations and cognitive differences are effective predictors of helping; confidence and self-esteem, for instance, are important personality dimensions under these circumstances (Batson et al., 1986; Midlarsky, 1984).

The role that personality plays in shaping perceptions of the situation is illustrated in the following study. As we have seen, people experience empathic or vicarious arousal and anxiety when they see another person in distress, and the intensity of this vicarious arousal/anxiety influences their willingness to help (Dovidio et al., 1991). Marks, Penner, and Stone (1982) investigated whether personality differences produce differences in how much empathic anxiety people experience when they see someone in distress. The personality characteristic Marks et al. examined was sociopathy. Sociopathy is almost the polar opposite of the other-person orientation associated with being helpful. According to Hare (1970), sociopaths are antisocial, egocentric, selfish individuals, who care little about the needs of others, and often feel little or no guilt or remorse when they hurt others. These are certainly not characteristics one would readily associate with helping. Subjects in this study by Marks et al. filled out a personality scale that measured sociopathy and, several weeks later, participated in an experiment in which they observed a person supposedly receiving painful electric shock. (He was, in fact, a confederate and was never shocked.) Subjects reported how much anxiety they felt while they watched the confederate receive shock. Subjects who were classified as high in sociopathy reported significantly less empathic anxiety than did those who were classified as low in sociopathy.

This personality characteristic also manifested itself in actual helping. To explain how and to illustrate this principle of interactionism, we need to describe the two conditions in the experiment. In the *contingent* condition, subjects were given the opportunity to stop the shock to the confederate by pushing a button on a panel in front of them; in the *noncontingent* condition, the subjects could not stop the shock by pressing the button. As you would expect, subjects responded much more rapidly in the contingent condition (when they could stop the shock and help the confederate) than in the noncontingent (when they could not). This shows the effect of the situational variable (i.e., contingency). But subjects high and low in sociopathy also reacted very differently to the opportunity to save the person from further shock. Figure 6.3 shows what happened. The low-

FIGURE 6.3
Low-sociopathic subjects respond faster when they can stop the shock administered to another person, whereas high-sociopathic subjects respond more slowly. (Based on data from Marks et al., 1982.)

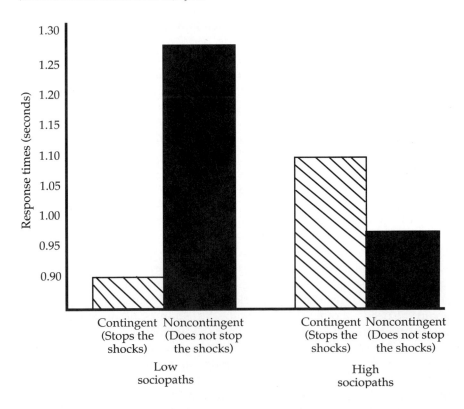

sociopathic subjects responded to the chance to stop the shock by responding significantly *faster* in the contingent than in the noncontingent condition (i.e., with shorter response times). But the high-sociopathic subjects actually responded *more slowly* in the contingent condition, where they could stop the shock to the confederate, than they did in the noncontingent condition, where they could not stop the shock to the confederate!

Besides telling us something about the kind of people we *wouldn't* want around if we were in trouble, this study illustrates that situational variables (the differences in contingencies) and personality traits (sociopathy) can jointly affect helping. The key to solving the puzzle of why people help is to make sure that you have both the situation and the person pieces available.

THE ANSWER: SUMMARY AND IMPLICATIONS

In this chapter we have considered the altruistic or prosocial personality. Does it exist, and what are the major components of it? With regard to the first question, we have seen that some people show prosocial tendencies that are stable across time and situations. This suggests that it is reasonable to talk about a prosocial personality. We used the results from two approaches to the study of personality to identify the traits that may make up this personality. The results obtained from these two approaches appear to converge in the identification of these traits. The first of them is being empathic; helpful, prosocial individuals are not only able to empathize with other people, they are inclined to do so. They are also oriented toward the well-being of other people, take responsibility for their welfare, and consider the effects of their actions on others. These characteristics relate to the important influences of perspective taking and moral reasoning on helping, which were discussed in the previous chapter. Finally, they believe that if they attempt to help someone, they will be successful.

Although it has not yet been determined whether people with a prosocial personality are engaging in truly altruistic (as opposed to egoistic) helping, they are certainly helpful individuals. We concluded the chapter by presenting the interactionist approach to the causes of social behaviors. Specifically, we proposed that helping behavior is determined by the personal characteristics of the helper *and* the nature of the circumstances in which the helping occurs. Thus, if we only used personality pieces or situational pieces to solve the puzzle, we would be unable to complete it. To understand helping we must understand the personal characteristics of people and the circumstances that surround them.

7

Help Wanted? Help Seeking: Actions and Reactions

❖

*I*n Chapter 1, we defined helping as an interpersonal process that involves both a person in need and a person who provides assistance. Thus far, we have focused almost exclusively on this process from the helper's point of view. In this chapter, we shift our perspective and consider helping from the point of view of the person in need, the recipient of some sort of assistance. As is usually true, changing our perspective on some issue makes us realize and appreciate its richness and complexity. For instance, the research on giving help seems to imply that helping is always good and, therefore, is always desired and appreciated by those who receive it. As we shall see, this is not necessarily the case.

THE QUESTION

Although helping, by definition, always involves some benefits for the recipient, people do not always seek the help they need. For example, Wills (1992) reported that well over 80 percent of people who have serious psychological problems do not seek professional help, even when this help would be provided at no cost to them. Similarly, in some laboratory experiments on help seeking, researchers have found that subjects who need help to successfully complete a task will often not ask for it. For example, DePaulo (1982) described an experiment in which men confronted with a mechanical task they could not solve were given the opportunity to ask another person for help with the task. Although the men knew that the person could help with the task, less than 10 percent asked the person for assistance.

Asking for help is not easy. Even though this man is not begging for a handout and is willing to work for what he needs, the psychological costs of asking for assistance from others are high. Because of these costs, many people will wait until they are truly desperate before they ask for help, or they may never ask for help at all. (AP/Wide World Photos)

These two examples should not, however, lead you to conclude that people in need never ask for help. There is evidence of considerable help seeking as well. For instance, Wills and DePaulo (1991) reported that about 50 percent of people with personal or psychological problems will seek informal help from a friend or family member. Similarly, Medvene (1992) found that most college students who had academic problems were quite willing to ask someone to help them with these problems.

Thus, the situation with regard to seeking help is very similar to that of giving help. Just as people sometimes give help and sometimes do not, people sometimes seek help and sometimes do not. This leads us to the two basic questions addressed in this chapter: (1) Why do people in need sometimes not ask for help? and (2) Why are people who receive help sometimes not grateful for the assistance they have received? Like many of the other aspects of helping and altruism, help seeking involves a difficult and complicated puzzle with many small pieces. To answer these two questions we must put the puzzle pieces in their correct places.

Imagine yourself in the following situation. You did not do well on your first chemistry test. Would you recognize that you need help and that others can provide it? Would you admit your problem to your friends? Would you seek help? If so, would it be from your instructor or one of your classmates? And how would you react if one of your classmates offered to tutor you, without your asking for help? This chapter concerns your responses in this situation and why they occur. Specifically, in the first portion of the chapter we examine the conditions that initially lead people to consider seeking help, the factors that affect whether they actually will ask for help, and how they decide whom they should ask for help. In the second section, we consider how people react to help from others and attempt to explain these reactions.

STUDYING HELP SEEKING: THE LABORATORY AND BEYOND

We begin with a brief consideration of the different settings in which psychologists study help seeking and examine how this might affect the answers we give to questions about help seeking. As you read in the previous chapters, researchers who attempted to answer questions about bystander intervention and other similar kinds of help *giving* have relied very heavily on the results of laboratory experiments on helping among strangers. Many of the people who study help *seeking* also use this kind of laboratory approach. However, there is also a considerable amount of nonlaboratory research on this aspect of prosocial behavior. It involves using surveys and interviews to learn about when and why people ask for help. For example, Dooley and Catalano (1984) conducted a telephone survey of people in the Los Angeles area and asked them whether they had an emotional problem during the previous three months and what they had done about it. Wilcox and Birkel (1983) asked recently divorced women to keep daily journals for four weeks and to record the problems they encountered and how they dealt with them. Both studies found that considerably more than 60 percent of the people surveyed requested help from friends and relatives. This can be contrasted with the results from laboratory studies of help seeking, in which the percentage of subjects who ask for help is often less than 20 percent (e.g., Nadler, 1987). Thus, if we are to find answers to the major questions of this chapter, we must first solve a related puzzle. Why do the results from the field studies and the laboratory experiments on help seeking differ?

Communal versus Exchange Relationships

Although a number of factors are probably responsible for these divergent findings, we believe that the major cause is a difference in the nature of the interpersonal relationships that are studied in the laboratory experiments and in the field surveys. The laboratory results are usually based on situations in which people are given the opportunity to seek help from strangers; on the other hand, the field results usually come from situations in which people are seeking help from relatives, friends, and other people with whom they have close relationships. The laboratory interactions are probably what Clark and Mills (1993) call *exchange relationships.* Exchange relationships are typically positive and friendly, but behavior in them is largely controlled by economic considerations. People in such a relationship are aware of and consider the effort they expend when they do something for another person, and they expect that such actions will be reciprocated. Similarly, they are aware that if the other person helps them, they owe that person something in return. Think about your relationships with your boss, a classmate with whom you are working on some class project, or a person who lives down the hall from you in the dormitory. These may be examples of exchange relationships.

In contrast, the help seeking usually described by the people who respond to the field surveys and interviews is likely to occur within *communal relationships,* in which people are less interested in the costs and benefits associated with their actions and more interested in the well-being of the other person. Because the parties involved in the relationship care about one another, they assume that kindnesses and favors will eventually be repaid (Webley & Lea, 1993) but do not keep close track of who owes what to whom. Additionally, because the other people in a communal relationship know one another fairly well, they are more willing to "let their guard down" and are (somewhat) less concerned about someone ridiculing or rejecting them if they disclose something negative about themselves. Your relationships with your parents, your romantic partner, and your roommate are all probably communal in nature.

As you might suspect, worries about whether we will be obligated to someone and concerns about what the person will think of us if we need her or his help are among the potential costs associated with asking for help. There is good reason to believe that these and other costs associated with help seeking will be lower in a communal than in an exchange relationship. As a result, help seeking may be more common in the close, communal relationships that people usually are thinking of when they respond in the field studies.

Social Support

Not only is the incidence of help seeking affected by the nature of the relationship between the person seeking and the person giving the help, but so is the kind of help that is given. When people ask a close friend for help, often they are requesting social support. Social support involves providing advice and help with a particular problem, as well as encouragement and comfort. The people who give this kind of help are usually called a person's *social-support network* (Nadler, 1986; Wills, 1991, 1992). Your parents, your roommate, your siblings, your friends from high school, your romantic partner, a coworker, or a member of the clergy may all be part of your social-support network.

Social support differs in several respects from most of the kinds of helping that have been discussed in the previous chapters. First, whereas the kinds of help discussed in these chapters usually involve helping a person to directly solve some sort of problem (e.g., fighting off an attacker, recovering a lost object), typically social support has two somewhat different goals. One of these is to give the person in need some help or advice that may directly lead to the solution of the problem *(instrumental support)*. The other goal is to give the person emotional or psychological support to help them deal with the stresses created by the problem *(emotional support)* (Wills, 1991). Helping an unemployed friend fill out a job application or lending the friend money until a job has been obtained are examples of instrumental support. Comforting a grieving relative, talking with a friend who has just ended a romantic relationship, and visiting a classmate who is in the hospital are examples of emotional support.

Second, whereas helping in response to an extreme emergency is almost equally likely to be provided to friends and strangers, social support is most likely to be provided to someone with whom the helper has a close personal relationship (McGuire, 1994). The third difference is extremely relevant to help seeking. People who need social support are likely to play an active role in determining the quantity and quality of this kind of aid; this is typically not true for the victim in some emergency situation (Barbee et al., 1993; Derlega, Barbee, & Winstead, 1994; Melamed & Brenner, 1990).

The benefits of social support. It appears that effective social support can provide substantial benefits to the help seeker. According to some researchers, good social-support networks reduce the absolute amount of stress that people experience in their lives. Additionally, effective social support may also provide a buffer for a person when he or she experiences stressful or negative life events (e.g., a physical illness, a divorce, the death of a loved one, losing a job) (Cohen & Wills, 1985).

There are findings to indicate that social support produces both benefits. People in social-support networks experience fewer and less severe stressful life events, and they are more likely to resolve small problems effectively before they evolve into major problems (Billings & Moos, 1982; Wills, 1991). For example, people with a good social-support system are more likely to comply with appropriate medical regimens that permit them to recover from a medical illness more rapidly (Wallston, Alagna, DeVellis, & DeVellis, 1983). Also, people who receive social support may be less likely to develop psychological and medical problems in the future. For example, Zeliony and Wills (1990) found that strong emotional support from friends opposed to drug use reduced the likelihood that people with a history of intravenous drug use would continue to engage in such behaviors. Social support may even have direct physical benefits. With regard to buffering, Baron, Cutrona, Hicklin, Russell, and Lubaroff (1990) studied people who were undergoing severe stress because their spouse had developed cancer. Baron et al. examined the immune responses of these people and found that those who reported high levels of social support were more resistant to certain kinds of diseases and infections than those who reported low levels of support.

This fairly lengthy exposition on the characteristics and benefits of social support in close relationships is not intended to suggest that other kinds of assistance are unimportant or of no benefit to the person receiving the help. There are many problems that will only be resolved because of the kindness of strangers, and the failure to seek this help can have very negative consequences for a person. Nor do we want to suggest that people will always seek social support when they have a problem. Some people fail to ask even close acquaintances for help, some have few acquaintances to ask, and some react very negatively to the help that is offered. Thus, we still need to find answers to the central questions in this chapter—why and when will people ask for help, and how do they react when they receive help?

SEEKING HELP: WHEN, WHY, AND FROM WHOM

In Chapter 3, we used a decision-tree model of emergency intervention to describe the decision-making process that potential helpers go through when deciding whether to give aid to others (Latane & Darley, 1970). Gross and McMullen (1983) have suggested that those in need go through a similar decision-making process when deciding whether to ask for help. Their model of the help-seeking process, which is presented in Figure 7.1, boils down to three basic questions:

1. Do I have a problem that help will alleviate?
2. Should I ask for help?
3. Who is most capable of providing the kind of help I need?

In this section, we consider how people arrive at answers to these three questions.

The decision-making process described by Gross and McMullen (1983) is not necessarily a sequential one, as their model might seem to imply at first. In many cases, a person may have time to think through

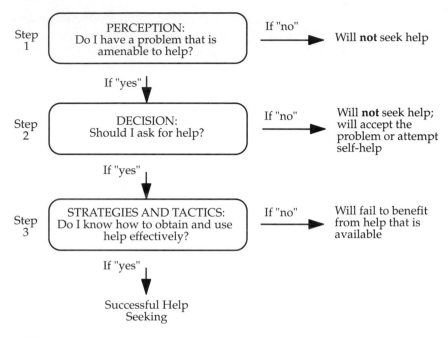

FIGURE 7.1
Steps in the help-seeking process. (Adapted from Gross & McMullen, 1983.)

various scenarios involving various sources of help and try to anticipate what would happen if help were solicited from each source. Because people in need are able to play out the various possibilities in their minds before actually having to make a commitment to a particular course of action, the anticipated outcomes for each decision not only may affect subsequent decisions but also may feed back to previous steps and change the entire decision process. Nonetheless, this model provides us with a framework to begin our examination of help seeking.

Do I Have a Problem? Defining the Help-Seeking Situation

As shown in Figure 7.1, before people ask for help, they must first define their situation as a problem that requires help. In general, if our lives are proceeding normally, we see no particular reason to seek help from others. It is when the unexpected happens or when things go seriously wrong that we begin to think about the need for help (Mechanic, 1968; Wong & Weiner, 1981). On the basis of our everyday experiences, we have each developed our own ideas of what is normal, and it is only when our experiences deviate from these personal norms that we begin to consider seeking help from others. For example, if I twist my ankle on my way to work, I may schedule an appointment with a physician to check for sprains or breaks. A professional football player may find an equally severe twist to be nothing more than a minor annoyance that is just part of the game, and simply run it off before reentering the contest.

The importance of recognizing that there is a problem for help seeking can be illustrated by examining the behavior of people who have a history of alcohol abuse. Betsy Thom (1986, 1987) studied the barriers to help seeking among people with alcohol-related problems. She conducted a survey of fifty British clients of a hospital-based, outpatient treatment center. These people had been heavy drinkers for at least five years before entering the treatment program. Denial that there was a drinking problem was a significant barrier to treatment for both male and female clients. In fact, Thom found that the patients' primary reason for entering treatment was not to treat drinking problems per se; rather they typically reported that they hoped that the treatment would eliminate other problems in their lives. Why did these people fail to recognize their drinking problem? Perhaps because of the gradual development of such problems, alcoholics deny there is any problem and do not seek help.

Should I Ask for Help? Making the Decision

Even if a person has recognized the existence of a problem that might be alleviated with outside help, the person must consider whether seeking help is really the best course of action. This decision takes into account a variety of considerations. One issue that must be faced is whether the help that could be requested is absolutely necessary for the problem to be solved or is simply convenient. If help is necessary to relieve the problem, then cost considerations enter the picture. If the costs for *not* asking for assistance are high and outweigh the costs *for* asking for help, people will be inclined to seek help. The more important solving the problem is for the person in need, the more costly it would be not to ask for assistance. Under these conditions, people will be even more motivated to seek help. If help is convenient but not necessary or if the problem is not seen as being important, the costs of asking for help (e.g., feelings of embarrassment or incompetence) inhibit asking for help. Of course, this is not the first time that considerations of cost have been raised in our discussion of helping behavior. The Piliavin et al. (1981) arousal: cost-reward model of emergency intervention (see Chapters 2 and 3) introduced the issue of the cost of helping versus not helping from the helper's point of view. Their model suggests that helpers weight the cost and benefits of the options available to them, and take the course that maximizes their payoff. According to Gross and McMullen (1983), those in need face a similar kind of dilemma: Am I better off asking for help and possibly accepting some embarrassment and social obligation, or is suffering through the difficulty while trying to solve my problems on my own a better course of action?

Once again, the literature on substance abuse provides us with an illustration of the concept of interest. In a study of seeking help for alcohol and substance abuse problems, Windle, Miller-Tutzauer, Barnes, and Welte (1991) surveyed over 27,000 adolescents from New York State. The teenagers were asked from whom would they seek help if they had a serious problem with alcohol and substance abuse. Overall, 10 percent of the respondents said they would not ask anyone for help. About 25 percent of the African Americans and Hispanic Americans under 14 years of age said that if they ever had a drug or alcohol problem, they would not ask anyone (e.g., friends, parents, or other adults) for help. Presumably this reluctance was due to the respondents' beliefs that asking for help would entail some considerable costs (e.g., ridicule from their friends, censure from their parents or other adults), and these costs outweighed any possible benefits that would come from asking for the needed help. Thus, many substance abusers may be reluctant to seek such assistance even after they recognize that they need help. This is a critical problem, because outside intervention is often necessary to eliminate the pattern of abuse. We should also point out that in this instance teenagers were saying that they would not seek help even from people with whom they were quite close (i.e., parents, friends). As we noted earlier, even in close relationships help seeking is not automatic.

These findings suggest that simply recognizing that a problem exists may not always be sufficient to motivate people to seek help. Usually decisions about help seeking involve the balance between the two forces depicted in Figure 7.2. The first is the motivation to achieve a specific

FIGURE 7.2
The decision about whether to seek help involves weighing the potential benefits and costs of taking action.

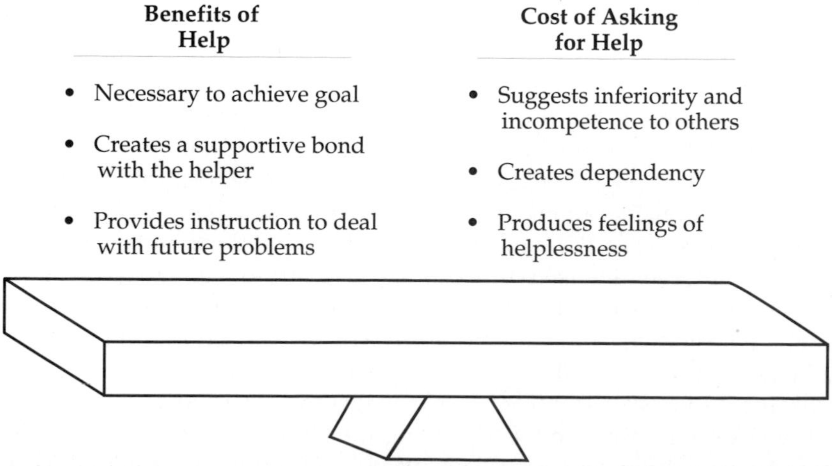

Benefits of Help	Cost of Asking for Help
• Necessary to achieve goal	• Suggests inferiority and incompetence to others
• Creates a supportive bond with the helper	• Creates dependency
• Provides instruction to deal with future problems	• Produces feelings of helplessness

objective, such as improving one's situation, alleviating some specific problem, or making oneself feel better. The second motivation is to maintain one's self-esteem and self-image—to feel positively about oneself and to be in control of one's life. Requesting assistance can often represent a potential threat and challenge to these beliefs. Therefore, a person has some important decisions to make before he or she actually asks for help.

According to Arie Nadler (1991), decisions about help seeking are influenced by (1) the characteristics of the person in need—some people are more inclined to seek help than are others; (2) the specific kind of assistance needed—there are some problems for which people readily seek help, there are other problems that they prefer to deal with alone; and (3) the potential source of the help—it is easier to ask some people for help than others. In the pages that follow we consider each of these.

Demographic Characteristics of the Person in Need

We saw in Chapter 6 that personal characteristics may affect a person's decision of whether to offer help. Similarly, there are personal characteristics that influence decisions about whether or not to ask for help. As noted above, asking for help may involve *personal* costs, such as feelings of loss of self-esteem, and *social* costs, relating to the impressions of others. People who value different things associate different personal and social costs with help seeking. Both demographic variables (i.e., gender, race, age, socioeconomic status) and personality characteristics (e.g., self-esteem) have been found to play important roles in determining whether a person will request aid. We examine the demographic variables first.

Sex and gender. One of the most frequently investigated demographic characteristics in the study of help seeking is the sex of the person seeking help. In this instance, the findings from the field studies and experiments are quite similar. Both of these research strategies usually find that women are significantly more likely to seek help than are men, even when their need for assistance is the same. Women seek help more than men for medical care, psychological counseling, substance abuse treatment, and educational and work-related assistance (e.g., Barbee et al., 1993; Corney, 1990; Johnson, 1988; Nelson-LeGall & Glor-Scheib, 1985; Smith & DeWine, 1991; Thom, 1986). These sex differences are even found among elementary school-age boys and girls (Barnett et al., 1990). Although such differences in help seeking could conceivably be explained by biological differences between the sexes (see Chapter 4), we believe that there is another, more social explanation. It is the manner in which men and women are socialized (Eagly & Crowley, 1986; Piliavin & Unger, 1985). Because men are expected to be independent and competent, help seeking is less socially desirable for men and more threatening to their self-esteem. Thus, it appears that gender and gender roles rather than bio-logical sex are responsible for differences in help seeking. As we discussed in Chapter 6, gender involves more than a person's biological sex; it involves the personal, legal, and social status of someone identified as male or female. A person's *gender role* was defined by Eagly and Crowley (1986) as a set of norms about how people should behave based on their presumed biological sex. (See Chapter 6.)

Recently, Anita Barbee and her associates (Barbee et al., 1993; Derlaga et al., 1994) have examined how gender roles affect the seeking of social support. As suggested earlier, Barbee believed that social support involves a dynamic, interactive process between the person who seeks this kind of help and those who provide it. The actions of the person who needs social support play a major role in the quantity and the quality of the support they receive. The research of Barbee and others indicates that gender roles affect both of these.

Recall from the model of help seeking presented earlier, before a per-son will ask for help she or he must recognize that a problem exists and that assistance is needed to solve it. With regard to this aspect of help seeking, men are more likely than women to see their problems as minor and under their own control. Men are also more likely than women to worry about people's reactions if they ask for help with a problem (Bruder-Mattson & Hovanitz, 1990). As we have noted, such differences are consistent with what we know about gender roles. Strength, compe-tence, and autonomy have traditionally been associated with the male gender role; dependence and naïveté have been associated with the fem-inine gender role. For example, men who request support from their work supervisor are viewed by others as less competent than women who ask for the same kind of help (Smith & DeWine, 1991). Thus, for a man who subscribes to the traditional male gender role, the social costs of asking for social support from even close associates may be too high. Seeking assis-tance could be taken as evidence that the man is not in control and, there-fore, is not living up to the masculine standards. Rather than suffer the potential embarrassment of asking for assistance, he decides to forego the help that he may need. A women seeking social support, however, may be perceived as satisfying her gender-role requirements while also securing the help that she may need (Barbee et al., 1993; Derlega et al., 1994; Good, Dell, & Mintz, 1989).

It also appears that women may simply be better than men at elicit-ing support from others. Reviews of the research literature indicate that the more feminine a person's gender-role orientation, the more empathic, socially skilled, emotionally expressive, and skilled at sending and receiv-ing nonverbal messages the person will be (Eagly, 1987; Eagly & Wood, 1991). Barbee et al. argued that these kinds of gender-related differences result in women being better than men at letting other people know when they need social support. For example, Gottlieb and Wagner (1991) com-pared husbands' and wives' attempts to elicit social support from their spouses. Wives were more likely than husbands to use emotional displays (e.g., smiling or pouting) to elicit social support from their spouses. Similarly, Sarason, Sarason, Hacker, and Basham (1985) found that relative to men, women used more eye contact and better voice quality when they sought social support.

Age. Help seeking also varies with age. Young children are not as likely as adults to shy away from seeking help when they are faced with new challenges (Shell & Eisenberg, 1992). One reason for this is that children are dependent on adults and assume that they are entitled to help and protection. In addition, because children younger than 8 years of age are not likely to make global judgments about their self-worth (Harter, 1986), concerns about self-esteem do not inhibit their help seeking. But, as children get older, they seem to become more reluctant to request help. By the second grade, some children begin to express concern about how others will view them if they seek help for schoolwork. They are also aware of specific social expectations: Girls, for example, say they fear that their parents and teachers will think they are "dumb" if they ask for assistance in math (Newman & Goldin, 1990).

This trend continues through adulthood. Older adults (particularly those over 60 years of age) are less likely to seek help than are younger adults (Veroff, 1981). Elderly people may be particularly concerned about maintaining a sense of personal independence and self-efficacy in their lives (Lieberman & Tobin, 1983). These feelings of control are important to their psychological and physical well-being (Langer, 1989; Langer & Rodin, 1976). Thus, just as men may not seek help for their problems in order to behave in a manner consistent with their traditional gender role, older people may be particularly reluctant to seek help in those areas of their lives in which they feel most vulnerable (Fox, 1984). Not coincidentally, these may be the areas in which their need is greatest.

Ethnicity. People from different ethnic groups may also show some differences in their willingness to seek help (e.g., Takeuchi, Leaf, & Kuo, 1988). For example, African-American adults are more likely than white American adults to seek formal help (i.e., mental health professionals, teachers, lawyers, social workers, and emergency medical personnel; Broman 1987; Broman, Neighbors, & Taylor, 1989). As members of an ethnic minority that is often the object of prejudice and discrimination, African Americans may simply experience more stress in their day-to-day lives than do whites. This appears to be true; studies that have compared stress levels in various ethnic groups have found that non-Hispanic whites report less stress than do African Americans, Puerto Ricans, or Mexican Americans (Kessler, 1979; Golding & Burnam, 1990).

In summary, demographic differences may produce different personal and social standards of behavior which play major roles in determining whether people will seek help for their problems. However, as we have noted before, we must be careful in interpreting these demographic differences. Unlike the methods used in experimental research, it is impossible to assign people randomly to different sex, socioeconomic class, age, or ethnic groups. Thus, it is best to think of the demographic variables as being correlates of help seeking and to remain cognizant that the factors that go along with being a certain sex or belonging to a particular ethnic group are often the true causes of differences in social behavior.

Personality Characteristics

Personality not only affects help giving (see Chapter 6), it may also influence the likelihood that help will be sought. We now consider two personality traits that have been found to be important in help seeking.

Self-esteem. Because the act of requesting help may challenge one's sense of control and perception of self-competence, individual differences in self-esteem would appear to be particularly relevant to this behavior. Who is *less* likely to seek help, people with low or high self-esteem? One line of reasoning suggests that it would be people of high self-esteem; they have more to lose by asking for help. Alternatively, it may be people of low self-esteem, who may feel even more vulnerable if they ask for help. In general, findings from both field and laboratory research supports the first argument. People with high self-esteem are less willing than people with low self-esteem to ask for help (e.g., Miller, 1985; Nadler & Fisher, 1986; Weiss & Knight, 1980; Wills & DePaulo, 1991). For instance, alcoholics with low self-esteem and abused women with low self-esteem are more likely to seek treatment or counseling (Frieze, 1979; Miller, 1985). Similarly, Nadler, Mayseless, Peri, and Chemerinski (1985) found that high self-esteem subjects are less likely to seek help on tasks that involve intellectual and cognitive abilities.

Of course, it is possible that people with high self-esteem seek help less often than those with low self-esteem because they do not believe they need it as much. Although this interpretation is plausible, it cannot explain all the results. Even in experiments that controlled for the amount of help needed (e.g., presenting subjects with an unsolvable problem), individuals higher in self-esteem were less likely to seek help (Nadler, 1986). Maintaining self-esteem seems particularly important to people who have a very positive self-image. Because of the potential damage of help seeking to their image of competence and control, these people are hesitant to seek assistance from others.

Following this logic, one would expect that the effects of self-esteem would interact with whether or not the help seeker could reciprocate the favor. Specifically, high self-esteem individuals should be more likely to ask the for help if they have a chance to pay the person back. Why? Because paying back the favor would enable the person to restore a positive self-image—he or she not only receives favors, but he or she *does* them as well. In the experiment just mentioned, Nadler (1986) measured self-esteem and manipulated whether the subjects believed that they would be able to reciprocate by later helping the person who helped them. Figure 7.3 shows the results of this experiment. Note that among the low self-esteem subjects, reciprocity had little effect on help seeking, but among the high self-esteem subjects the belief that they would be able to reciprocate the favor greatly increased their willingness to ask for help.

Is it wise for high self-esteem people to be reluctant to seek help? Perhaps not always. Weiss and Knight (1980) conducted a study in which, as expected, low self-esteem subjects requested more help than high self-esteem subjects. More important, Weiss and Knight also found that, as a result of asking for help, the products that the low self-esteem subjects produced in the study were actually better than the products of the self-sufficient, high self-esteem subjects. If one is willing to accept a small

FIGURE 7.3
High self-esteem subjects seek more help when they believe that they can later reciprocate aid than when they cannot; low self-esteem people seek help regardless of the opportunity to reciprocate. (Adapted from Nadler, 1986.)

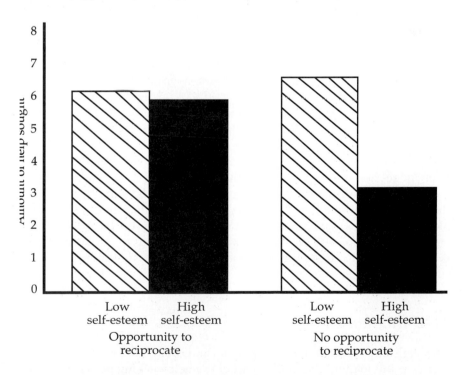

threat to one's self-image in the short term by asking for help, one may realize the long-term benefit of helping. Weiss and Knight argue that help seeking in such a situation may demonstrate the "utility of humility."

We would be remiss in our examination of self-esteem and help seeking if we did not also consider whether this personality characteristic affects help seeking in close relationships. In a study of college students, Caldwell and Reinhart (1988) found that students with high self-esteem, were somewhat *more* likely to receive social support from their families than were students with low self-esteem. We suspect this was because students with high self-esteem had good relations with their families and did not feel that their self-esteem would be threatened by asking their parents or siblings for help. So high levels of self-esteem are not always associated with less help seeking.

Shyness. Another personality trait that appears to be related to help seeking is shyness. Indeed, in his book on shyness, Philip Zimbardo (1977) argued that one of the most serious consequences of being shy is an unwillingness to ask for help. People who are shy usually have low self-esteem (Cheek, Malchior, & Carpentieri, 1986), but there is more to shyness than just low self-esteem. Shy individuals are also anxious and unsure of themselves in social situations and often try to avoid interacting with others (Wills & DePaulo, 1991). This social anxiety even seems to affect people's ability to obtain aid from their social-support network. Caldwell and Reinhart (1988) found a negative relationship between social anxiety and the amount of social support college students received from friends, especially friends of the other sex. Similarly, DePaulo, Dull, Greenberg, and Swaim (1989) found that shy people were especially unlikely to ask for help when the other person was a member of the opposite sex.

An additional reason why shy individuals may be reluctant to seek help is because they fear that either they will do poorly in the interaction with the helper or the helper may simply reject their request. This latter fear has some basis in fact. DePaulo et al. found that shy people were less likely to get help from a member of the opposite sex. This may have been a case of a self-fulfilling prophecy; that is, because the shy people expect their requests to be rejected, they act in a manner that makes this more likely. As Barbee (1990) has noted, in the case of social support, the manner in which people ask for support and their reactions to the support that is offered strongly affects the behavior of the person who can provide the support.

The Situation and Help Seeking

Although individual differences play an important role in help seeking, there are still many pieces of this part of the help-seeking puzzle missing.

As is true with almost all social behaviors, the situation also exerts a strong influence on help seeking. For example, as we have already mentioned, the ability to reciprocate the help has a great impact on whether a person will ask for help. In general, the less able a person is to repay a favor, the less likely he or she is to ask for help (Morris & Rosen, 1973; Nadler, 1991; Wills, 1992). Also, if asking for help has the effect of making a large number of other people aware of the help seeker's problem, help seeking decreases (Wills & DePaulo, 1991). It is for this reason that people with problems sometimes turn to impersonal sources for help.

Seeking impersonal help can reduce the psychological costs of requesting aid (e.g., embarrassment, threat to self-esteem and one's sense of personal control), because little or no social comparison takes place when impersonal help is used (Tesser, 1988). The success of crisis hotlines for providing aid to rape and assault victims or to those considering suicide has been attributed, in part, to the anonymity that such programs provide the callers (Hill & Harmon, 1976; Raviv, Raviv, & Yunowitz, 1989).

Despite the advantage of minimizing psychological costs, the disadvantages of impersonal sources involves the quality of help provided. Because of the nature of these sources, communication is less open and interactive. The help received may therefore not be satisfying. Thus, although there are some circumstances under which impersonal help may be preferable, in many cases those in need prefer help from other *people* if the problem to be solved is a significant one.

The nature of the problem. One major situational determinant of whether people will seek help and the kind of help they will seek is the specific problem they confront. Some problems make it less likely that people will ask for help. Abraham Tesser and his associates (1988) have found that feeling inferior to a comparable or similar person on a dimension that is important to one's self-concept is much more threatening than feeling less competent than a dissimilar person. Imagine yourself in such a situation—a classmate, who went to the same high school as you did, can easily solve a mathematics problem that has you totally befuddled. You would probably feel inadequate because someone similar to you can solve the problem, but you cannot. Further, because asking for help may imply lower competence, you may be reluctant to ask this similar person for help under these circumstances.

Nadler (1987) conducted an experiment that provides empirical support for this idea. The subjects were Israeli high school students who were either high or low in self-esteem. Their task was to solve some very difficult, almost unsolvable, anagrams within three minutes. After they had worked on the anagrams and had not solved them, they were given the chance to ask another subject of the same sex for help. Although, in fact, this person did not exist, subjects believed that they would see him or her later on. Nadler manipulated two variables in this experiment. First, he led some subjects to believe they were very similar to the potential helper and others to believe they were not similar. Second, he told some subjects that performance on the anagram task was highly correlated with intelligence and academic achievement, but he told others that performance depended on a person's mood and luck. In Nadler's terms, he manipulated the *ego-centrality* of the task. A task that involves some central and important aspect of a person's character or personality, such as their intelligence, is high in ego-centrality. The dependent measure was a composite score based on the amount of help the subjects requested.

Nadler predicted that subjects would be threatened by the possibility that they needed help on a task that was central to their character. Asking for help from someone who was similar to them would intensify these feelings of inadequacy, because seeking help would force them to compare their performance to a similar person who evidently did not need help on the task. Therefore, they would be reluctant to ask for help. These feelings would, of course, be greatest among the subjects who were high in self-esteem. Figure 7.4 presents the results of Nadler's experiment. As predicted, when the task was ego-central, subjects were less likely to ask the similar person for help. Figure 7.4 also shows that this effect was much stronger for high than low self-esteem subjects (also see Nadler, Fisher, & Ben-Itzhak, 1983; Nadler & Fisher, 1986). Evidently when a task is very relevant to a person's self-image or self-esteem and asking for help would threaten these, people may be more motivated to look and feel good than to solve the problem. This appears to provide another example of Weiss and Knight's (1980) concept of the utility of humility.

It must be recognized, however, that in this experiment the potential helper, while similar to the help seeker, was still a stranger. Would similarity affect help seeking among close friends in the same manner? Apparently not; many studies of social support suggest that people are more willing to ask similar others (i.e., relatives and friends) for help with problems than they are to ask dissimilar others (i.e., professionals). For example, Wills (1992) reported that people with personal or emotional problems were two to three times more likely to ask for informal help from people in their social support than to ask for help from a professional. Even when people seek organized formal support for a specific problem, they are as likely to join a self-help group comprised of people with the same problem (e.g., an alcoholic joining Alcoholics Anonymous) as they are to go to a professional who treats such problems. In 1990, it was estimated that from 10 to 15 million Americans (about 6 percent of all the people in the United States) were members of such self-help groups (Leerhsen, Lewis, Pomper, Davenport, & Nelson, 1990).

So, we have an inconsistency with regard to the effects of similarity on help seeking. Similarity inhibits help seeking among strangers and facilitates help seeking among close friends. Fortunately, earlier in the chapter, a reasonable explanation of this difference was provided. Recall

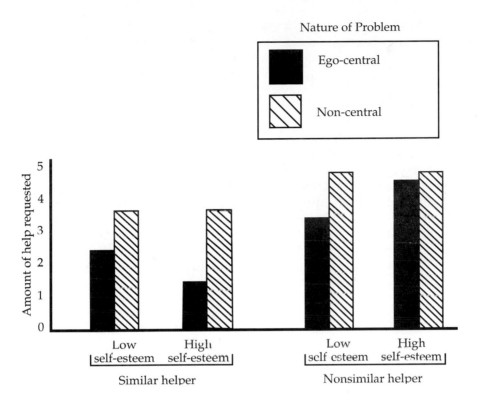

FIGURE 7.4
People are less likely to seek help from a person who is more similar to them, particularly when they have high self-esteem and the task performance is seen as central to their self-image. (Adapted from Nadler, 1987.)

the distinction between an exchange relationship and a communal relationship. Whereas the people in Nadler's experiment probably (correctly) saw themselves in an exchange relationship with a similar *stranger*, people are likely to see their relationship with similar friends and relatives as a communal one. In such relationships, help seekers may feel that they can expose their weaknesses and problems to others without a great deal of fear that they will be ridiculed or rejected.

There is another aspect to how problem characteristics can affect help seeking. It seems that people react differently to problems which affect parts of their lives. Studies of when and how people react to these problems provide us with both theoretical and practical information about help seeking. In the next section, we examine help seeking in response to three different kinds of problems: academic, medical, and psychological.

Academic problems. If you are like most students, you occasionally need some assistance in order to grasp a difficult concept in class or solve a particularly confusing problem. In such circumstances, there are two strategies that you might use to understand the concept or solve the problem. First, you might simply go to classmates and ask them if they would complete the problem for you or allow you to copy their work. Karabenick and Knapp (1988) refer to this as *executive help seeking*, which they define as "help seeking that is designed to decrease the cost of completing tasks by enlisting the aid of others" (p. 221). Alternatively, you might go to your classmate and ask for a little hint or advice about how to approach the problem. This is called *instrumental help seeking*, which focuses on understanding the process for finding the solution rather than simply obtaining the correct answer. This distinction is not unlike the old adage that if you give people fish, they will eat for a day, but if you teach them how to fish, they will be able to feed themselves forever.

The benefits of instrumental help seeking, if it is appropriate and reciprocal, may go well beyond its academic value. It can also improve social

In academic settings, receiving help from a teacher is a generally accepted part of the learning process and should not threaten the student's self-image. In this case, the teacher is providing instrumental help that is intended to help. (AP/Wide World Photos)

relations. As we saw in Chapter 1, *cooperation* relates to the give and take of individual resources to achieve a collective goal. *Cooperative learning* activities in classroom settings involve the mutual sharing of information and expertise in which each person gives and receives help from others (see Aronson & Gonzalez, 1988; Johnson, Johnson, Tiffany, & Zaidman, 1983). Not only is this method educationally effective, but the reciprocal help giving and receiving that occurs in cooperative learning may be a very effective strategy for improving race relations in desegregated schools (McConahay, 1981; Slavin, 1990).

In contrast to the social benefits of mutual, instrumental helping relationships, executive help seeking may be detrimental to peer relations. For example, Sharon Nelson-LeGall and her colleagues (e.g., Nelson-LeGall & Glor-Scheib, 1986) found that executive help seeking was maladaptive, particularly when the student had not made a good faith effort to solve the problems alone. Students who sought help under these conditions were held in lower regard by their peers. In contrast, students who were more restrained in their requests for help and sought instrumental aid only after they had given it the "good old college try" were the ones who were viewed more positively.

The potential impact of academic help seeking on one's social and self-image suggests that people who need help the most may be the ones least likely to seek it. What is the relationship between academic need and help seeking? In one study, researchers asked over 600 students what grade they expected to receive in their introductory psychology course and what kinds of help they had sought and actually obtained during the semester (Karabenick & Knapp, 1988). Intuition might suggest that those students with the greatest need (that is, those making the lowest grades) would be the ones most likely to seek help and that those students in the least need (that is, those making high grades) should be among the least likely to seek help. But this was not what the study found. Although students who expected to receive poor grades recognized that they were in serious need of help, they were no more likely than "A" students to actually seek help from their professor, tutors, or friends. The students who sought help most frequently were those in the middle of the grade distribution. For poor students, asking for help may be a public acknowledgment of their lack of competence and control. Students who do poorly in their courses may make self-defeating attributions to account for their performances. These students may rationalize that there is nothing that can be done to improve their situation and, as a consequence, they may experience a feeling of learned helplessness. These expectations of future failure coupled with the negative emotions engendered by the helplessness may lead to withdrawal from the very activities that could help them most.

Medical problems. Because of the potential threat to one's very survival, medical problems represent particularly critical need situations.

Ostrove and Baum (1983) provided an overview of when people will seek help for medical problems. They distinguished between *curative* and *preventive* help seeking. The former involves seeking medical help because of some current or ongoing problem; the latter involves seeking medical help to prevent future problems. We will focus primarily on curative actions because they represent clearer examples of seeking medical help.

As you might suspect, the presence of clear symptoms is the primary determinant of whether a person will seek curative medical help. Symptoms that are numerous, severe, and interfere with the person's daily activities are likely to result in a visit to the doctor or clinic. In contrast, symptoms that a person has experienced frequently and with which he or she is familiar are unlikely to result in the seeking medical help unless the person has adopted a "sick role." People who adopt this role view themselves are being in chronically poor health and see all their symptoms as requiring medical attention. Such individuals are likely to visit their physician or health clinic quite often.

It should be noted that people may also seek medical help for non-medical problems. For example, Wills and DePaulo (1991) observed that people with psychological and personal problems often seek professional help from a physician rather than a mental health professional. Moreover, there is strong evidence that people with mental health problems are much more likely to seek help for their medical ailments than are those without mental health problems (Shapiro et al., 1984).

Although people are more likely to seek formal, professional help for medical problems than for psychological problems, when confronted with serious medical problems, people frequently turn to their friends and families as well. A recent longitudinal survey of how 530 homosexual men coped with their concerns about HIV and AIDS is illustrative of this kind of help seeking (Hayes, Catania, McKusick, & Coates, 1990). Homosexual men who were HIV-negative or who had not been tested sought help mainly from their peers. In contrast, AIDS-diagnosed respondents sought help more often and from a wider range of sources. Although they saw their peers as the most helpful group, they actively solicited assistance from professionals and family as well.

Why is it that homosexual men who are HIV-negative or who have not been tested are less likely to use professional and medical services than homosexual men with diagnosed cases of AIDS? Feelings of personal threat and the costs of asking versus not asking for help may be the key to this puzzle. Because of the strong negative stigmas attached to homosexuality and AIDS in our society (Pryor, Reeder, & McManus, 1991), many gay men may fear seeking help for medical problems associated with either of these characteristics. This fear prevents them from seeking help from strangers. Once they *know* they have AIDS, the perceived social costs associated with seeking help are probably far outweighed by the perceived medical and physical costs of not seeking treatment. Thus, the person may be more willing to seek assistance from a wider range of potential helpers.

Psychological problems. Psychological problems are quite pervasive; approximately one person in five in the United States receives professional help for psychological problems. But as suggested above, many more people do not seek professional help they need because of their concerns about how others will perceive them (Wills, 1992). Thus, we see once again that short-term concerns about one's image may prevent people from taking action that may be in their long-term best interest. There are several additional factors that influence whether people will seek psychological assistance.

Not surprisingly, the severity of the psychological problem plays a major role in an individual's decision of whether to seek help. For example, it has been found that women who were more debilitated by their depression were more likely to seek help from a psychological professional (Dew, Dunn, Bromet, & Schulberg, 1988). Just as the cost of helping plays a major role in determining whether the potential helper will provide assistance (see Chapter 2), the anticipated costs of *not* getting help are important in determining whether people seek assistance. Serious and undeniable psychological impairment can thus trigger the help-seeking process.

Second, as suggested earlier, the controllability of the problem is critical. People are motivated to seek help when they believe that they are losing control of an important aspect of their lives that is ultimately controllable. College students who use their university's psychological services tend to see themselves as the primary cause of their problems but also as being *personally* unable to solve or control these problems (Simoni, Adelman, & Nelson, 1991). Nevertheless, if problems persist and become so serious that people come to believe that they are uncontrollable, they will no longer be motivated to seek help. People may simply decide to give up.

Wolcott (1986) surveyed nearly 300 recently divorced people about their help-seeking actions prior to divorce. Although they all recognized the seriousness of their problems, she found that about half the respondents did not seek formal assistance to help save their marriages. Why not? The primary thing that differentiated these couples from those that did seek help was their beliefs about whether they could do anything to avoid a divorce; that is, whether they had any control over the solution of their marital problems. The people who did not seek help believed that the relationship could not be saved and that "things" could not be changed. Thus, there was no need to seek help. Interestingly, even though the marriages of those who sought professional help (from marriage counselors, psychologists, the clergy, or other professionals) also ended in divorce, these people reported benefiting from having had an opportunity to express their feelings and from the support they had received. Whether the severity of the problems experienced by couples who sought or did not seek help was different is not clear; what is important is that they *perceived* the controllability of their situations differently and reacted accordingly on the basis of those perceptions.

Beliefs held about mental health providers and services are a third critical dimension of help seeking for psychological problems. In contrast to fifty or even twenty-five years ago, there are a substantial number of mental health professionals in most communities who could provide help with personal and psychological problems. Yet no more than 20 percent of people with such problems turn to these professional helpers; instead they seek assistance from friends, family members, members of the clergy, and medical doctors (Wills, 1992; Wills & DePaulo, 1991).

It is likely that traditional stigmas associated with having psychological problems prevent many people from seeking formal assistance (Sibicky & Dovidio, 1986). In general, the more negatively people feel about having psychological problems, the less likely they will be to seek help from mental health professionals. Further, even those who seek professional assistance often do it at unnecessary expense. To avoid potential stigmatization, they will pay for it privately rather than use insurance benefits for mental health care provided by their employers (Sobel, 1981).

Cultural changes have taken place over the years, and the stigma attached to seeing a mental health professional has declined. For example, in one study, subjects evaluated college students who had sought professional help for their psychological problems more positively than students who had the same problems but did not seek assistance (Dovidio, Fishbane, & Sibicky, 1985). Thus, although this stigma still exists, it is not as prevalent as it once was. As a result, increasing numbers of people have sought psychological/counseling services they need to help them cope with their problems (Horwitz, 1987). But as we have noted repeatedly, it still seems to be a relatively underused kind of helping.

Although there are many other variables that can affect the person's decision to ask for help, we must leave this aspect of help seeking and turn to the third part of Gross and McMullen's model—decisions about who the help seeker wants to provide the help.

Seeking Help: Whom Shall I Ask?

The last step in the help seeker's decision-making process concerns how to actually implement the decision to seek help (Gross & McMullen, 1983). Once the decision has been made to seek help, the person must decide whom to ask for help. Sometimes there may be no options available in terms of help from others. But in other circumstances, the person in need may have several alternatives from which to choose. There may be different costs associated with seeking help from different sources, and these costs are central to this decision.

One possible way to minimize the social costs of seeking help (e.g., the impressions of others) is to choose impersonal help; the requester is able to minimize the costs by eliminating the social costs of helping. But as noted earlier, impersonal, inanimate sources of help (e.g., self-help books on a particular problem) may not always be very useful for solving one's problems. Thus, in most instances, people in need turn to personal sources—other people. But what kind of people do they choose? Which source a person chooses is again determined by the trade-off between the amount of material assistance and the threat to one's feelings of competence and control.

Similarity to the help provider. Surveys of help seeking for personal and psychological problems strongly indicate that we are likely to ask our friends, or at least people who are similar to us, for assistance for many of our problems. According to Wills (1992), people who seek help for psychological problems are about five times as likely to seek it from their friends, other family members, or other acquaintances as they are to seek it from professionals. Of course, we also know that in laboratory experiments subjects are often reluctant to ask similar others for help.

We do not need to spend much time on this issue here. Recall from our earlier discussions that these differences are probably due to differences in the nature of the relationship between the person asking for help and the potential helper. For a number of reasons, researchers usually arrange experiments so that the participants do not know the person whom they must ask for help, even if he or she is presented as similar to them. Thus, subjects have not had and do not expect to have a close, long-term relationship with this person. As a result, there is no history of having helped the person or any expectation that such opportunities will arise in the future. Further, this is an *exchange relationship,* in which favors must be repaid and saving face is important. One consequence of this is that people are reluctant to seek help from similar people.

Before we leave this matter, however, we want to be sure that we do not overstate the differences in the findings obtained inside the laboratory and those obtained outside the laboratory. For example, both approaches indicate that help seekers are concerned about their self-image when they ask for help. Recall the nonlaboratory studies of school children asking for help with their schoolwork. DePaulo et al. (1989) and Newman and Goldin (1990) both found that children were often concerned about looking dumb if they asked for help. This is essentially what Nadler (1987) found in his laboratory experiment on people seeking help with problems high in ego-centrality. Moreover, in recent years researchers have begun to conduct laboratory experiments on help seeking among friends (see Barbee, 1990; Barbee et al., 1993; Derlega et al., 1994). The experiments that use friends as subjects produce the kinds of results that the field research on help seeking would predict. Namely, similarity between the requester and potential provider typically does not inhibit a person's willingness to seek help. So, in the final analysis, we find convergence between laboratory and field studies of help seeking. Similarity is likely to inhibit help seeking when the potential provider is a stranger or the parties are in an exchange relationship; it is likely to facilitate helping in a communal relationship.

Social comparison. Another characteristic of the potential helper that may influence help seekers' choices is how they compare themselves to that person. If they are making the request primarily because they want the person to help them solve a problem and improve themselves, they will probably choose someone with more competence, expertise, or information about the matter at hand than they possess. This is called an *upward comparison*—we compare ourselves to someone who is doing better than we are (Medvene, 1992). In contrast, if people's self-esteem is seriously threatened by the problem and they want to bolster their self-image, they will probably make a *downward comparison*—we select someone with less experience or expertise than us, who is not doing as well as we are with the problem (Taylor & Lobel, 1989; Wills, 1983).

If a person is threatened by a problem, but makes an upward comparison in choosing a helper, this may produce what Wills (1983) has called the *paradox of help seeking*—the person seeks help from someone who could threaten his or her self-image and cause further self-devaluation. What do people actually do when seeking help? Although laboratory experiments suggest a preference for downward comparisons, there is evidence from field studies that help seekers are also interested in finding someone who can actually help them solve their problems and thus may strike a balance between upward and downward comparisons.

For example, Medvene (1992) examined college students' preferences for selecting someone to help them with their academic and social problems. They were asked to choose among several different potential helpers. Among their choices were other students with the same problems as theirs, who were either better, worse, or equal to them in their ability to solve them (so-called similar peers), other students who did not have the same problems but who did have formal training and expertise in solving these problems (trained paraprofessionals), and professional experts in the problem area.

The students' choices reflected concern for both self-improvement and for their self-image. Specifically, by far the most frequent choice for a helper (50 percent for academic problems; 58 percent for social problems) was a similar peer who was *better* at solving their problems than the help seekers. The most common reason the students gave for doing this was that it would lead to self-improvement. The fact that they chose the best peer supports this claim. But notice that they did not select the *most* qualified individuals—the paraprofessionals or the professionals. Medvene suggests that this preference represents a compromise between self-improvement and self-enhancement concerns. He further notes that this is the kind of choice usually found in field studies of help seeking. For example, when people join support groups such as Alcoholics Anonymous, they are given a sponsor, someone further along in the treatment program who is able to help them (an upward comparison), but very soon they agree to serve as a sponsor themselves, helping someone not as far along in the recovery process as they are (a downward comparison; Medvene, 1992).

Summary

We began this chapter by noting that seeking help is at least as complex a process as giving help. Even before we could address the first question of interest, it was necessary to consider the relationship between the help seeker and the potential help giver, and to recognize that this plays an important role in when and how people ask for help, and the kind of help they receive. Help seeking is much more common among close friends and people in communal relationships than among strangers and people in exchange relationships. And when friends help one another, the kind of help they are most likely to give is social support that helps a person solve the problem or cope with the stresses created by the problem.

But whether we are considering strangers or friends, people who appear to be in need of assistance do not always ask for help. Why? To answer this question we used Gross and McMullen's decision-tree model of help seeking. This model proposes that before asking for help, the person makes three interrelated decisions. The first is whether a problem exists that requires help. If there is a problem, the person must decide whether seeking help for it is really the best course of action. If seeking help is the best course, then the person must decide whom to ask for this help.

The major dilemma for the help seeker in the last two decisions is the conflict between the need to improve his or her situation and the need to preserve his or her self-image. The three major things that affect estimates of these rewards and costs are the personal attributes of the person in need, the situation in which help would be given, and characteristics of the potential helper. With regard to the first of these, we saw that both demographic (e.g., age, gender) and personality characteristics (e.g., self-esteem, shyness) of the potential recipient affect estimates of the costs of asking for help versus the costs of not asking for help. For example, high self-esteem individuals usually see help as much more threatening to their self-image than do low self-esteem people.

The characteristics of the situation were also shown to affect help-seeking decisions. One of these characteristics is the extent to which the problem reflects upon the self and the social image of the person in need. If the problem is one that is directly relevant to the traits and characteristics that are central to these images (i.e., high in ego-centrality), it is unlikely that the person will ask for help. Another characteristic of the situation that affects help seeking is the ability to reciprocate the favor; people are generally reluctant to ask for help if they believe they will be expected to repay it but feel they will be unable to do so.

The decision about whom to ask for help is strongly influenced by the characteristics of the potential helper. If people in need must rely on another person to provide the necessary help, they will try to keep the self-image and social impression costs as low as possible. They will usually choose friends with whom they have long-standing, communal relationships. In such relationships, a single request for help should have relatively little impact on the way they are evaluated by the helper and others. But, even in these relationships, people are sensitive to the threat to their self-image of asking for help. Often they will prefer to ask someone who can provide help without being *too* threatening to their self-esteem rather than ask the most competent person for help.

Thus, we see that just as potential helpers weigh the costs of helping and not helping (see Chapter 2), potential recipients weigh the costs of asking for aid against the potential benefits of receiving help. If the recipient believes the costs of asking a certain person for help outweigh the benefits, the recipient will refrain from asking that person for the help, even though an observer may clearly recognize the need. Help seeking (or the failure to seek help) is probably a more difficult puzzle for an outside observer to understand than is help giving. This is because the costs considered by the recipient are often egocentrically based; that is, the costs reflect the recipient's personal feelings and perceptions of how he or she would feel if help were given. The recipient may fail to fully take into account the objective benefits that might accrue if help were given. This leads us to the second question in this chapter: Why do people sometimes react negatively to being helped?

RECIPIENTS' REACTIONS TO HELP

Once the person in need has received help, there are still social and psychological consequences that must be considered if we are to complete the help-seeking puzzle. On the one hand, it seems that the recipient should be pleased that the problem has been confronted and dealt with successfully. One would expect the recipient to be thankful for the helper's contributions and appreciative of the assistance. This is certainly the expectation of many egoistically motivated helpers who may have offered the assistance primarily to make themselves feel good and who are looking for a word of thanks to bolster their own self-image (see Chapter 3). On the other hand, the recipient may experience self-doubts about his or her competence and feel that the relationship with the helper has been changed as a result of the help received. These consequences are the costs that were considered when deciding whether or not to ask for assistance, and these reactions represent the "bill" that comes due after the help has been received.

Consider the following situation. You are playing a game similar to Monopoly, in which you invest money in the stock market. The rules of the game are such that if your stocks increase in value, you win a large amount of money. If the value of your stocks decline, however, and you lose a certain amount, you are eliminated from the game. Initially, you will play this game by yourself, but later in the game you will compete against another player who is in an adjoining room. Your investments do not go well, and soon you are facing elimination from the game. At this point, you receive an envelope that you did not ask for from the other player. The envelope contains enough money for you to continue the game. How do you feel? Elated at your good fortune or threatened by this unsolicited help?

Nadler, Altman, and Fisher (1979) placed subjects in this situation and compared their mood and self-image (e.g., how intelligent they thought they were) to the mood and self-image of subjects who were in the same situation but did not receive this unsolicited help. Nadler et al. found that the subjects' reactions to the help depended on their self-esteem. As we would expect, high and low self-esteem subjects reacted quite differently. Unexpected, unsolicited help improved the mood and self-image of the low self-esteem subjects, relative to the no-help group. But among the high self-esteem subjects, helping hurt both their mood and their self-image. Nadler and Mayseless (1983) suggest that the unsolicited help that subjects received in this experiment had this effect on the high self-esteem subjects because it was inconsistent with their self-image of being highly competent, independent individuals who had considerable control over what happened to them. But such negative reactions to help are not confined to high self-esteem individuals. Any individual who perceives help as threatening rather than supportive is likely to react negatively to it.

Arie Nadler and Jeffrey Fisher have proposed a comprehensive model that attempts to predict and explain people's positive and negative reactions in situations such as these. It is called the threat to self-esteem model of reactions to help (Fisher, Nadler, & Whitcher-Alagna, 1982; Nadler & Fisher, 1986) and is presented in Figure 7.5. We shall use this model to help us answer the last question in this chapter—why are people sometimes not pleased when they receive help with a problem?

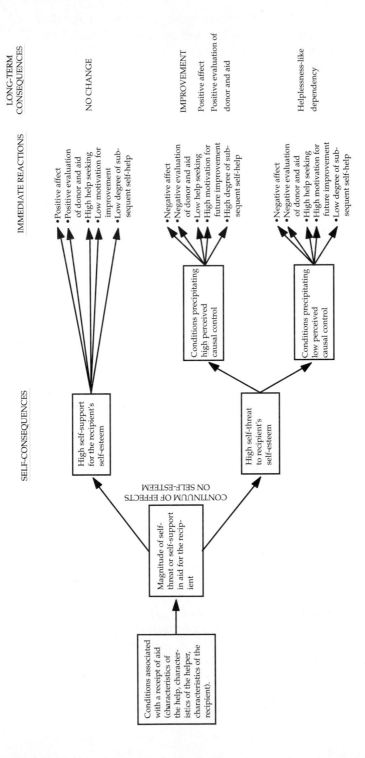

FIGURE 7.5
Schematic diagram of the threat × control model of reaction to help. [From "The role of threat to self-esteem and perceived control in recipient reaction to help: Theory development and empirical validation." A. Nadler & J. D. Fisher (1986). In L. Berkowitz (Ed.), *Advances in experimental social psychology*, Vol. 19, p. 95, San Diego, CA: Academic Press. Copyright 1986 by Academic Press. Reprinted by permission.]

Threat to Self-Esteem Model

The threat to self-esteem model provides a comprehensive description of how people react to help that they receive from others. The components of the model integrate the results of many of the studies that have been presented in this chapter. A very important premise of the model is its assumption that receiving help is neither all good nor all bad; it is the relative amounts of self-threat and self-support that ultimately determine a particular recipient's reaction to being helped. The model begins by considering the kind of help that is given, the person who gives it, and the person who receives it (see the box on the far left of Figure 7.5). As we have seen, these variables individually and in combination affect how the recipient perceives being helped. Helping can either been seen as threatening or supportive by the recipient (the next set of boxes in the model). Let us examine each of these reactions.

Threatening help. Think back to a time when you were younger. How many times did you respond to efforts of help from your brother or sister by saying, "Leave me alone! Let me do it myself." Many times reactions such as these to others' offers to help may seem overly negative and unjustifiable to others. Nevertheless, the threat to self-esteem model predicts this response. In general, people are most likely to see help as threatening when it (1) comes from someone who is socially comparable to the recipient; (2) threatens the recipient's freedom and autonomy; (3) implies an obligation to repay the favor, but provides no opportunity to do so; (4) suggests that the recipient is inferior to and dependent upon the helper; (5) is received for an ego-central task; and (6) is inconsistent with the positive aspects of the recipient's self-concept. Such help produces defensiveness and negative feelings in the recipient. Thus, people often respond defensively to help from a brother or sister, particularly when they normally feel more dominant and competent to their sibling but have low-esteem relative to their peers (Searcy & Eisenberg, 1992).

Similarly, although peer tutoring is now popular in many schools, it may sometimes have adverse psychological consequences. DePaulo and her colleagues (1989) found that many fourth graders feel threatened by peer tutoring. These children tend to react in two different ways. Those who believe that they are capable of doing better on their own try even harder. However, those who feel that they are unable to master the material respond by giving up and doing very poorly on the task. Why do people respond in these different ways? Three general theories of social behavior can be used to explain why acts of helping may sometimes be seen as threatening and to predict how people react to this threat. They are equity theory, reactance theory, and attribution theory.

Equity theory, which was discussed in Chapter 3, proposes that people involved in an interaction desire and expect that the outcomes from the interaction will be proportional to the resources each person has expended. Those who give a lot, get a lot; those who give little, get little. Equity theory is usually used to explain people's negative reactions when they do not get enough from an exchange, but it can also be used to explain negative reactions when they get too much from an exchange. Unsolicited or excessive help is one such situation (Hatfield & Sprecher, 1983). Recipients who think that they have received more than they deserve may feel overbenefited, and this can evoke feelings of guilt and the expectation that at some point they may be punished for this. The recipient is motivated to eliminate these aversive reactions by restoring equity. One obvious solution (and perhaps the preferable one) would be to reciprocate the favor as quickly as possible (Walster et al., 1978). But when the help cannot be easily reciprocated, equity theory suggests that people may dislike someone *because* that person helped them. For example, in a cross-cultural study, participants in Sweden, Japan, and the United States felt negatively toward people who helped them when there was no opportunity to repay the helper (Gergen, Morse, & Bode, 1974). This finding may help to explain why nations receiving foreign aid from the United States may develop anti-American attitudes. Similarly, in personal relations, helping may have negative consequences for the recipient and for the relationship between him or her and the person who gives the help.

A second theoretical explanation of these negative reactions to being helped is contained in *reactance theory* (Brehm, 1966; Brehm & Brehm, 1981). This theory of human motivation posits that people value their freedom and will attempt to reassert their freedom of choice whenever they feel it has been threatened. In the context of reactions to aid, recipients may feel that their behavioral freedom has been limited by help that they receive, because now they are, in some way, obligated to the helper. For example, in some cases, aid may be given with some limitations imposed. Has anyone ever offered you help *on the condition* that you do something for them? Although the intent of the person's actions may have been charitable, you were probably less than delighted at the prospects of receiving such assistance.

Finally, attribution theory provides yet another explanation of why people see some kinds of help as threatening. *Attribution theory* is concerned with how people make judgments about the causes of behavior (Heider, 1958; Jones & Davis, 1965; Jones & McGillis, 1976; Kelley, 1967, 1973). The context in which the help is offered can affect the recipient's attributions about a helper's real intentions. For example, suppose that you are in a debate and your opponent continually tries to clarify the moderator's questions for you. Rather than perceiving this as helpful behavior, the attribution that you are most likely to make is that your rival is trying to make you look incompetent. No prosocial motives will be attributed to the rival. However, if a person offers help with no obvious ulterior motives, altruistic attributions may be made, and positive evaluations of the donor should result.

Although these attributional processes may affect recipients' own judgments of the helper, recipients may also use attribution processes to try to determine the cause of their unfortunate predicament in the first place. The answer to this question may have significant implications for the help seeker's self-image (Tessler & Schwartz, 1972). For example, imagine that you are unable to solve some problem, but this is not your fault (e.g., an instructor in a chemistry class has gotten confused and given you a homework assignment that is much too difficult for anyone in the class to complete). Under these conditions, you can reasonably attribute your trouble to the difficulty of the task. You can receive help with little concern that others will make negative attributions about you, and you will be able to maintain a positive self-image. Now imagine that everyone else can easily solve the problem that is causing you trouble. Attribution theory suggests that you should attribute your trouble to your personal shortcomings. As a result, you may react negatively to even the most well-intended help.

Claude Steele (1992) discusses one implication of this process for people of color. In particular, he proposes that programs designed to be helpful but which primarily emphasize the deficiencies of a particular group create a "suspicion of inferiority" for recipients. This suspicion, if it is compounded by traditional stereotypes, is especially detrimental to participants' self-esteem. As a consequence, affirmative action programs may have many benefits for targeted groups, but they may also have damaging negative effects on the self-esteem of the beneficiaries (Major & Crocker, 1993).

Supportive help. Of course, it is also possible that the help will be seen as supportive. Supportive help is pretty much the polar opposite of threatening help: It usually comes from a noncomparable donor, it does not threaten the recipient's freedom and autonomy, it does not communicate inferiority or dependence, and it is much more consistent with the recipient's positive self-concept. The model proposes that supportive help produces a nondefensive reaction and positive feelings in the recipient (Fisher, Nadler, & Whitcher-Alagna, 1982, 1983; Nadler & Fisher, 1986).

Self-consequences and immediate reactions. The next part of the threat to self-esteem model considers how people react to help that is perceived as threatening or as supportive. As you can see in Figure 7.5, if the help is seen as supportive (the arrow in the figure that goes up), this has the self-consequences of providing support for the recipient's self-esteem. This, in turn, produces certain immediate reactions, such as a good mood in the recipient, good feelings about the helper, more help seeking, and a decrease in the tendency to engage in self-help and self-improvement.

However, if the help is seen as threatening (the arrow that goes down), this challenges the recipient's self-esteem and produces quite different immediate reactions. The specific character of these reactions depends on how this help affects the recipient's sense of control over the problem. If it *increases* the sense of control (arrow going up), the recipient will react negatively to the help and the helper and will be less likely to seek help from others; instead, the recipient will engage in more self-help and self-improvement and become more independent. Threatening help that *decreases* the sense of control (arrow going down) produces negative reactions toward the help and the helper as well, but it also produces an increase in help-seeking and decrease in self-help. Recipients become more dependent and continue to seek help because they believe that they cannot solve their problems on their own.

Long-term consequences. The final part of the model concerns the long-term consequences of receiving help. If the help is supportive of recipient's self-esteem, these consequences are the same as the immediate reactions—positive feelings about being helped and little inclination toward self-help. The long-term effects of help that threatens a person's self-esteem depends on how this action also affects the person's sense of control. If the aid is seen as threatening but *increases* the recipient's sense of control, there are negative immediate reactions, but later these feelings become positive. Why? It is because the help has enabled the person to feel that he or she can solve the problem and thus has improved the person's self-image. The person is a more competent, independent individual. For example, earlier we asked you to place yourself in a hypothetical situation where you could not solve a math problem, but a classmate could. Now imagine that the classmate who had no trouble with the problem tells you that she wants to show you how to solve it. This may be very threatening to you; but if, in the course of helping you, she gives you information that makes you "see the light" and realize how to solve this particular problem and other similar ones, this may increase your sense of control and self-confidence in dealing with mathematics. As a result your long-term reactions to this help will be positive.

Assistance that is threatening and *decreases* the sense of control produces negative immediate reactions and long-term feelings of helplessness and dependency. It convinces people that they need help to solve problems because they are not very competent. They continue to seek help, but this causes them considerable distress.

Extensions of the model. Nadler and Fisher originally developed this model to provide a comprehensive framework to describe how adults react to help. More recently, Shell and Eisenberg (1992) have adapted the threat to self-esteem model to explain how children react to being helped. There are, however, several differences between the original model and

Shell and Eisenberg's modified version of it. The major difference involves the effects of social-cognitive development on reactions to being helped. Specifically, the latter model proposes that a recipient's initial reaction to being helped (i.e., whether the help is seen as threatening or supportive) partially depends upon where the recipient is in social and cognitive development. As discussed earlier in Chapter 5, the cognitive development of young children (under 8 or 9 years) is still in its early stages, and they do not explain their own behavior and the behavior of others in the same ways as do adults. As a result, they do not react to being helped in the same ways as adults. For example, they respond very favorably to a helper even when they know the helper was told to offer them assistance, and they do not necessarily evaluate themselves negatively when they require help with some task (Shell & Eisenberg, 1992).

Another difference between the original model and the one proposed by Shell and Eisenberg was due to the context in which children usually are helped. Much of the help that children receive comes from someone whom they *expect* and *want* to help them—someone with whom they have a close and intimate relationship, such as a parent. As you have learned from our earlier discussions of communal exchanges, helping in these relationships is less likely to produce a negative reaction in the recipient. Thus, children may be less likely than adults to react negatively to being helped.

Despite these changes, Shell and Eisenberg agree with the basic premises of the original threat to self-esteem model. If help threatens a child's self-esteem and decreases his or her sense of control, it will produce feelings of dependency and helplessness in the child and an increased reliance on others for help with problems. Like adults, children will dislike the help they receive and the person who provides it.

THE ANSWER: SUMMARY AND IMPLICATIONS

In the final portion of the chapter, we considered the psychological impact that asking for help and receiving it can have on the recipient. We saw that these reactions can be negative or positive. Help that threatens the recipient's self-image and social image makes the recipient feel badly about himself or herself, the helper, and the help that is given. People may have negative reactions to receiving help because of concerns about equity, reactions to threats to their freedom and autonomy, or explanations of their behavior that would reflect poorly on them. But reactions to help are not always negative, and the threat to self-esteem model suggests the circumstances under which recipients will feel good about being helped. According to this model, in the long run, help that produces the most positive consequences for recipients is help that may initially challenge their self-esteem, but also makes them recognize that they have control over their environment. This gives them the sense of confidence, competence, and willingness to seek help when it is really needed and not to feel badly about this.

All the pieces of the puzzle are in place, and now we are ready to answer the questions that began this chapter. With regard to the first question, people sometimes do not seek the help that observers think they need because the person desires to maintain a positive self-image, and being helped in certain situations by certain individuals might threaten this. In some instances, this results in the person not asking for any help; in other instances, help is requested only from certain people; and, in still other instances, only certain types of help are solicited. The specific action people take depends on their relationship with the potential helper, their own personal attributes, the nature of the problem they confront, and the characteristics of the person who might help them. In most instances, the people we ask for help is someone with whom we have a long-term, fairly intimate relationship.

The second major question asked in this chapter was, Why are people not always pleased when someone helps them? The answer to it is quite similar to the answer to the first question. People will react negatively to help if the help threatens their self-image. The portion of the puzzle dealing with reactions to help has several additional pieces, however. Some kinds of help—those that increase a person's sense of control—may initially threaten the person and cause negative immediate emotional reactions, but they may also motivate people to work harder to improve themselves and to become more independent. The long-term reactions to this kind of help will be positive. Perhaps this is something we need to keep in mind when others offer to help us and when we offer help to them. One is reminded of Mark Twain's comment about how his parents got smarter and their advice got better as *he* got older! Maybe the same thing is true about the quality of some of the help we are offered but do not take.

Most of the questions we have posed about individuals giving and receiving help to one another have been answered. Most of the pieces in the individual puzzles we have described are now in their correct places and fit together without too much effort. But before we can turn to the final chapter and the questions we cannot answer and the puzzles that presently cannot be solved, we must return to one other aspect of helping and altruism. Because we were all trained as social psychologists, we have approached helping and altruism from the usual perspective for psychologists—we have considered helping and being helped at the individual or one-to-one level. To put it more formally, our "unit of analysis" has been the individual. Our colleagues in sociology and other disciplines (e.g., economics, political science) would point out, however, that there is also helping at the collective level—large groups of individuals banding together to address problems of common concern and acts of helping by individuals that benefit a large number of people. We consider the phenomenon of collective helping in the next chapter.

8

Cooperation and Collective Helping

❖

For most of this book we have concentrated on helping by individuals. More specifically, we have mainly considered one-on-one helping—one victim and one helper, who are usually strangers to one another—under circumstances that occur more or less unexpectedly. We have not yet addressed the societal context in which helping takes place. As psychologists usually do, we have focused on individuals rather than groups; in this chapter, however, we take a more collectivist view of helping. We consider people's helping behavior as it affects and is affected by their social group, their communities, and social institutions at large. In addition, we identify both similarities and differences between this type of prosocial action and the individual, spontaneous reactions that have been the focus of much of the previous chapters. And there are important differences. The puzzle of the type of helping that is the focus this chapter is more like a Rubik's Cube than the jigsaw puzzle metaphor we have been using. In collective helping, there is a greater interdependence between one person's actions and the actions of those around him or her, and the connection between the person's actions and the society in which he or she lives is one that cannot be broken. As John Donne said over 350 years ago:

> No man is an island, Intire of itself;
> Every man is a peece of the Continent,
> . . . Any man's death diminishes me,
> Because I am involved in mankind; and therefore
> Never send to know for whom the bell tolls,
> It tolls for thee.

THE QUESTION

We address two fundamental questions in this chapter. First, how can we encourage people to act prosocially when, in the short run, it may be in their best interests to be selfish? An example of this conflict is the issue of recycling. In terms of time and effort, it is easier not to recycle but instead to throw out cans, glass bottles, cardboard, newspapers, and plastics along with the rest of the trash. After all, it takes time and effort to sort containers and tie up newspapers and cardboard. In the short run, recycling is costly and thus *not* in one's interest.

If nobody recycles, however, there are long-term, negative consequences for each of us. There will be higher taxes to pay for the disposal of these waste products and new landfills will be needed in which to bury them. More natural resources (e.g., trees) will need to be consumed, which endangers other parts of the environment and ecosystem. At some time in the future, the world will probably face a shortage of these resources and may be unable to replenish them. This kind of problem is called a *social dilemma*, which we discussed briefly in Chapter 1. A social dilemma involves a conflict between an individual's desire to obtain the best personal (selfish) outcomes and the desire to maximize collective (e.g., group or societal) outcomes (Komorita & Parks, 1994; Liebrand, Wilke, & Messick, 1992). The first section of this chapter considers social dilemmas and asks the question of how we can get people to act prosocially when it may appear not to be in their immediate personal interests.

Whereas the section on social dilemmas highlights important conceptual issues in the decisions that *individuals* make in laboratory research, the second section of this chapter examines these and other principles in *collective action*—working to improve one's community. Most people agree that there is a growing need for individuals to contribute time and effort for the welfare of others. As federal and state governments find themselves less able or less willing to deal with mounting social problems, more private citizens will have to take this responsibility on themselves. How can we increase the number of people willing to assume this responsibility? To answer this question, we need to learn about the kinds of people who give their time and energy to the betterment of society and what motivates them.

SOCIAL DILEMMAS

Social dilemmas are conflicts between alternative courses of action that pit an individual's best interest against the best interest of some group, or collectivity, of which the individual is a member. Such conflicts are perhaps best illustrated by "the tragedy of the commons," which we also mentioned in Chapter 1. The commons tragedy was first described in the early nineteenth century by Lloyd (1833; cited by Dawes, 1975) and brought to the attention of contemporary researchers in many disciplines by a biologist, Garrett Hardin (1968). According to the story, citizens of a small New England community were permitted to graze their cattle on the town's common land (the commons). The only cost for grazing these cattle was depletion of the common pasture land, which was effectively shared by the community as a whole. Each citizen who chose to take advantage of the opportunity profited individually from the cattle that he or she privately owned but grazed on the public commons. In this situation, an individual's most rational course of action was to graze as many additional cattle as possible on the commons. This individually rational choice applied to each member of the community.

When too many citizens of the community decided to pursue this individual course of action, however, the cumulative consequences were tragic. So many cattle were brought to the commons that it was over-grazed, the grass was destroyed, the commons was lost as a resource, and the whole community suffered. Hardin views this final outcome of the commons dilemma as being inevitable: "Ruin is the destination toward which all men rush, each pursuing his own best interest in a society that believes in the freedom of the commons. Freedom in a commons brings ruin to all" (1968, p. 1244). In the pages that follow, we will consider the accuracy of Hardin's pessimistic viewpoint and under what circumstances people may choose to act prosocially.

Social dilemmas have two fundamental characteristics: (1) each individual receives a higher payoff for defecting from what is in the group's best interest (e.g., using all the available resources for one's own advantage) than for cooperating, no matter what the other individuals in the society do, but (2) all individuals are better off if they *all cooperate* than if they *all defect* (Dawes, 1980). As we saw in Chapter 2, situational features have a strong impact on individuals' decisions to spontaneously help another person. Situations also play an important role in how people respond to social dilemmas.

Although characteristics of specific dilemmas may vary greatly, there are three major types of social dilemmas. In general, people make different types of decisions as a function of whether there is a potential gain or loss. They are more willing to forgo potential gains than to give up resources they already possess. This is also an important distinction for types of social dilemmas. Social dilemmas can involve people's decisions to take resources that are available; these are called *take-some dilemmas*. There are two types of take-some social dilemmas: (1) resource management dilemmas that deal with *how much* people will use or abuse existing resources, and (2) social traps that focus on *trade-offs over time*, specifically the potential long-term negative effects of actions that are rewarding in the short run. The third type of dilemma is a *give-some*, or public goods, *dilemma* and involves how much of some personal resource people are willing to *give* to achieve some greater, collective good. These types of social dilemmas are but a few examples of the social dilemmas that face us everyday. Once the basic notion of a social dilemma is understood, we can find them everywhere. We only need to read the morning newspaper or watch the evening news to see multiple examples of apparently rational individual choices that lead to social, political, business, and environmental disasters for the collective group.

What can be done to encourage prosocial behavior and concern for the greater good in a social dilemma? Unlike the theories of spontaneous helping, such as Latané and Darley's decision-tree model or the arousal: cost-reward model introduced in Chapter 2, there are few comprehensive theories of behavior in social dilemmas. However, the research on spontaneous, individual helping may provide some clues to this part of the puzzle. We found in Chapter 2 that people weigh the costs and rewards associated with helping as they make their decisions. Perceptions of these costs and benefits may be influenced directly by varying the consequences of taking action (e.g., increasing personal danger) or indirectly by affecting a person's interpretation of the situation based on the behavior of other bystanders. The relationship of the bystander to the person in need is also important. The closer this connection, the more costly it is *not* to help, and consequently the more helpful people become. In addition, as we considered in Chapter 6, there are significant individual differences in the perceptions of costs and benefits and, thus, in how helpful different people are. In the next section we examine how these principles apply to actions in social dilemmas.

Determinants of Behavior in Social Dilemmas

Research on social dilemmas is extensive, and coverage of this area and related topics in cooperation and conflict merits a book by itself (see Komorita & Parks, 1994; see also Pruitt & Carnevale, 1993; Worchel & Simpson, 1993). Therefore, we provide a brief overview here primarily to illustrate the similarities between spontaneous helping and these types of collective actions. We consider four aspects of behavior in social dilemmas that directly relate to the processes we have considered throughout this book: the costs associated with various actions, social influence, the connection to others, and individual and cultural differences.

Costs and consequences. When people are in a social dilemma and have to decide whether to take the prosocial course of action, they consider the payoffs associated with immediate and long-term consequences of their actions. This should not be surprising by this point in the book. We have already seen that potential helpers and those in need of help engage in cost-benefit analyses when making their decisions; there is no reason to suspect that those in dilemmas would be any different. If people do not believe that their behavior will have a significant impact on the long-term consequences for the group, they will have little incentive to cooperate. For example, does it really matter whether you set your thermostat in the winter at 68 degrees or 65 degrees? If you were the only person to choose the higher temperature, there probably would be no real problem; the extra natural gas or electricity that you would consume to heat your house would have no meaningful impact on the world's energy reserves. But as we saw in the discussion above, it is the collective consequences of everyone choosing the higher setting that really matters.

Similarly, if people believe that their personal payoffs will be substantially higher if they defect than if they cooperate, it is unlikely that they will take the prosocial route. As the discrepancy increases, the motivation to defect becomes greater.

The influence of others. When psychologists, sociologists, or economists think about social dilemmas, they analyze the situation and think about it in terms of a payoff matrix that specifies exactly what will happen if everyone cooperates, if everyone defects, and all the possibilities in between. Using this type of analysis, they can then specify the optimal solution to the dilemma. But how do ordinary people make their decisions? Do they go through such a comprehensive analysis, or do they look for decision-making shortcuts to determine how they should act? In a series of studies on resource management dilemmas, Schroeder and his colleagues (Schroeder, Jensen, Reed, Sullivan, & Schwab, 1983) examined these questions. Subjects played a game in which they "harvested" poker chips worth different point values from a common resource pool over several trials; these points could be exchanged for money at the end of the game, so subjects were motivated to maximize their individual point totals. Each subject could keep all the points he or she individually took from the pool, but each member of a group would also be credited with the points remaining in their common resource pool (if any) at the end of the session.

Because of the way that the consequences were arranged, the optimal solution to this dilemma from the *group's* point of view was for each player to take the low-valued chips from the pool during the game, so that everyone would share the large point pool at the end of the game. The subjects were prohibited from communicating with one another and, therefore, were unable to discuss the pros and cons of the possible strategies or to coordinate their actions. But the subjects had been given sufficient information to determine the optimal strategy on their own and had been tested to ensure that they understood the nature of the dilemma situation. Rather than do a thorough analysis, however, they took a shortcut: they chose to imitate the actions of the other group members. They watched others taking high-value chips from the pool and quickly followed suit, leaving fewer points to be shared in the pool. As a result, their payoffs were less than they would have been had the subjects not gone for the immediate, individual payoff.

Why did these subjects pursue this self-defeating strategy? Recall from Chapter 2 how other bystanders can influence a person's decision to help in an emergency by influencing the interpretation of the event or permitting diffusion of responsibility to occur. Like the subjects in Latané and Darley's emergency intervention studies, participants in this resource management dilemma relied on the actions of others to define the situation, abdicating their personal responsibility to decide how to act. Whereas the pluralistic ignorance of Latané and Darley's subjects led to inaction, the pluralistic ignorance of subjects in these studies led to a "feeding frenzy" of overconsumption from the resource pool that would have ultimately proved disastrous to all members of the group.

There are other behaviors in social dilemmas that are similar to behaviors in emergencies. For instance, people in social dilemmas behave in a less socially responsible manner and a resource is depleted more rapidly when it is shared by several individuals than when it is controlled by one person (Martichuski & Bell, 1991). This is analogous to the bystander effect in emergencies. In addition, the larger the group (Brewer & Kramer, 1986) and the more anonymous people feel (Allison, McQueen, & Schaerfl, 1992; Kerr, 1989), the more likely a resource will be exploited and the more likely people will be to free ride—that is, attempt to benefit from the group's actions without contributing (Kerr & Bruun, 1983; Kerr & MacCoun, 1985). Thus, there are strong parallels between spontaneous helping and cooperation in social dilemmas.

As we saw in Chapter 2, the presence of others does not always reduce prosocial action. If others communicate information that the situation is serious and that people should help, people are often more likely to help than if they were alone. Similarly, communication might facilitate cooperative action in social dilemmas in some situations. For instance, in the Schroeder et al. studies the subjects were specifically prohibited from talking with one another. Without the opportunity to speak with one another to discuss strategies, coordinate actions, share information, or develop common expectations, individual concerns dominated people's considerations and led to individual defections rather than to cooperation. What would have happened if Schroeder et al.'s subjects could have spoken with one another?

Research by Dawes, McTavish, and Shaklee (1977) provides some answers to this question. These researchers had eight-person groups play a social dilemma game in which each person made only one decision. Before making their choices, however, some groups were allowed to talk about the social dilemma problem, while other groups were permitted to discuss an irrelevant topic or simply work quietly and individually on an irrelevant task. As you might expect, the groups in which subjects could talk among themselves showed higher rates of cooperation than groups that were not allowed to discuss the dilemma problem. However, just talking with others in one's group did nothing to elicit greater cooperation; becoming acquainted with other group members does not appear to be sufficient to arouse concern for the common good. Instead, cooperation is the result of group members using one another's knowledge to gain a better understanding of the dilemma situation and to determine what course of action should be taken, just as they tried to do in the Schroeder et al. studies. When communication is effective, the results can be dramatic. Even ten minutes of communication can double the amount of cooperation in a group and thereby double the value of outcomes to each person (Orbell, van de Kragt, & Dawes, 1988).

Subsequent research shows some additional benefits from permitting communication among group members. In some public goods dilemmas, members of the group must collectively contribute some minimum amount (the provision point) or else the good will not be provided. These are called *step-level* public goods dilemmas, because of the all-or-none nature of the payoff. In step-level public goods situations, communication allows group members to follow a cooperative strategy in which a subset of the group is specifically designated as the ones who are to contribute (the so-called minimal contributing set; Orbell et al., 1988) to ensure that the public good will be provided. Those designated then know that their contribution is absolutely critical for achieving the provision point. Under these circumstances, defections are extremely rare among those selected to be members of the minimal contributing set.

Relationship to others. If group members are able to communicate with one another, discover that they share similar characteristics with other group members, or feel that they all share a common fate, the group may develop a sense of belongingness and affiliation with each other. This sense of belongingness and affiliation may be accompanied by a shift of focus from self-concern to heightened concern for the well-being of the group as a whole. Kramer and Brewer (1984) reported an experiment in which participants were led to focus on either a subordinate group identity (e.g., the fact that they were college students and some other subjects in the study were not) or a superordinate identity (e.g., the fact that all the subjects in the study were residents of the same city). These students played a resource management dilemma game, with another subgroup of subjects (elderly residents of the same city who were working at another location). When the commons began to deteriorate, participants who were focused on their subordinate identity as students became greedier; those who were focused on their identity as part of a superordinate group did not. This pattern was stronger for men than for women. As we observed in earlier chapters of this book, people behave more prosocially toward others whom they see as part of their own group.

Individual and cultural differences. Like spontaneous helping, the fact that situational and social factors are potent determinants of responses does not negate the substantial importance of personality variables (Glance & Huberman, 1994). In addition, there appears to be a direct link between helpful and cooperative personalities. People who are characteristically helpful tend to act in socially responsible ways in social dilemmas (Liebrand & van Run, 1985).

Whereas research on individual differences in helping has examined a large number of personality variables, research on individual differences in reactions to social dilemmas has mostly focused on one set of characteristics—an actor's social values. Liebrand (1984, 1986) identified four kinds of actors on the basis of their social values: altruists, cooperators, individualists, and competitors. They differ in their preferences for allocating resources to themselves and others. For example, both altruists and cooperators essentially have prosocial motivations, but altruists give more weight to others' outcomes than to their own, whereas cooperators give roughly equal consideration to their own and others' outcomes. Individualists consider only their own outcomes, ignoring what the payoffs (good or bad) for others would be. Competitors try to maximize their own outcomes relative to the outcomes of others, even if it means accepting a lower personal payoff in order to beat the coactors by a larger margin!

Why do these four kinds of people behave so differently in social dilemmas? Cunha (1985) found that their levels of trust and trustworthiness were important variables. Trust relates to how much faith they put in others' prosocial actions; trustworthiness involves how much they can be trusted by others to behave consistently and cooperatively. Competitive subjects are usually very low on measures of trust. Thus, their actions appear to be driven by fear and suspicion; they do not believe that they can trust others to make the cooperative choice. Individualists, cooperators, and altruists, all of whom are high on trust, seem to be motivated largely by possible profit. But individualists, who are low in trustworthiness, are willing to exploit others in pursuit of profit; altruists and cooperators are not.

As with spontaneous helping, there are also consistent differences among cultures in cooperativeness. Charles McClintock and his colleagues have examined these differences using one type of social dilemma (McClintock, 1974; McClintock & Nuttin, 1969; Toda, Shinotsuka, McClintock, & Stech, 1978). Their subjects were Anglo-American, Mexican-American, Japanese, and Greek children in the second, fourth, and sixth grades. Figure 8.1 presents the percentage of children who chose a competitive response in the social dilemma. Several trends are apparent. First, at least in this situation, competition is the typical response across all cultures. Second, different cultures reflect different levels of competitiveness. Among sixth graders, Japanese and Greek children are the most competitive and Mexican-American children are the least competitive. Third, age has an even stronger impact than culture. The prevalence of competitive responses increases across all cultures from the second to fourth to the sixth grade. However, these trends do not necessarily continue into adulthood. Knight, Dubro, and Chao (1985) have proposed that cooperation is a more complex process than competition and,

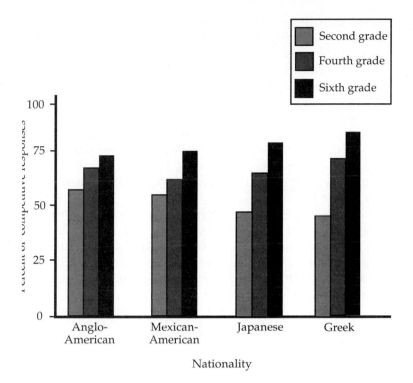

FIGURE 8.1
Cooperativeness and competitiveness vary as a function of culture and age.
(Adapted from Komorita & Parks, 1994).

because of limited cognitive capacities, children first learn competitiveness. Later, with cognitive and social maturation, cooperativeness becomes more common.

In summary, this discussion of the determinants of behavior in social dilemmas suggests several ways to promote greater cooperation. Making the positive consequences of cooperation more salient, exposing actors to cooperative models, encouraging discussions among group members, emphasizing the actors' common fate, and trying to socialize more people to have more prosocial values are obvious steps that could be taken. However, these solutions may take long periods of time to implement or require social interventions that may not be very practical. What other ways can cooperation for the general good be encouraged?

Structural Solutions to Dilemmas

Unlike most of the spontaneous helping situations that we have considered in this book, naturally occurring social dilemmas take place over an extended period of time. Thus, there may be processes for inducing cooperation that are unique to social dilemmas and are not related to the mechanisms involved in individual helping situations. For example, those caught in a social dilemma may decide to take a direct approach by imposing *structural solutions*. They realize that they need to change the very nature of the dilemma situation if they have any hope of reducing defections and promoting greater cooperation. As a consequence, they might decide to select a superordinate authority (or leader) to make the allocation decisions (e.g., Platt, 1973) or to privatize the common resource so that each individual will be personally responsible for managing a small section of the pool (Cass & Edney, 1978). What structural solutions often do is to eliminate the individual versus group conflict—essentially eliminating the root of the dilemma.

What leads groups to be willing to impose structural solutions upon themselves? David Messick, Charles Samuelson, and their colleagues (Messick et al., 1983; Samuelson & Messick, 1986a, 1986b; Samuelson, Messick, Rutte, & Wilke, 1984) found that groups were more willing to elect a leader to manage resource allocations if the common resource pool was being depleted than if it were being satisfactorily managed by the group. That is, if the group's outcome was acceptable, there was no need or interest in changing the status quo; only when things start to get bad are group members willing to hand over control to a leader.

In another study, Rutte, Wilke, and Messick (1987) found that the nature of the dilemma affected the structural solutions that actors choose. Actors were more likely to elect a leader in a take-some (resource management) dilemma than in a give-some (public goods) game. Rutte et al. explained this difference by proposing that while people are unwilling to hand over control of their privately owned resources (as is the case in give-some games), they are willing to have a leader take control of a common resource that has to be protected for all (as is the case in take-some games). The former action is seen as threatening to their individual freedom; the latter action is not.

Summary

Social dilemmas represent an important part of the puzzle of helpful, prosocial behaviors. Unlike many of the other prosocial actions we have discussed in previous chapters, there are clear benefits to the actor for the other-oriented, helpful actions. That is, if individuals can be induced to act in the long-term best interests of the collective, they too will benefit. In contrast to spontaneous helping by an individual in emergencies, prosocial behavior in a social dilemma is an interdependent or collective phenomenon: The outcome of this action does not depend on how any one individual behaves but on how a group of people act. The successful solution requires that some critical mass of people act for the common good, whether it be conserving the common resource or contributing to a public good. But getting people to act in this manner is not easy. The temptations to defect by taking too much or giving too little are great. We have seen that the extent to which people will engage in short-term selfish behaviors as opposed to prosocial actions is influenced by many factors reflecting the complexity of the social dilemma part of the prosocial behavior puzzle.

Because social dilemmas involve collective actions, they may seem somewhat far removed from the kinds of helping and altruistic actions that were discussed in the earlier chapters. But, as we have seen, there are a number of points of continuity between them. The connection between collective and individual action will become even more evident in the next section, in which we discuss a very common (perhaps the most common) kind of helping—donating one's time or money (or both) for the benefit of others. The decision as to whether one should volunteer time or money is really a kind of public good dilemma. Whether or not you contribute to some charity, you can receive its benefits. But the remarkable thing is that despite the short-term advantage of withholding one's resources from the public good, many people do give freely and seem to expect little in the way of tangible rewards. Who are these people, and why do they act so prosocially?

DONATING AND VOLUNTEERING: GIVING TO THE THIRD SECTOR

The decisions involved in social dilemmas in the laboratory research discussed in the first part of this chapter, although often difficult, are usually limited by the nature of the experimental situation. For example, the experimenter is often the ultimate source of rewards for participants. The situation in society is more complex. There are three sources, or sectors, that provide goods and services to individuals (Weisbrod, 1975). The first is the *private* or *market* sector; it supplies private goods—things that individuals or families can purchase and use alone, such as television sets or cars. The motivation for providing these goods is normally profit; companies make money from these purchases. The second, or *public* sector, is usually the government, and it provides public goods that most people want (such as national defense, parks, disaster relief, and elementary and secondary education) but cannot provide for themselves. The motivation here is also straightforward; the government exists to serve the people. In order to prevent the kind of free riding discussed in the previous section, laws are passed to ensure that everyone is taxed for the cost of these services, even though some individuals may not want some of them.

Weisbrod used the term *third sector* to describe the final source of the goods and services that people receive. The third sector is comprised of people and organizations engaging in voluntary actions without substantial support from either the private or public sectors of the economy. It

BOX 8.1

Is Social Responsibility Good for Business? Corporate Philanthropy

Although the primary activity of large corporations is to produce goods for the first or private sector of the economy, they also contribute to the third sector. In 1990, corporate contributions for charitable and similar purposes were $5.9 billion (United States Bureau of the Census, 1992). This may seem impressive, but it is only 7 percent of what individuals donated in the same year. As Galaskiewicz (1985) pointed out, corporations have never approached the limits of giving permitted by Internal Revenue Service rules. In the 1980s, corporations were allowed to deduct up to 10 percent of their pretax income for charitable donations, but the national average for corporations at that time was about 1 percent.

There is great regional variability in corporate giving. For example, in the 1970s, thirty-three of the thirty-seven corporations that gave 5 percent of their income to charities were from the Minneapolis and St. Paul, Minnesota, area. How can we understand both the overall low level and the regional differences?

One reason appears to be modeling and/or social pressure similar to the kind that influences the behavior of individuals. Consider the corporations from the Minneapolis/St. Paul area. Galaskiewicz found that there has been a Five Percent Club (i.e., they should donate 5 percent of their pretax income) in Minneapolis since 1976, when it started with twenty-three firms as members; by 1982, sixty-two companies were members. Thus, corporate contributions may be made in the hope of winning the esteem and recognition of the local business elite. The closer a firm's executives were to the philanthropic elite, the more they donated.

Galaskiewicz also found a great deal of peer pressure, negative reciprocity (If

supplies important products and services that are too large and costly to be private goods but that the government is unwilling or unable to provide. Examples of these kinds of public goods include research centers for specific diseases, special facilities for disadvantaged or specially challenged people, educational television, and symphony orchestras (see Box 8.1). The need for contributions to the public welfare by the third sector is increasing in the United States (Douglas, 1983). As recent taxpayer revolts demonstrate, citizens are growing increasingly unwilling to support government services that they believe will not directly benefit them or will benefit only a small segment of society. Thus, if these needs are to be met, they will have to be provided by the third sector. But, what moti-

BOX 8.1 continued

you don't donate to my charity, I won't donate to yours), and the perception that soliciting and contributing were "rituals that helped to integrate businessmen into the local civic culture" (p. 220). In another study conducted in Great Britain, Moore and Richardson (1988) noted that corporate responsibility had been increasing in Great Britain, and they concluded, in agreement with Galaskiewicz, that peer-group pressure was a major cause of the increase in corporate responsiveness to social issues.

A second strong possibility is perceived self-interest. For example, Galaskiewicz found that the largest corporate donors were those who believed it was in their economic self-interest to do so (e.g., If we give money to charities, it will help preserve the free enterprise system). Galaskiewicz also found that companies which gave more money to charity were seen as more successful by the executives of other companies, and there is reason to believe that both perceptions are correct.

Clarkson (1988) analyzed the corporate responsibility of thirty-two corporations in Canada. A major finding was that economic performance was strongly related to rated level of corporate responsibility, with the most financially successful firms showing the most proactive approach to social issues. Those Canadian companies that emphasized the bottom line at the expense of their social responsibilities had economic performances that were below average. In defense of his argument that corporate responsibility can *lead* to profit, Clarkson claimed that several of the successful companies he studied had a history of social responsibility that *preceded* their current levels of economic success.

Thus, it would appear that normative pressures and enlightened self-interest may be major causes of socially responsible behavior by large corporations. Normative pressures can increase social responsibility, but it is largely because such pressures lead corporate officers to perceive that socially responsible behavior is in the corporation's own best interest. Corporations do not feel empathy or have group-oriented feelings. Corporate philanthropy, however valuable it is, is not altruism.

vates this third sector? And how does it relate to the individual motivations for helping that we have considered in this book?

In the pages that follow, we will discuss the people who contribute to the third sector. Although we will use the general term *volunteer* to describe them, members of the third sector do more than just donate money or work a few hours for some charity. Some of the people we will discuss are full-time social activists who dedicate their lives to improve the conditions of other members of society; others are individuals who, as part of their jobs, provide informal psychological and personal support to those with whom they come in contact.

As noted in Chapter 3, a substantial number of people engage in such activities, but an even greater number do not. So, we have another puzzle to solve. What differentiates the people who contribute to the third sector from those who do not? What motivates people to give their time, money, and energy for the benefit of others in their community? This, of course, is not the first time we have asked these questions about helpful people. But the issues here are different. Whereas much of the previous material has been concerned with an individual's willingness to engage in spontaneous, short-term helping of strangers, here we will focus on people's willingness to engage in long-term, deliberative helping of neighbors, friends, and members of their families. Like spontaneous helping, long-term deliberative helping is very common in our society (Radley & Kennedy, 1992). In 1990, about 20 percent of the people in the United States stated that they performed volunteer work and about 75 percent of the households in the United States reported giving money to charity (Independent Sector, 1990).

We begin our attempt to solve this part of the helping puzzle by considering the demographic characteristics of those who contribute their time and money to the public good. Understanding *who* helps may provide clues about *why* people help. Furthermore, individual differences appear to be very important in this area; there are substantial differences between those who contribute to the third sector and those who do not. For example, in a 1990 study of volunteerism in the United States, it was found that 64 percent who gave money to charity also worked as volunteers and, generally, the more they gave, the more they volunteered. By contrast, only 26 percent of noncontributors worked as volunteers (Independent Sector, 1990).

Demographic Characteristics

As you may recall from Chapter 6, a demographic characteristic is some aspect of a person's background or personal characteristics that concerns that person's physical or social status. What kinds of characteristics might be related to volunteering and donating? Chapter 2 demonstrated that people are less likely to help when helping is more costly. Thus, people who have more resources (e.g., money or time) may be more likely to contribute to the third sector because it is easier (i.e., relatively less costly) for them to give. This may be part of the puzzle, but it does not provide the complete picture. Interpersonal relations may also be influential. Chapters 3 to 6 illustrated the importance of empathy in helping. These findings suggest that volunteers may be more attuned to the needs of others or have stronger connections to the community. But how well do these findings for spontaneous, short-term helping predict planned, long-term commitments?

Resources and contributions. People of different levels of socioeconomic status and educational achievement and of different races, ages, and gender possess different amounts of resources in our society. These differences may provide some people with greater opportunities to help their communities than others. The question that we focus on in this part of the chapter is thus, Do people who have more to give give more? In general, the answer is yes.

Socioeconomic status is strongly related to donating both time and money. For instance, wealthier people are more likely to volunteer their time to charities. One possible reason for this is that among people in lower income brackets, time is money in a much more direct sense than it is for those who have higher incomes. People of lower socioeconomic status are typically paid by the hour. Donating time would therefore involve sacrificing personal wages as well as personal effort. In contrast, people in higher income brackets are usually on salary and thus may have greater flexibility in terms of the specific hours they work. Because donating time is less costly to them, they may be more likely to volunteer. Personal wealth is also related to donating money. Wealthier households give more money. People at different levels of the social-status hierarchy, therefore, appear to have different opportunities to engage in helping acts. However, the greater opportunity of wealthier people to donate their time and money is not the entire story (Unger, 1991). Despite the fact that wealthy people may be expected to adhere to social norms that mandate that they not only engage in philanthropy but also give their time for the betterment of others in their community (noblesse oblige), wealthier households do not necessarily give more money in terms of percentage of their total income. On average, families that make less than $20,000 per year and more than $75,000 per year give the highest percentage of their total incomes to charities (Independent Sector, 1990). Thus, as we will see, other influences besides available resources are involved in contributions to the third sector.

Education, which is related to socioeconomic status and thus available resources, is also related to how much people contribute to the third sector. As educational level increases, so does the amount of money a person donates and the likelihood that a person will work as a volunteer (Reddy, 1980; United States Department of Labor, 1990). However, as we saw before, having more resources may be part of the explanation, but it is not the whole story; education is related to giving in ways beyond the effects of wealth. More highly educated people tend to develop different attitudes toward specific types of giving. For example, people with more education are not more likely to make religious donations. They are, however, particularly likely to make contributions to a specific kind of third-sector activity, blood donations—a type of giving in which people of different educational backgrounds have equal opportunity and resources.

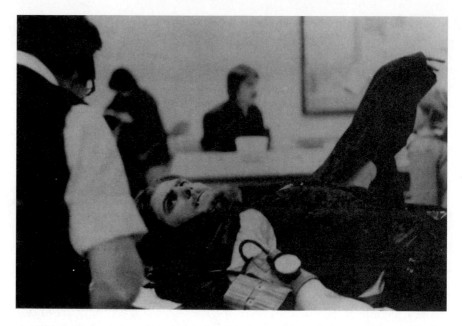

A college student gives blood dressed as a vampire to help others lighten up about the costs of donating. Demographic characteristics of potential donors and their relations with those who might benefit appear to influence their willingness to contribute.

Blood donors are most likely to be people with at least some college education and who hold white-collar or professional jobs (Piliavin & Callero, 1991). Thus, education appears to influence giving in ways that cannot be explained simply in terms of available resources.

Robert Bellah and his colleagues (1985) have suggested another reason why financially secure, well-educated individuals are usually the greatest contributors to the third sector. On the basis of several case studies of small communities in the United States, these researchers concluded that many middle- and upper-class Americans initially put their personal and career concerns before community involvement. Once they have achieved success in their work, however, they find they want more from their lives, something from which they can attain joy. Thus, according to Bellah et al., successful individuals contribute to their communities because this gives them something more than just a successful career. With wealth and education comes a need for other, less tangible goals and rewards.

Perhaps because race and ethnicity are related to socioeconomic differences in the United States, they may also be related to contributions to the third sector. Minority group members, who tend to have lower socioeconomic status and levels of education than majority group members, are underrepresented in all areas of formalized contributions and volunteering. For example, whereas about 22 percent of whites reported working as volunteers, less than 12 percent of African Americans and 10 percent of Hispanic Americans report engaging in volunteer work (United States Department of Labor, 1990). Many minority group members feel alienated from the major institutions of society, seeing them as dominated by white, Anglo culture and as being unfriendly to outsiders (National Conference of Christians and Jews, 1994). As a consequence, although a great deal of informal helping does occur within minority communities, these efforts are less likely to occur through formal, third-sector channels.

The curvilinear relationship between age and charitable contributions may be explained, in a large part, by differences in people's resources for giving. People in their forties and fifties give more than either younger or older people. Young people have less disposable income; older people are worried about their retirement. A very similar pattern is found in volunteering; over 50 percent of the people who volunteer their time to third-sector organizations are between 35 and 55 years old (United States Department of Labor, 1990). Nevertheless, as with race and ethnicity, focusing only on formal contributions to the third sector overlooks the significant amount of assistance that elderly people give in other ways (Midlarsky, 1991). For instance, 55 percent of the residents in a community for the elderly reported that they regularly provide informal assistance to others (Chappell & Havens, 1983), much higher than the percentage who formally volunteer their time for charity. In addition, although the amount of money donated tends to decrease among people in their sixties and older, the likelihood that people will donate something continues to increase with age (Midlarsky & Hannah, 1989).

We have already discussed the role of gender in other kinds of helping (see Chapter 6), so we will only briefly touch on it here with respect to longer-term, planned giving. Traditionally, men have given more money, and women have given more time (United States Department of Labor, 1990). One reason for this is again available resources. Historically, gender and wealth have been correlated, such that men typically have had more money to give. Until recently, women have often worked without pay in the home and have had more free time. All these tendencies are changing as our social structure in relation to gender changes; thus, we might expect the patterns of donations and charitable action to change as society moves closer to equality of the sexes. However, to the extent that attitudes and orientations toward others are involved, these changes may occur very slowly. As we discussed in Chapter 6, gender not only influences whether a person will offer assistance, but also the type of help that is given. Men typically help in a more direct, instrumental, and less personally involved manner (as would be the case with donating money); women are more likely to provide emotional support and personal forms of assistance (as would be the case with volunteering time). Gender differences in giving money and time may therefore persist because of traditional gender roles even as men's and women's socioeconomic resources converge.

Religion also is an important influence in encouraging more general prosocial actions. A central aspect of religious teachings involves an individual's connections to others. As we saw in Chapter 1, prosocial values and norms are taught by virtually every religious denomination, and attendance at services and participation in religious activities also give individuals access to social networks and information. Does this affect contributions to the third sector? It certainly influences donations to religious organizations. In the United States, the most likely recipient of charitable contributions is a religious organization. In 1990, over 53 percent of the donations from individuals and 65 percent of the donations from corporations and foundations went to religious organizations (Independent Sector, 1990; United States Bureau of the Census, 1992).

In general, people who are members of religious congregations give both more money and more time to charitable enterprises in general than do people who are not members of congregations (Hodgkinson, Weitzman, & Kirsch, 1990). In addition, Hodgkinson et al. (1990) found that church members donated a higher proportion of their income and gave to a larger number of charities. Membership in a religious organization was even a greater influence on the amount donated than was actual income (although it is not clear in their analysis how much of this charitable giving was specifically to religious causes). Overall, the more people went to church, the more they gave, and members of religious organizations also reported more volunteering. There are, however, limits. Piliavin, Lee, and Call (1992) have found that religious activity and religious identity are associated with a person's identity as a helper in terms of donating money and time, but not in terms of donating blood.

It is important to recognize that religious congregations serve important functions in their communities and around the world. Much of the organization of delivery of services (e.g., foreign relief, shelters for the homeless) is accomplished by religious congregations, which provide not only the money and the volunteer labor but also the leadership and the facilities where the services are provided. Religious organizations are critical in linking individuals to their communities in ties of service. The injunction to "love thy neighbor" seems to be alive and well in our religious congregations.

In summary, the research on demographic differences in helping does suggest, consistent with the cost-benefit analysis presented in Chapter 2, that the more people have, the more they will give. This applies to both money and time. However, having resources is not the entire explanation. For each of the demographic characters we have considered, people's attitudes and orientation toward others also appear to play an important role. In the next section we consider how and why these connections to others influence long-term, planned forms of helping.

Relations to Others

Demographic factors may indirectly affect people's willingness to contribute to the public good by their influence on what we think about others and how sensitive we are to their needs. When we discussed the social
dilemma research, we noted that smaller groups, groups with face-to-face
communication, and groups that had a more all-inclusive view of who
was part of their community solved their resource management problems
more effectively. Demographic differences among people may similarly
relate to differences in their sense of belonging to a community and thus
to their willingness to contribute to the public good. In general, as we
have seen in the other chapters of this book, the more connected people
feel to others, the more likely they may be to contribute to the welfare of
the group as a whole. In this part of the chapter, we examine how community, culture, and religion relate to willingness to work for the welfare
of others.

A sense of community involves feelings of connectedness and association. Thus, as there are urban-rural differences in spontaneous helping
(Chapter 2), there may be parallel differences in the long-term kinds of
helping that takes place among friends, neighbors, and relatives. Do city
dwellers and people from rural areas also differ in this kind of helping?
The great southern American novelist, Thomas Wolfe, once wrote that city
dwellers "have no manners, no courtesy, no consideration for the rights of
others, and no humanity" (1940, p. 240). Sociological theorists (e.g.,
Simmel, 1950) have described those who live in cities as alienated and
unresponsive to the needs of others. Indeed, people who live in urban
environments are less likely to volunteer their time and money for the
general welfare of others (Amato, 1993; Steblay, 1987). One reason for this
difference involves the importance of different norms for helping
(Chapter 3) in cities and towns. Whereas people in rural communities are
guided more strongly by feelings of general responsibility toward others,
urban dwellers adhere more to the norm of reciprocity (you scratch my
back, I'll scratch yours). One consequence of this norm is that in large
cities, those who cannot give help are less likely to receive it. For example,
Amato (1993) found that elderly urban dwellers, who often are unable to
reciprocate help, were helped less than other age groups. This was not the
case in rural areas.

Returning to our main question, does living in an urban environment
interfere with our feelings of responsibility toward everyone or only
toward strangers? Even within cities, it might be possible to develop a
sense of community with others, such as with relatives and friends. Thus,
one's larger residential environment may have little impact on longer-
term helping relationships within this more private community. The data,
illustrated in Figure 8.2, support this reasoning. Using a sample of over
13,000 families in the United States, Amato (1993) found that people from
large cities and from small towns were equally willing to help friends and

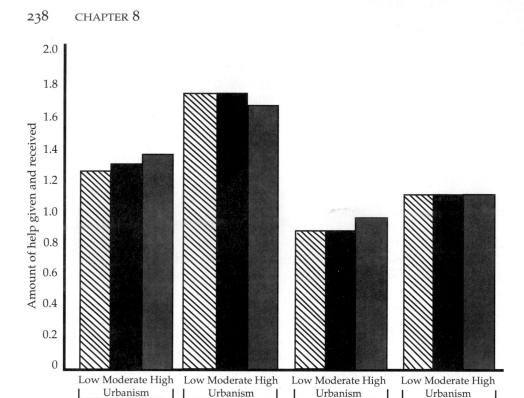

FIGURE 8.2
Receiving assistance from and giving help to friends and relatives is not affected by urbanism. (Adapted from Amato, 1993.)

family members (see also Korte, 1980). There was also no overall difference in the amount of help reported to be given and received from friends and family in cities of different sizes or between cities and small towns (see Figure 8.2). Thus, what distinguishes the prosocial actions of people in urban and rural settings is what they define as their community.

International relations. Another kind of third-sector helping involves providing aid to others specifically outside one's community, such as foreign aid to governments or to individuals in need. It is a fact of the late twentieth century that many of the have-not or developing nations are highly dependent on the industrialized nations, such as the United States. Despite this great need, Americans are not supportive of the idea of foreign aid. Over 75 percent of the respondents to a nationwide survey in 1991 reported that they believed that the government spends too much money on foreign aid, and this sentiment has been increasing over time (Davis & Smith, 1991). As we have seen in earlier chapters of this book (e.g., Chapter 2) and similar to urban-rural differences in helping, as physical and psychological distance between a helper and the potential recipient of the help increases, willingness to help with money or time decreases.

Research on international helping behavior comes from a series of experiments by Taormina and his colleagues (Taormina, 1984; Taormina & Messick, 1983; Taormina, Messick, Iwawaki, & Wilke, 1988) that focused on judgments of foreign-aid deservingness. Because the respondents were all college students, the results shed little light on the ways in which such policy decisions are actually made. However, these studies can tell us about individuals' personal predispositions to help and the bases for these attitudes. For example, Taormina and Messick (1983) found that needier countries (based on average personal incomes), countries similar to the United States (i.e., democracies rather than dictatorships), and countries in which the aid was expected to be effective were seen as being the most deserving.

Similar factors affect people's willingness to give money and time to organizations designed to help individuals in developing countries (Ting, 1992). These data came from a survey carried out in 1987 in the twelve nations that make up the European Community. As with foreign aid, people were more willing to volunteer their time and donate money when the developing country's need was perceived to be greater and when the assistance was anticipated to be more effective. However, experience with and interest in the third world played an important role; people with more experience and interest perceived greater need and greater effectiveness of helping. That is, feelings of connectedness to these communities appeared to influence people's perceptions of need and of the effectiveness of helping, which in turn related to their willingness to contribute time and money. Similarly, there is evidence that having experience with charities (e.g., having received services) is related to one's involvement in charitable activities (Lee, 1992; Piliavin & Callero, 1991). In general, as with the urban-rural differences, people differ in their sense of community and connectedness, and those who perceive stronger links with others respond more prosocially to their needs.

Situational cues can also increase people's tendencies to help individuals in other countries. For example, direct requests for help increase the costs for not helping and therefore increase the likelihood that a person will help (Chapter 2). Witnessing helpful models facilitates helping by making prosocial norms salient (Chapters 3 and 5). Ting thus proposed that individual differences in experience with the third world and interest in the third world would combine with modeling (e.g., knowing that others were helping) and having been asked to help to increase international helping. All four of these factors were found to influence subjects' attitudes toward foreign aid. As illustrated in Figure 8.3, nearly 80 percent of respondents who were high on experience, interest, and modeling said

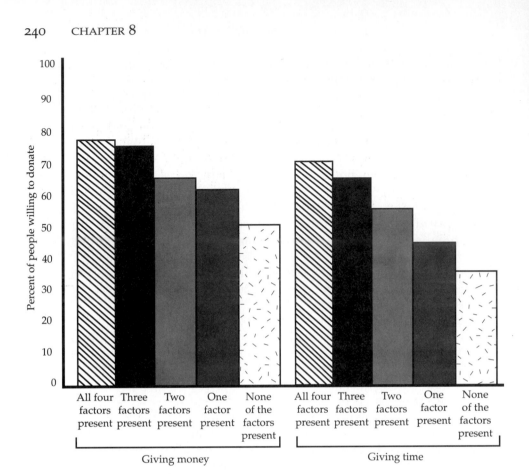

FIGURE 8.3
Greater willingness to donate money and time to third-world countries is related to higher levels of interest in and experience with the third world, modeling, and being directly asked. (Data from Ting, 1993.)

they would be willing to give money (or to give more money than they already gave), while less than half those who were low on all four of the variables said they would be willing to give money. The effect was even stronger for giving time: Over 70 percent of those high on the first three factors said they would give time, whereas less than 40 percent of the inexperienced, disinterested people who neither were asked nor had observed others helping said they would be willing to do so.

As we noted in Chapter 6, however, cultures vary substantially in their members' willingness to help individual members of other groups. Do different cultures have different reactions to assisting foreign countries? Taormina et al. (1988) explored this issue in a study using subjects from the Netherlands, Japan, and the United States. They also considered separately the effectiveness of aid for meeting the objectives of the country giving it and for the need of the country receiving it. In general, the results were similar to those found in Taormina and his colleagues' previous studies; a country's need, similarity of the country to one's own, perceived effectiveness of aid for one's own country, and perceived effectiveness of assistance for the other country were all positively related to attitudes toward foreign aid. However, as expected, there were cultural differences. For American and Japanese students, the potential benefits to one's own country were more important in determining their decisions than the benefits to the country that would receive the aid. In contrast, the effectiveness of the aid in providing benefits to the *recipient* was the single most important factor influencing the Dutch students' judgments. In other words, the Dutch, whose culture tends to be more tolerant and accepting of others, were primarily motivated by the desire to satisfy the needs of the other country; Americans and Japanese were more likely to see foreign aid as a means to help their countries attain their own political and economic goals.

There are also significant cultural differences in response to receiving aid. As we discussed in Chapter 7, receiving help may be threatening to an individual's self-esteem. When there is no opportunity to reciprocate helping, people tend to respond negatively to the helper and to the assistance, and they experience a loss of self-esteem (Gergen, Ellsworth, Maslach, & Seipel, 1975). A similar principle may apply to foreign aid. Countries that have received foreign aid from the United States and are unable to reciprocate in an appropriate way may develop negative attitudes toward the aid and the United States. This process would help explain why some countries demonstrate strong anti-American sentiment even while they are still receiving foreign aid from the United States. However, the likelihood of this reaction differs across cultures. Reactions of this type are substantially more negative in Scotland, the United States, Korea, and South Africa than in China and Japan (Moghaddam et al., 1993). Gergen and his colleagues (Gergen, Morse, & Gergen, 1980) have proposed that Buddhist teachings in Japan and China, which condemn self-centered orientations and personal esteem, may make aid of this type less personally threatening. Once again, views of connectedness to others—in this case, culturally determined—affect the nature of long-term, planned helping in systematic ways that parallel what we know about more spontaneous helping.

To summarize this section, a person's relationship to others is strongly and consistently related to longer-term, nonspontaneous helping. This effect, which is influenced by one's residential environment, attitudes toward other countries, culture, and religion, is important over and above the influence of having more resources. The social ties that bind people together promote prosocial relationships. Whether people define their community as their family, their town, their country, or humankind in general, people are more willing to donate their time and money to people within that community than those outside of it. However, contributing one's time and money to charity is only one way in which people can contribute to the third sector. In the next section, we will examine some less common ways of helping one's community and the people who live in it.

Helping the Community

For most of this chapter we have been talking about everyday or mundane types of helping. However, contributions to the third sector can be much more dramatic. In this section, we will consider one of the more extraordinary ways in which individuals can contribute to the public good—through social and political movements. We will argue that many social movements may represent a kind of political and social altruism.

Community activism. The continuity among social movement activism, volunteerism, and personal helping can be seen in responses of many communities to the AIDS crisis. Kayal (1993) provides a case study of one such response in his book, *Bearing Witness: Gay Men's Health Crisis and the Politics of AIDS*. The Gay Men's Health Crisis (GMHC) group was initially founded by members of the gay community to make people more aware of the AIDS epidemic and to raise money for research. What was the motivation behind this effort? The organization was other-oriented, in the sense that most of those who were initially active in the organization did not have AIDS. Yet, in the sense of identification with those afflicted in the gay community, personal interests were involved. As the GMHC grew, its focus shifted to the care and support of persons with AIDS, and its impact now reaches far beyond the gay community. The ranks of volunteers now include many heterosexual women (but not men) and lesbians. The motives of these people are varied. Some say that their motives are essentially altruistic, but most mention personal rewards. The great majority of the GMHC volunteers claim that they get more from their participation than they give.

Although people may report a wide range of reasons for becoming involved in these large-scale, community-oriented helping activities, there may be commonalities in the types of motivations (Chapter 3) and the kinds of people (Chapter 6) involved. In 1987, William Berkowitz wrote a collection of brief biographies of people who became prosocial activists in their communities. He called these people *local heroes*. For example, Homer Fahrner, a retired engineer, deplored the fact that elderly people were starving while produce rotted in the California fields; therefore, he started the Senior Gleaners, who collect and distribute this food to needy people. Among the other heroes were Bill and Helen Sample, who wanted to make the last days of dying children a little happier and started the Sunshine Foundation; Curtis Sliwa, the founder of the Guardian Angels, a group that fights urban crime; and Candy Lightner, who started Mothers Against Drunk Driving (MADD).

Some of these people seemed to be motivated solely by altruistic concerns, and some seemed to be motivated by self-interest. For example, Homer Fahrner was not poor, and the Samples had no sick children. But Curtis Sliwa did live in a dangerous urban area, and Candy Lightner's daughter was killed by a drunk driver. Whatever their reasons for starting these groups, many other people have been helped by the organizations initiated by these local heroes. It is clear that the drive that kept all these heroes going was not based solely on self-interest but rather on a determination to solve problems that caused other people to suffer or to accomplish goals that would improve the life of the collectivity. In other words, all these individuals were focused on some community—either an actual local community or some community of interest, such as sick children or hungry people.

What kind of people become local heroes? There are more differences between Berkowitz's heroes than there are similarities. Some are affluent, others poverty stricken; there are men and women, rural and urban residents, elderly and young people. Berkowitz suggests, however, that these people do have several characteristics in common: few familial obligations, strong parental influence, a spiritual background, and the political ethic of the 1960s. Personality similarities included naïveté (not realizing what they were getting themselves into!), high energy coupled with the ability to pace themselves, and a boundless capacity for humor. Two additional characteristics struck Berkowitz, however. First, these local heroes displayed strong emotions: They had experienced excitement about the issue that made them want to "jump out of their seats" and anger that made them want to really "kick butt." Second, the heroes had a strong belief in and reliance upon traditional virtue; that is, commitment, tolerance for criticism, hard work, optimism, persistence, and the willingness to take a risk for a good cause. Note here, as elsewhere in this chapter, that there are similarities between long-term and spontaneous helping. The two important characteristics of local heroes resemble two of the central characteristics that define the altruistic personality in Chapter 6: strong emotional response (related to empathy) and the belief that one's efforts will be successful.

Community-oriented helping can also occur spontaneously. The need for help can arise rapidly and unexpectedly, for example during natural disasters. Often, the response must be swift to be effective. This type of community-oriented helping is considered in the next section.

Helping in disasters. In recent years, we have seen dramatic examples of people's willingness to help their communities. In 1993, as the waters of the Mississippi and Missouri rivers threatened to destroy cities and towns along their banks, thousands of people worked to save these

These people came together to place sandbags on the banks of the Mississippi River in an effort to protect the town of Hardin, Illinois, from the ravages of the flood of 1993. Most volunteers were trying to save their own homes and businesses, but many other volunteers came from areas not threatened by the flood. It is interesting to note that the volunteers recognized the value of trying to save the community as a whole rather than trying to protect only their own property—the only viable solution to this social dilemma. (Kevin Horan for U.S. News & World Report)

communities. Some people helped shore up the levees with sand bags, some offered shelter to the people displaced by the flood, and others made sure that all these helpers were well-fed and had a place to rest. In 1994, we witnessed dramatic rescue efforts in the aftermath of the Los Angeles earthquake. Helping in the time of a disaster is a time-honored tradition. Again we ask, who helps and why? Dynes and Quarantelli (1980) reviewed a large number of studies on responses to disasters. They defined a disaster as an event that occurs within a specific time and location that produces conditions "whereby the continuity of the structure and processes of social units becomes problematic" (p. 340). What this sociological jargon means is that in a disaster—such as a flood, a tornado, or an earthquake—nothing works the way it is supposed to and people have to improvise.

Generally, individuals become very helpful in disasters. For example, following a severe tornado in White County, in Arkansas, in 1952, 27 percent of the adults in the affected communities, including roughly half of all the men in the impacted area, participated in rescue efforts directed toward strangers and acquaintances, typically giving one to six hours of help to those in need. In a study following a massive flood in Wilkes-Barre, Pennsylvania, in 1972, 24 percent of those interviewed reported doing related volunteer work during the recovery period for some federal, state, or local community organization. There were multiple volunteers from 4.5 percent of households in the area, and these households supplied almost 20 percent of all volunteers (Dynes & Quarantelli, 1980). These findings are consistent with laboratory research demonstrating that sharing a common stressful situation increases helpfulness to others in the same situation (Batson et al., 1979; Dovidio & Morris, 1975).

But, specifically, who are these individuals? Disaster volunteers tend to be relatively young men, married with children. Characteristically, they have high-level jobs, are upper-middle or middle class, and are well integrated into the community. This list of social characteristics suggests that individuals who help in disasters are located in a particular place in the community's social structure. That is, they typically occupy positions of responsibility in a community and, thus, are expected by others and by themselves to help when catastrophes strike (Dynes & Quarantelli, 1980). As we saw in Chapter 2, people are more likely to help in emergency situations when responsibility is focused on them. Similarly, with respect to natural disasters, a community's social structure rather than the characteristics of particular individuals may be the most important determinant of who helps in a disaster and who does not.

One important aspect of natural disasters that distinguishes them from laboratory situations, which are very limited in duration, is that the continuous stress produced by these events may exhaust the personal and material resources of potential helpers. Because members of one's social-support network must also cope with the community disaster, social support becomes weakened over time. Thus, natural disasters can cause psychological damage to victims in two ways. First, they can have an immediate impact on the psychological well-being of victims through direct damage to people and their possessions. For example, Kaniasty and Norris (1993) found that personal losses produced by severe floods that occurred in Kentucky in 1981 had intense, but short-term effects on victims. Victims who suffered greater losses became more depressed. Second, disasters can create further, long-term problems by producing a deterioration in social support. As social support becomes depleted, people's capacity to cope with stress declines. The effects of community destruction from the Kentucky flood, for instance, adversely affected social-support networks for up to eighteen months after the disaster occurred (Kaniasty, Norris, & Murrell, 1990). The loss of this social support, particularly from nonrelatives, then made victims more susceptible to depression (Kaniasty & Norris, 1993). These findings not only confirm the importance of social support, which we discussed in Chapter 7, they also reveal some of the limitations of laboratory research for understanding the full range of helping behaviors. In the next section, we consider other types of helping that extend beyond that studied in the laboratory.

Informal helpers. Much of this book has concerned informal helpers, untrained people who help spontaneously either inside or outside the laboratory. Social support is another form of informal help, although it may be more long term. In contrast to these informal helpers, there are many occupations that are organized around providing help to others: fire fighters, police officers, social workers, clinical psychologists, and medical personnel. These individuals make their living helping others solve their problems, and they typically have formal training that allows them to handle problems in their areas of expertise. However, members of these formal helping professions provide only a small percentage of the help that is ultimately given to those in need.

In between the spontaneous, untrained helpers and the professional helpers is another, often overlooked type of helper. These people are practitioners in occupations not normally defined as helping professions who often may step in to serve helping functions. Because the people who hold such jobs are involved in one-on-one contact with clients and have the opportunity to identify the needs of these clients, they sometimes become informal helpers. There is research from both the United States and Germany concerning job-related helpers: taxi drivers, beauticians, masseurs, bartenders, even mail carriers, meter readers, and sales personnel. According to Nestmann (1991), the "so-called role- or job-related helpers are not formally forced by their occupational roles to help. But it seems that a lot of everyday help giving and social support is embedded in their services" (p. 224).

Cowen (1982) and his colleagues used both face-to-face interviews and questionnaires to find out about informal helping by hairdressers, lawyers, industrial foremen, and bartenders. Hairdressers reported an average of twenty-five minutes of conversation with their customers and said that about a third of the customers discussed moderate-to-serious problems with them. Although Cowen's sample of lawyers worked on a very small number of family cases (i.e., divorce, custody), the lawyers

TABLE 8.1 MOST FREQUENTLY HEARD PROBLEMS FOR FOUR JOB-RELATED HELPING PROFESSIONS

Rank	Bartenders	Lawyers	Supervisors	Hairdressers
1.	Jobs	Anger with spouse	Problems with fellow workers	Difficulties with children
2.	Marital problems	Depression	Opportunities for advancement	Physical health
3.	Finances	Managing contact with spouse	Dissatisfaction with job	Marital problems
4.	Sex	Difficulties with children	Finances	Depression
5.	Depression	Emotional/psychological	Difficulties with children *and* Physical health	Anxiety

Adapted from Cowen (1982, p. 389).

reported that there were extensive discussions of the clients' personal problems in about 40 percent of their cases.

The topics discussed were broadest among bartenders and hairdressers; lawyers dealt mainly with problems and consequences of divorce, and foremen with work and career difficulties (see Table 8.1). Nevertheless, in all four occupations, informal helpers consistently and repeatedly gave emotional support and provided active advice and help giving as a consequence of the nature of their jobs.

Nestmann (1991) also reported an extensive study of informal helping among taxi drivers, hairdressers, bartenders, and masseurs. More than 95 percent of those interviewed reported either having clients mention problems or having provided help or support to them. In addition to surveys and interviews, Nestmann's data included direct observations of helping exchanges and analyses of the conversations that took place. For example, one source of data was a month-long daily record of interactions in a corner bar, and another was a set of sixty recorded conversations with taxi drivers. These convert, direct observations corroborated the self-report data, finding frequent mention of problems by customers and supportive responses from the workers. Some of the people interviewed even mentioned trying to elicit problems from regular customers whom they observed to be upset or "down." As Nestmann states, "Everyday helpers are not restricted to reactive behavior, but also can stimulate and undertake help processes actively and on their own initiative" (p. 234).

These examples of informal helpers serve to underscore the point made several times in this section—it may be *where* we are in the social structure as much as *who* we are as individuals that affect our participation in both formal and informal helping activities.

A Functional Analysis of Volunteerism

Demographic analyses and case histories of prosocial behaviors such as donating and volunteering are often very interesting, but they are typically deficient in one important respect. They can tell us *who* engages in a behavior (and perhaps even where and when), but they can only indirectly suggest *why* these people do it. Thus, if we are to solve the particular puzzle of why people do or do not contribute to the public goods of the third sector, we must also consider their motivations.

Mark Snyder and his associates (Snyder, 1992b; Clary & Orenstein, 1991; Clary & Snyder, 1991; Omoto & Snyder, 1990) have used what they called a *functional analysis* to explain why people volunteer. A functional analysis of social behavior attempts to understand such behavior by identifying the purposes it serves for the person who engages in it—the "personal and social needs, plans, goals, and functions that are being served . . . [these] actions" (Clary & Snyder, 1991, p. 123). People can engage in the same kind of actions for very different reasons. As Table 8.2 indicates,

TABLE 8.2   THE FUNCTIONS OF VOLUNTEERISM: SAMPLE ITEMS FROM THE VOLUNTEER FUNCTIONS QUESTIONNAIRE

Value-expressive: Volunteerism is motivated by the volunteer's values about the welfare of others; it allows for the expression of personality characteristics and convictions that are part of the volunteer's self-concept.
• I am concerned about people less fortunate than me.

Social adjustive: Volunteerism is motivated by the volunteer's desire to fit in with and get along well with members of his or her reference group; it is a response to social pressure.
• People I'm close to want me to volunteer.

Ego-defensive: Volunteerism serves to help volunteers cope with inner conflicts and anxieties concerning their personal worth and competence; it makes a volunteer feel that he or she is a good person who will receive help if needed.
• Doing volunteer work relieves me of some of the guilt over being more fortunate than others.

Knowledge: Volunteerism is motivated by intellectual curiosity about the people that are helped and being a helper; it also may provide the volunteer with the opportunity to learn new skills and competencies or improve existing ones.
• Volunteering allows me to gain a new perspective on things.

the four primary needs that volunteering can satisfy are value-expressive, social adjustive, ego-defensive, and knowledge.

Consistent with this functional analysis, studies of volunteers (e.g., Allen & Rushton, 1983; Independent Sector, 1988; Anderson & Moore, 1978) suggest that different people have different reasons for engaging in this activity. National surveys suggest that the most common reason for volunteering seems to be value-expressive—volunteers are concerned about the welfare of other people. But volunteering also seems to be motivated by ego-defensive functions for many people. For example, Anderson and Moore (1978) reported that about 50 percent of the volunteers they interviewed gave "feeling useful and needed" as one of the major reasons why they volunteered. This motive may often lead people to volunteer their assistance in dramatic and risky ways. Many of the people who helped to rescue Jews during the Holocaust reported that these actions enhanced their self-images and reinforced their humanitarian values (Anderson, 1993).

Omoto and Snyder (1990; see also Snyder & Omoto, 1992a, 1992b) have conducted long-term studies of volunteers who work for groups that help people with AIDS. They found that people who were motivated by a value-expressive function were more willing to have direct contact with AIDS patients (by serving as buddies for them) than were people who were motivated by social-adjustive and ego-defensive functions. After a year, however, people whose initial motivations were to enhance their own self-esteem and personal development were *more* likely to still be volunteers than were people who were initially motivated by their desire to help others. Snyder (1992a) speculates that this may have been because the people who helped for selfish reasons may have initially had fewer illusions about the unpleasant aspects of helping AIDS patients (e.g., their physical deterioration as the disease progressed). He suggested, "Ironically, . . . it may be those volunteers who themselves are motivated by the most selfish of motivations who, in the long run, end up offering the greatest benefits to other people and making the most altruistic contributions to society" (1992a, p. 15).

A functional analysis of volunteerism may be of more than just theoretical interest. Imagine you are trying to get some classmates to join you in working for some charity. It would be useful to recognize that different people may be motivated by different reasons to join, for example, a group of people who rehabilitate impoverished people's homes. Some volunteers may use the volunteer activity to satisfy their needs to help others, some may use it to make social contacts with the other volunteers, and some may even use it to learn more about carpentry and home repair. If your goal is to get as many volunteers as possible, then you would want to try a number of different appeals and, if possible, tailor your appeals to the idiosyncratic motivations of potential volunteers.

THE ANSWER: SUMMARY AND IMPLICATIONS

In the first part of this chapter, we considered the problem of social dilemmas—situations in which actions that are in the immediate best interest of the individual are contrary to the long-term best interests of the group. Social dilemmas clearly demonstrate the interdependency that exists in groups of people and the need for cooperative efforts to maximize the payoffs for all concerned. Such situations are pervasive throughout our lives, and finding ways to promote greater concern for the well-being of the larger community is becoming more critical as the pools of scarce resources decrease and the demands on them increase.

As we have seen, numerous factors contribute to the problems inherent in social dilemmas. People often only think about the immediate rewards that selfish actions will bring them or the selfish actions of other people who share the dilemma. They fail to consider the long-term consequences and subsequently find themselves trapped by their actions. Unfortunately, people often want to get their fair share even if it means depleting a common resource pool or failing to provide some needed public good.

But it is possible to get people to act prosocially and cooperatively in a social dilemma. If people are able to coordinate their actions by discussing the nature of the social dilemma and recognizing that everyone faces the same common fate, individualistic responses are tempered, and greater cooperation occurs. However, these possible solutions are often difficult to achieve, and other strategies must be employed to save common resources. The implementation of structural solutions, such as appointing a leader who will administer the allocation of resources to protect the common pool, forces those involved to restrain their consumption. It may be that only by relinquishing some freedoms can everyone prosper. But if dramatic steps are not taken in many of the social dilemmas that exist today, we may have to confront Hardin's pessimistic prediction about people in a social dilemma: "Ruin is the destination toward which all men rush, each pursuing his own best interest in a society that believes in the freedom of the commons. Freedom in the commons brings ruin to all" (1968, p. 1244).

The second question in this chapter concerns another prosocial behavior that occurs in a collective context, volunteerism. How can it be maintained and increased? Voluntary private contributions to the welfare of the community represent an extremely important form of prosocial behavior. Indeed, in many respects, they may be as important as the interpersonal, one-to-one kinds of helping that were discussed in the earlier chapters. In recent years, the importance of these kinds of actions has increased because the willingness and ability of governmental agencies to provide certain public goods has declined. To understand *how* we can increase volunteerism, we must understand *why* people contribute to the third sector of the economy. There are a large number of pieces to this puzzle.

Demographic characteristics play an indirect role by giving people the ability and opportunity to contribute, by placing them in a certain role within a community and, sometimes, by affecting their feeling of belonging to a community. Volunteerism may also, in part, result from a person attempting to satisfy certain personal needs, including selfish ones. Although most contributions consist of donating small amounts of time or money, this kind of prosocial behavior can also take more dramatic forms. For example, some people contribute to the common good by becoming political activists or helping at the time of disasters. These behaviors, like donating and volunteering, seem to be influenced by both the social structure of a community and the activists' personal characteristics.

If we wish to increase the number of people willing to contribute to the public good, we probably need to recognize that altruistic motivations may not play a major role in these actions. Participating in the third sector is something people, voluntary associations, religious organizations, and corporations do for themselves as much as for others. Despite some sacrifices, this kind of work is, by its nature, rewarding. Wendy Kaminer (1984) says, "Paid work is simply a matter of earning a living. Volunteering is 'doing something you are about'" (p. 217). Studs Terkel (1975) wrote, "Most of us have jobs that are too small for our spirit. Jobs are not big enough for people . . . most of us are looking for a calling" (p. xxix). Working to improve the lives of others is such a calling. And if only a few of those volunteers become local heroes, they can make fundamental changes in society. In some instances, activism can be altruism; but even if this behavior is driven by solely egoistic motives, it would still constitute a very valuable contribution to the world in which we live.

9

Looking Backward, Looking Ahead

———— ❖ ————

*I*n the previous chapters we have examined important theoretical and practical questions about helping and altruism. It is now time to step back, take a broader perspective, and figure out what we really know. In this chapter, we begin by restating the questions that have guided our investigation of helping and providing brief answers to them. Rather than simply leaving these "facts" in isolation, in the second part of the chapter we attempt to integrate what we know in two general models of prosocial behavior. These models are most relevant to informal, unplanned, and short-term helping situations but may also be extended to more long-term and formal relationships. Then, in the final section of this chapter, we move beyond the pieces of the puzzle considered in the previous chapters and identify some new ones. We explore some theoretical and practical questions about prosocial behavior that have not yet been fully addressed in a systematic way within the field. But success in such an effort requires an understanding of current knowledge about when people help and why. What do we know about prosocial behavior?

THE QUESTIONS AND OUR ANSWERS TO THEM

In this section we review the questions about helping and altruism that began each of the previous chapters and present brief summaries of the answers that were given to them. The answers represent highlights of the major conclusions that were reached in response to each question. We present these questions and answers once more here because we believe it will help the reader to better understand and evaluate the integrative models that we subsequently propose. The questions and their answers are not intended to substitute for the chapter summaries or to suggest that the questions that have been asked can be answered in a few simple sentences. It is hoped that one lesson this book has conveyed to you is that, although it is possible to solve puzzles about human behavior, the solutions are rarely simple or straightforward. Pieces may appear to go together at first, but later we often find gaps and spaces and realize that the pieces do not fit in the way we originally thought they would. The answers that follow are simplified versions of the full answers that appear in the chapters, representing what we presently believe to be true. With this caveat in mind, let us turn to the questions we have addressed so far.

When Will People Help?

- Before bystanders offer help, they must decide that something is wrong, that another person's help is required to solve the problem, and that they have personal responsibility to provide this help. Then they have to decide whether they can provide the kind of

We certainly hope that your understanding of the helping and altruism literature will make you more responsive to the needs of others rather than offer another excuse not to get involved. (© 1994 by Sidney Harris.)

"Don't worry about it. It's probably just another one of those sociological experiments."

assistance that is needed. Only if the answer to each of these questions is yes will the bystanders help.

- When presented with a potential helping opportunity, people weigh the costs and rewards associated with various courses of action. Besides helping directly, people can help indirectly (e.g., call someone else for help), reinterpret the situation as one that does not require their personal assistance, or simply leave the scene. People will help directly when they believe that helping represents the most cost-effective action, considering all the interests involved.

What Motivates People to Offer Help?

There is no single thought or feeling that motivates all acts of helping. At least four separate processes produce motivations to help.

- People are sometimes motivated to help because they have learned through direct experiences and by observing others that helping will produce both tangible and intangible benefits for them. People will seek these rewards particularly when they are feeling sadness or other negative states.
- People's emotions and feelings also motivate helping. People typically experience empathic arousal when they see someone in distress. Usually (but not invariably), this arousal increases the motivation to help. This motivation may be egoistic and self-serving. By eliminating the other person's problem, helping can reduce the negative feelings that people experience as a result of the other's distress.
- In circumstances in which there are feelings of connectedness between the bystander and the person in need, the motivation to help can originate from a feeling of empathic concern about the other person. Empathic concern motivates altruistic helping, in which the primary goal is to improve the other person's welfare.
- Social and personal norms about what is appropriate or acceptable behavior may also motivate people to help. People may be motivated to help because they feel external or internal pressure to comply with these norms.

Are Humans Prosocial and Altruistic by Nature?

- There is reason to believe that humans may be genetically predisposed to be helpful. There are at least two evolutionary processes that could produce such tendencies in humans: kin selection and reciprocal altruism. Kin selection produces prosocial tendencies because helping one's kin can increase the likelihood that the helper's relatives will survive and reproduce some of his or her genes, even if the helper dies without reproducing. Reciprocal altruism may have this effect because helping an unrelated person can increase the likelihood that the altruist will receive aid from people he or she has helped, which also increases the altruist's chances of surviving and reproducing.

- Among humans, genes do not directly cause prosocial actions. Instead, genes provide humans with the capacity and inclinations to engage in such behaviors. The innate abilities to empathize with other humans and to effectively communicate one's emotions and feelings serve this function for prosocial behaviors. Although these abilities are substantially influenced by heredity, learning experiences influence them as well. This appears to be especially true of empathy, which is often taught and fostered by parents.

Does Prosocial Behavior Change as People Mature?

- As humans mature, they usually become more other-oriented and intrinsically motivated to help. Two interrelated developmental processes are responsible for these changes: social learning and social-cognitive development. Social learning involves direct reinforcement, observing other people, and direct instruction. Through these processes, children learn that helping is socially valued. Social-cognitive development involves maturational changes in the way children think about the causes of their own behaviors and of the actions of others. As children mature in the way they think about helping and being helped, the reasons why they help also change.
- Both social learning and social-cognitive development produce changes in moral reasoning—judgments about right and wrong. As children mature, moral reasoning usually becomes more prosocial and other-oriented; others' needs and welfare become more important at more advanced levels of moral reasoning.

Are Some People More Helpful than Others?

- There are stable individual differences in the willingness to help others. Demographic and social characteristics, such as sex and gender, are related to differences in helping. In many instances, men and women react differently to someone in need of help.

These differences not only involve whether assistance is offered but also the ways in which help is given. These male-female differences are due, in part, to socialization and norms about how members of each gender should behave. People are most likely to help in ways that are consistent with these gender-role norms.

- Characteristically helpful and nonhelpful people also differ with respect to personality traits. Helpful people are inclined to be empathic individuals, who are concerned about and willing to accept responsibility for the well-being of others. Helpful people are also individuals who have a sense of self-efficacy—they believe that if they attempt to do something they will succeed.

- Prosocial behavior is jointly determined by personal characteristics and the nature of the situation in which the helping could occur. Some types of people will help more in some kinds of situations and less in others.

When Will People Ask for Help and How Do They React When They Receive It?

- Before asking for help, potential help seekers make decisions similar to those made by potential helpers. They must decide if a problem really exists and if it could be solved with help from another person. If the answer to each of these questions is yes, then they must decide which person is most capable of providing this help.

- Decisions about when to ask for help and whom to ask are greatly influenced by concerns about self-esteem. People will ask for help if doing this does not threaten their self-esteem. As a result, people are usually reluctant to ask for help with a problem that involves a central aspect of their personality or character. This reluctance to ask for help may be reduced if the help seeker has a long-term, close relationship with the potential help provider or believes that the favor can be reciprocated.

- Self-esteem considerations strongly influence people's reactions to receiving help. Help that threatens self-esteem will produce immediate negative reactions. Help that increases a person's sense of control over the problem, however, will produce long-term positive reactions and increase independence in solving subsequent problems.

What Makes People Willing to Contribute to the Betterment of Others?

- In general, people will act cooperatively and contribute to the betterment of society when they believe it is in their self-interest to do so. People are unlikely to cooperate in situations in which they will immediately benefit from being selfish—even if selfishness may cause negative consequences for them and others in the long run. Communicating with other people or identifying with them can increase voluntary cooperation, but sometimes it is necessary to create stronger situational incentives to promote cooperation within the group.

- There are many reasons why people contribute time and money to charities. For some people, the primary motivation is altruistic, but for many more the motivation is egoistic. Volunteering can satisfy personal needs. This personal benefit can even outweigh the costs associated with charitable activities that involve considerable time, effort, and money, and sometimes require a long-term commitment.

These short and very simple answers represent the most basic pieces of the puzzle of altruistic and helpful behaviors. However, throughout this book we have attempted not only to identify the pieces of the puzzle but also to show how they fit together. Therefore, in the next section we try to put these answers and other pieces together in a completed puzzle that reveals the "big picture" of the causes of prosocial behavior.

PUTTING THE PIECES OF THE PUZZLE TOGETHER

Before we begin the endeavor, we want to make it clear that the models we introduce in this section concern only *help giving*. We believe that help seeking is a very important aspect of helping and altruism, and many of the elements of our models are related to frameworks for help seeking and reactions to aid, such as the one developed by Nadler, Fisher, and their colleagues (see Figure 7.5). Because most of this book has focused on help giving, however, we will focus our models on this phenomenon. In addition, these models are perhaps most appropriate for understanding acts of spontaneous helping. Given that the bulk of the helping research has investigated bystander intervention and other varieties of informal helping, it should not be surprising that our models would show a similar emphasis. However, we do not believe that it would be difficult to adapt our models to account for more formal or planned prosocial behavior, including the collectivist helping that we discussed in Chapter 8.

As you read about our two general models of prosocial behavior, there are three things to keep in mind. First, although the material that follows comes from the chapters you have read, we will be organizing it in new and different ways. Second, we will not include all the individual facts, findings, and theories we have covered in this book; the concepts we present here are intended to summarize the information we have presented thus far. We are trying to synthesize what we know about helping and altruism. Therefore, we will usually not reference specific research findings or studies that may be related to the point being made; these contributions have already been acknowledged in the previous chapters of this book, and additional referencing may prove distracting.

Finally, parts of the models represent as yet untested theories of prosocial behavior. A useful scientific model not only integrates what is already known about the subject but also suggests new hypotheses that need to be tested. Although the scientific study of helping and altruism has been proceeding for almost seventy years, researchers have still not identified all of the pieces and, with the accumulation of new evidence, some of the pieces may not fit as well as they originally believed. But advances in science always begin with approximations to knowledge, in which scientists gradually gain an understanding of the phenomena they study. Sometimes it is two steps forward and one step back; we believe that the models that follow represent steps forward. Only time and further study will show whether we are right.

Affective and Cognitive Models of Helping

Humans are feeling and thinking beings. Both affect (emotions, feelings) and cognition (thoughts) strongly influence our behavior. One view of how affect and cognition influence human behavior, proposed by Robert Zajonc (1980), is that affect and cognition are separate systems. Although these systems can (and undoubtedly do) influence each other, they often provide humans with independent sources of information about what has happened and independent guides as to how they should act. We rely on both affective and cognitive information in making our decisions, but they may tell us different things.

We believe that the most effective way of getting the big picture about helping and altruism is to divide prosocial actions into those best explained by affective processes and those best explained by cognitive processes (see Figure 9.1). Therefore, we will be presenting an affective model of helping and a separate cognitive model of helping. We must quickly add, however, that in the real world it is often impossible to look at a prosocial act and say that it is definitely an example of affective or of cognitive helping. The world is not divided this neatly. We have separated the processes for purposes of simplicity and clarity, but several of the processes (e.g., classical conditioning, standards of fairness) have both affective and cognitive aspects. In addition, you should keep in mind that feelings can influence thoughts and vice versa. We will consider these mutual influences at the conclusion of this section.

Zajonc (1980) proposed that affective reactions are more basic and primitive than cognitive responses and typically occur first (cf. Lazarus, 1982). Thus, we present the affective bases of helping first and then turn our attention to the cognitive bases.

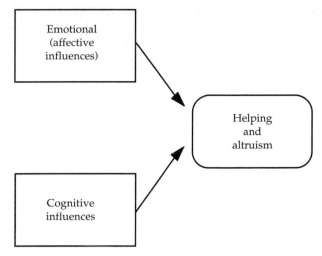

FIGURE 9.1
Determinants of helping and altruism.

Affective Bases of Helping

Figure 9.2 contains our model of the affective bases of helping. A brief word about the figure. A single arrow indicates a causal relationship between the elements in the model; for example, the arrow between "Empathic Reactions" and "Distress and Upset" indicates that the former causes the latter. Bidirectional arrows with heads pointing in both directions represent reciprocal influences; that is, one element influences and is also influenced by the other.

On the left-hand side of the model are innate, genetically based human characteristics we believe represent the origins of affective helping in humans. On the right-hand side are the three major motivations for affectively based prosocial actions (see also Batson, 1991). The goal of the model is to link these two sides. A basic premise of this model is that affective kinds of helping are, *in part*, caused by tendencies we have inherited from our ancestors. That is, we believe there is sufficient evidence that humans are genetically predisposed to react to distress in another person in ways that may cause them to help that person. The first part of the model presents the mechanisms responsible for this.

Inherent capacities and abilities. The neurological structures that are responsible for feelings and emotions (i.e., the limbic system) are, evolutionarily, among the oldest in the human brain. If there is an evolutionary basis for helping and altruism, the mechanisms for translating these genetic predispositions into behavior are likely to involve emotions. As Zajonc (1980) proposed, "Affect is the first link in the evolution of complex adaptive functions" (p. 156). In Chapter 4, we suggested that the genetic origins of helping and altruism may lie in *spontaneous communication* (i.e., the general tendency of humans to communicate their emotions). This innate tendency may have given rise to other more specific kinds of communication between humans, such as empathy. *Empathy* is a fundamental affective response of people to the problems and distress of others; even newborn infants display empathic reactions to the cries of other infants within their first forty-eight hours of life.

Our model proposes that spontaneous communication and empathy probably provided the capacities and abilities needed for the two genetic selection processes that could lead to the evolution of helpful and altruistic tendencies in humans—kin selection and reciprocal altruism.

Genetic selection processes. The notion of *kin selection*, as it applies to affectively based helping, is that some of our ancestors were genetically predisposed to help their relatives or kin. As explained in Chapter 4, the key to the survival of some trait or characteristic in a species is whether it contributes to the reproductive success of individuals who possess that characteristic. Thus, even altruists who died before they had offspring could have contributed to the reproductive success of their genetic characteristics by helping relatives (with whom they shared these genetic characteristics) survive and reproduce. If helpers' actions greatly increased the chances of their genetic relatives' survival and reproduc-

FIGURE 9.2
Affective bases of helping.

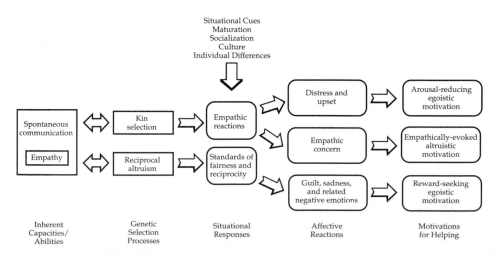

tion, then now-dead altruists would still have succeeded in transmitting a portion of their genes to future generations. Some of these genes would predispose people to be particularly responsive to distress in those close to them.

We believe that spontaneous communication and, more specifically, empathy greatly facilitate the process of kin selection. The spontaneous communication approach suggests that people will communicate most often and most effectively with those with whom they share positive interactive relations. These people are typically family members or others who live in close proximity. Thus, people are more likely to experience empathy in response to the needs of others with whom they are close because they are better able to communicate emotionally with them. As we discussed in Chapters 3 and 4, the research on emotional empathy is consistent with this premise. Humans and other animals are particularly likely to become more physiologically aroused by the problems, crises, and emergencies of others who are physically or psychologically close to them.

Note that not only does empathy facilitate kin selection, but the beneficiaries of kin selection are also likely to be people whose relatives were especially sensitive to the feelings of others. Thus, empathy is both an antecedent and a consequence of kin selection; this is why there is a bidirectional arrow between these boxes in Figure 9.2.

The other genetic selection process in the model is *reciprocal altruism*— mutual helping that increases the likelihood that unrelated but cooperating individuals will survive. The model indicates that successful reciprocal altruism also depends on affective communication and empathy. For reciprocal altruism to benefit helpers and their descendants, a potential helper must not only be able to effectively and efficiently recognize that another person needs help but also correctly distinguish between (1) those people who will reciprocate the aid and (2) potential cheaters who will accept the assistance but not reciprocate by helping. The individuals who are best at making this discrimination are also likely to be quite good at spontaneous communication and quite empathic. Why? Because they need to communicate effectively their expectations to the recipient of their help *and* perceive his or her true intentions accurately. Effective communication skills and empathy facilitate both of these. If reciprocal altruism increases the reproductive success of those who practice it effectively, it would increase the incidence of genetically based concern for reciprocity and fairness in interpersonal exchanges. Because reciprocal altruism would also increase the reproductive success of empathic individuals, the model also includes a bidirectional relationship between spontaneous communication (empathy) and reciprocity.

Situational responses. The next part of the model concerns people's reactions when they see another person in need. We believe there are two interrelated kinds of situational responses to the distress of another person: *empathic reactions* and *activation of standards about fairness and reciprocity*. These reactions are partly the product of the genetic predispositions we have been discussing, but they are also strongly influenced by more immediate and social causes. Evolutionary psychologists and behavioral geneticists recognize the importance of environmental, social, and cultural influences in determining whether genetically based predispositions will be expressed in immediate reactions to some event or stimulus in a person's environment, and this stage represents these social influences.

These influences, which are represented by the arrow at the top of Figure 9.2, include the immediate situational and social context, and maturation, socialization, culture, and individual differences. We examined how situational and social influences affect the responsiveness of individuals to others' needs in Chapter 2. Empathic reactions to someone in need are more likely to be triggered by some situations (e.g., clear emergencies) than by others. The nature of the social relationship between a potential helper and a victim can also have substantial impact on empathic reactions and feelings about fairness. In long-term relationships, the role of empathy tends to increase, while the importance of short-term reciprocation decreases.

Changes that occur within individuals over time and individual differences in personal characteristics also influence affective processes in helping. The research reviewed in Chapters 4 and 5 demonstrated that there are systematic *maturational changes* in people's capacity to experience empathy. As we noted earlier, newborns display a very primitive form of empathy within the first two days of life. By the age of 2, children are capable of experiencing basic forms of affective empathy. Cognitive empathy appears to take quite a bit longer to develop, but by the time children have reached puberty, most of them are capable of experiencing adultlike affective and cognitive empathic reactions.

In Chapter 5, we discussed how cultural factors and socialization can produce group and individual differences in reactions to someone in distress. For example, among those reared in collectivistic cultures in which group (rather than individual) achievement is a primary value, people are more responsive to the needs of members of their own group and less sensitive to the needs of members of other groups. With regard to family socialization, parental models are critical. Recall from Chapters 5 and 6 that many of the people who risked their lives to save Jews in Europe during World War II had parents with strong prosocial morals. There is also evidence that warm and nurturing parents tend to have nurturing children.

As we discussed in Chapter 6, there are also significant individual differences in the extent to which people experience empathy. These differences may result from variations in family experiences, social modeling, and gender socialization, although genetic factors appear to be involved as well. For example, the twin studies discussed in Chapter 4 indicated that a substantial proportion of individual differences in empathy were related to genetic heritage. Furthermore, supporting the premise that genetic influences are expressed primarily through emotional mechanisms, affective empathy has a greater heritability component than does cognitive empathy.

The other situational response concerns feelings about what is fair and just treatment of a person. The immediate (proximal) and more distant (distal) causes discussed above also affect a person's feelings about what is fair and just and how strongly he or she reacts to violations of these standards. Thus, just as empathic reactions produce certain affective reactions to a person in need of help, so does the activation of standards about fairness and reciprocity.

Affective reactions. The next part of the model concerns the potential helper's affective reactions to the situation and the person in need of help. As discussed in Chapter 3 and illustrated in Figure 9.2, affective reactions to potential helping situations can be experienced in a variety of ways. Through the process of empathy, people may experience negative emotional states such as *personal distress* and *upset*. These negative emotions are influenced directly by situational cues (e.g., emergencies) and by personal characteristics (e.g., people who are dispositionally unable to control their level of arousal are likely to experience negative arousal; Eisenberg et al., 1994).

Empathy can produce other affective reactions as well. Under some circumstances, people may feel *empathic concern* (e.g., feelings of compassion and concern for a victim). Empathy is most likely to generate empathic concern when there is a special bond between a potential helper and the person in need. This bond may result from characteristics of the immediate situation (e.g., perceptions of shared fates or focusing on the other person's feelings), a long-term personal relationship between the people involved or, even genetic relatedness, as suggested by evolutionary theories.

The other affective reaction identified by our model is the consequence of violating the potential helper's standards of *fairness and reciprocity* (see Chapter 3). Social standards of fairness, such as the norm of reciprocity, are universal across cultures, and people are generally motivated to act in ways that maintain these standards of fairness. For example, people will help others more when they have previously been helped themselves. In addition, the helper may be motivated by negative emotions, such as the guilt they experience when they violate these standards. Feelings of guilt may motivate us to help others in an effort to restore the general balance of fairness or to help to "repair" our self-image. Similarly, when we observe unjustified harm to others, we may experience sadness.

People may have very different reactions when they focus their attention on the person responsible for the violation of their standards of fairness. In such cases, people tend to experience a different set of negative emotions (e.g., anger) that reduce the likelihood of prosocial behavior toward the perpetrator of the violation. It is important to note that people do not react negatively to unfair or unjust actions simply because someone has broken some rule or norm. Rather they have concern for action that violates and challenges deeply held and fundamental principles about what is right and what is wrong. Anthropologists call such principles *mores*. All societies of which we are aware have mores about treating others fairly. Such mores are probably the result of both our evolutionary heritage and the things humans have learned about what they need to do to get along with one another. These lessons are culturally transmitted from one generation to another; they affect our ongoing behavior through our emotional reactions to the people who are the perpetrators of injustice and those who are the victims of the injustice.

Motivations for helping. Affective reactions directly influence the last component of the model—the motivations for helping. There are at least three distinct motivations for helping (see Chapter 3; also Batson, 1991). The motivation to help that is produced by distress and upset is primarily *egoistic*: People help in order to relieve their own discomfort aroused by observing the distress of another. Nevertheless, as the arousal: cost-reward model (see Chapters 2 and 3) suggests, one's own needs and the needs of others frequently become intertwined through the mechanism of affective empathy.

According to the empathy-altruism hypothesis, the affective reaction of empathic concern may elicit a truly *altruistic* motivation, in which the primary goal of the help given is to improve the other person's welfare. Thus, our model proposes that there are some prosocial actions that are truly other-oriented and solely motivated by an altruistic concern for another person's well-being. But as we noted in Chapter 3, altruistically motivated helping is probably much less common than egoistically motivated helping.

Like the motivation produced by distress and upset, the motivation produced by feelings such as guilt and sadness is also *egoistic*. These affective reactions lead to helping primarily because the person believes that helping will make him or her feel better by eliminating the negative mood or will produce some rewarding outcome. This portion of our affective model of helping is primarily based on the negative-state relief model and other similar models (see Chapter 3), which propose that people have learned that helping is often an effective way of making themselves feel better.

In summary, the affective bases of helping depicted in Figure 9.2 are likely to have their origins in genetic predispositions that have been shaped by long-term evolutionary forces. These genetic tendencies are expressed in affective mechanisms related to empathy and emotional reactions associated with adherence to or violations of standards of fairness and reciprocity. As current theories of behavioral genetics suggest, however, these genetic predispositions do not automatically or completely determine our actions. Social, environmental, cultural, and personal factors influence the extent to which people exhibit these emotional reactions as well as the specific nature of the emotion (e.g., empathic concern versus personal distress) that they experience. These emotions then determine whether helping is *altruistically motivated* (the result of empathic concern) or *egoistically motivated* (the result of distress, guilt, or sadness), or whether people will help at all (a consequence of anger).

What kinds of prosocial behavior are best explained by a model of the affective bases of helping? We believe that this model is most applicable to informal, unplanned, and short-term acts of helping. It also is likely to explain helping among friends and family members—people who are likely to evoke strong emotions in the helper. Furthermore, affect exerts its strongest influence when another person is in extreme distress or great danger. In these situations, it is probably helpers' hearts rather than their heads that determine their actions.

Cognitive Bases of Helping

As we said earlier, humans are both feeling and thinking beings, and thus affect is not the whole story of helping. The capacity for higher-level thought and reasoning distinguishes humans from other animals. Although there may be a strong affective basis of helping rooted in our evolutionary history, cognitive processes can also have a significant and perhaps an even more important influence on helping. Figure 9.3 summarizes the major cognitive mechanisms discussed in the previous chapters. As the figure illustrates, this kind of helping depends primarily on a potential helper's assessments of the costs and benefits associated with offering help. Our task is to explain how the other parts of the model affect this critical decision.

Acquisition processes.   This model places much less emphasis on genetic or inherited factors than does the model of affectively based helping. Instead, the distal causes of cognitively based helping are social and cultural influences on a person's thoughts about helping. Differences in families, social environments, and cultures produce differences among people with respect to direct-learning experiences, the social models to which they have been exposed, and the cultural and social values they have learned. From a cognitive perspective, people learn about helping and how to be helpful in the same ways they learn other social behaviors. As we saw in Chapter 5, direct learning (by classical conditioning and operant learning) is important. Children frequently learn that they should help others by receiving tangible rewards for helping. Children (and

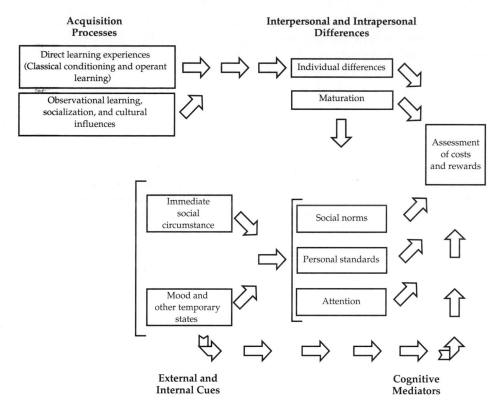

FIGURE 9.3
Cognitive bases of helping.

adults) are strongly influenced by observational (social) learning. By watching prosocial models, children can not only learn that helping is valued but also *how* to help and what happens to them when they help.

Of course, people's socialization experiences and culture also affect the way they think about helping. Individual families and entire cultures can differ in what they teach a child about helping. For example, American and Hindu Indian cultures evidently differ in what they teach children about repaying favors; Indians are more likely than Americans to believe that one has a moral (as opposed to a legal) responsibility to reciprocate favors (Miller & Bersoff, in press). These variations in personal and cultural histories can obviously lead to individual differences in thoughts about helping.

Interpersonal and intrapersonal differences. The second set of variables in the model concern more immediate and proximal causes of helping decisions. Cognitive processes, like affective processes, may be influenced by the personality characteristics and social roles of the potential helper, which have been shaped by the learning and socialization processes just described.

The next variable, maturational changes in cognitive processes, was considered in Chapter 5. Young children are cognitively egocentric: They find it difficult to learn to be helpful because they lack the cognitive ability to imagine themselves in another person's situation and truly appreciate another person's problem or needs. As children mature, they develop the necessary cognitive skills to perceive events from another person's perspective. As a result, they are better able to understand when and how to help. Similar changes occur in actual helping. External and tangible rewards for helping become less important as children mature. By late adolescence (around the age of 15 or 16), most people have developed personal, intrinsic motivations for helping, which directly and indirectly affect cognitively based kinds of helping.

External and internal cues. When a helping situation arises, the *transitory moods and feelings* of a potential helper and the immediate social circumstances come into play. As we discussed in Chapters 2 and 3, positive and negative moods can directly influence assessments of the costs and rewards of offering help. For example, people in good moods may help more because their positive mood makes them think more about the positive consequences of helping others. Chapters 2 and 3 also provided considerable evidence about the effects of *immediate situational factors* on helping. Such situational factors have a very important and direct influence on a potential helper's assessment of the rewards and costs of helping. Recall, for example, the concept of diffusion of responsibility (Chapter 2); when there are other people who also see the person in distress and could offer help, their presence substantially lowers a person's estimates of the costs of not offering help. As a consequence, helping is reduced.

Cognitive mediators. In Figure 9.3, we propose that personal characteristics and immediate social circumstances indirectly affect cognitive kinds of helping through a limited number of cognitive responses. These are *social norms, personal standards*, and *focus of attention*, which we discussed in Chapter 3.

Social norms are widely held expectations about what is and is not acceptable behavior. These expectations have their roots in individual differences in social and cultural experiences, as the path of arrows from the "Acquisition Processes" stage of the model indicates. Through personal experiences and observational learning, people learn about the social norms that their society or group values (e.g., the norm of social responsibility—helping those dependent on you, and the norm of reciprocity—helping others who have helped you). But there is also direct and implicit communication with other people in the same circumstances through which individuals learn what norms are operative in this specific situation and what response is expected of them. Thus, observers' learning experiences and the immediate situation contribute to their understanding of which social norms are most relevant in a particular situation.

Whereas social norms provide general guidelines about what people should do across a range of situations, personal standards relate to an individual's own ideals and feelings of moral obligation (see Chapters 3 and 5). Personal standards are intimately related to a person's self-concept, and there may be considerable variation in personal standards within the same culture. Moreover, maturational processes affect the extent to which personal norms affect judgments about helping. For example, among young children who have not yet developed a stable sense of self, personal standards are not important determinants of helping. However, by the age of 8 or 9, they begin to make internal attributions about their own helpfulness and the helpfulness of others, and personal norms begin to play a greater role in helping decisions.

The third cognitive mediator in the model concerns where potential helpers focus their *attention* when another person is in need. All the personal and situational variables we have been discussing influence the extent to which people pay attention to the needs of others as well as to their own needs. For example, because of different socialization experiences, men and women may attend differently to the needs of others (see Chapter 6), with women traditionally being more socially sensitive. With regard to temporary moods, positive affect leads people to attend more to others, while some negative states (e.g., depression) make them less attentive. In terms of the effects of the immediate circumstance, we saw in Chapter 2 that in overly stimulating environments people are usually less attentive to the needs of others.

Decisions about helping. According to the model presented in Figure 9.3, social norms, personal standards, and attention directly affect the final and most critical cognitive mediator, an observer's *assessment of the costs and rewards* associated with the decision about whether or not to help. A cost-reward analysis of helping assumes an economic view of human behavior—people are motivated to maximize rewards and minimize costs. This represents a decidedly egoistic perspective toward the motivation of helping, one in which people are assumed to be mainly concerned about their own self-interest. The arousal: cost-reward model of emergency intervention (see Chapter 2) is perhaps the most explicit in incorporating these considerations into the decision to help, identifying two basic categories of costs and rewards relevant to a helping decision. One category involves personal costs (e.g., injury) and potential rewards (e.g., praise) for helping. The other category considers the costs for the person not receiving help; this category includes both personal costs (e.g., blame from others, guilt) and empathic costs (e.g., negative feelings associated with empathizing with a person who remains in distress) for non-intervention. The arousal: cost-reward approach also recognizes some flexibility in the responses that people can make when their help is needed. As noted earlier, depending on their perceptions of the most favorable balance of costs and rewards, people may decide to help directly, to help indirectly, or not to offer any help.

In summary, cognitively determined helping has its distal causes in learning and socialization experiences and its more immediate causes in the personal characteristics of potential helpers and the characteristics of the situations in which help might be given. Personal characteristics, maturational processes, temporary mood states, and immediate social circumstances directly influence assessments of the costs of and rewards for helping. These factors may also indirectly affect these assessments through their influence on social norms, personal standards, and focus of attention. Ultimately, the potential helper considers the perceived costs and rewards for various courses of action when making the final decision whether to help.

We believe that this cognitive model, like the affective model of helping presented earlier, can explain many acts of spontaneous, unplanned, and informal helping that occur among friends and even relatives. But we believe that the cognitive model is much more useful than the affective model in explaining the kinds of collective prosocial and cooperative actions that were discussed in Chapter 8. As noted in the questions and answers section of this chapter, the research presented in that chapter strongly suggests that decisions to contribute time or money to public goods or charities are most often determined by cost-reward calculations. Volunteers and contributors are usually individuals who have decided that it is in their own long-term best interests, as well as the long-term best interests of others in the community, to engage in work for the public good. Thus, we believe that most (but perhaps not all) actions of this type represent cognitively based forms of helping.

Affect and Cognition

Before we conclude our discussion of the two models, it is important to explicitly recognize that although we can talk about affective bases and cognitive bases of helping separately, the products of these processes are typically interrelated in the decisions that people make. For instance, the degree to which we experience affective empathy strongly influences the cognitive assessment of costs for not helping when we are deciding what action we should take. The more unpleasant the arousal we experience by empathizing with a person in distress, the greater will be the anticipated costs for not helping and, as a consequence, the more likely we will be to help.

Similarly, assessments of costs can influence the level of arousal that a person experiences. Suppose you see someone fall into a fast-flowing river—you immediately become aroused and distressed. Then you notice that the victim is your brother! The guilt, shame, and sorrow that you anticipate if you were to do nothing makes you even more aroused and upset. This higher level of unpleasant arousal may now impel you to immediate action. You may not know exactly what to do, but you know you must do *something*.

Alternatively, alterations of the perception of costs for helping may eventually reduce the amount of arousal you experience. Recall yet again the Kitty Genovese incident to which we have returned time and again throughout this book. The costs for direct help for the bystanders were high (e.g., the possibility of being stabbed if they intervened), and the costs for not helping were high (e.g., her death). One way such "high cost for helping—high cost for not helping" dilemmas can be relieved is by reinterpreting or redefining the situation, as described by the arousal: cost-reward model. The observers of Kitty Genovese's murder did just this by diffusing responsibility. By convincing themselves that someone else would help, bystanders could come to believe that the emergency was over. By construing the situation in this way, their level of arousal could be decreased, further reducing the likelihood of helping. Although there is a dramatic difference between *believing* that someone else will help and *knowing* that someone has helped, the effects on a bystander's arousal and, consequently, his or her motivation to help may be similar.

The mutual influence of affect and cognition can also occur at a more fundamental level. As we observed in Chapter 3, high levels of arousal can influence how we perceive situations and our assessment of costs and rewards. Specifically, high levels of arousal focus our attention very narrowly on the most important, central stimuli at the expense of less important, peripheral stimuli. We process the most important information thoroughly and exhaustively, but we may largely ignore the peripheral information that is available. People who have been in a car accident sometimes report that they can provide vivid details about the hood ornament or shape of the bumper on the oncoming car—the central stimuli in the situation. But they recall almost nothing about what was happening on either side of them—the peripheral information. As we saw in Chapters 3 and 4, the impact of this focusing process on helping can be profound. People who are unable to rationally assess the full range of costs in the situation because of their extreme levels of arousal may help impulsively. Because this type of impulsive helping is nonrational, it can jeopardize the lives of both the bystander and the person in need in some cases. Ironically, the problem here is not too much apathy but instead too much empathy.

In summary, decisions about whether to help are based on both affective and cognitive processes. Although these systems can operate independently, they usually combine to determine our behavior. Their influences can be direct and obvious (e.g., by arousal increasing the costs for not helping) or more indirect (e.g., by arousal influencing how information is processed). The research on helping and altruism can be assembled into a clearly discernible, although still sometimes complicated picture. Nevertheless, some important pieces to the puzzle are still missing. In the next section, we consider where we might look for these missing pieces.

SOME UNANSWERED QUESTIONS

The two complementary models depicted in Figures 9.2 and 9.3 summarize and integrate much of what we now know about the determinants of helping and altruism. They represent our attempt to provide a coherent description of when and why people help. Although descriptive models are important and useful, in science, models or theories that only summarize previous findings are less valuable than those that also suggest new questions. Consider Einstein's special and general theories of relativity: They not only provided coherent syntheses of previous theories and experiments in physics, but they also generated important new avenues of inquiry (Hawking, 1988; Will, 1986). These two related theories have stimulated thousands of experiments in physics since they were proposed. Obviously, even in our most grandiose moments, we do not place the models presented in this chapter in the same category (or even on the same time-space continuum) as Einstein's theories. But we do believe that they can be used to generate a number of new theoretical and empirical questions about altruism and helping. In this final section, we use the models for this purpose.

With a Little Help from Our Friends . . .

Although each of the authors brought different experiences, backgrounds, and interests to this book, we recognize that there are still other perspectives on the causes and consequences of helping and altruism. Therefore, we contacted our colleagues throughout the world and asked: "What do you think are the one or two most important theoretical or applied questions about helping and altruism that you think remain unanswered and demand our continued attention?" Some of the questions they posed are included along with our own. We begin with our version of the nature-nurture question.

The Nature and Nurturance of Empathy and Helping

As our affective model (Figure 9.2) suggests, the capacity for empathy is a critical component (perhaps even the most critical component) for understanding helping and altruism. Questions concerning how people acquire and develop this capacity are therefore fundamental ones. The answers to these questions need to consider genetic, biological, and environmental influences.

How do genes influence empathy and helping? In our affective model, we propose that there is an evolutionary, genetic basis for human empathic capacities. But, how does our genetic heritage become translated into specific feelings and actions when we see someone in distress? Questions about genetic influences have extremely complex and difficult answers. Consider, for example, a characteristic that we know is largely determined by heredity—our height. Scientists still do not understand exactly how the genes for height actually influence how tall we become. The answer for helping behavior will probably be even more complex. Furthermore, it is difficult to know where to begin to find the answer. Researchers currently know very little about the specific mechanisms by which genes influence empathic reactions to specific situations or how genetic differences might produce differences in general empathic tendencies. Nevertheless, we have some clues.

As we noted in Chapter 4, Buck and Ginsburg (1991) believe that a genetic predisposition toward spontaneous communication may be the underlying mechanism for empathy. These researchers see the communicative gene as being at the root not only of altruism but also of all social behavior. They argue that the establishment of affective communication and social bonding must necessarily precede the acquisition of cognitive skills associated with prosocial action. Thus, the communicative gene may be the key to understanding this aspect of prosocial behavior. It creates the ability to communicate emotionally, which is the skill that is necessary for empathy to occur. Nevertheless, the relationship between general emotional communication skills and empathy is not yet well understood; additional evidence on this topic could help clarify how genes influence our capacity for empathy.

Although the processes proposed by Buck and Ginsburg (1991) are plausible and merit additional psychological research, it is also possible that the genetic basis for empathy and helping is more direct. That is, there may be an empathic or altruistic gene (or set of genes). Molecular biology might shed additional light on this matter. The Human Genome

Project is a massive, fifteen-year project funded by the United States government to identify the location and function of all the genes in the human genome. The methodology currently being used to identify the genes responsible for certain physical and mental disorders is potentially applicable to the identification of the genes that influence emotional reactivity, empathic capacities, and altruism. So far, only about 5 percent of the over 100,000 genes in humans have been mapped (*The New York Times*, December 28, 1993). Thus, there is ample opportunity for these genetic mapping techniques to discover the way in which certain genes affect empathy and altruism in humans. However, it is not necessary to wait for the results of the Human Genome Project to ask the next question.

How do biology and physiology influence empathy? Empathy does not have to be specifically genetically programmed for biological structures and functions to influence this process. And, there is very good reason to believe that, independent of genetics, both neurological and biochemical factors are involved in the ability to experience empathy and the manner in which it is experienced. Research in clinical neuropsychology indicates that when individuals with damage to certain portions of the right hemisphere of the brain are shown pictures of people portraying different emotions (e.g., anger, sadness), they have great difficulty identifying the emotion the other person is experiencing and in feeling such emotions themselves. This finding strongly suggests that such individuals would have great difficulty experiencing empathy in response to another person's distress (Borod, 1992; Cimino, Behner, & Allen, 1994). Despite this apparent link between brain function and empathic capacity, little research has examined neuropsychological influences on empathic reactions to distress in others. Similarly, biochemical processes may be involved. Levels of testosterone, for instance, are related to various forms of social behavior, such as dominance and aggressiveness (Dabbs, Riad, & Lathangue, 1992). Thus, it is possible that the different kinds of empathic arousal described in the affective model of helping (i.e., distress, empathic concern, sadness) are associated with different patterns of biochemical as well as neurological activity.

Evidence of genetic and biological influences on empathy would not mean that our genetic heritage "forces" us to behave in certain ways or that biology determines our destiny. It certainly would not imply that empathy can totally be explained by biological processes. As DeKay and Buss (1992) noted, a common misconception about evolutionary and biological approaches to human behavior is that they view humans as "robotlike automatons, rigidly programmed by genes to carry out activities that are inflexible and impermeable to environmental, social, and cultural influences" (p. 186). Instead, current thinking about evolution and behavioral genetics recognizes the importance of environmental, social, and cultural influences in determining whether genetically based predis-

BOX 9.1

Empathy and Helping

Ross Buck (University of Connecticut): "The nature of and relationship of communicative and selfish genes needs to be considered. I suspect that both exist and that they are the ultimate origins of affiliative and agonistic tendencies. There are no altruistic genes. Altruism is based upon communicative genes."

Michael Cunningham (University of Louisville, Kentucky): "What are the individual evolutionary advantages versus disadvantages of various levels of empathy and helpfulness? Do nice guys really finish last, in terms of having shortened lives and leaving fewer surviving offspring than selfish people? Is there a genetic pattern of empathy and altruism that provides an optimal balance of long-term self-interest versus social interest?"

David Rosenhan (Stanford University): "There are clearly biological roots to prosocial behavior. They need to be understood, not only for themselves, but because the biological determinants of prosocial behavior are likely to be the same determinants of other behaviors, thereby linking prosociality to other domains."

Ervin Staub (University of Massachusetts): "I believe that in some circumstances, a feeling of responsibility in addition to empathy is important for helping to occur. The relative importance of the two and the conditions under which each may be especially influential remains to be demonstrated."

positions will be expressed in immediate behaviors. Thus, there is also a need for further study of the role of a person's environment and learning experiences in the development of empathy and prosocial behavior (see Box 9.1), which leads us to the next question.

In what ways does culture affect empathy and helping? Because we are normally so totally immersed in our own culture, we often find it difficult to adopt other cultural perspectives. Frequently, it does not even occur to us that there are other cultural perspectives. Nevertheless, our culture exerts a profound influence on how we view ourselves and how we relate to other people, and there are substantial differences among different cultures. For example, perceiving a sharp distinction between oneself and others may be a distinctly Western cultural orientation (Markus & Kitayama, 1991). In Western culture, we typically see ourselves as individuals with unique sets of characteristics that make us distinct from others. In contrast, Markus and Kitayama describe the emphasis of non-Western cultures as involving "connectedness": the self is viewed primarily in connection with others. In these cultures, "one's behavior is [viewed as] determined, . . . [and] organized by what the actor perceives to be the thoughts, feelings, and actions of *others* in the relationship" (Markus & Kitayama, 1991, p. 227; italics in original). This fundamental connection between the self and others is likely to have a significant influence on a person's capacity to empathize with others and on other prosocial orientations. As we saw in Chapter 8, religion is also an element of culture that is influential in the inculcation of helping attitudes and connections to others.

In both our affective and the cognitive models, we have identified cultural factors as important influences on empathy and the ultimate decision to help. In the affective model, culture directly affects both empathic reactions and the standards that an individual considers when determining the "fairness" of some outcome. In the cognitive model, culture indirectly affects social norms and personal standards, which, in turn, affect the assessment of the costs and rewards of helping. Nevertheless, relatively little attention has actually been paid to cross-cultural differences in helping (see Moghaddam, Taylor, & Wright, 1993). This task has apparently been left primarily to sociologists and anthropologists. A recent review by Alan Fiske (1991), however, has reminded us that these cultural factors are extremely important determinants of helping and altruism. Additionally, Fiske's analysis suggests that the debate about whether helping is motivated by altruistic or egoistic motives may represent an overly simplistic and provincial Western view of helping and altruism. For example, he argues that an analysis of how humans relate and interact in many non-Western cultures indicates that, "it is invalid to assume that all human behavior is driven by selfish individualism" (p. 180); rather there may be multiple motives for prosocial behavior that go far beyond the egoism versus altruism debate. Thus, one important question to pursue is, How do societies differ in their views of the causes and consequences of prosocial actions? The answer to this question could place prosocial behavior in a broader context, which might ultimately reveal additional factors that play major roles in helping, altruism, and other forms of prosocial behavior.

Although such an enterprise would greatly improve our scientific understanding of prosocial behavior, there are other, more practical reasons for this activity as well. It has become almost trite to point it out, but the world *is* getting smaller; we are becoming a global village. As a result, our individual and collective lives will increasingly be affected by people from cultures different from our own. For these interactions to be positive and mutually beneficial, we need to understand and appreciate what people from these cultures do and do not believe are prosocial thoughts, feelings, and actions.

Just as we need to learn more about how and why people from different cultures may differ with regard to prosocial thoughts, feelings, and actions, we also have to become more knowledgeable about such differences among individuals within the same culture. Although researchers now readily acknowledge the significant impact of individual differences on helping (see Chapter 6), we still know relatively little about this issue as compared to what we know about situational influences on helping (see Chapter 2).

How do individual differences affect helping? Both the affective and cognitive models propose (see Figures 9.2 and 9.3) that individual differences in personal characteristics directly and indirectly affect prosocial actions. As you read in Chapter 6, researchers have begun to identify what personal characteristics influence prosocial behavior, but they know relatively little about *how* these characteristics influence helping, how they relate to more general personal characteristics, and what the origins of these individual differences are. We believe that the question about the origins of individual differences in prosocial tendencies is particularly important. To be sure, in Chapters 4 and 5 we discussed some general mechanisms and processes that appear to be responsible for differences among people in prosocial tendencies (e.g., inherited tendencies, the behavior of models, moral reasoning, social and cognitive development), but the specific manner in which these processes produce lasting individual differences in prosocial tendencies remains largely unknown.

At present, the best we can do is to identify certain parental characteristics or social circumstances that are correlated with prosocial propensities. As you are aware, correlation does not imply causation. That is, although we can document that a parent's moral actions are related to a child's helpfulness, usually we cannot conclude that this aspect of the parent's behavior specifically caused the child to grow to be a relatively helpful individual. At the very least, more longitudinal studies in which the same people are observed over extended periods of time are needed to better understand the processes involved. Work on the development of intervention strategies designed to increase the incidence of spontaneous positive, other-oriented actions among children and adults, besides their practical value, would be even more directly informative about the causal relationships.

In addition, new theoretical models are needed that attempt to explain how prosocial tendencies develop. These models could place helping in a larger context of individual differences. For instance, temperamental factors related to an individual's ability to regulate mood may play an important role in how people experience empathic arousal and thus may influence their motivations to help (Eisenberg et al., 1994). In contrast to the relatively small number of comprehensive models of individual differences in helping, there are a large number of fairly sophisticated models of antisocial behavior (especially aggression). We believe that it is as important to gain an understanding of what makes some people more helpful than others as it is to learn why some people are more aggressive than others. Indeed, understanding the former may even help us to better understand the latter.

In summary, despite all that we know about empathy and helping, there is still much to learn, particularly about the processes involved in the development of prosocial orientations (see Box 9.2). We need to ask about how empathy and other prosocial tendencies originate and develop in humans and about the interplay between biological and social processes. Of special interest are the mechanisms responsible for the commonalities and the differences in humans' capacity to experience both cognitive and emotional empathy.

Of course, understanding the origins and causes of empathy would not answer all the questions relevant to the affective model of helping. If we return to Figure 9.2, we see the model suggests that the different motives for helping provide critical links between empathic responses and helping. We now turn to questions related to the motivations that produce helping and altruism.

Motivations for Helping

Among the psychologists who study helping and altruism, there are few topics that have generated more interest and debate than the question of what motivates people to help. As we indicated in the affective model (Figure 9.2) and discussed at length in Chapter 3, there are at least three distinct motives for helping. Strong empirical support for the two egoistic paths has been obtained, and there is little controversy about the existence of egoistic motives for helping. However, the third path, the altruistic path, has been the subject of more controversy. Nevertheless, we are persuaded by the current research on this topic that, under some conditions, helping can be primarily motivated by the helper's altruistic concern for the well-being of the other person. As a result, additional research on this specific issue is probably not needed. (This view, however, is not uniformly shared by other helping researchers; see Box 9.3.) Still, the need for additional research concerning what motivates people to help would be valuable. Important questions remain about the relative frequency of altruistic and egoistic helping, the determinants of altruistic motivation, and the impact of altruistic motivation on how people help.

How common is altruism? Although the evidence for the existence of true altruism seems compelling, current research sheds little light on the relative frequency of egoistic versus altruistic helping outside the laboratory. We suspect that the frequency of egoistic helping is substantially greater than altruistic helping, but this view is based more on our consideration of the sheer number of conditions (e.g., empathic concern for the victim, low-to-moderate costs of helping) that must be present for truly

BOX 9.2

Differences in Prosocial Tendencies: Causes and Consequences

Michael Cunningham (University of Louisville, Kentucky): "One aspect of patience may be the capacity to continue to be helpful in the fact of frustration, such as a recipient who spurns ones' initial helpfulness. How is patience, and persistence in helping, developed?"

Nancy Eisenberg (Arizona State University): "One question is the relative contributions of nature (e.g., genetic factors, including temperamental factors) and socialization to the development of prosocial behavior. A second question is what aspects of socialization are most related to prosocial development."

William Graziano (Texas A&M University): "Is there such thing as an 'Altruistic Personality'; that is, are there persons who regularly incur costs to benefit others without any motive, conscious or unconscious, to benefit themselves? What are the socialization antecedents of persons who have the tendency toward altruism, expressing it occasionally and how do the socializing agents make these experiences 'stick'? Turning to the dark side, what quality lets some people be immune to the suffering and distress of persons around them?"

Elizabeth Midlarsky (Columbia University): "What are the patterns of develop-

ment of altruism across the lifespan? Are the manifestations of altruism qualitatively different at different ages?"

Sidney Rosen (University of Georgia): "There is increasing empirical evidence that helpers react negatively when their initial efforts to help are rebuffed, as evidenced by expressions of negative affect and attributional activity that casts the needy rejecter in an unfavorable light. But we have yet to identify (a) those factors (in the situation, the helpers, or the recipients) that determine whether the helpers will persist in the effort to overcome the recipients' resistance; and (b) what impact an extensive personal history of such rebuffs has on rejected helpers' self-images of competence at helping and of altruistic concern."

Ervin Staub (University of Massachusetts): "I believe we already have a reasonable understanding of the childhood origins of helping and altruism. We don't know, however, what experiences might develop caring, helping, and altruism in people who had harsh or abusive environments as children. Do the conditions that contribute to resiliency also contribute to caring, helping, and altruism?"

altruistic helping to occur. Alternatively, altruism might be much more common than the research would lead us to believe. Most of the research on helping has involved laboratory interactions among strangers rather than among relatives or close friends, but most of our daily interactions involve friends and family members for whom altruistic motivations are more likely to be aroused. Studying helping and altruism in more natural settings has several potential practical and theoretical benefits. With regard to the possible practical value of such research, it might identify techniques that could be used to improve personal relationships among people; with regard to the theoretical value, it would also provide tests of existing theories of helping in nonlaboratory settings and yield new information about the causes and consequences of egoistic and altruistic motivations to help. The next question considers one aspect of the consequences.

How do different motivations influence the ways in which people help? Much of the research on helping has examined people's responses in very constrained situations. For example, sometimes people have a choice simply to return a lost object or not; other times, they are asked how many hours or how much money they will donate to a cause or person. However, outside the laboratory, the decision is rarely so cut and dried. Think of the last time you were in a potential helping situation. There were probably many ways that you could have chosen to help, and you probably spent as much time and energy deciding what to do as you did deciding whether you should do something. The issue of how people help is thus an important but frequently overlooked one.

It is possible that people with different motivations will choose to help others in different ways. People who are motivated by egoistic reasons may be primarily concerned with short-term efforts that will provide the most immediate personal gratification (self-reward) or personal relief from the other's distress (arousal reduction) with the least effort. Their actions may tend to be superficial and perfunctory. Furthermore, although the helper's desires and the other person's needs may coincide, this may not always be the case. For example, if you are asked to help someone with a mathematics assignment, it may be rewarding and relatively easy for you to simply do the problem for the person. In the long term, however, it would probably be more beneficial for the other person (although more difficult and time-consuming for you) if you made sure that they understood how to solve the problem on their own (see Chapter 7). In contrast, altruistically motivated helpers may be very sensitive to the long-term consequences of their actions for the recipient and less concerned about a "quick-fix" for the problem. As a consequence, they may be more likely to make a deeper commitment that could even involve some significant short-term costs. Thus, although we know quite a bit

BOX 9.3

Motivations for Helping

Robert Cialdini (Arizona State University): "When we empathize with another's suffering, we hurt in a way that frequently leads to helping. For me, the most important question in the scientific study of helping action today is: 'What is the nature of that empathically generated hurt? Is it ultimately selfless or selfish?' The answer would be inordinately instructive about the character of human nature."

Michael Cunningham (University of Louisville, Kentucky): "It is clear that relatives and friends can provide more rewards for helping, and more costs for not helping, than can strangers. As a consequence, most helping for such people is automatic rather than deliberate. Yet generosity is not unlimited, even for kin. At what level of costs do people evaluate the rewards versus costs when they are considering helping their relatives and friends? Are there actuarial data indicating how long high intensity helping will be given to people of various relationships (paraplegic friend, declining parent, mentally retarded child, etc.)?"

William Graziano (Texas A&M University): "How do we define altruism and its underlying intent? Is there any good way to deal with the problem of equating altruism with intent? We may need a tough-minded philosopher to help us with this question."

Jurek Karylowski (University of North Florida): "The most important theoretical question that needs to be answered regards an interplay between empathy and anticipatory guilt (or anticipatory self-satisfaction) in motivating helping. At some level the factors are antagonistic, yet at another level they complement each other."

Melvin Lerner (Washington University): "How are the processes involved in the empathy-caring-helping reactions related to those underlying the sense of deservingness and justice?"

Mark Snyder (University of Minnesota): "There is a distinction between energizing effects—what moves people to action, and directive influences—what channels their action along one course or another. We need to disentangle questions of what prompts people to help and questions of what determines the forms that helping takes. Over time, energizing and directive influences may be somewhat different in prompting helping and sustaining it."

Richard Sorrentino (University of Western Ontario, Canada): "Is there really such a thing as an altruistic motive? I think not. Is empathy the key to unselfish or genuine altruistic behavior? I think it could be."

Ervin Staub (University of Massachusetts): "More work is needed in this area, including work that shows how bystanders can recruit others to join them in action. This is especially important when helping by one person would be dangerous, making it less likely that any one person will act."

about when people will help, more research is needed to understand how people decide what kind of help they will provide. We also need to consider more fully what helping means from the recipient's point of view as well as from the helper's. This brings us to the next issue and set of questions.

The Long-Term and Indirect Impact of Prosocial Actions

Research on what motivates people to offer help has usually focused only on the immediate benefits that helping produces for the helper (e.g., reduction of arousal) and the recipient. As we noted earlier, even these actions tend to be highly constrained by the experimental situation. Is it possible that prosocial actions might have additional positive or negative consequences? This leads us to consider some more specific questions about the consequences of helping.

How do the motivations for helping and altruism influence other forms of social behavior? Batson (1991) has suggested that empathic concern can produce other positive outcomes besides altruistically motivated helping. Among those he enumerated are the inhibition of aggression, reduction of racial tension, conflict in classroom situations, reduction of international tension, and reduction of domestic violence. It is also possible that the positive effects of egoistic motivations may not generalize to the same extent as the effects of altruistic motivation. These possibilities seem worthy of further study.

Is helping healthy? Research on helping has typically focused on the immediate rewards for helping—rewards that can be measured in a one-hour laboratory experiment. It is possible that helping also has long-term cumulative benefits for the helper. Because helping is socially valued and demonstrates one's positive impact on the social environment, it may enhance self-esteem and feelings of self-efficacy, and such feelings are integral aspects of good psychological health. In the short term, this seems to be the case. People who regularly help others also report feeling a sense of stimulation, warmth, and increased energy while helping and a sense of relaxation, freedom from stress, and enhanced self-worth after helping (Luks, 1992; see also Chapter 5). Helping others can also distract people from their own problems and help put their problems in proper perspective. As Midlarsky (1991) concluded, "Helping others can be a means for productive and successful coping with a variety of life stresses" (p. 238). But what about the long term? Are helpful people happier, less likely to become depressed, more self-confident, and better socially adjusted? Some studies suggest that this may be the case (see Midlarsky, 1991;

Penner et al., in press), but clearly much more research is needed particularly to determine whether helpfulness improves one's mental health or being mentally healthy increases one's helpfulness.

In addition to these direct psychological benefits of helping, helping may have indirect social benefits. Helping others normally improves the social welfare of one's group and may create ties with other people that ultimately contribute to our own well-being. As we noted in Chapter 7, people with strong social-support networks are better able to cope with a wide variety of psychological, social, and physical problems. In essence, helping others now may provide a type of "social insurance" for when we need help in the future.

As we consider the possible long-term benefits of helping, we must entertain another possibility. Are there negative consequences of helping? As we saw in Chapter 7, from the perspective of recipients, there is potentially a dark side to helping. Under some conditions, they experience a decrease in self-esteem and feelings of personal control. But could there also be negative consequences of helping for the helper?

What are the potential negative consequences to helpers for helping? In Chapter 2, we examined many of the potential costs for helping to the benefactor, such as personal danger, discomfort, and embarrassment. Once again, current research has focused mainly on the immediate consequences. Unforeseen, long-term negative effects are also possible. In addition, there may be circumstances in which being compassionate and helpful does not produce the best outcome for either the helper or the recipient of help. The problem of *codependency* is one such case.

Originally, codependency was a term used to describe the spouses (usually wives) of alcoholics who supported their alcoholic partners by helping them hide their drinking from others and taking over many of the functions they once performed. Later, however, the term was broadened to describe any excessive and unhealthy preoccupation with another person's problems (Beattie, 1987). There is considerable skepticism among mental health professionals as to whether there really is such a disorder as codependence, and we share these reservations. Indeed, we know of only one well-controlled empirical study that shows codependent individuals may act in the manner proposed by Beattie (Lyon & Greenberg, 1991). Nonetheless, it may be productive for researchers to further consider how and why some people can become so concerned about the welfare of another that they fail to consider whether their actions on that person's behalf are, in fact, detrimental to themselves, to the recipient, or to both.

Another case of helping too much may be *futile care*. Imagine someone in the late eighties whose physical health and mental alertness have degenerated substantially over the past few years; the person is in a coma and likely near death. Is it appropriate from a moral or ethical perspective for the person's physician to use extremely valuable and scarce medical resources to maintain this person's physiological functions a few more years? What if the resources needed to prolong this person's life could be used to bring a 30-year-old person back to full health? Furthermore, once these "heroic" medical efforts have begun, legal constraints often make it very difficult and painful for family members to the take a person off life support even when this treatment is clearly futile. Throughout the book, we have implicitly and explicitly assumed that helping someone is always the best thing to do, but what would be the best thing to do in this instance? Whereas laboratory research tends to simplify problems, the answers to questions such as these are very complicated—if there are any answers at all. Many different decisions could be reached, each with its own rationale and a different set of costs and consequences. Thus, it is important that future research on helping consider these broader, longer-term, and more complicated effects of helping on the helper and on others.

Research of this type may also improve the quality of social-policy decisions. For example, the resources available for medical care are finite. It is ultimately a zero-sum game; the more resources devoted to one type of care, the less that are available for other types. As unpleasant as we may find it, in the very near future, decisions about how money, personnel, and equipment for medical treatments should be allocated will probably be based on cost-benefit analyses similar to those described in the helping models.

Such questions are already being asked and will become even more prominent as the United States moves toward a managed health-care system. For example, the state of Oregon has proposed a radically new plan to determine the medical treatments for which its Medicaid system would provide payment (*U.S. News and World Report*, August 10, 1992). In the plan, 709 medical procedures are ranked on the basis of such factors as the severity of the illness, the likelihood of the patient's improvement, and the cost of the procedure. Based on available funds, a cutoff line is established and medical treatments that fall below the line are not covered by the state. The goal of this plan (which is essentially a structural solution to this social dilemma; see Chapter 8) is to ration medical care fairly and efficiently so that 100,000 people presently not covered in the state's Medicaid system would have access to treatment for their most serious medical problems. Perhaps helping researchers, along with medical ethicists, economists, and other professionals, can use insights drawn from their understanding of prosocial behavior to assist in the formulation of plans such as these and ensure that they provide ethical, humane, and rational solutions to such agonizing problems.

The questions we have been discussing have been generated primarily from our affective and cognitive models of helping, but there are other important questions about helping and altruism not directly suggested by these models. We now present some of these questions. They move us beyond the helper's perspective and individual acts of helping to a somewhat broader conception of helping and prosocial behavior.

Beyond the Models

Whenever help is given, someone must be the recipient of that help. In some cases, help is received spontaneously from a benefactor who recognizes the victim's need. In other cases, however, people try to hide their need from others and refrain from seeking help that would ameliorate their problems. We considered reasons why individuals might not seek help from other individuals at some length in Chapter 7. We believe that this issue also needs to be considered at a societal level.

What can be done to increase the likelihood that people will utilize institutional help? At a practical level, learning the answers to this question should enable social service organizations to become more user-friendly. As we discussed in Chapter 7, one of the major impediments to seeking help is the perceived cost (e.g., threat to self-esteem, anticipated sense of future responsibility). Bureaucratic systems often ignore or fail to appreciate the impact that their systems may have on the people whom they are supposed to serve. They sometimes institute policies and procedures that inhibit potential clients from using their services. As a consequence, smaller initial problems (e.g., access to adequate prenatal health care) may become larger and more costly problems for both individuals and society as time passes. As the saying goes, "an ounce of prevention is worth a pound of cure." Changes in an organization's procedures that are sensitive to the client's needs can thus help ensure that these needs are satisfactorily addressed while problems are still small and manageable. For example, in a study conducted among Mexican-American residents of Los Angeles, Medvene and Lin (1992) found that conducting self-help groups in Spanish and recruiting participants through ethnic agencies lowered organizational barriers and greatly increased participation rates among the residents of the community. Conceptually, understanding the dynamics of the helping relationship between institutions and society should provide more explicit links to sociological analyses of behavior. The social in social psychology applies to an understanding of society as well as an appreciation of the behavior of individuals (see Box 9.4). This leads us to the next question.

How are prosocial actions at the group or collective level similar or different than those at the individual level? As we discussed in Chapter 8, prosocial behavior need not be restricted to dyadic interactions; prosocial action may be taken at the group level as well. In this domain, one

BOX 9.4

Seeking and Receiving Help

Elizabeth Midlarsky (Columbia University): "Do people who give help find it easier or more difficult to seek help? In particular, what is the relationship between help-giving and help-seeking as people become frail and dependent in late life?"

Arie Nadler (Tel-Aviv University, Israel): "An important research concern is help seeking research in cross-cultural perspective. Recent theorizing on the self suggests that many of the findings in the help seeking literature are limited to Western cultures. Whereas independent cultures are likely to be characterized by patterns of under-utilization of help, interdependent cultures are likely to be characterized by patterns of over-utilization of help (see Markus & Kitayama, 1991). To avoid a strictly Westernized social psychology of help-seeking and receiving we need to further explore these cross-cultural implications. Another important avenue of research is the link between dependency and social stigma. Individuals who seek help may pay the toll of being stigmatized by onlookers, and those who help them. Sometimes the fact that a person is seeking help is viewed as evidence of his or her high motivation and determination to overcome obstacles. At other times, the same behavior is viewed as evidence of that individual's incompetence and dependence on others. What variables mediate these perceptions? Finally, help seeking can sometimes be a maladaptive behavior. This would occur when the individual in need 'over'- or 'under'-utilizes available resources. What are the conditions that allow individuals in need to adequately analyze the social situation they are in, and seek help accordingly?"

Ervin Staub (University of Massachusetts): "We could use some good work on what actions by individuals who need help might increase the likelihood that they receive help."

---

important issue concerns the strategies that might be used to encourage people to volunteer their time, money, and energies to long-term projects that benefit their communities. In the social influence literature, there are numerous examples of techniques that can be used to induce individuals to donate time or money for charitable organizations (e.g., Cialdini, 1993). In general, these techniques take advantage of many of the same variables that promote helping a person in distress. And like emergency interventions, donations made under these circumstances are often spontaneous, unplanned, short-lived, and represent a response to a direct request. As we discussed in Chapter 8, however, volunteerism is usually a nonspontaneous form of prosocial action that often involves an extended commitment to some activity. As such, volunteer actions may be best understood (and promoted) by studying the decision-making processes of volunteers, as well as the personal characteristics and circumstances that affect decisions about volunteering for some activity. Clary and Snyder's (1991) functional analysis of volunteerism, which focuses on the different functions volunteering may serve for the person who volunteers (see Chapter 8), suggests one promising approach to this issue. A consideration of helping at a collective level also suggests related issues.

Given the apparent immediate benefits of selfishness, under what conditions will people cooperate collectively, and how do these principles relate to intergroup behavior? The issue of individuals cooperating collectively relates to our discussion of social dilemmas in Chapter 8. Recent and not-so-recent history suggest that trying to force cooperation to the exclusion of personal interests may not be the best way. Hardin's (1977) cardinal rule of policy is, "Never ask a person to act against his own self-interest" (p. 27). But Hardin (1968) also believes that "mutual coercion, mutually agreed upon" may be the only viable way out of the myriad of social dilemmas that now plague our society. By this he means that people must voluntarily agree to seek and accept structural solutions to the problems that confront them collectively (e.g., pollution control, water shortages, inadequate medical care, increased violence among young people). Although each individual may be asked to make sacrifices in terms of what would be the absolute best outcome for him or her personally, society will benefit as a whole and, in the long run, so will the individual.

More recent writing (see Mansbridge, 1990) suggests that Hardin's view may be overly pessimistic. Analyses of voting behavior, for example, consistently indicate that individuals will choose their ideology over their personal economic self-interest in many situations. That is, well-to-do liberals frequently vote for candidates who promise to "soak the rich" because they believe it is the right thing to do. And fair-minded whites vote for civil rights and affirmative action, even though it may cause them to experience more competition in the marketplace.

Finally, we believe that it would be productive for researchers to move beyond examining helping and cooperation among individuals to investigating these phenomena between groups. People have both social identities, relating to their identification with important groups, and personal identities, relating to their unique qualities and characteristics. These identities have different consequences on our reactions to others (Tajfel, 1970; Turner, Hogg, Oakes, Reicher, & Wetherell, 1987). People who focus on their social identity, for instance, have a more positive evaluation of members of one's own group and the tendency to see members of other groups as being alike. The activation of one's social identity may also arouse competitive motivations to see one's group in a more favorable position and to act in ways that give one's group a social or material advantage. The implications of these intergroup processes on empathy

BOX 9.5

Collective Forms of Helping and Altruism

Melvin Lerner (Washington University): "Questions about the 'Heroic Motive' (Meindl & Lerner, 1983, 1984) raise some important issues and need to be pursued. What are the psychological processes or conditions which make all of us potential 'heroes' or 'terrorists'; that is, engaging in extreme acts in the service of a sacred cause?"

Norman Miller (University of Southern California): "Upward links to more molar processes are needed. Theoretical and empirical progress in work on social justice, bargaining and negotiation, and social dilemmas needs to be integrated with work on helping. Researchers who work in areas of prejudice and intergroup relations need to consider intergroup prosocial behavior as well as antisocial attitudes and behavior. Are there asymmetries between prosocial and antisocial action at the group level? Will the greater competitiveness between groups than individuals be matched by circumstances in which groups are more cooperative than individuals? Or is there an individual/group discontinuity with respect to prosocial behavior?"

David Rosenhan (Stanford University): "We treat prosocial behavior as individual behavior, often seeking the determinants on the individual. What if one construed it as a group behavior?"

and helping are likely to be important, but they remain largely unexplored. Examination of this issue promises, conceptually, to link the study of helping and altruism to more general social psychological theorizing and, perhaps, to contribute more practical strategies for reducing intergroup conflict (see Box 9.5).

One recent paper suggests that there is a complex relationship among one's sense of self, one's attachment to one's group, and the nature of one's prosocial motivation. Jarymowicz (1992) found that individuals who are unable to separate their self-concepts from their perceptions of others in their own social group—people with low self-other differentiation—are motivated to help primarily by the need to feel good about themselves (endocentric motivation). Those with a more differentiated sense of self are more likely to be motivated by the desire to make others feel better (exocentric motivation). These exocentric individuals are better able to take the perspective of those in an out-group and consequently to be more responsive to their needs.

SUMMARY AND CONCLUSION

Much of this chapter has been a summary of the questions we have asked and the answers we have found as we explored the literature of helping and altruism. Therefore, we will not restate these conclusions yet again. The models that were proposed, although not explicitly presented in the previous chapters, should serve this purpose. Again, we note that affective and cognitive processes are neither psychologically or physiologically independent; feelings influence cognition and vice versa in prosocial behavior and in almost all other kinds of social behavior.

As we reach the end of the book, we find that we have answered many questions and solved several puzzles. However, one clear message of this chapter is that much remains to be done to understand fully the processes that converge to directly and indirectly determine (1) whether a prosocial action will occur, (2) what the nature of that action will be, and (3) what its consequences will be. We have tried to identify some of the issues that deserve further attention. Nevertheless, we acknowledge that, even with the help of our colleagues' contributions, it is very unlikely that we exhausted the list of theoretical and practical questions that need to be answered. If we have done our job and piqued your interest in helping and altruism, you may have already formulated many questions we have overlooked. Attempting to understand the psychology of helping and altruism is not just an academic exercise carried out for the entertainment and employment of social psychologists and other social scientists. We sincerely believe that if we can understand the causes of prosocial behavior, then our society will be able to address more effectively the broad range of grave problems that currently confront us. We hope that this book has taught you something about some of these causes and encourages you to address some of the questions that remain unanswered.

Learning about prosocial behavior and writing about helping and altruism has made each of us personally more aware of what it means to help and to be helped. As a result, we believe we have become more sensitive and responsive to the needs of others. We hope that, as a product of reading this book, you too have gained an increased sense of the need to consider the welfare of others in your everyday life. If so, this has been a worthwhile effort.

Bibliography

Abrahams, R. D. (Ed.). (1985). *Afro-American folktales: Stories from black traditions in the New World*. New York: Pantheon.

Ahammer, I. M., & Murray, J. P. (1979). Kindness in the kindergarten: The relative influence of role playing and prosocial television in facilitating altruism. *International Journal of Behavioral Development*, 2, 133–157.

Ainsworth, M. D. S. (1973). The development of infant-mother attachment. In B. M. Caldwell & H. N. Riccuiti (Eds.), *Review of child development research* (Vol. 3, pp. 1–91). Chicago: University of Chicago Press.

Alcock, J. (1989). *Animal behavior* (4th ed.). Sunderland, MA: Sinauer Associates.

Allen, H. (1970). Unpublished study cited in B. Latané & J. M. Darley, *The unresponsive bystander: Why doesn't he help?* New York: Appleton-Century-Crofts.

Allen, N., & Rushton, J. P. (1983). The personality of community volunteers. *Journal of Voluntary Action Research*, 9, 1183–1196.

Allison, S. T., McQueen, L. R., & Schaerfl, L. M. (1992). Social decision-making processes and the equal partitionment of shared resources. *Journal of Experimental Social Psychology*, 28, 23–42.

Amato P. R. (1993). Urban-rural differences in helping friends and family members. *Social Psychology Quarterly*, 56, 249–262.

Anderson, J. C., & Moore, L. (1978). The motivation to volunteer. *Journal of Voluntary Action Research*, 7, 232–252.

Anderson, V. L. (1993). Gender differences in altruism among Holocaust rescuers. *Journal of Social Behavior and Personality*, 8, 43–58.

Archer, R. L. (1984). The farmer and the cowman should be friends: An attempt at reconciliation with Batson, Coke, and Psych. *Journal of Personality and Social Psychology*, 46, 709–711.

Archer, R. L., Diaz-Loving, R., Gollwitzer, P. M., Davis, M. H., & Foushee, H. C. (1981). The role of dispositional empathy and social evaluation in the empathic mediation of helping. *Journal of Personality and Social Psychology*, 46, 786–796.

Arlitt, A. H. (1930). *Psychology of infancy and early childhood*. New York: McGraw-Hill.

Arnold, E. (1967). *A night of watching*. New York: Fawcett.

Aronfreed, J. (1970). Socialization of altruistic and sympathetic behavior: Some theoretical and experimental analyses. In J. Macaulay & L. Berkowitz (Eds.), *Altruism and helping behavior* (pp. 103–123). New York: Academic Press.

Aronfreed, J., & Paskal, V. (1965). *Empathy, altruism, and the conditioning of positive affect*. Unpublished manuscript, University of Pennsylvania, Philadelphia.

Aronson, E., & Gonzalez, A. (1988). Desegregation, jigsaw, and the Mexican-American experience. In P. A. Katz & D. Taylor (Eds.), *Towards the elimination of racism: Profiles in controversy*. New York: Plenum.

Ausubel, N. (Ed.). (1948). *A treasury of Jewish folklore*. New York: Crown.

Badcock, C. R. (1986). *The problem of altruism*. Oxford, England: Basil Blackwell.

Bandura, A. (1977). *Social learning theory*. Englewood Cliffs, NJ: Prentice-Hall.

Bandura, A. (1986). *Social foundations of thought and action*. Englewood Cliffs, NJ: Prentice-Hall.

Bar-Tal, D. (1982). Sequential development of helping behavior: A cognitive-learning approach. *Developmental Review, 2*, 101–124.

Bar-Tal, D., & Raviv, A. (1982). A cognitive-learning model of helping behavior development: Possible implications and applications. In N. Eisenberg (Ed.), *The development of prosocial behavior* (pp. 199–217). New York: Academic Press.

Bar-Tal, D., Raviv, A., & Leiser, T. (1980). The development of altruistic behavior: Empirical evidence. *Developmental Psychology, 16*, 516–524.

Barbee, A. P. (1990). Interactive coping: The cheering up process in close relationships. In S. Duck (Ed.), *Personal relationships and social support* (pp. 45–65). London: Sage.

Barbee, A. P., Cunningham, M. R., Winstead, B. A., Derlega, V. J., Gulley, M. R., Yankeelov, P. A., & Druen, P. B. (1993). Effects of gender role expectations on the social support process. *Journal of Social Issues, 49*, 175–190.

Barnett, M. A. (1987). Empathy and related responses in children. In N. Eisenberg & J. Strayer (Eds.), *Empathy and its development* (pp. 146–162). Cambridge: Cambridge University Press.

Barnett, M. A., Sinisi, C. S., Jaet, B. P., Bealer, R., Rodell, P., & Saunders, L. C. (1990). Perceiving gender differences in children's help-seeking. *Journal of Genetic Psychology, 151*, 451–460.

Baron, R. S., Cutrona, C. E., Hicklin, D., Russell, D. W., & Lubaroff, D. M. (1990). Social support and immune function among spouses of cancer patients. *Journal of Personality and Social Psychology, 59*, 344–352.

Barton, E. J., & Osborne, J. G. (1978). The development of classroom sharing by a teacher using positive practice. *Behavior Modification, 2*, 231–251.

Bates, J. (1989). Concepts and measures of temperament. In G. Kohnstamm, J. Bates, & M. Rothbart (Eds.), *Temperament in childhood* (pp. 3–26). New York: Wiley.

Batson, C. D. (1983). Sociobiology and the role of religion in promoting prosocial behavior: An alternative view. *Journal of Personality and Social Psychology, 45*, 1380–1385.

Batson, C. D. (1987). Prosocial motivation: Is it ever truly altruistic? In L. Berkowitz (Ed.), *Advances in experimental social psychology* (Vol. 20, pp. 65–122). New York: Academic Press.

Batson, C. D. (1991). *The altruism question: Toward a social-psychological answer*. Hillsdale, NY: Erlbaum.

Batson, C. D., Batson, J. G., Griffitt, C. A., Barrientos, S., Brandt, J. R., Sprengelmeyer, P., & Bayly, M. J. (1989). Negative-state relief and the empathy-altruism hypothesis. *Journal of Personality and Social Psychology, 56*, 922–933.

Batson, C. D., Batson, J. G., Slingsby, J. K., Harrell, K. L., Peekna, H. M., & Todd, R. M. (1991). Empathic joy and the empathy-altruism hypothesis. *Journal of Personality and Social Psychology, 61,* 413–426.

Batson, C. D., Bolen, M. H., Cross, J. A., Neuringer-Benefiel, H. E. (1986). Where is the altruism in the altruistic personality? *Journal of Personality and Social Psychology, 50,* 212–220.

Batson, C. D., Dyck, J. L., Brandt, J. R., Batson, J. G., Powell, A. L., McMaster, M. R., & Griffitt, C. (1988). Five studies testing two new egoistic alternatives to the empathy-altruism hypothesis. *Journal of Personality and Social Psychology, 55,* 52–77.

Batson, C. D., Fultz, J., Schoenrade, P. A., Paduano, A. (1987). Critical self-reflection and self-perceived altruism: When self-reward fails. *Journal of Personality and Social Psychology, 53,* 594–602.

Batson, C. D., & Oleson, K. C. (1991). Current status of the empathy-altruism hypothesis. In M. S. Clark (Ed.), *Review of personality and social psychology: Vol. 12. Prosocial behavior* (pp. 62–85). Newbury Park, CA: Sage.

Batson, C. D., O'Quin, K., Fultz, J., Vanderplas, M., & Isen, A. (1983). Influence of self-reported distress and empathy on egoistic versus altruistic motivation to help. *Journal of Personality and Social Psychology, 45,* 706–718.

Batson, C. D., Pate, S., Lawless, H., Sparkman, P., Lambers, S., & Worman, B. (1979). Helping under conditions of threat: Increased "we-feeling" or ensuring reciprocity. *Social Psychology Quarterly, 42,* 410–414.

Baumeister, R. F., Chesner, S. P., Sanders, P. S., & Tice, D. M. (1988). Who's in charge here? Group leaders do lend help in emergencies. *Personality and Social Psychology Bulletin, 14,* 17–22.

Beaman, A. L., Cole, C. M., Preston, M., Klentz, B., & Steblay, N. M. (1983). Fifteen years of foot-in-the-door research: A meta-analysis. *Personality and Social Psychology Bulletin, 9,* 181–186.

Beattie, M. (1987). *Codependent no more.* New York: HarperCollins.

Bell, P. A., Fisher, J. D., Baum, A., & Greene, T. (1990). *Environmental psychology* (3rd ed.). Fort Worth, TX: Holt, Rinehart, & Winston.

Bellah, R. N., Madsen, R., Sullivan, W. M., Swidler, A., & Tipton, S. M. (1985). *Habits of the heart: Individualism and commitment in American life.* Berkeley: University of California Press.

Bengston, V. (1985). Diversity and symbolism in grandparental roles. In V. Bengston & J. Robertson (Eds.), *Grandparenthood* (pp. 11–25). Beverly Hills, CA: Sage.

Benson, P. L., Karabenick, S. A., & Lerner, R. M. (1976). Pretty pleases: The effects of physical attractiveness, race, and sex on receiving help. *Journal of Experimental Social Psychology, 12,* 409–415.

Berkowitz, L. (1972). Social norms, feelings, and other factors affecting helping behavior and altruism. In L. Berkowitz (Ed.), *Advances in experimental social psychology* (Vol. 6, pp. 63–108). New York: Academic Press.

Berkowitz, L., & Daniels, L. R. (1963). Responsibility and dependency. *Journal of Abnormal and Social Psychology, 66,* 429–436.

Berkowitz, L., & Daniels, L. R. (1964). Affecting the salience of the social responsibility norm: Effect of past help on the responses to dependency relationships. *Journal of Abnormal and Social Psychology, 68,* 275–281.

Berkowitz, W. (1987). *Local heroes.* Lexington, MA: Lexington Books.

Bickman, L. (1971). The effect of another bystander's ability to help on bystander intervention in an emergency. *Journal of Experimental Social Psychology, 7,* 367–379.

Bickman, L., & Kamzan, M. (1973). The effect of race and need on helping behavior. *Journal of Personality and Social Psychology, 89,* 73–77.

Bickman, L., Teger, A., Gabriele, T., McLaughlin, C., Berger, M., & Sunaday, E. (1973). Dormitory density and helping behavior. *Environment and Behavior, 5,* 465–490.

Bierhoff, H. W., Klein, R., & Kramp, P. (1991). Evidence for the altruistic personality from data on accident research. *Journal of Personality, 59,* 263–280.

Billings, A., & Moos, R. (1982). Social support and functioning among community and clinical groups: A panel model. *Journal of Behavioral Medicine, 5,* 295–311.

Blake, J. A. (1978). Death by hand grenade: Altruistic suicide in combat. *Suicide and Life-Threatening Behavior, 8,* 46–59.

Borgida, E., Conner, C., & Manteufel, L. (1992). Understanding living kidney donation: A behavioral decision-making perspective. In S. Spacapan & S. Oskamp (Eds.), *Helping and being helped* (pp. 183–212). Newbury Park, CA: Sage.

Borod, J. C. (1992). Interhemispheric and intrahemispheric control of emotion: A focus on brain damage. *Journal of Consulting and Clinical Psychology, 60,* 339–348.

Borofsky, G. L., Stollack, G. E., & Messé, L. A. (1971). Sex differences in bystander reactions to physical assaults. *Journal of Experimental Social Psychology, 7,* 313–318.

Bowlby, J. (1969). *Attachment and loss: Vol. 1. Attachment.* New York: Basic Books.

Boykin, A. W. (1983). The academic performance of Afro-American children. In J. T. Spence (Ed.), *Achievement and achievement motives.* San Francisco: Freeman.

Brehm, J. W. (1966). *A theory of psychological reactance.* New York: Academic Press.

Brehm, S. S., & Brehm, J. W. (1981). *Psychological reactance: A theory of freedom and control.* New York: Academic Press.

Brewer, M. B., & Kramer, R. M. (1986). Choice behavior in social dilemmas: Effects of social identity, group size, and decision framing. *Journal of Personality and Social Psychology, 50,* 543–549.

Brody, G. H., & Shaffer, D. R. (1982). Contributions of parents and peers to children's moral socialization. *Developmental Review, 2,* 31–75.

Broman, C. L. (1987). Race differences in professional help seeking. *American Journal of Community Psychology, 15,* 473–489.

Broman, C. L., Neighbors, H. W., & Taylor, R. J. (1989). Race differences in seeking help from social workers. *Journal of Sociology and Social Welfare, 16,* 109–123.

Bruder-Mattson, S. F., & Hovanitz, C. A. (1990). Coping and attributional styles as predictors of depression. *Journal of Clinical Psychology, 46,* 557–565.

Buck, R., & Ginsburg, B. (1991). Spontaneous communication and altruism: The communicative gene hypothesis. In M. S. Clark (Ed.), *Review of personality and social psychology: Vol. 12. Prosocial behavior* (pp. 149–175). Newbury Park, CA: Sage.

Byrne, D. (1971). *The attraction paradigm.* New York: Academic Press.

Caldwell, R. A., & Reinhart, M. A. (1988). The relationship of type of personality to individual differences in the use and type of social support. *Journal of Social and Clinical Psychology, 6,* 140–146.

Callero, P. L. (1985/1986). Putting the social in prosocial behavior: An interaction-ist approach to altruism. *Humboldt Journal of Social Relations, 13,* 15–34.

Campbell, D. T. (1975). On the conflicts between biological and social evolution and between psychology and moral tradition. *American Psychologist, 30,* 1103–1126.

Caporael, L. R., & Brewer, M. B. (Eds.). (1991). Issues in evolutionary psychology. *Journal of Social Issues, 47* (3).

Carlo, G., Eisenberg, N., Troyer, D., Switzer, G., & Speer, A. L. (1991). The altruis-tic personality: In what contexts is it apparent? *Journal of Personality and Social Psychology, 61,* 450–458.

Carlson, M., & Miller, N. (1987). Explanation of the relation between negative mood and helping. *Psychological Bulletin, 102,* 91–108.

Carnevale, P. J., Pruitt, D. G., & Carrington, P. I. (1982). Effects of future depen-dence, liking, and repeated requests for help on helping behavior. *Social Psychology Quarterly, 45,* 9–14.

Cass, R. C., & Edney, J. J. (1978). The commons dilemma: A simulation testing the effects of resource visibility and territorial division. *Human Ecology, 6,* 371–386.

Chambers, J. H., & Ascione, F. R. (1987). The effects of prosocial and aggressive video games on children's donating and helping. *Journal of Genetic Psychology, 148,* 499–505.

Chambre, S. M. (1987). *Good deeds in old age: Volunteering by the new leisure class.* Lexington, MA: Lexington Books.

Chandler, M., Fritz, A. S., & Hala, S. (1989). Small-scale deceit: Deception as a marker of two-, three-, and four-year olds' early theories of mind. *Child Development, 60,* 1263–1277.

Chappell, N., & Havens, B. (1983). Who helps the elderly person? In W. Peterson & J. Quadragno (Eds.), *Social bonds in later life* (pp. 21–227). Beverly Hills, CA: Sage.

Charng, H. W., Piliavin, J. A., & Callero, P. L. (1988). Role-identity and reasoned action in the prediction of repeated behavior. *Social Psychology Quarterly, 51,* 303–317.

Cheek, J. M., Malchior, L. A., & Carpentieri, A. M. (1986). Shyness and self concept. In L. M. Hartman & K. R. Blankstein (Eds.), *Advances in the study of commu-nication and affect: Vol. 2. Perception of self in emotional disorder and psychother-apy* (pp. 113–131). New York: Plenum.

Cialdini, R. B. (1993). *Influence: Science and practice* (3rd ed.). New York: HarperCollins.

Cialdini, R. B., Darby, B. K., & Vincent, J. E. (1973). Transgression and altruism: A case for hedonism. *Journal of Experimental Social Psychology, 9,* 502–516.

Cialdini, R. B., & Fultz, J. (1990). Interpreting the negative mood/helping litera-ture via *mega*-analysis: A contrary view. *Psychological Bulletin, 107,* 210–214.

Cialdini, R. B., & Kenrick, D. T. (1976). Altruism as hedonism: A social develop-ment perspective on the relationship of negative mood state and helping. *Journal of Personality and Social Psychology, 34,* 907–914.

Cialdini, R. B., Kenrick, D. T., & Baumann, D. J. (1982). Effects of mood on proso-cial behavior in children and adults. In N. Eisenberg (Ed.), *The development of prosocial behavior* (pp. 339–359). New York: Academic Press.

Cialdini, R. B., Schaller, M., Houlihan, D., Arps, K., Fultz, J., & Beamen, A. L.

(1987). Empathy-based helping: Is it selflessly or selfishly motivated? *Journal of Personality and Social Psychology, 52,* 749–758.

Cimino, C., Behner, G., & Allen, M. (1994, February). *Asymmetries in emotional processing: A comparison of right hemisphere, valence, and preparatory models.* Paper presented at the meeting of the International Neuropsychological Society, Cincinnati, OH.

Clark, M. S., & Mills, J. (1993). The difference between communal and exchange relationships: What is and what is not. *Personality and Social Psychology Bulletin, 19,* 684–691.

Clark M. S., Mills, J., & Corcoran, D. (1989). Keeping track of needs and inputs of friends and strangers. *Journal of Personality and Social Psychology, 15,* 533–542.

Clark, R. D., III. (1976). On the Piliavin and Piliavin model of helping behavior: Costs are in the eye of the beholder. *Journal of Applied Social Psychology, 6,* 322–328.

Clark, R. D., III, & Word, L. E. (1972). Why don't bystanders help? Because of ambiguity? *Journal of Personality and Social Psychology, 24,* 392–400.

Clark, R. D., III, & Word, L. E. (1974). Where is the apathetic bystander? Situational characteristics of the emergency. *Journal of Personality and Social Psychology, 29,* 279–287.

Clarkson, M. B. E. (1988). Corporate social performance in Canada, 1976–1986. In L. E. Preston (Ed.), *Research in corporate social performance and policy* (Vol. 10, pp. 241–266). Greenwich, CT: JAI Press.

Clary, E. G., & Orenstein, L. (1991). The amount and effectiveness of help: The relationship of motives and abilities to helping behavior. *Personality and Social Psychology Bulletin, 17,* 58–64.

Clary, E. G., & Snyder, M. (1991). A functional analysis of altruism and prosocial behavior: The case of volunteerism. In M. S. Clark (Ed.), *Review of personality and social psychology: Vol.12. Prosocial behavior* (pp. 119–148). Newbury Park, CA: Sage.

Cohen, S., & Wills, T. A. (1985). Stress, social support, and the buffering hypothesis. *Psychological Bulletin, 98,* 310–357.

Colby, A., & Damon, M. (1992, August). *Development of extraordinary moral commitment.* Paper presented at the annual meeting of the American Psychological Association, Washington, DC.

Colby, A., & Kohlberg, L. (1987). *The measurement of moral judgment: Vol 1. Theoretical foundations and research validation.* Cambridge, England: Cambridge University Press.

Colby, A., Kohlberg, L., Gibbs, J., & Lieberman, M. (1983). A longitudinal study of moral judgment. *Monographs of the Society for Research in Child Development, 48* (1–2, Serial No. 200).

Cook, M., & Mineka, S. (1989). Observational conditioning of fear to fear-relevant vs. fear-irrelevant stimuli in rhesus monkeys. *Journal of Abnormal Psychology, 98,* 448–459.

Cook, M., & Mineka, S. (1990). Selective associations in the observational conditioning of fear in the monkey. *Journal of Experimental Psychology: Animal Behavior Processes, 16,* 372–389.

Corney, R. (1990). Sex differences in general practice attendance and help seeking for minor illness. *Journal of Psychosomatic Research, 34,* 525–534.

Cowen, E. L. (1982). Help is where you find it. Four informal helping groups. *American Psychologist, 37,* 385–395.

Crockenberg, S. B., & Litman, C. (1990). Autonomy as competence in 2 year olds: Maternal correlates of child defiance, compliance, and self-assertion. *Developmental Psychology, 26,* 961–971.

Cunha, D. (1985). *Interpersonal trust as a function of social orientation.* Unpublished doctoral dissertation, University of Delaware, Newark.

Cunningham, M. R. (1983, August). *Altruism and attraction from a sociobiological perspective.* Paper presented at the annual meeting of the American Psychological Association, Anaheim, CA.

Cunningham, M. R. (1985/1986). Levites and brother's keepers: A sociobiological perspective on prosocial behavior. *Humboldt Journal of Social Relations, 13,* 35–67.

Cunningham, M. R., Steinberg, J., & Grev, R. (1980). Wanting to and having to help: Separate motives for positive mood and guilt-induced helping. *Journal of Personality and Social Psychology, 38,* 181–192.

Curry, R. L. (1988). Influence of kinship on helping behavior in Galápagos mockingbirds. *Behavioral Ecology and Sociobiology, 22,* 141–152.

Dabbs, J. M., Riad, J. K., & Lathangue, L. A. (1992, August). *Harsh facial regard of high testosterone males.* Paper presented at the annual meeting of the American Psychological Association, Washington, DC.

Daniels, A. K. (1988). *Invisible careers: Women civic leaders from the volunteer world.* Chicago: University of Chicago Press.

Darley, J., & Batson, C. D. (1973). From Jerusalem to Jericho: A study of situational and dispositional variables in helping behavior. *Journal of Personality and Social Psychology, 27,* 100–108.

Darley, J. M., & Latané, B. (1968). Bystander intervention in emergencies: Diffusion of responsibility. *Journal of Personality and Social Psychology, 8,* 377–383.

Davis, J. A., & Smith, T. W. (1991). *General social surveys, 1972–1991: Cumulative codebook.* Chicago: National Opinion Research Center.

Davis, M. H. (1980). Measuring individual differences in empathy. *JSAS Catalog of Selected Documents in Psychology, 10,* 85.

Davis, M. H. (1983). Empathic concern and muscular dystrophy telethon: Empathy as a multidimensional construct. *Personality and Social Psychology Bulletin, 9,* 223–229.

Davis, M. H. (1994). *Empathy: A social psychological approach.* Madison, WI: Brown & Benchmark.

Davis, M. H., Luce, C., & Kraus, S. J. (in press). The heritability of characteristics associated with dispositional empathy. *Journal of Personality.*

Dawes, R. M. (1975). Formal models of dilemmas in social decision-making. In M. F. Kaplan & S. Schwartz (Eds.), *Human judgment and decision processes* (pp. 87–108). New York: Academic Press.

Dawes, R. M. (1980). Social dilemmas. *Annual Review of Psychology, 31,* 169–193.

Dawes, R. M., McTavish, J., & Shaklee, H. (1977). Behavior, communication, and assumption about other people's behavior in a commons dilemma situation. *Journal of Personality and Social Psychology, 35,* 1–11.

DeKay, W. T., & Buss, D. (1992). Human nature, individual differences, and the importance of context: Perspectives from evolutionary psychology. *Current Directions in Psychological Science, 6,* 184–189.

DePaulo, B. M. (1982). Social-psychological processes in informal help seeking. In T. A. Wills (Ed.), *Basic processes in helping relationships.* New York: Academic Press.

DePaulo, B. M. (1992). Nonverbal behavior and self-presentation. *Psychological Bulletin, 111*, 203–243.

DePaulo, B. M., Dull, W. R., Greenberg, J. M., & Swaim, G. W. (1989). Are shy people reluctant to ask for help? *Journal of Personality and Social Psychology, 56*, 834–844.

Derlega, V. J., Barbee, A. P., & Winstead, B. A. (1994). Friendship, gender and social support. In B. R. Burelson, T. L. Albrecht, & I. G. Sarason (Eds.), *The communication of social support: Messages, interactions, relationships, and community* (pp. 136–150). Newbury Park, CA: Sage.

Deutsch, F. M., & Lamberti, D. M. (1986). Does social approval increase helping? *Personality and Social Psychology Bulletin, 12*, 149–157.

Deutsch, M., & Gerard, H. (1955). A study of normative and informational social influence. *Journal of Abnormal and Social Psychology, 51*, 629–636.

Dew, M. A., Dunn, L. O., Bromet, E. J., & Schulberg, H. C. (1988). Factors affecting help-seeking during depression in a community sample. *Journal of Affective Disorders, 14*, 223–234.

Dooley, D., & Catalano, R. (1984). Why the economy predicts help-seeking: A test of competing explanations. *Journal of Health and Social Behavior, 25*, 160–176.

Douglas, J. (1983). *Why charity? The case for a third sector.* Beverly Hills, CA: Sage.

Dovidio, J. F. (1984). Helping behavior and altruism: An empirical and conceptual overview. In L. Berkowitz (Ed.), *Advances in experimental social psychology* (Vol. 17, pp. 361–427). New York: Academic Press.

Dovidio, J. F. (1993, October). *Androgyny, sex roles, and helping.* Paper presented at the convention of the Society of Experimental Social Psychology, Santa Barbara, CA.

Dovidio, J. F., Allen, J., & Schroeder, D. A. (1990). The specificity of empathy-induced helping: Evidence for altruism. *Journal of Personality and Social Psychology, 59*, 249–260.

Dovidio, J. F., Fishbane, R., & Sibicky, M. E. (1985). Perceptions of people with psychological problems: Effects of seeking counseling. *Psychological Reports, 57*, 1263–1270.

Dovidio, J. F., & Gaertner, S. L. (1981). The effects of race, status, and ability on helping behavior. *Social Psychology Quarterly, 44*, 192–203.

Dovidio, J. F., & Gaertner, S. L. (1983). The effects of sex, status, and ability on helping behavior. *Journal of Applied Social Psychology, 13*, 191–205.

Dovidio, J. F., & Gaertner, S. L. (1993). Stereotypes and evaluative intergroup bias. In D. M. Mackie & D. L. Hamilton (Eds.), *Affect, cognition, and stereotyping: Interactive processes in group perception.* San Diego, CA: Academic Press.

Dovidio, J. F., Mann, J., & Gaertner, S. L. (1989). Resistance to affirmative action: The implications of aversive racism. In F. A. Blanchard & F. J. Crosby (Eds.), *Affirmative action in perspective* (pp. 83–103). New York: Springer-Verlag.

Dovidio, J. F., & Morris, W. N. (1975). Effects of stress and commonality of fate on helping behavior. *Journal of Personality and Social Psychology, 31*, 145–149.

Dovidio, J. F., Piliavin, J. A., Gaertner, S. L., Schroeder, D. A., & Clark, R. D., III. (1991). The Arousal: Cost-reward model and the process of intervention: A review of the evidence. In M. S. Clark (Ed.), *Review of personality and social psychology: Vol. 12. Prosocial behavior* (pp. 86–118). Newbury Park, CA: Sage.

Drake, A. W., Finkelstein, S. N., & Sopolsky, H. M. (1982). *The American blood supply.* Cambridge, MA: MIT Press.

Dutton, D. G., & Aron, A. (1989). Romantic attraction and generalized liking for others who are sources of conflict-based arousal. *Canadian Journal of Behavioural Science, 21,* 246–257.

Dutton, D. G., & Lake, R. A. (1973). Threat of own prejudice and reverse discrimination in interracial situations. *Journal of Personality and Social Psychology, 28,* 94–100.

Dutton, D. G., & Lennox, V. L. (1974). Effect of prior "token" compliance on subsequent interracial behavior. *Journal of Personality and Social Psychology, 29,* 65–71.

Dyck, J. L., Batson, C. D., Oden, A., & Weeks, J. L. (1989, April). *Another look at altruism in the altruistic personality: Hers and his.* Paper presented at the meeting of the Midwestern Sociological Association, St. Louis, MO.

Dynes, R. R., & Quarantelli, E. L. (1980). Helping behavior in large-scale disasters. In D. H. Smith & J. Macaulay (Eds.), *Participation in social and political activities* (pp. 339–354). San Francisco: Jossey-Bass.

Eagly, A. H. (1987). *Sex differences in social behavior: A social-role interpretation.* Hillsdale, NJ: Erlbaum.

Eagly, A. H., & Crowley, M. (1986). Gender and helping behavior: A meta-analytic view of the social psychological literature. *Psychological Bulletin, 100,* 283–308.

Eagly, A. H., & Wood, W. (1991). Explaining sex differences in social behavior: A meta-analytic perspective. *Personality and Social Psychology Bulletin, 17,* 306–315.

Easterbrook, J. A. (1959). The effect of emotion on cue utilization and the organization of behavior. *Psychological Review, 66,* 183–201.

Eccles, J. P. (1991). Gender role socialization. In R. Baron & W. G. Graziano (Eds.), *Social psychology* (pp. 160–191). Fort Worth, TX: Holt, Rinehart, & Winston.

Edelmann, R. J., Childs, J., Harvey, S., Kellock, I., & Strain-Clark, C. (1984). The effect of embarrassment on helping. *Journal of Social Psychology, 124,* 253–254.

Edelmann, R. J., Evans, G., Pegg, I., & Tremain, M. (1983). Responses to physical stigma. *Perceptual and Motor Skills, 57,* 294.

Eibl-Eibesfeldt, I. (1989). *Human ethology.* New York: Aldine de Gruyter.

Eisenberg, N. (1982). The development of reasoning regarding prosocial behavior. In N. Eisenberg (Ed.), *The development of prosocial behavior* (pp. 219–249). New York: Academic Press.

Eisenberg, N. (1986). *Altruistic emotion, cognition and behavior.* Hillsdale, NJ: Erlbaum.

Eisenberg, N. (1992). *The caring child.* Cambridge, MA: Harvard University Press.

Eisenberg, N., & Fabes, R. A. (1990). Empathy: Conceptualization, measurement and relation to prosocial behavior. *Motivation and Emotion, 14,* 131–149.

Eisenberg, N., & Fabes, R. A. (1991). Prosocial behavior and empathy: A multimethod developmental perspective. In M. S. Clark (Ed.), *Review of personality and social psychology: Vol. 12. Prosocial behavior* (pp. 34–61). Newbury Park, CA: Sage.

Eisenberg, N., Fabes, R. A., Miller, P. A., Shell R., Shea, R., & May-Plumee, T. (1990). Preschoolers' vicarious emotional responding and their situational and dispositional prosocial behavior. *Merrill-Palmer Quarterly, 36,* 507–529.

Eisenberg, N., Fabes, R. A., Murphy, B., Karbon, M., Maszk, P., Smith, P., O'Boyle, C., & Suh, K. (1994). The relations of emotionality and regulation to dispositional and situational empathy-related responding. *Journal of Personality and Social Psychology, 66,* 776–797.

Eisenberg, N. A., Fabes, R. A., Schaller, M., Carlo, G., & Miller, P. (1991). The relations of parental characteristics and practices to children's vicarious emotional responding. *Child Development, 62,* 1393–1408.

Eisenberg, N., & Lennon, R. (1983). Sex differences in empathy and related capacities. *Psychological Bulletin, 94,* 100–131.

Eisenberg, N., & Miller, P. (1987). The relation of empathy to prosocial and related behaviors. *Psychological Bulletin, 101,* 91–119.

Eisenberg, N., Miller, P., Shell, R., McNally, S., & Shea, C. (1991). Prosocial development in adolescence: A longitudinal study. *Developmental Psychology, 27,* 849–857.

Eisenberg, N., Shell, R., Pasternack, J., Lennon, R., Beller, R., & Mathy, R. M. (1987). Prosocial development in middle childhood: A longitudinal study. *Developmental Psychology, 23,* 712–718.

Eisenberg-Berg, N. (1979). Development of children's prosocial moral judgment. *Developmental Psychology, 15,* 128–137.

Eisenberg-Berg, N., & Neal, C. (1981). Effects of identity of the story character and cost of helping on children's moral judgment. *Personality and Social Psychology Bulletin, 7,* 17–23.

Eisenberg-Berg, N., & Roth, K. (1980). The development of children's prosocial moral judgment: A longitudinal follow-up. *Developmental Psychology, 16,* 375–376.

Enzle, M. E., & Harvey, M. D. (1979). Recipient mood states and helping behavior. *Journal of Experimental Social Psychology, 15,* 170–182.

Erdoes, R., & Ortiz, A. (Eds.). (1984). *American Indian myths and legends* (pp. 252–253). New York: Pantheon Books.

Essock-Vitale, S. M., & McGuire, M. T. (1985). Women's lives viewed from an evolutionary perspective. II. Patterns of helping. *Ethology and Sociobiology, 6,* 155–173.

Eysenck, M. V. (1977). *Human memory: Theory, research, and individual differences.* Oxford, England: Pergamon Press.

Fabes R. A., Eisenberg, N., & Eisenbud, L. (1993). Behavioral and physiological correlates of children's reactions to others in distress. *Developmental Psychology, 29,* 655–664.

Fabes, R. A., Eisenberg, N. A., Karbon, M., Bernzweig, J., Speer, A. L., & Carlo, G. (1994). Socialization of children's vicarious emotional responding and prosocial behavior: Relations with mothers' perceptions of children's emotional reactivity. *Developmental Psychology, 30,* 44–55.

Fabes, R. A., Eisenberg, N., & Miller, P. A. (1990). Maternal correlates of children's vicarious emotional responsiveness. *Developmental Psychology, 26,* 639–648.

Fabes, R. A., Fultz, J., Eisenberg, N., May-Plumlee, T., & Christopher, F. S. (1989). Effects of rewards on children's prosocial motivation: A socialization study. *Developmental Psychology, 25,* 509–515.

Feldman, N. S., & Ruble, D. N. (1981). The development of person perception: Cognitive versus social factors. In S. S. Brehm, S. M. Kassin, & F. X. Gibbons (Eds.), *Developmental social psychology* (pp. 191–206). New York: Oxford University Press.

Feldman, R. (1968). Response to a compatriot and foreigner who seek assistance. *Journal of Personality and Social Psychology, 10*, 202–214.

Festinger, L. (1954). A theory of social comparison processes. *Human Relations, 7*, 117–140.

Fisher, J. D., Nadler, A., & Whitcher-Alagna, S. (1982). Recipient reactions to aid. *Psychological Bulletin, 91*, 27–54.

Fisher, J. D., Nadler, A., & Whitcher-Alagna, S. (1983). Four conceptualizations of reactions to aid. In J. D. Fisher, A. Nadler, & B. M. DePaulo (Eds.), *New directions in helping: Vol. 1. Recipient reactions to aid* (pp. 51–84). San Diego, CA: Academic Press.

Fiske, A. P. (1991). The cultural relativity of selfish individualism: Anthropological evidence that humans are inherently sociable. In M. S. Clark (Ed.), *Review of personality and social psychology: Vol. 12. Prosocial behavior* (pp. 176–214). Newbury Park, CA: Sage.

Flavell J. H. (1985). *Cognitive development*. Englewood Cliffs, NJ: Prentice-Hall.

Foss, R. (1983). Community norms and blood donation. *Journal of Applied Social Psychology, 13*, 281–291.

Fox, J. W. (1984). Sex, marital status and age as social selection factors in recent psychiatric treatment. *Journal of Health and Social Behavior, 25*, 394–405.

Freedman, J. L., & Fraser, S. C. (1966). Compliance without pressure: The foot in the door technique. *Journal of Personality and Social Psychology, 4*, 195–202.

Freetly, A. H. (1991). *Defining rape: Perceptions of non-consensual sexual intercourse by varying levels of intimacy*. Unpublished master's thesis, University of Wisconsin–Madison.

Frey, D. L., & Gaertner, S. L. (1986). Helping and the avoidance of inappropriate interracial behavior: A strategy that perpetuates a nonprejudiced self-image. *Journal of Personality and Social Psychology, 50*, 1083–1090.

Friedrich, L. K., & Stein, A. H. (1975). Prosocial television and young children: The effects of verbal labeling and role playing on learning and behavior. *Child Development, 46*, 27–38.

Friedrich-Cofer, L. K., Huston-Stein, A., Kipnis, D. M., Susman, E. J., & Clewett, A. S. (1979). Environmental enhancement of prosocial television content: Effects of interpersonal behavior, imaginative play, and self-regulation in a natural setting. *Developmental Psychology, 15*, 637–646.

Frieze, I. H. (1979). Perceptions of battered wives. In I. H. Frieze, D. Bar-Tal, & J. S. Carroll (Eds.), *Attribution theory: Applications to social problems*. San Francisco: Jossey-Bass.

Froming, W. J., Allen, L., & Jensen, R. (1985). Altruism, role-taking, and self-awareness: The acquisition of norms governing altruistic behavior. *Child Development, 56*, 1223–1228.

Fultz, J., Batson, C. D., Fortenbach, V. A., McCarthy, P. M., & Varney, L. L. (1986). Social evaluation and the empathy-altruism hypothesis. *Journal of Personality and Social Psychology, 50*, 761–769.

Fultz, J., Schaller, M., & Cialdini, R. B. (1988). Empathy, sadness, and distress: Three related but distinct vicarious affective responses to another's suffering. *Personality and Social Psychology Bulletin, 14*, 312–325.

Gaertner, S. L., & Bickman, L. (1971). Effects of race on the elicitation of helping behavior. *Journal of Personality and Social Psychology, 20*, 218–222.

Gaertner, S. L., & Dovidio, J. F. (1977). The subtlety of white racism, arousal, and helping behavior. *Journal of Personality and Social Psychology, 35,* 691–707.

Gaertner, S. L., & Dovidio, J. F. (1986). The aversive form of racism. In J. F. Dovidio & S. L. Gaertner (Eds.), *Prejudice, discrimination, and racism* (pp. 61–90). Orlando, FL: Academic Press.

Galaskiewic, J. (1985). *Social organization of an urban grants economy: A study of business philanthropy and nonprofit organizations.* New York: Academic Press.

Garvey, C. (1990). *Play.* Cambridge, MA: Harvard University Press.

Gelfand, D. M., & Hartmann, D. P. (1982). Response consequences and attributions: Two contributors to prosocial behavior. In N. Eisenberg (Ed.), *The development of prosocial behavior* (pp. 167–196). New York: Academic Press.

George, J. M. (1991). The effects of positive mood on prosocial behaviors at work. *Journal of Applied Psychology, 76,* 497–513.

Gergen, K. J., Ellsworth, P., Maslach, C., & Seipel, M. (1975). Obligation, donor resources, and reactions to aid in three cultures. *Journal of Personality and Social Psychology, 31,* 390–400.

Gergen, K. J., Gergen, M. M., & Meter, K. (1972). Individual orientations to prosocial behavior. *Journal of Social Issues, 8,* 105–130.

Gergen, K. J., Morse, S. J., & Bode, K. A. (1974). Overpaid or overworked? Cognitive and behavioral reactions to inequitable rewards. *Journal of Applied Social Psychology, 4,* 53–58.

Gergen, K. J., Morse, S. J., & Gergen, M. M. (1980). Behavior exchange in cross-cultural perspective. In H. C. Triandis & R. W. Brislin (Eds.), *Handbook of cross-cultural psychology: Vol. 15. Social psychology* (pp. 121–153). Boston: Allyn & Bacon.

Ghiselin, M. T. (1974). *The economy of nature and the evolution of sex.* Berkeley: University of California Press.

Gibbons, F. X. (1990). Self-attention and behavior: A review and theoretical update. In M. P. Zanna (Ed.), *Advances in experimental social psychology* (Vol. 23, pp. 249–303). San Diego, CA: Academic Press.

Gilligan, C. (1982). *In a different voice.* Cambridge, MA: Harvard University Press.

Glance N. S., & Huberman, B. A. (1994, March). The dynamics of social dilemmas. *Scientific American,* pp. 76–81.

Glassman, R. B., Packel, E. W., & Brown, D. L. (1986). Green beards and kindred spirits: A preliminary mathematical model of altruism toward nonkin who bear similarities to the giver. *Ethology and Sociobiology, 7,* 107–115.

Glick, P., DeMorest, J. A., & Hotze, C. A. (1988). Keeping your distance: Group membership, personal space, and requests for small favors. *Journal of Applied Social Psychology, 18,* 315–330.

Goethals, G. R., & Darley, J. M. (1987). Social comparison theory: Self-evaluation and group life. In B. Mullen & G. R. Goethals (Eds.), *Theories of group behavior* (pp. 21–47). New York: Springer-Verlag.

Goffman, E. (1959). *The presentation of self in everyday life.* Garden City, NY: Doubleday Anchor.

Goldberg, L. R. (1993). The structure of phenotypic personality traits. *American Psychologist, 48,* 26–34.

Golding, J. M., & Burnam, M. A. (1990). Stress and social support as predictors of depressive symptoms in Mexican-Americans and non-Hispanic whites. *Journal of Social and Clinical Psychology, 9,* 268–287.

Good, G. E., Dell, D. M., & Mintz, L. B. (1989). Male role and gender role conflict: Relations to help seeking in men. *Journal of Counseling Psychology, 36,* 295–300.

Goranson, R., & Berkowitz, L. (1966). Reciprocity and responsibility reactions to prior help. *Journal of Personality and Social Psychology, 3,* 227–232.

Gottlieb, B. H., & Wagner, F. (1991). Stress and support processes in close relationships. In J. Eckenroade (Ed.), *The social context of coping* (pp. 165–188). New York: Plenum.

Gouldner, A. (1960). The norm of reciprocity: A preliminary statement. *American Sociological Review, 25,* 161–178.

Graziano, W. G., & Eisenberg, N. H. (in press). Agreeableness: A dimension of personality. In S. Briggs, R. Hogan, & W. Jones (Eds.), *Handbook of personality psychology.* San Diego, CA: Academic Press.

Gross, A. E., & McMullen, P. A. (1983). Models of the help seeking process. In B. M. DePaulo, A. Nadler, & J. D. Fisher (Eds.), *New directions in helping: Vol. 2. Help seeking* (pp. 47–73). New York: Academic Press.

Grusec, J. E. (1982). The socialization of altruism. In N. Eisenberg (Ed.), *The development of prosocial behavior* (pp. 139–166). New York: Academic Press.

Grusec, J. E. (1991a). The socialization of empathy. In M. S. Clark (Ed.), *Review of personality and social psychology: Vol. 12. Prosocial behavior* (pp. 9–33) Newbury Park, CA: Sage.

Grusec, J. E. (1991b). Socialization of concern for others in the home. *Developmental Psychology, 27,* 338–342.

Grusec, J. E., & Goodnow, J. J. (1994). Impact of parental discipline methods on the child's internalization of values. *Developmental Psychology, 30,* 4–19.

Grusec, J. E., Kuczynski, L., Rushton, J. P., & Simutis, Z. M. (1978). Modeling, direct instructions, and attributions: Effects of altruism. *Developmental Psychology, 14,* 51–57.

Grusec, J. E., & Lytton, H. (1988). *Social development: History, theory, and research.* New York: Springer-Verlag.

Grusec, J. E., & Redler, E. (1980). Attribution, reinforcement, and altruism: A developmental analysis. *Developmental Psychology, 16,* 525–534.

Grusec, J. E., Saas-Kortsaak, P., & Simutis, Z. M. (1978). The role of example and moral exhortation in the training of altruism. *Child Development, 49,* 920–923.

Hamilton, W. D. (1964). The genetic evolution of social behavior. *Journal of Theoretical Biology 7,* 1–52.

Hardin, G. (1968). The tragedy of the commons. *Science, 162,* 1243–1248.

Hardin, G. (1977). *The limits of altruism.* Bloomington, IN: Indiana University Press.

Hare, R. D. (1970). *Psychopathy: Theory and research.* New York: Wiley.

Harris, M. B., & Bays, G. (1973). Altruism and sex roles. *Psychological Reports, 32,* 1002.

Harris, M. B., Benson, S. M., & Hall, C. L. (1975). The effects of confession on altruism. *Journal of Social Psychology, 102,* 197–208.

Harter, S. (1986). Processes underlying the construct, maintenance, and enhancement of the self-concept in children. In J. Suls & A. Greenwald (Eds.), *Psychological perspectives on the self* (Vol. 3, pp. 137–181). Hillsdale, NJ: Erlbaum.

Hatfield, E., & Sprecher, S. (1983). Equity theory and recipients' reactions to aid.

In J. Fisher, A. Nadler, & B. M. Depaulo (Eds.), *New directions in helping: Vol 1. Recipient's reaction to aid* (pp. 113–143). New York: Academic Press.

Hawking, S. (1988). *A brief history of time.* New York: Bantam.

Hayes, R. B., Catania, J. A., McKusick, L., & Coates, T. J. (1990). Help-seeking for AIDS-related concerns: A comparison of gay men with various HIV diagnoses. *American Journal of Community Psychology, 18,* 743–755.

Hearold, S. (1986). A synthesis of 1043 effects of television on social behavior. In G. Comstock (Ed.), *Public communications and behavior* (Vol. 1, pp. 65–133). New York: Academic Press.

Hedge, A., & Yousif, Y. H. (1992). Effects of urban size, urgency, and cost of helpfulness: A cross-cultural comparison between the United Kingdom and the Sudan. *Journal of Cross-Cultural Psychology, 23,* 107–115.

Heider, F. (1958). *The psychology of interpersonal relationships.* New York: Wiley.

Hill, F. E., & Harmon, M. (1976). The use of telephone tapes in telephone counseling program. *Crisis Intervention, 7,* 88–96.

Hodgkinson, V. A., Weitzman, M. S., & Kirsch, A. D. (1990). From commitment to action: How religious involvement affects giving and volunteering. In R. Wuthnow & V. A. Hodgkinson (Eds.), *Faith and philanthropy in America* (pp. 93–114). San Francisco: Jossey-Bass.

Hoffman, M. L. (1970). Conscience, personality and socialization techniques. *Human Development, 13,* 90–126.

Hoffman, M. L. (1975). Altruistic behavior and the parent child relationship. *Journal of Personality and Social Psychology, 31,* 937–943.

Hoffman, M. L. (1977). Sex differences in empathy and related behaviors. *Psychological Bulletin, 34,* 712–722.

Hoffman, M. L. (1978). Physiological and biological perspectives on altruism. *International Journal of Behavioral Development, 1,* 323–339.

Hoffman, M. L. (1981). Is altruism part of human nature? *Journal of Personality and Social Psychology, 40,* 121–137.

Hoffman, M. L. (1984). The measurement of empathy. In C. E. Izard, J. Kagan, & R. B. Zajonc (Eds.), *Emotions, cognitions, and behavior* (pp. 103–131). Cambridge, England: Cambridge University Press.

Hoffman, M. L. (1990). Empathy and justice motivation. *Motivation and Emotion, 14,* 151–172.

Hoffman, M. L. (1994). Discipline and internalization. *Developmental Psychology, 30,* 26–28.

Holloway, S., Tucker, L., & Hornstein, H. A. (1977). The effects of social and nonsocial information on interpersonal behavior of males: The news makes news. *Journal of Personality and Social Psychology, 35,* 514–522.

Hoover, C. W., Wood, E. E., & Knowles, E. S. (1983). Forms of social awareness and helping. *Journal of Experimental Social Psychology, 18,* 577–590.

Hopper, J. R. (1991). Recycling as altruistic behavior: Normative and behavioral strategies to expand participation in a community recycling program. *Environment and Behavior, 23,* 195–220.

Hornstein, H. A. (1970). The influence of social models on helping behavior. In J. Macaulay & L. Berkowitz (Eds.), *Altruism and helping behavior* (pp. 29–42). New York: Academic Press.

Hornstein, H. A. (1982). Promotive tension: Theory and research. In V. J. Derlega & J. Grzelak (Eds.), *Cooperation and helping behavior: Theories and research* (pp. 229–248). New York: Academic Press.

Horwitz, A. V. (1987). Help-seeking processes and mental health services. *New Directions for Mental Health Services, 36*, 33–45.

Hume, R. E. (1959). *The world's living religions*. New York: Scribner.

Humphrey, G. (1923). The conditioned reflex and elementary social reaction. *Journal of Abnormal and Social Psychology, 17*, 113–119.

Hunt, M. (1990). *The compassionate beast*. New York: Morrow.

Huston, T., Geis, G., & Wright, R. (1976, June). The angry samaritan. *Psychology Today*, pp. 61–64, 85.

Huston, T., Ruggiero, M., Conner, R., & Geis, G. (1981). Bystander intervention into crime: A study based on naturally occurring episodes. *Social Psychology Quarterly, 44*, 14–23.

Independent Sector. (1988). *Giving and volunteering in the United States: Findings from a national survey*. Washington, DC: Author.

Independent Sector. (1990). *Giving and volunteering in the United States*. Washington, DC: Author.

Isen, A. M. (1970). Success, failure, attention, and reaction to others: The warm glow of success. *Journal of Personality and Social Psychology, 15*, 294–301.

Isen, A. M. (1993). Positive affect and decision making. In M. Lewis & M. Haviland (Eds.), *Handbook of emotion* (pp. 261–267). New York: Guilford.

Isen, A. M., Clark, M., & Schwartz, M. (1976). Duration of the effect of good mood on helping: "Footprints in the sands of time." *Journal of Personality and Social Psychology, 34*, 385–393.

Isen, A. M., & Levin, P. F. (1972). Effect of feeling good on helping: Cookies and kindness. *Journal of Personality and Social Psychology, 21*, 384–388.

Isen, A. M., Shalker, T. E., Clark, M., & Karp, L. (1978). Affect, accessibility of material in memory, and behavior. *Journal of Personality and Social Psychology, 36*, 1–12.

Israel, A. C. (1978). Some thoughts on the correspondence between saying and doing. *Journal of Applied Behavior Analysis, 11*, 271–276.

Israel, A. C., & Brown, M. S. (1979). Effects of directiveness of instructions and surveillance on the production and persistence of children's donations. *Journal of Experimental Child Psychology, 27*, 250–261.

Jarymowicz, M. (1992). Self, we, and other(s): Schemata, distinctiveness, and altruism. In P. M. Oliner, S. P. Oliner, L. Baron, L. A. Blum, D. L. Krebs, & Smolenska (Eds.), *Embracing the other: Philosophical, psychological, and historical perspectives on altruism* (pp. 194–212). New York: NYU Press.

Johnson, D. W., Johnson, R. T., Tiffany, M., & Zaidman, B. (1983). Are low achievers disliked in a cooperative situation? A test of rival theories in a mixed ethnic situation. *Contemporary Educational Psychology, 8*, 189–200.

Johnson, F. L., & Aries, E. J. (1983). Conversational patterns among same-sex pairs of late adolescent close friends. *Journal of Genetic Psychology, 142*, 225–238.

Johnson, G. R. (1986). Kin selection, socialization, and patriotism: An integrating theory. *Politics and the Life Sciences, 4*(2), 127–154.

Johnson, M. E. (1988). Influences of gender and sex role orientation on help-seeking attitudes. *Journal of Psychology, 122*, 237–241.

Johnson, R. C., Danko, G. P., Darvill, T. J., Bochner, S., Bowers, J. K., Huang, Y. H., Park, J. Y., Pecjak, V., Rahim, A. R. A., & Pennington, D. (1989). Cross-cultural assessment of altruism and its correlates. *Personality and Individual Differences, 8*, 855–868.

Jones, E. E., & Davis, K. E. (1965). From acts to dispositions: The attribution process in person perception. In L. Berkowitz (Ed.), *Advances in experimental social psychology* (Vol. 2, pp. 219–266). New York: Academic Press.

Jones, E. E., & McGillis, D. (1976). Correspondent inference and the attribution cube: A comparative reappraisal. In J. Harvey, W. Ickes, & R. Kidd (Eds.), *New directions in attribution theory* (pp. 389–420). Hillsdale, NJ: Erlbaum.

Kahn, A. (1986). *No contest: The case against competition*. Boston: Houghton Mifflin.

Kahn, A., & Tice, T. (1973). Returning a favor and retaliating harm: The effects of stated intention and actual behavior. *Journal of Experimental Social Psychology 9*, 43–56.

Kaminer, W. (1984). *Women volunteering*. Garden City, NY: Anchor Press.

Kaniasty, K., & Norris, F. H. (1993). A test of the social support deterioration model in the context of a natural disaster. *Journal of Personality and Social Psychology, 64*, 395–408.

Kaniasty, K., Norris, F. H., & Murrell, S. A. (1990). Received and perceived social support following a natural disaster. *Journal of Applied Social Psychology, 35*, 85–114.

Karabenick, S. A., & Knapp, J. R. (1988). Help seeking and the need for academic assistance. *Journal of Educational Psychology, 80*, 406–408.

Kayal, P. (1993). *Bearing witness: Gay men's health crisis and the politics of AIDS*. Boulder, CO: Westview Press.

Kelley, H. H. (1967). Attribution theory in social psychology. In D. Levine (Ed.), *Nebraska symposium on motivation, 15*, 192–238.

Kelley, H. H. (1973). The process of causal attributions. *American Psychologist, 28*, 107–128.

Kelley, K., & Byrne, D. (1976). Attraction and altruism: With a little help from my friends. *Journal of Research in Personality, 10*, 59–68.

Kerr, N. L. (1989). Illusions of efficacy: The effects of group size on perceived efficacy in social dilemmas. *Journal of Experimental Social Psychology, 25*, 287–313.

Kerr, N. L., & Bruun, S. E. (1983). Dispensability of member effort and group motivation losses: Free-rider effects. *Journal of Personality and Social Psychology, 44*, 78–94.

Kerr, N. L., & MacCoun, R. J. (1985). Role expectations in social dilemmas: Sex roles and task motivation in groups. *Journal of Personality and Social Psychology, 49*, 1547–1556.

Kessler, R. (1979). Stress, social status, and psychological distress. *Journal of Health and Social Behavior, 20*, 259–272.

Kestenbaum, J., Farber, E., & Sroufe, L. A. (1989). Individual differences in empathy among preschoolers: Relation to attachment history. *New Directions for Child Development, 44*, 51–64.

Knight, G. P., Dubro, A. F., & Chao, C. C. (1985). Information processing and the development of cooperative, competitive, and individualistic social values. *Developmental Psychology, 21*, 37–45.

Kohlberg, L. (1963). The development of children's orientations toward a moral order: I. Sequence in the development of moral thought. *Vita Humana, 6*, 11–33.

Kohlberg, L. (1985). *The psychology of moral development*. San Francisco: Harper & Row.

Komorita, S. S., & Parks, C. D. (1994). *Social dilemmas*. Madison, WI: Brown & Benchmark.

Korte, C. (1969). Group effects on help-giving in an emergency. *Proceedings of the Seventy-seventh Annual Convention of the American Psychological Association, 4,* 383–384.

Korte, C. (1980). Urban-nonurban differences in social behavior and social psychological models of urban impact. *Journal of Social Issues, 36,* 29–51.

Kramer, R. M., & Brewer, M. B. (1984). Effects of group identity on resource use in a simulated commons dilemma. *Journal of Personality and Social Psychology, 46,* 1044–1057.

Kramer, R. M., & Brewer, M. B. (1986). Social group identity and the emergence of cooperation in resource conservation dilemmas. In A. M. Wilke, D. M. Messick, & C. G. Rutte (Eds.), *Experimental social dilemmas* (pp. 205–234). Frankfurt am Main: Verlag Peter Lang.

Krebs, D. (1982). Psychological approaches to altruism: An evaluation. *Ethics, 92,* 447–458.

Krebs, D. (1987). The challenge of altruism in biology and psychology. In C. Crawford, M. Smith, & D. Krebs (Eds.), *Sociobiology and psychology: Ideas, issues, and applications* (pp. 81–118). Hillsdale, NJ: Erlbaum.

Krebs, D., & Miller, D. T. (1985). Altruism and aggression. In G. Lindzey & E. Aronson (Eds.), *Handbook of social psychology* (3rd ed.) (Vol. 2, pp. 1–71). New York: Random House.

Krupat, E., & Guild, W. (1980). Defining the city: The use of objective and subjective measures for community description. *Journal of Social Issues, 36,* 9–28.

Kunz, P. R., & Woolcott, M. (1976). Season's greetings: From my status to yours. *Social Science Research, 5,* 269–278.

Langer, E. J. (1989). *Mindfulness*. Reading, MA: Addison-Wesley.

Langer, E. J., & Rodin, J. (1976). The effects of choice and enhanced personal responsibility for the aged: A field experiment in an institutional setting. *Journal of Personality and Social Psychology, 34,* 191–198.

Latané, B., & Dabbs, J. M. (1975). Sex, group size and helping in three cities. *Sociometry, 18,* 180–194.

Latané, B., & Darley, J. M. (1970). *The unresponsive bystander: Why doesn't he help?* New York: Appleton-Century-Crofts.

Latané, B., Nida, S. A., & Wilson, D. W. (1981). The effects of group size on helping behavior. In J. P. Rushton & R. M. Sorrentino (Eds.), *Altruism and helping behavior: Social, personality, and developmental perspectives* (pp. 287–313). Hillsdale, NJ: Erlbaum.

Lazarus, R. S. (1982). Thought on the relations between emotion and cognition. *American Psychologist, 37,* 1019–1024.

Leahy, R. L. (1979). Development of conceptions of prosocial behavior: Information affecting rewards given for altruism and kindness. *Developmental Psychology, 15,* 34–37.

Lee, L. (1992). *Factors that influence donor identities: A comparison of three types of donating*. Unpublished Master's thesis, University of Wisconsin, Madison.

Leek, M., & Smith, P. K. (1989). Phenotypic matching, human altruism, and mate selection. *Behavioral and Brain Sciences, 12,* 534–535.

Leek, M., & Smith, P. K. (1991). Cooperation and conflict in three-generation families. In P. K. Smith (Ed.), *The psychology of grandparenthood: An international perspective* (pp. 177–194). London: Routledge.

Leerhsen, C., Lewis, S., Pomper, S., Davenport, L., & Nelson, M. (1990, February 5). Unite and conquer. *Newsweek*, pp. 50–55.

Lepper, M. (1981). Intrinsic and extrinsic motivation in children: The detrimental effects of superfluous social controls. In W. A. Collins (Ed.), *Minnesota symposium on child psychology* (Vol. 14, pp. 115–214). Hillsdale, NJ: Erlbaum.

Lerner, M. J. (1980). *The belief in a just world: A fundamental delusion*. New York: Plenum.

Leung, K. (1988). Theoretical advances in justice behavior: Some cross-cultural inputs. In M. H. Bond (Ed.), *The cross-cultural challenge to social psychology* (pp. 218–239). Newbury Park, CA: Sage.

Lewin, K. (1936). *Principles of topological psychology*. New York: McGraw-Hill.

Lieberman, M. A., & Tobin, S. S. (1983). *The experience of old age: Stress, coping and survival*. New York: Basic Books.

Liebert, R. M., & Sprafkin, J. (1988). *The early window: The effects of television on children and youth*. New York: Pergamon.

Liebrand, W. B. G. (1984). The effect of social motives, communication and group size on behavior in an *n*-person multi-stage mixed-motive game. *European Journal of Social Psychology, 14*, 239–264.

Liebrand, W. B. G. (1986). The ubiquity of social values in social dilemmas. In A. M. Wilke, D. M. Messick, & C. G. Rutte (Eds.), *Experimental social dilemmas* (pp. 113–133). Frankfurt am Main: Verlag Peter Lang.

Liebrand, W. B. G., & van Run, G. J. (1985). The effects of social motives on behavior in social dilemmas in two cultures. *Journal of Experimental Social Psychology, 21*, 86–102.

Liebrand, W. B. G., Wilke, H. A., & Messick, D. M. (Eds.). (1992). *Social psychological approaches to social dilemmas*. Tarrytown, NY: Pergamon Press.

Lindzey, G. (Ed.). (1954). *Handbook of social psychology*. Cambridge, MA: Addison-Wesley.

Lindzey, G., & Aronson, E. (Eds.). (1969). *Handbook of social psychology* (2nd ed.). Cambridge, MA: Addison-Wesley.

Lindzey, G., & Aronson, E. (Eds.). (1985). *Handbook of social psychology* (3rd ed.). New York: Random House.

Lipscomb, T. J., McAllister, H. A., Bregman, N. J. (1985). A developmental inquiry into the effects of multiple models on children's generosity. *Merrill-Palmer Quarterly, 31*, 335–344.

Lockard, J. S., & Paulhus, D. L. (1988). *Self-deception: An adaptive mechanism?* Englewood Cliffs, NJ: Prentice-Hall.

London, P. (1970). The rescuers: Motivational hypotheses about Christians who saved Jews from the Nazis. In J. Macaulay & L. Berkowitz (Eds.), *Altruism and helping behavior* (pp. 241–250). New York: Academic Press.

Lopreato, J. (1981). Toward a theory of genuine altruism in *Homo sapiens*. *Ethology and Sociobiology, 2*, 113–126.

Luks, A. (1992). *The healing power of doing good: The health and spiritual benefits of helping others*. New York: Fawcett Columbine.

Lyon, D., & Greenberg, J. (1991). Evidence of that codependency in women with an alcoholic parent: Helping out Mr. Wrong. *Journal of Personality and Social Psychology, 61*, 435–439.

Ma, H. (1985). Cross-cultural study of altruism. *Psychological Reports, 57*, 337–338.

Macaulay, J. R. (1970). A shill for charity. In J. Macaulay & L. Berkowitz (Eds.), *Altruism and helping behavior* (pp. 43–60). New York: Academic Press.

Macaulay, J. R., & Berkowitz, L. (Eds.). (1970). *Altruism and helping behavior*. New York: Academic Press.

MacDonald, K. (1984). An ethological-social learning theory of the development of altruism: Implications for human sociobiology. *Ethology and Sociobiology, 5*, 97–109.

Machiavelli, N. (1950). *The prince*. New York: Modern Library. (Original work published 1513).

MacLean, P. D. (1973). *A triune concept of the brain and behavior*. Toronto, Canada: University of Toronto Press.

MacLean P. D. (1985). Evolutionary psychiatry and the triune brain. *Psychological Brain, 15*, 219–221.

Mails, T. E. (1988). *Secret Native American pathways: A guide to inner peace*. Tulsa, OK: Council Oaks Books.

Main, M., & Weston, D. R. (1981). The quality of the toddler's relationship to mother and to father: Related to conflict behavior and the readiness to establish new relationships. *Child Development, 52*, 932–940.

Major, B., & Crocker, J. (1993). Social stigma: The consequences of attributional ambiguity. In D. M. Mackie & D. L. Hamilton (Eds.), *Affect, cognition, and stereotyping: Interactive processes in group perception* (pp. 345–370). San Diego: Academic Press.

Mallozzi, J., McDermott, V., & Kayson, W. A. (1990). Effects of sex, type of dress, and location on altruistic behavior. *Psychological Reports, 67*, 1103–1106.

Mansbridge, J. (Ed.). (1990). *Beyond self-interest*. Chicago: University of Chicago Press.

Manucia, G. K., Baumann, D. J., & Cialdini, R. B. (1984). Mood influences in helping: Direct effects or side effects? *Journal of Personality and Social Psychology, 46*, 357–364.

Marcus, P. (1973). *Survey of Lansing employee perceptions of capital area United Way: Report #1: Givers and nongivers*. Unpublished paper, Department of Sociology, Michigan State University.

Markus, H. R., & Kitayama, S. (1991). Culture and the self: Implications for cognition, emotion, and motivation. *Psychological Review, 98*, 224–253.

Marks, E. L., Penner, L. A., & Stone, A. W. (1982). Helping as a function of empathic responses and sociopathy. *Journal of Research in Personality, 16*, 1–20.

Martichuski, D. K., & Bell, P. A. (1991). Reward, punishment, privatization, and moral suasion in a commons dilemma. *Journal of Applied Social Psychology, 21*, 1356–1369.

Martin, G. B., & Clark, R. D., III. (1982). Distress crying in infants: Species and peer specificity. *Developmental Psychology, 18*, 3–9.

Marwell, G., Aiken,. M. T., & Demerath, N. J., III. (1987). The persistence of political attitudes among 1960's civil rights activists. *Public Opinion Quarterly, 51*, 359–375.

Marwell, G., & Ames, R. (1981). Economists free ride, does anyone else? Experiments on the provision of public goods, IV. *Journal of Public Economics, 15*, 295–310.

Mathews, K. E., & Canon, L. K. (1975). Environmental noise level as a determinant of helping behavior. *Journal of Personality and Social Psychology, 32*, 571–577.

Matthews, K. A., Batson, C. D., Horn, J., & Rosenman, R. H. (1981). "Principles in his nature which interest him in the fortune of others . . .": The heritability of empathic concern for others. *Journal of Personality, 49,* 237–247.

McCall, G. J., & Simmons J. L. (1978). *Identities and interactions.* New York: Free Press.

McClintock, C. G. (1974). Development of social motives in Anglo-American and Mexican-American children. *Journal of Personality and Social Psychology, 29,* 348–354.

McClintock, C. G., & Nuttin, J. (1969). Development of competitive game behavior across two cultures. *Journal of Experimental Social Psychology, 5,* 203–218.

McConahay, J. B. (1981). Reducing racial prejudice in desegregated schools. In W. D. Hawley (Ed.), *Effective school desegregation: Equity, quality, and feasibility* (pp. 35–53). Beverly Hills, CA: Sage.

McDougall, W. (1936). *Social Psychology* (23rd ed.). London: Metheun. (Original work published 1908).

McGovern, L. P. (1976). Dispositional social anxiety and helping behavior under three conditions. *Journal of Personality, 44,* 84–97.

McGovern, L. P., Ditzian, J. L., & Taylor, S. P. (1975). The effect of one positive reinforcement on helping behavior. *Bulletin of the Psychonomics Society, 5,* 421–423.

McGuire, A. M. (1994). Helping behaviors in the natural environment: Dimensions and correlates of helping. *Personality and Social Psychology Bulletin, 20,* 45–56.

McMillen. D. L., Sanders, D. Y., & Solomon, G. S. (1977). Self-esteem, attentiveness, and helping behavior. *Personality and Social Psychology Bulletin, 3,* 257–261.

Mechanic, D. (1968). *Medical sociology.* London: Collier-MacMillan.

Medvene, L. J. (1992). Self-help groups, peer helping, and social comparison. In S. Spacapan & S. Oskamp (Eds.), *Helping and being helped: Naturalistic studies* (pp. 49–82). Newbury Park, CA: Sage.

Medvene, L. J., & Lin, K. (1992). Developing a recruitment strategy to increase the participation of Mexican-Americans in family support groups. In L. J. Medvene (Chair), *From scenarios to self-help groups: Current research on helping relationships.* Symposium presented at the convention of the American Psychological Association, Washington, DC.

Meindl, J. R., & Lerner, M. J. (1983). The heroic motive: Some experimental demonstrations. *Journal of Experimental Social Psychology, 19,* 1–20.

Meindl, J. R., & Lerner, M. J. (1984). Exacerbation of extreme responses to an outgroup. *Journal of Personality and Social Psychology, 47,* 71–84.

Melamed, B. G., & Brenner, G. F. (1990). Social support and chronic medical stress: An interaction-based approach. *Journal of Social and Clinical Psychology, 9,* 104–117.

Meltzoff, A. N. (1985). The roots of social and cognitive development: Models of man's original nature. In T. M. Field & N. A. Fox (Eds.), *Social perception in infants* (pp. 1–30). Norwood, NJ: Ablex.

Messick, D. M., Wilke, H., Brewer, M. B., Kramer, R. M., Zemke, P. E., & Lui, L. (1983). Individual adaptations and structural change as solutions to social dilemmas. *Journal of Personality and Social Psychology, 44,* 294–309.

Midlarsky, E. (1984). Competence and helping. In E. Staub, D. Bar-Tal, J. Karylowski, & J. Reykowski (Eds.), *Development and maintenance of prosocial behavior* (pp. 291–308). New York: Plenum.

Midlarsky, E. (1985/1986). Helping during the Holocaust: The role of political, theological and socioeconomic identification. *Humboldt Journal of Social Relations, 13,* 285–305.

Midlarsky, E. (1991). Helping as coping. In M. S. Clark (Ed.), *Review of personality and social psychology: vol. 12. Prosocial behavior* (pp. 238–264). Newbury Park, CA: Sage.

Midlarsky, E., & Hannah, M. E. (1985). Competence, reticence, and helping by children and adolescents. *Developmental Psychology, 21,* 534–541.

Midlarsky, E., & Hannah, M. E. (1989). The generous elderly. *Psychology and Aging, 4,* 346–351.

Mikolay, D., Dovidio, J. F., Ellyson, S. L., Maggiano, N. A., & Keating, C. F. (1989, March). *Androgyny as a mediating variable in helping behavior.* Paper presented at the annual meeting of the Eastern Psychological Association, Boston, MA.

Milgram, S. (1970). The experience of living in cities. *Science, 167,* 1461–1468.

Miller, J. G. (in press). Cultural diversity in the morality of caring: Individually-oriented versus duty-based interpersonal moral codes. *Cross-Cultural Research.*

Miller, J. G., & Bersoff, D. M. (in press). Cultural influences on the moral status of reciprocity and the discounting of endogenous motivation. *Personality and Social Psychology Bulletin.*

Miller, N., & Carlson, M. (1990). Valid theory-testing: Meta-analyses further question the negative state relief model of helping. *Psychological Bulletin, 107,* 215–225.

Miller, W. R. (1985). Motivation for treatment: A review with a special emphasis on alcoholism. *Psychological Bulletin, 98,* 84–107.

Moghaddam, F. M., Taylor, D. M., & Wright, S. C. (1993). *Social psychology in cross-cultural perspective.* New York: Freeman.

Monson, T. C., Hesley, J. W., & Chernick, L. (1982). Specifying when personality traits can and cannot predict behavior: An alternative to abandoning the attempt to predict single-act criteria. *Journal of Personality and Social Psychology, 43,* 385–399.

Moore, B. S., & Eisenberg, N. (1984). The development of altruism. *Annals of Child Development, 1,* 107–174.

Moore, C., & Richardson, J. J. (1988). The politics and practice of corporate responsibility in Great Britain. In L. E. Preston (Ed.), *Research in corporate social performance and policy* (Vol. 10, pp. 267–290). Greenwich, CT: JAI Press.

Moore, J. (1984). The evolution of reciprocal sharing. *Ethology and Sociobiology, 5,* 4–14.

Morgan, C. J. (1985). Natural selection for altruism in structured populations. *Ethology and Sociobiology, 6,* 211–218.

Moriarty, T. (1975). Crime, commitment, and the responsive bystander: Two field experiments. *Journal of Personality and Social Psychology, 31,* 370–376.

Morris, D. (1967). *The naked ape.* London: Constable.

Morris, S. C., III, & Rosen, S. (1973). Effects of felt adequacy and opportunity to reciprocate on help-seeking. *Journal of Experimental Social Psychology, 9,* 265–276.

Moss, M. K., & Page, R. A. (1972). Reinforcement and helping behavior. *Journal of Applied Social Psychology, 2,* 360–371.

Mueller, C. W., & Donnerstein, E. (1981). Film-facilitated arousal and prosocial behavior. *Journal of Experimental Social Psychology, 17,* 31–41.

Mueller, C. W., Donnerstein, E., & Hallam, J. (1983). Violent films and prosocial behavior. *Personality and Social Psychology Bulletin, 9*, 83–89.

Munekata, H., & Ninomiya, K. (1985). The development of prosocial moral judgments. *Japanese Journal of Educational Psychology, 33*, 157–164.

Murchison, C. A. (Ed.). (1935). *Handbook of social psychology.* Worcester, MA: Clark University Press.

Myers, D. (1993). *Social psychology* (4th ed.). New York: McGraw-Hill.

Nadler, A. (1986). Self esteem and the seeking and receiving of help: Theoretical and empirical perspectives. In B. Maher & W. Maher (Eds.), *Progress in experimental personality research* (Vol. 14, pp. 115–163). New York: Academic Press.

Nadler, A. (1987). Determinants of help seeking behavior: The effects of helper's similarity, task centrality and recipient's self esteem. *European Journal of Social Psychology, 17*, 57–67.

Nadler, A. (1991). Help-seeking behavior: Psychological costs and instrumental benefits. In M. S. Clark (Ed.), *Review of personality and social psychology: Vol. 12. Prosocial behavior* (pp. 290–311). Newbury Park, CA: Sage.

Nadler, A., Altman, A., & Fisher, J. D. (1979). Helping is not enough: Recipient's reactions to aid as a function of positive and negative self-regard. *Journal of Personality, 47*, 615–628.

Nadler, A., & Fisher, J. D. (1986). The role of threat to self-esteem and perceived control in recipient reaction to help: Theory development and empirical validation. In L. Berkowitz (Ed.), *Advances in experimental social psychology* (Vol. 19, pp. 81–122). San Diego, CA: Academic Press.

Nadler, A., Fisher, J. D., & Ben-Itzhak, S. (1983). With a little help from my friend: Effect of single or multiple act aid as a function of donor and task characteristics. *Journal of Personality and Social Psychology, 44*, 310–321.

Nadler, A., & Mayseless, O. (1983). Recipient self-esteem and reactions to help. In J. D. Fisher, A. Nadler, & B. M. DePaulo (Eds.), *New directions in helping: Vol. 1. Recipient reactions to aid* (pp. 167–188). New York: Academic Press.

Nadler, A., Mayseless, O., Peri, N., & Chemerinski, A. (1985). Effects of opportunity to reciprocate and self-esteem on help-seeking behavior. *Journal of Personality, 53*, 23–35.

National Conference of Christians and Jews. (1994, March 3). Survey reported in "Poll shows a gap in how races relate." News Service Reports, *Syracuse Post Standard*, pp. A1, A4.

Nelson-LeGall, S., & Glor-Scheib, S. (1985). Help-seeking in elementary classrooms: An observational study. *Contemporary Educational Psychology, 10*, 58–71.

Nelson-LeGall, S., & Glor-Scheib, S. (1986). Academic help seeking and peer relations in school. *Contemporary Educational Psychology, 11*, 187–193.

Nestmann, F. (1991). Role-related helping: Natural helpers in the service sector. In L. Montada, & H. W. Bierhoff (Eds.), *Altruism in social systems* (pp. 224–249). Lewiston, NY: Hogrefe and Huber.

Newman, R. S., & Goldin, L. (1990). Children's reluctance to seek help with schoolwork. *Journal of Educational Psychology, 82*, 92–100.

Nisbett, R. E. (1980). The trait construct in lay and professional psychology. In L. Festinger (Ed.), *Retrospections in social psychology* (pp. 109–130). New York: Oxford.

Ohmman, A., & Dimberg, U. (1978). Facial expressions as conditional stimuli for electrodermal responses: A case of "preparedness"? *Journal of Personality and Social Psychology, 36,* 1251–1258.

Oliner, S. P., & Oliner, P. M. (1988). *The altruistic personality: Rescuers of Jews in Nazi Europe.* New York: Free Press.

Omoto, A. M., & Snyder, M. (1990). Basic research in action: Volunteerism and society's response to AIDS. *Personality and Social Psychology Bulletin, 16,* 152–166.

Orbell, J. M., van de Kragt, A. J. C., & Dawes, R. M. (1988). Explaining discussion-induced cooperation. *Journal of Personality and Social Psychology, 54,* 811–819.

Ostrove, N. M., & Baum, A. (1983). Factors influencing medical help-seeking. In A. Nadler, J. D. Fisher, & B. M. Depaulo (Eds.), *New directions in helping: Vol. 3. Applied perspectives on help-seeking and receiving* (pp. 107–130). New York: Academic Press.

Otten, C. A., Penner, L. A., & Altabe, M. N. (1991). An examination of therapists' and college students' willingness to help a psychologically distressed person. *Journal of Social and Clinical Psychology, 10,* 102–120.

Otten, C. A., Penner, L. A., & Waugh, G. (1988). That's what friends are for: The determinants of psychological helping. *Journal of Social and Clinical Psychology, 7,* 34–41.

Pearce, J. L. (1983). Participation in voluntary associations: How membership in a formal organization changes the rewards of participation. In D. H. Smith (Ed.), *International perspectives on voluntary action research* (pp. 148–156). Washington, DC: University Press of America.

Pearce, P. L., & Amato, P. R. (1980). A taxonomy of helping: A multidimensional scaling analysis. *Social Psychology Quarterly, 43,* 363–371.

Penner, L. A., & Craiger, J. P. (1991, August). *The altruistic personality: A case of multiple identities?* Paper presented at the annual meeting of the American Psychological Association, San Francisco, CA.

Penner, L. A., Dertke, M. C., & Achenbach, C. J. (1973). The flash system: A field study of altruism. *Journal of Applied Social Psychology, 3,* 362–373.

Penner, L. A., & Fritzsche, B. A. (1993). Magic Johnson and reactions to people with AIDS: A natural experiment. *Journal of Applied Social Psychology, 23,* 1035–1050.

Penner, L. A., & Fritzsche, B. A. (1993, August). *Measuring the prosocial personality: Four construct validity studies.* Paper presented at the annual meeting of the American Psychological Association, Toronto, Canada.

Penner, L. A., Fritzsche, B. A., Craiger, J. P., & Freifeld, T. (in press). Measuring the prosocial personality. In J. N. Butcher & C. D. Spielberger (Eds.), *Advances in personality assessment* (Vol. 10). Hillsdale, NJ: LEA.

Piaget, J. (1932/1965). *The moral judgment of the child.* New York: Free Press.

Piaget, J., & Inhelder, B. (1971). *Mental imagery in the child.* New York: Basic Books.

Pietromonaco, P., & Nisbett, R. E. (1982). Swimming upstream against the fundamental attribution error: Subjects' weak generalizations from the Darley and Batson study. *Social Behavior and Personality, 10,* 1–4.

Piliavin, I. M., Piliavin, J. A., & Rodin, J. (1975). Costs, diffusion, and the stigmatized victim. *Journal of Personality and Social Psychology, 32,* 429–438.

Piliavin, I. M., Rodin, J., & Piliavin, J. A. (1969). Good samaritanism: An underground phenomenon? *Journal of Personality and Social Psychology, 13,* 289–299.

Piliavin, J. A. (1990). Why they "Give the gift of life to unnamed strangers": A review of research on blood donors since Oswalt (1977). *Transfusion, 30,* 444–459.

Piliavin, J. A., & Callero, P. L. (1991). *Giving blood: The development of an altruistic identity.* Baltimore: Johns Hopkins University Press.

Piliavin, J. A., & Charng, H. W. (1990). Altruism: A review of recent theory and research. *Annual Review of Sociology, 16,* 27–65.

Piliavin, J. A., Dovidio, J. F., Gaertner, S. L., & Clark, R. D., III. (1981). *Emergency intervention.* New York: Academic Press.

Piliavin, J. A., Lee, L., & Call, V. (1992, July). *The development of identities for giving time, money, and blood.* Paper presented at the First Joint Meeting of the Society of Experimental Social Psychology and the European Association of Experimental Social Psychology, Lewven, Belgium.

Piliavin, J. A., & Piliavin, I. M. (1972). The effects of blood on reactions to a victim. *Journal of Personality and Social Psychology, 23,* 253–261.

Piliavin, J. A., Piliavin, I. M., & Broll, L. (1976). Time of arousal at an emergency and likelihood of helping. *Personality and Social Psychology Bulletin, 2,* 273–276.

Piliavin, J. A., & Unger, R. K. (1985). The helpful but helpless female: Myth or reality? In V. O'Leary, R. K. Unger, & B. S. Wallston (Eds.), *Women, gender and social psychology* (pp. 149–186). Hillsdale, NJ: Erlbaum.

Plato. (1952). *Laws* (B. Jowett, Trans.). Chicago: Encyclopedia Britannica.

Platt, J. (1973). Social traps. *American Psychologist, 28,* 641–651.

Plomin, R., DeFries, J. C., & McClearn, G. E. (1990). *Behavioral genetics, a primer* (2nd ed.). New York: Freeman.

Pomazal, R. S., & Clore, G. L. (1973). Helping on the highway: The effects of dependency and sex. *Journal of Applied Social Psychology, 3,* 160–164.

Porter, R. H. (1987). Kin recognition: Functions and mediating mechanisms. In C. Crawford, M. Smith, & D. Krebs (Eds.), *Sociobiology and psychology* (pp. 175–204). Hillsdale, NJ: Erlbaum.

Porter, R. H., Cernoch, J. M., and Balogh, R. D. (1984). Recognition of neonates by facial-visual characteristics. *Pediatrics, 74,* 501–504.

Porter, R. H., Cernoch, J. M., & Balogh, R. D. (1985). Odor signatures and kin recognition. *Physiology and Behavior, 34,* 445–448.

Porter, R. H., Cernoch, J. M., & McLaughlin, F. J. (1983). Maternal recognition of neonates through olfactory cues. *Physiology and Behavior, 30,* 151–154.

Pruitt, D. G., & Carnevale, P. J. (1993). *Negotiation in social conflict.* Pacific Grove, CA: Brooks/Cole.

Pryor, J. B., Reeder, G. D., & McManus, J. A. (1991). Fear and loathing in the workplace: Reactions to AIDS infected co-workers. *Personality and Social Psychology Bulletin, 17,* 133–139.

Rabow, J., Newcomb, M. D., Monto, M. A., & Hernandez, A. C. R. (1990). Altruism in drunk driving situations: Personal and situational factors in helping. *Social Psychology Quarterly, 53,* 199–213.

Radke-Yarrow, M. R., & Zahn-Waxler, C. (1984). Roots, motives, and patterns in children's prosocial behavior. In E. Staub, D. Bar-Tal, J. Karylowski, & J. Reykowski (Eds.), *Origins and maintenance of prosocial behaviors* (pp. 81–100). New York: Plenum.

Radke-Yarrow, M. R., Zahn-Waxler, C. J., & Chapman, M. (1983). Children's proso-cial dispositions and behavior. In E. M. Hetherington (Ed.), *Handbook of child psychology: Vol. 4. Socialization, personality and social development* (pp. 469–546). New York: Harper & Row.

Radley, A., & Kennedy, M. (1992). Reflections upon charitable giving: A compari-son of individuals from business, "manual," and professional backgrounds. *Journal of Community and Applied Social Psychology, 2,* 113–129.

Raven, B. H., & Rubin, J. Z. (1983). *Social psychology* (2nd ed.). New York: Wiley.

Raviv, A., Bar-Tal, D., & Lewis-Levin, T. (1980). Motivations for donation behavior by boys of three different ages. *Child Development, 51,* 610–613.

Raviv, A., Raviv, A., & Yunovitz, R. (1989). Radio psychology and psychotherapy: A comparison of client attitudes and expectations. *Professional Psychology: Research and Practice, 20,* 1–7.

Reddy, R. D. (1980). Individual philanthropy and giving behavior. In D. H. Smith & J. Macaulay (Eds.), *Participation in social and political activities* (pp. 370–399). San Francisco: Jossey-Bass.

Regan, D. T. (1971). Effect of a favor on liking and compliance. *Journal of Experimental Social Psychology, 7,* 627–639.

Regan, D. T., Williams, M., & Sparling, S. (1972). Voluntary expiation of guilt: A field experiment. *Journal of Personality and Social Psychology, 24,* 42–45.

Ridley, M., & Dawkins, R. (1984). The natural selection of altruism. In J. Rushton & R. Sorrentino (Eds.), *Altruism and helping behavior: Social, personality, and developmental perspectives.* Hillsdale, NJ: Erlbaum.

Rokeach, M., & Mezei, L. (1966). Race and shared belief as factors in social choice. *Science, 151,* 167–172.

Romer, D., Gruder, C. L., & Lizzardo, T. (1986). A person-situation approach situ-ation to altruistic behavior. *Journal of Personality and Social Psychology, 51,* 1001–1012.

Rosenhan, D. L. (1969). Some origins of concern for others. In P. H. Mussen, J. Langer, & M. Covington (Eds.), *Trends and issues in developmental psychology.* New York: Holt, Rinehart, & Winston.

Rosenhan, D. L. (1970). The natural socialization of altruistic autonomy. In J. Macaulay & L. Berkowitz (Eds.), *Altruism and helping behavior* (pp. 251–268). New York: Academic Press.

Rosenhan, D. L., Salovey, P., & Hargis, K. (1981). The joys of helping: Focus of attention mediates the impact of positive affect on helping. *Journal of Personality and Social Psychology, 40,* 899–905.

Ross, L., & Nisbett, R. E. (1991). *The person and the situation: Perspectives on social psychology.* New York: McGraw-Hill.

Rothstein, S. I., & Pierotti, R. (1988). Distinctions among reciprocal altruism, kin selection, and cooperation and a model for the initial evolution of beneficent behavior. *Ethology and Sociobiology, 9,* 189–209.

Ruble, D. N., & Rholes, W. S. (1983). The development of children's perceptions and attributions about their social world. In J. H. Harvey, W. Ickes, & R. F. Kidd (Eds.), *New directions in attribution research* (Vol. 3). Hillsdale, NJ: Erlbaum.

Rushton, J. P. (1975). Generosity in children: Immediate and long term effects of modeling, preaching, and moral judgment. *Journal of Personality and Social Psychology, 31,* 459–466.

Rushton, J. P. (1982). Social learning theory and the development of prosocial behavior. In N. Eisenberg (Ed.), *The development of prosocial behavior* (pp. 77–105). New York: Academic Press.

Rushton, J. P. (1984). The altruistic personality: Evidence from laboratory, naturalistic and self-report perspectives. In E. Staub, D. Bar-Tal, J. Karylowski, & J. Reykowski (Eds.), *Development and maintenance of prosocial behavior*. New York: Plenum.

Rushton, J. P. (1989). Genetic similarity, human altruism, and group selection. *Behavioral and Brain Science, 12,* 503–518.

Rushton, J. P., & Campbell, A. C. (1977). Modeling, vicarious reinforcement and extraversion on blood donating in adults: Immediate and long term effects. *European Journal of Social Psychology, 7,* 297–306.

Rushton, J. P., Fulker, D. W., Neale, M. C., Nias, D. K. B., & Eysenck, H. J. (1986). Altruism and aggression: The heritability of individual differences. *Journal of Personality and Social Psychology, 50,* 1192–1198.

Rushton, J. P., Russell, R. J. H., & Wells, P. A. (1984). Genetic similarity theory: Beyond kin selection altruism. *Behavioral Genetics, 14,* 179–193.

Rushton, J. P., & Teachman, G. (1978). The effects of positive reinforcement, attributions, and punishment on model induced altruism in children. *Personality and Social Psychology Bulletin, 4,* 322–325.

Rutte, C. G., Wilke, H. A. M., & Messick, D. M. (1987). Scarcity or abundance caused by people or the environment as determinants of behavior in the resource dilemma. *Journal of Experimental Social Psychology, 15,* 208–216.

Sagi, A., & Hoffman, M. L. (1976). Empathic distress in the newborn. *Developmental Psychology, 12,* 175–176.

Salovey, P. (1992). Mood-induced self-focused attention. *Journal of Personality and Social Psychology, 62,* 699–707.

Salovey, P., Mayer, J. D., & Rosenhan, D. L. (1991). Mood and helping: Mood as a motivator of helping and helping as a regulator of mood. In M. S. Clark (Ed.), *Review of personality and social psychology: Vol. 12. Prosocial behavior* (pp. 215–237). Newbury Park, CA: Sage.

Samuelson, C. D., & Messick, D. M. (1986a). Alternative structural solutions to resource dilemmas. *Organizational Behavior and Human Decision Processes, 37,* 139–155.

Samuelson, C. D., & Messick, D. M. (1986b). Inequities in access to and use of shared resources in social dilemmas. *Journal of Personality and Social Psychology, 51,* 960–967.

Samuelson, C. D., Messick, D. M., Rutte, C. G., & Wilke, H. (1984). Individual and structural solutions to resource dilemmas in two cultures. *Journal of Personality and Social Psychology, 47,* 94–104.

Sarason, B. R., Sarason, I. G., Hacker, T. A., & Basham, R. B. (1985). Concomitants of social support: Social skills, physical attractiveness, and gender. *Journal of Personality and Social Psychology, 49,* 469–480.

Savin-Williams, R. C. (1987). *Adolescence: An ethological perspective.* New York: Springer-Verlag.

Savin-Williams, R. C., Small, S., & Zeldin, R. S. (1981). Dominance and altruism among adolescent males: A comparison of ethological and psychological methods. *Ethology and Sociobiology, 2,* 167–176.

Schachter, S., & Singer, J. E. (1962). Cognitive, social, and physiological determinants of emotional state. *Psychological Review, 69,* 379–399.

Schaller, M., & Cialdini, R. B. (1988). The economics of empathic helping: Support for a mood management motive. *Journal of Experimental Social Psychology, 24*, 163–181.

Schlenker, B. R., Dlugolecki, D. W., & Doherty, K. (1994). The impact of self-presentations on self-appraisals and behavior: The power of public commitment. *Personality and Social Psychology Bulletin, 20*, 20–34.

Schmidt, G., & Weiner, B. (1988). An attribution-effect-action theory of behavior: Replications of judgments of help-giving. *Personality and Social Psychology Bulletin, 14*, 610–621.

Schmitt, D. R., & Marwell, G. (1972). Withdrawal and reward reallocation as responses to inequity. *Journal of Experimental Social Psychology, 8*, 207–221.

Schroeder, D. A., Dovidio, J. F., Sibicky, M. E., Matthews, L. L., & Allen, J. L. (1988). Empathy and helping behavior: Egoism or altruism. *Journal of Experimental Social Psychology, 24*, 333–353.

Schroeder, D. A., Jensen, T. D., Reed, A. J., Sullivan, D. K., & Schwab, M. (1983). The actions of others as determinants of behavior in social trap situations. *Journal of Experimental Social Psychology, 19*, 522–539.

Schwartz, S. H. (1977). Normative influences on altruism. In L. Berkowitz (Ed.), *Advances in experimental social psychology* (Vol. 10, pp. 222–280). New York: Academic Press.

Schwartz, S. H., & Howard, J. A. (1981). A normative decision-making model of altruism. In J. P. Rushton & R. M. Sorrentino (Eds.), *Altruism and helping behavior: Social, personality, and developmental perspectives* (pp. 189–211). Hillsdale, NJ: Erlbaum.

Schwartz, S. H., & Howard, J. A. (1982). Helping and cooperation: A self-based motivational model. In V. J. Derlega & J. Grzelak (Eds.), *Cooperation and helping behavior: Theories and research* (pp. 327–353). New York: Academic Press.

Schwartz, S. H., & Howard, J. A. (1984). Internalized values as motivators of altruism. In E. Staub, D. Bar-Tal, J. Karylowski, & J. Reykowski (Eds.), *Development and maintenance of prosocial behavior* (pp. 229–255). New York: Plenum.

Searcy, E., & Eisenberg, N. (1992). Defensiveness in response to aid from a sibling. *Journal of Personality and Social Psychology, 62*, 422–433.

Segal, N. L. (1984). Cooperation, competition, and altruism within twin sets: A reappraisal. *Ethology and Sociobiology, 5*, 163–177.

Segal, N. L. (1991, April). *Cooperation and competition in adolescent MZ and DZ twins during the Prisoners' Dilemma Game.* Paper presented at the meeting of the Society for Research in Child Development, Seattle, WA.

Segal, N. L. (1993). Twin sibling, and adoption methods: Test of evolutionary hypotheses. *American Psychologist, 48*, 943–956.

Selman, R. L. (1980). *The growth of interpersonal understanding.* Orlando, FL: Academic Press.

Settle, T. (1993). Fitness and altruism: Traps for the unwary, bystander and biologist alike. *Biology and Philosophy, 8*, 61–84.

Shapiro, S., Skinner, E. A., Kessler, L. G., Von Korff, M., German, P. S., Tischler, G. L., Leaf, P. J., Benham, L., Cottler, L., & Regier, D. A. (1984). Utilization of health and mental health services: Epidemiologic catchment area sites. *Archives of General Psychiatry, 41*, 971–978.

Shell, R., & Eisenberg, N. (1992). A developmental model of recipient's reactions to aid. *Psychological Bulletin, 111*, 413–433.

Sherman, P. W. (1981). Kinship demography, and Belding's ground squirrel nepotism. *Behavioral Ecology and Sociology, 8*, 604–606.

Sherman, P. W. (1985). Alarm calls of Belding's ground squirrels to aerial predators: Nepotism or self-preservation? *Behavioral Ecology and Sociobiology, 17*, 313–323.

Shotland, R. L. (1992). A theory of the causes of courtship rape: Part 2. *Journal of Social Issues, 48*, 127, 144.

Shotland, R. L., & Heinold, W. D. (1985). Bystander response to arterial bleeding: Helping skills, the decision-making process, and differentiating the helping response. *Journal of Personality and Social Psychology, 49*, 347–356.

Shotland, R. L., & Huston, T. L. (1979). Emergencies: What are they and how do they influence bystanders to intervene? *Journal of Personality and Social Psychology, 37*, 1822–1834.

Shotland, R. L. & Straw, M. (1976). Bystander response to an assault: When a man attacks a woman. *Journal of Personality and Social Psychology, 34*, 990–999.

Sibicky, M. E., & Dovidio, J. F. (1986). Stigma of psychological therapy: Stereotypes, interpersonal reactions and the self-fulfilling prophecy. *Journal of Counseling Psychology, 33*, 148–154.

Sibicky, M. E., Schroeder, D. A., & Dovidio, J. F. (in press). Empathy and helping: Considering the consequences of intervention. *Basic and Applied Social Psychology.*

Siebenalar, J. B., & Caldwell, D. K. (1956). Cooperation among adult dolphins. *Journal of Mammology, 37*, 410–414.

Sills, D. L. (1957). *The volunteers.* Glencoe, IL: Free Press.

Simmel, G. (1950). The metropolis and mental life. In K. H. Wolff (Ed.), *The sociology of Georg Simmel.* New York: Free Press.

Simmons, R. G., Marine, S. K., & Simmons, R. L. (1977). *Gift of life: The effect of organ transplantation on individual, family, and societal dynamics.* New Brunswick, NJ: Transaction Books.

Simner, M. L. (1971). Newborn's response to the cry of another infant. *Developmental Psychology, 5*, 136–150.

Simoni, J. M., Adelman, H. S., & Nelson, P. (1991). Perceived control, causality, expectations and help-seeking behaviour. *Counseling Psychology Quarterly, 4*, 37–44.

Slavin, R. E. (1980, September). *Cooperative learning and desegregation.* Paper presented at the annual meeting of the American Psychological Association, Montreal.

Slavin, R. E. (1990, December/January). Research on cooperative learning: Consensus and controversy. *Educational Leadership*, pp. 52–54.

Smith, C. L., Gelfand, D. M., Hartmann, D. P., & Partlow, M. E. P. (1979). Children's causal attributions regarding help giving. *Child Development, 50*, 203–210.

Smith, G. L., & DeWine, S. (1991). Perceptions of subordinates and requests for support: Are males and females perceived differently when seeking help? *Group and Organizational Studies, 16*, 408–427.

Smith, K. D., Keating, J. P., & Stotland, E. (1989). Altruism reconsidered: The effect of denying feedback on a victim's status to empathic witnesses. *Journal of Personality and Social Psychology, 57*, 641–650.

Smith, R. E., Smythe, L., & Lien, D. (1972). Inhibition of helping behavior by a similar or dissimilar nonreactive fellow bystander. *Journal of Personality and Social Psychology, 23*, 414–419.

Snyder, M. (1992a). *Basic research and practical problems: The promise of a functional personality and social psychology.* Paper presented at the annual meeting of the American Psychological Association, Washington, DC.

Snyder, M. (1992b). Of persons and situations, of personality and social psychology. *Psychological Inquiry, 3*, 94–98.

Snyder, M., & Omoto, A. M. (1992a). Volunteerism and society's response to the HIV epidemic. *Current Directions in Psychological Science, 1*, 113–116.

Snyder, M., & Omoto, A. M. (1992b). Who helps and why? In S. Spacapan & S. Oskamp (Eds.), *Helping and being helped: Naturalistic studies* (pp. 213–239). Newbury Park, CA: Sage.

Sobel, D. (1981, August 4). Thousands with mental health insurance choose to pay own bill. *The New York Times*, III 1:1.

Sober, E. (1988). What is evolutionary altruism? *Special Issue of Journal of Philosophy* [Special issue: M. Matthen & B. Linsky (Eds.), Philosophy and biology], *14*, 75–100.

Sober, E. (1992). The evolution of altruism: Correlation, cost and benefit. *Biology and Philosophy, 7*, 177–188.

Sroufe, L. A., Cooper, R. G., & DeHart, G. B. (1992). *Child development its course and nature.* New York: McGraw-Hill.

Staub, E. (1971). Helping a person in distress: The influence of implicit and explicit "rules" of conduct on children and adults. *Journal of Personality and Social Psychology, 17*, 137–144.

Staub, E. (1974). Helping a distressed person: Social, personality, and stimulus determinants. In L. Berkowitz (Ed.), *Advances in experimental social psychology* (Vol. 7, pp. 293–341). New York: Academic Press.

Staub, E. (1981). *Positive social behavior and morality: Vol. 1. Social and personal influences.* New York: Academic Press.

Staub, E. (1992). The origins of caring, helping and nonaggression: Parental socialization, the family system, schools, and cultural influence. In S. Oliner & P. Oliner (Eds.), *Embracing the other: Philosophical, psychological, and theoretical perspectives on altruism* (pp. 390–412). New York: New York University Press.

Steblay, N. M. (1987). Helping behavior in rural and urban environments: A meta-analysis. *Psychological Bulletin, 102*, 346–356.

Steele, C. (1992). Race and the schooling of black Americans. *The Atlantic, 269*(4), 68–78.

Stein, D. D., Hardyck, J. A., & Smith, M. B. (1965). Race *and* belief: An open and shut case. *Journal of Personality and Social Psychology, 1*, 281–289.

Sterling, B., & Gaertner, S. L. (1984). The attribution of arousal and emergency helping: A bidirectional process. *Journal of Experimental Social Psychology, 20*, 286–296.

Straus, M. A., Gelles, R. J., & Steinmetz, S. K. (1980). *Behind closed doors: Violence in the american family.* New York: Anchor Press.

Stryker, S. (1980). *Symbolic interactionism: A social structural version.* Menlo Park: Benjamin/Cummings.

Swinyard, W. R., & Ray, M. L. (1979). Effects of praise and small requests on receptivity to direct-mail appeals. *Journal of Social Psychology, 108*, 177–184.

Tajfel, H. (1970). Experiments in intergroup discrimination. *Scientific American, 223*, 96–102.

Takeuchi, D. T., Leaf, P. J., & Kuo, H. S. (1988). Ethnic differences in the perception of barriers to help-seeking. *Social Psychiatry and Psychiatric Epidemiology, 23*, 273–280.

Tanner, J. (1966). *Growth at adolescence*. Oxford: Blackwell Scientific.

Taormina, R. J. (1984). *Foreign aid deservingness and allocation: Group versus individual decision-making*. Unpublished doctoral dissertation, University of California, Santa Barbara.

Taormina, R. J., & Messick, D. (1983). Deservingness for foreign aid: Effects of need, similarity, and estimated effectiveness. *Journal of Applied Social Psychology, 13*, 371–391.

Taormina, R. J., Messick, D., Iwawaki, S., & Wilke, H. (1988). Cross-cultural perspectives on foreign aid deservingness decisions. *Journal of Cross-Cultural Psychology, 19*(4), 387–412.

Taylor, S. E., & Lobel, M. (1989). Social comparison activity under threat: Downward comparison. *Psychological Review, 96*, 569–575.

Terkel, S. (1975). *Working*. New York: Avon.

Tesser, A. (1988). Toward a self-evaluation maintenance model of social behavior. In L. Berkowitz (Ed.), *Advances in experimental social psychology* (Vol. 21, pp. 181–227). New York: Academic Press.

Tessler, R. C., & Schwartz, S. H. (1972). Help-seeking, self-esteem, and achievement motivation: An attributional analysis. *Journal of Personality and Social Psychology, 21*, 318–326.

Thom, B. (1986). Sex differences in help-seeking for alcohol problems. I. The barriers to help-seeking. *British Journal of Addiction, 81*, 777–788.

Thom, B. (1987). Sex differences in help-seeking for alcohol problems: II. Entry into treatment. *British Journal of Addiction, 82*, 989–997.

Thomas, G. C., & Batson, C. D. (1981). Effect of helping under normative pressure on self-perceived altruism. *Social Psychology Quarterly, 44*, 127–131.

Thomas, G. C., Batson, C. D., & Coke, J. S. (1980). Do good samaritans discourage helpfulness?: Self-perceived altruism after exposure to highly helpful others. *Journal of Personality and Social Psychology, 40*, 194–200.

Thompson, R. A. (1987). Empathy and emotional understanding: The early development of empathy. In N. Eisenberg & J. Strayer (Eds.), *Empathy and its development* (pp. 119–146). Cambridge, England: Cambridge University Press.

Tietjan, A. (1986). Prosocial reasoning among children and adults in a Papua New Guinea society. *Developmental Psychology, 22*, 861–868.

Tiger, L., & Fox, R. (1971). *The imperial animal*. New York: Holt, Rinehart, & Winston.

Ting, J-C. (1992). *Experience, interest, modeling, and being asked to help: A four factor model of international helping*. Unpublished master's thesis. University of Wisconsin.

Toda, M., Shinotsuka, H., McClintock, C. G., & Stech, F. (1978). Development of competitive behavior as a function of culture, age, and social comparison. *Journal of Personality and Social Psychology, 36*, 835–839.

Toi, M., & Batson, C. D. (1982). More evidence that empathy is a source of altruistic motivation. *Journal of Personality and Social Psychology, 43*, 281–292.

Trivers, R. L. (1971). The evolution of reciprocal altruism. *Quarterly Review of Biology, 46*, 35–37.

Turner, J. C., Hoff, M. A., Oakes, P. J., Reicher, S. D., & Wetherell, M. S. (1987). *Rediscovering the social group: A Self-categorization theory*. Oxford, England: Basil Blackwell.

Turner, R. H. (1978). The role and the person. *American Journal of Sociology, 84*, 1–23.

Unger, L. (1991). Altruism as a motivation to volunteer. *Journal of Economic Psychology, 12*, 71–100.

Unger, R. K., & Crawford, M. (1992). *Women and gender: A feminist psychology*. Philadelphia: Temple University Press.

United States Bureau of the Census. (1992). *Statistical abstract of the United States, (1992)* (112th ed.). Washington, DC: Author.

United States Department of Labor. (1990, March 29). *U.S. Bureau of Labor Statistics News*, pp. 90–154.

Vaughan, K. B., & Lanzetta, J. T. (1980). Vicarious instigation and conditioning of facial expressive and autonomic responses to a model's expressive display of pain. *Journal of Personality and Social Psychology, 38*, 909–923.

Veroff, J. B. (1981). The dynamics of help-seeking in men and women: A national survey study. *Psychiatry, 44*, 189–200.

Vine, I. (1983). Sociobiology and social psychology: Rivalry or symbiosis? *British Journal of Social Psychology, 22*, 1–11.

Wallston, B. S., Alagna, S. W., DeVellis, B. M., & DeVellis, R. F. (1983). Social support and physical health. *Health Psychology, 2*, 367–391.

Walster, E., Walster, G. W., & Berscheid, E. (1978). *Equity: Theory and research*. Boston: Allyn & Bacon.

Walton, M. D., Sachs, D., Ellington, R., Hazlewood, A., Griffin, S., & Bass, D. (1988). Physical stigma and the pregnancy role: Receiving help from strangers. *Sex Roles, 18*, 323–331.

Warren, P. E., & Walker, I. (1991). Empathy, effectiveness, and donations to charity: Social psychology's contribution. *British Journal of Social Psychology, 30*, 325–337.

Webley, P., & Lea, S. E. G. (1993). The partial unacceptability of money in repayment for neighborly help. *Human Relations, 46*, 65–76.

Wegner, D. M., & Crano, W. D. (1975). Racial factors in helping behavior: An unobtrusive study. *Journal of Personality and Social Psychology, 32*, 901–905.

Weiner, B. (1980). A cognitive (attribution)-emotion-action model of motivated behavior: An analysis of judgments of help-giving. *Journal of Personality and Social Psychology, 39*, 186–200.

Weiner, B. (1986). *An attributional theory of motivation and emotion*. New York: Springer-Verlag.

Weiner, B., Perry, R. P., & Magnusson, J. (1988). An attributional analysis of reactions to stigmas. *Journal of Personality and Social Psychology, 55*, 738–748.

Weisbrod, B. (1975). Towards a theory of the non-profit sector. In E. Phelps (Ed.), *Altruism, morality, and economic theory* (pp. 171–195). New York: Russell Sage.

Weiss, H. M., & Knight, P. A. (1980). The utility of humility: Self-esteem, information search and problem solving efficiency. *Organizational Behavior and Human Performance, 25*, 216–223.

West, S. G., Whitney, G., & Schnedler, R. (1975). Helping a motorist in distress: The effects of sex, race, and neighborhood. *Journal of Personality and Social Psychology, 31*, 691–698.

White, J. W., & Sorenson, S. B. (1992). Adult sexual assault: An overview of the research. *Journal of Social Issues, 48*, 1–9.

Whiting, B. B., & Edwards, C. P. (1988). *Children of different worlds: The formation of social behavior*. Cambridge, MA: Harvard University Press.

Whiting, B. B., & Whiting, J. J. M. (1975). *Children of six cultures*. Cambridge: Harvard University Press.

Wicklund, R. A. (1975). Objective self-awareness. In L. Berkowitz (Ed.), *Advances in experimental social psychology* (Vol. 8, pp. 233–275). San Diego, CA: Academic Press.

Wilcox, B. L., & Birkel, R. C. (1983). Social networks and the help-seeking process: A structural perspective. In A. Nadler, J. Fisher, & B. M. DePaulo (Eds.), *New directions in help seeking: Vol. 3. Applied perspectives on help-seeking and -receiving* (pp. 235–255). New York: Academic Press.

Will, C. (1986). *Was Einstein right? Putting general relativity theory to the test*. New York: Basic Books.

Williamson, G., & Clark, M. S. (1989). Effects of providing help to another and of relationship type on the provider's mood and self-evaluation. *Journal of Personality and Social Psychology, 56*, 722–734.

Wills, T. A. (1983). Social comparison in coping and help seeking. In B. M. DePaulo, A. Nadler, & J. D. Fisher (Eds.), *New directions in helping: Vol. 2. Help seeking* (pp. 109–142). New York: Academic Press.

Wills, T. A. (1991). Social support and interpersonal relationships. In M. S. Clark (Ed.), *Review of personality and social psychology: Vol. 12. Prosocial behavior* (pp. 265–289). Newbury, CA: Sage.

Wills, T. A. (1992). The helping process in the context of personal relationships. In S. Spacapan & S. Oskamp (Eds.), *Helping and being helped: Naturalistic studies* (pp. 17–48). Newbury Park CA: Sage.

Wills, T. A., & DePaulo, B. M. (1991). Interpersonal analysis of the help-seeking process. In C. R. Snyder & D. R. Forsyth (Eds.), *Handbook of social and clinical psychology* (pp. 350–375). New York: Pergamon.

Wilson, D. S. (1992). On the relationship between evolutionary and psychological definitions of altruism and selfishness. *Biology and Philosophy, 7*, 61–68.

Wilson, D. W., & Kahn, A. (1975). Rewards, costs, and sex differences in helping behavior. *Psychological Reports, 36*, 31–34.

Wilson, J. P. (1976). Motivation, modeling, and altruism: A person × situation analysis. *Journal of Personality and Social Psychology, 34*, 1078–1086.

Windle, M., Miller-Tutzauer, C., Barnes, G. M., & Welte, J. (1991). Adolescent perceptions of help-seeking resources for substance abuse. *Child Development, 62*, 179–189.

Wispé, L. G. (Ed.). (1978). *Altruism, sympathy, and helping*. New York: Academic Press.

Wispé, L. G., & Freshley, H. B. (1971). Race, sex, and sympathetic helping behavior: The broken bag caper. *Journal of Personality and Social Psychology, 17*, 59–65.

Wolcott, I. H. (1986). Seeking help for marital problems before separation. *Australian Journal of Sex, Marriage and Family, 7*, 154–164.

Wolfe, T. (1940). *The web and the rock*. Garden City, NY: Sundial Press.

Wong, P., & Weiner, B. (1981). When people ask "why" questions and the heuristics of attributional search. *Journal of Personality and Social Psychology, 40,* 650–663.

Worchel, S., & Simpson, J. A. (Eds.). (1993). *Conflict between people and groups: Causes, processes, and resolutions.* Chicago, IL: Nelson-Hall.

Yakimovich, D., & Saltz, E. (1971). Helping behavior: The cry for help. *Psychonomic Science, 23,* 390–400.

Yinon, Y., & Landau, M. O. (1987). On the reinforcing value of helping behavior in a positive mood. *Motivation and Emotion, 11,* 83–93.

Younger, J. (1993, December 2). Fishy short cut to mapping human genome. *The New York Times,* pp. B7, B9.

Zahn-Waxler, C., Radke-Yarrow, M., & King, R. (1979). Child rearing and children's prosocial initiations toward victims of distress. *Child Development, 50,* 319–330.

Zahn-Waxler, C., Radke-Yarrow, M., Wagner, E., & Chapman, M. (1992a). Development of concern for others. *Developmental Psychology, 28,* 126–136.

Zahn-Waxler, C., Robinson, J. L., & Emde, R. N. (1992b). The development of empathy in twins. *Developmental Psychology, 28,* 1038–1047.

Zajonc, R. B. (1980). Feeling and thinking: Preferences need no inferences. *American Psychologist, 35,* 151–175.

Zeliony, R. D., & Wills, T. A. (1990, August). *Predictors of AIDS risk in methadone patients.* Paper presented at the meeting of the American Psychological Association, Boston.

Zillman, D. (1983). Transfer of excitation in emotional behavior. In J. T. Cacioppo & R. E. Petty (Eds.), *Social psychophysiology: A sourcebook* (pp. 215–240). New York: Guilford.

Zimbardo, P. G. (1977). *Shyness: What it is, what to do about it.* Reading, MA: Addison-Wesley.

Name Index

Abrahams, R. D., 4
Achenbach, C. J., 163
Adelman, H. S., 205
Ahammer, I. M., 146
Aiken, M. T., 172
Ainsworth, M. D. S., 147
Alagna, S. W., 188
Alcock, J., 103
Aliquipiso, 4
Allen, H., 43
Allen, J., 82
Allen, L., 129
Allen, M., 273
Allen, N., 177, 249
Allison, S. T., 244
Altabe, M. N., 177
Altman, A., 211
Amato, P. R., 16, 18, 237
Anderson, J. C., 249
Anderson, V. L., 249
Archer, R. L., 79
Aries, E. J., 163
Aristotle, 10
Arlitt, A. H., 114
Arnold, E., 173
Aron, A., 73
Aronfreed, J., 119–121, 142
Aronson, E., 13, 14, 203
Arps, K., 67
Ausubel, N., 8

Ba Yua, 4
Badcock, C. R., 107
Balogh, R. D., 106, 107
Bandura, A., 63, 146, 175
Bar-Tal, D., 128–132, 134, 135, 140
Barbee, A. P., 162, 188, 193, 194, 198, 207
Barnes, G. M., 192
Barnett, M. A., 113, 193
Baron, R. S., 189
Barrientos, S., 82, 83
Barton, E. J., 149
Basham, R. B., 195

Bass, D., 50
Bates, J., 94
Batson, C. D., 9, 18, 19, 21, 43, 45, 64, 74–83, 99, 113, 118, 153, 169, 179–181, 245, 259, 264, 281
Batson, J. G., 79–83
Baum, A., 31, 204
Baumann, D. J., 67, 69, 128
Baumeister, R. F., 38
Bayly, M. J., 83
Bays, G., 164
Bealer, R., 193
Beaman, A. L., 67, 154
Beattie, M., 282
Behner, G., 273
Bell, P. A., 31, 224
Bellah, R. N., 234
Beller, R., 135
Ben-Itzhak, S., 200
Bengston, V., 155
Benham, L., 204
Benson, P. L., 48, 50
Benson, S. M., 68
Berger, M., 30
Berkowitz, L., 85, 87, 177
Berkowitz, W., 242, 243
Bernzweig, J., 119
Berscheid, E., 85, 86
Bersoff, D. M., 266
Bickman, L., 30, 38, 50
Bierhoff, H. W., 178
Billings, A., 188
Birkel, R. C., 186
Blake, J. A., 108
Bochner, S., 159
Bode, K. A., 241
Bolen, M. H., 179
Bond, M., 49
Borgida, E., 41, 111
Borod, J. C., 273
Borofsky, G. L., 164, 165
Bowers, J. K., 159
Bowlby, J., 147
Boykin, A. W., 4

Brandt, J. R., 80
Bregman, N. J., 146
Brehm, J. W., 214
Brehm, S. S., 214
Brenner, G. F., 188
Brewer, M. B., 104, 224, 225
Brody, G. H., 145
Broll, L., 29
Broman, C. L., 195
Bromet, E. J., 205
Brown, D. L., 107
Brown, M. S., 149
Bruder-Mattson, S. F., 194
Bruun, S. E., 224
Buck, R., 120, 121, 124, 272, 274
Burnam, M. A., 195
Buss, D., 93, 273
Byrne, D., 48

Caldwell, D. K., 99
Caldwell, R. A., 198
Call, V., 236
Callero, P. L., 59, 60, 148, 154, 155, 234, 239
Campbell, A. C., 152
Campbell, D. T., 4
Canon, L. K., 30
Caporael, L. R., 104
Carlo, G., 118, 119, 178
Carlson, M., 69
Carnevale, P. J., 85, 222
Carpentieri, A. M., 198
Carrington, P. I., 85
Cass, R. C., 228
Catalano, R., 186
Catania, J. A., 204
Cernoch, J. M., 106, 107
Chambre, S. M., 60
Chandler, M., 139
Chao, C. C., 226
Chapman, M., 116, 137
Chappell, N., 235
Charng, H. W., 155, 175
Cheek, J. M., 198
Chemerinski, A., 196
Chernick, L., 180
Chesner, S. P., 38
Childs, J., 46
Christopher, F. S., 143
Cialdini, R. B., 64, 66–69, 74, 75, 79, 81, 82,
    128–131, 134, 280, 285
Cimino, C., 273
Clark, M., 37, 47, 124, 187
Clark, R. D., III, 15, 34, 41, 42, 73, 87, 114
Clarkson, M. B. E., 231
Clary, E. G., 248, 286
Clewett, A. S., 147
Clore, G. L., 163
Coates, T. J., 204
Cohen, S., 188
Coke, J. S., 153

Colby, A., 133, 134, 175
Cole, C. M., 154
Confucius, 7
Conner, C., 41, 111
Conner, R., 161
Constanzo, P., 152
Cook, M., 120
Cooper, R. G., 94
Corcoran, D., 124
Corney, R., 193
Cottler, L., 204
Cowen, E. L., 246
Craiger, J. P., 177
Crano, W. D., 50
Crawford, M., 164
Crockenberg, S. B., 145
Crocker, J., 215
Cross, J. A., 179
Crowley, M., 159–163, 193, 194
Cunha, D., 226
Cunningham, M. R., 64–66, 110, 113, 121, 194,
    274, 278, 280
Curry, R. L., 109
Cutrona, C. E., 189

Dabbs, J. M., 164, 273
Damon, M., 175
Daniels, A. K., 60
Daniels, L. R., 85, 87, 177
Danko, G. P., 159
Darby, B. K., 67
Darley, J. M., 14, 21, 22, 27–33, 36–38, 40, 43, 52,
    55, 56, 169, 189, 222, 224
Darvill, T. J., 159
Darwin, C., 95, 100
Davenport, L., 200
Davis, J. A., 238
Davis, K. E., 214
Davis, M. H., 79, 113, 118, 139, 176, 177
Dawes, R. M., 221, 224, 225
Dawkins, R., 19, 98–100
DeFries, J. C., 93
DeHart, G. B., 94
DeKay, W. T., 93, 273
Dell, D. M., 194
Demerath, N. J., III, 172
DeMorest, J. A., 46
Denny, R. O., 26, 34, 50, 58
DePaulo, B. M., 107, 184, 185, 196–199, 204, 206,
    207, 213
Derlega, V. J., 188, 194, 207
Dertke, M. C., 163
Deutsch, F. M., 46
Deutsch, M., 32
DeVellis, B. M., 188
DeVellis, R. F., 188
Dew, M. A., 205
DeWine, S., 193, 194
Diaz-Loving, R., 79
Dimberg, U., 120

Ditzian, J. L., 46
Dlugolecki, D. W., 107
Doherty, K., 107
Donnerstein, E., 73
Dooley, D., 186
Dopheide, M., 1
Douglas, J., 230
Dovidio, J. F., 14, 15, 42, 43, 48–52, 55, 64, 70–72, 81, 82, 113, 157, 163, 171, 175, 181, 206, 245
Drake, A. W., 60
Druen, P. B., 194
Dubro, A. F., 226
Dull, W. R., 198
Dunn, L. O., 205
Dutton, D. G., 50, 51, 73
Dyck, J. L., 79, 179
Dynes, R. R., 244, 245

Eagley, A. H., 159–163, 193, 194
Easterbrook, J. A., 73
Eccles, J. P., 161
Edelmann, R. J., 46, 50
Edney, J. J., 228
Edwards, C. P., 148
Eibl-Eibesfeldt, I., 95
Einstein, A., 271
Eisenberg, N., 63, 70, 71, 113, 118, 119, 134–137, 140, 142, 143, 145, 147, 149, 152, 162, 171, 176–179, 194, 213, 216, 217, 263, 276, 278
Eisenberg-Berg, N., 134
Eisenbud, L., 70, 71, 119, 145
Ellington, R., 50
Ellsworth, P., 241
Ellyson, S. L., 163
Emde, R. N., 118
Enzle, M. E., 88
Erdoes, R., 4
Essock-Vitale, S. M., 111
Evans, G., 50
Eysenck, H. J., 118
Eysenck, M. V., 73

Fabes, R. A., 63, 70, 71, 113, 118, 119, 140, 143, 145, 148, 162
Fahrner, H., 242, 243
Farber, E., 148
Feldman, N. S., 140
Feldman, R., 49
Festinger, L., 36
Finkelstein, S. N., 60
Fishbane, R., 206
Fisher, J. D., 31, 193, 200, 211, 215, 216
Fiske, A. P., 91, 130, 142, 275
Flavell, J. H., 139
Fools Crow, 7
Fortenbach, V. A., 79
Foss, R., 39
Foushee, H. C., 79
Fox, J. W., 195
Fox, R., 91

Fraser, S. C., 153, 154
Freedman, J. L., 153, 154
Freetly, A. H., 165
Freifeld, T., 177
Freshley, H. B., 50
Freud, S., 83
Frey, D. L., 50, 87
Friedrich, L. K., 147
Friedrich-Cofer, L. K., 147
Frieze, I. H., 196
Fritz, A. S., 139
Fritzsche, B. A., 48, 177, 179
Froming, W. J., 129
Fulker, D. W., 118
Fultz, J., 45, 67, 69, 75, 79, 143, 153

Gabriele, T., 30
Gaertner, S. L., 15, 42, 48, 50, 51, 55, 70, 71–73, 87, 175
Galaskiewic, J., 230, 231
Garvey, C., 85
Geis, G., 161, 181
Gelfand, D. M., 143
Gelles, R. J., 165
Genovese, K., 13, 14, 16, 21, 25, 27, 36, 37, 43, 54–58, 157, 160, 165, 270
George, J. M., 86
Gerard, H., 32
Gergen, K. J., 171, 214, 241
Gergen, M. M., 171, 241
German, P. S., 204
Ghiselin, M. T., 98
Gibbons, F. X., 89
Gibbs, J., 133
Gilligan, C., 141
Ginsburg, B., 120, 121, 124, 272
Glance, N. S., 225
Glassman, R. B., 107
Glick, P., 46
Glor-Scheib, S., 193, 203
Goethals, G. R., 36
Goffman, E., 107
Goldberg, L. R., 3
Goldin, L., 195, 207
Golding, J. M., 195
Gollwitzer, P. M., 79
Gonzalez, A., 203
Good, G. E., 194
Goodnow, J. J., 145
Goranson, R., 85
Gottleib, B. H., 194
Gouldner, A., 85
Graziano, W. G., 171, 178, 179, 278, 280
Greenberg, J., 198, 282
Greene, T., 31
Grev, R., 66
Griffin, S., 50
Griffitt, C., 82
Gross, A. E., 189, 191, 206, 209
Gruder, C. L., 110, 180

Grusec, J. E., 62, 63, 141–145, 147–152
Guild, W., 39
Gulley, M. R., 194

Hacker, T. A., 195
Hala, S., 139
Hall, C. L., 68
Hallam, J., 73
Hamilton, W. D., 100
Hannah, M. E., 46, 155, 235
Hardin, G., 221, 250, 286
Hardyck, J. A., 50
Hare, R. D., 181
Hargis, K., 47
Harmon, M., 199
Harrell, K. L., 81
Harris, M. B., 68, 164
Harter, S., 195
Hartmann, D. P., 143
Harvey, M. D., 88
Harvey, S., 46
Hatfield, E., 214
Havens, B., 235
Hawking, S., 271
Hayes, R. B., 204
Hazlewood, A., 50
Hearold, S., 147
Hedge, A., 29
Heider, F., 150, 214
Heinold, W. D., 40
Hernandez, A. C. R., 41
Hesley, J. W., 180
Hicklin, D., 189
Hill, F. E., 199
Hitler, A., 172
Hobbes, T., 11
Hodgkinson, V. A., 236
Hoffman, M. L., 63, 64, 71, 113–115, 144, 145, 174
Hogg, M. A., 286
Holloway, S., 48
Hoover, C. W., 89
Hopper, J. R., 88
Horn, J., 118
Hornstein, H. A., 48, 63, 64, 152
Horwitz, A. V., 206
Hotze, C. A., 46
Houlihan, D., 67
Hovanitz, C. A., 194
Howard, J. A., 55, 88, 89
Huang, Y. H., 159
Huberman, B. A., 225
Hume, R. E., 7
Humphrey, G., 114
Hunt, M., 91, 174, 175
Huston, T., 31, 161, 181
Huston-Stein, A., 147

Inhelder, B., 139
Isen, A. M., 45–48
Israel, A. C., 149

Iwawaki, S., 239

Jaet, B. P., 193
Jarymowicz, M., 287
Jegerski, J., 110
Jensen, R., 129
Jensen, T. D., 223
Johnson, D. W., 203
Johnson, F. L., 163
Johnson, Magic, 48
Johnson, M. E., 193
Johnson, R. T., 203
Jones, E. E., 214

Kahn, A., 20, 46, 85
Kaminer, W., 251
Kamzan, M., 50
Kaniasty, K., 245, 246
Karabenick, S. A., 48, 202, 203
Karbon, M., 119
Karp, L., 47
Karylowski, J., 280
Kayal, P., 242
Kayson, W. A., 48
Keating, C. F., 163
Keating, J. P., 47, 80
Kelley, H. H., 150, 214
Kelley, K., 48
Kellock, I., 46
Kennedy, M., 232
Kenrick, D. T., 67, 128–130
Kerr, N. L., 224
Kessler, L. G., 204
Kessler, R., 195
Kestenbaum, J., 148
King, R., 118
Kipnis, D. M., 147
Kirsch, A. D., 236
Kitayama, S., 274, 275, 285
Klein, R., 178
Klentz, B., 154
Knapp, J. R., 202, 203
Knight, G. P., 226
Knight, P. A., 196–198, 200
Knowles, E. S., 89
Kohlberg, L., 133, 134, 141
Komorita, S. S., 220, 222
Korte, C., 38, 238
Kramer, R. M., 224, 225
Kramp, P., 178
Kraus, S. J., 118
Krebs, D., 18, 100, 104
Krupat, E., 39
Kuczynski, L., 149
Kunz, P. R., 85
Kuo, H. S., 195

Lake, R. A., 50
Lambers, S., 245

Lamberti, D. M., 46
Landau, M. O., 67
Langer, E. J., 195
Lanzetta, J. T., 71
Lao-Tze, 7, 8
Latané, B., 14, 21, 22, 27, 28–33, 36–38, 40, 41, 52, 55, 56, 164, 189, 222, 224
Lathunga, L. A., 273
Lawless, H., 245
Lazarus, R. S., 258
Lea, S. E. G., 187
Leaf, P. J., 195, 204
Leahy, R. L., 138
Lee, L., 148, 236, 239
Leek, M., 107
Leerhsen, C., 200
Leiser, T., 131
Lennon, R., 135, 162
Lennox, V. L., 51
Lepper, M., 144
Lerner, R. M., 48
Leung, K., 49
Levin, P. F., 47
Lewin, K., 167, 180
Lewis, S., 200
Lewis-Levin, T., 135
Lieberman, M., 133, 195
Liebert, R. M., 146
Liebrand, W. G. B., 220, 226
Lien, D., 36
Lightner, C., 243
Lin, K., 284
Lindzey, G., 13, 14
Lipscomb, T. J., 146
Litman, C., 145
Lizzadro, T., 180
Lobel, M., 208
Lockard, J. S., 79
London, P., 148, 174
Lopreato, J., 107
Lubaroff, D. M., 189
Luce, C., 118
Lui, L., 228
Luks, A., 281
Lyon, D., 282
Lytton, H., 145

Ma, H. -K., 88
Macaulay, J. R., 18, 152
MacCoun, R. J., 224
MacDonald, K., 113
Machiavelli, N., 10
MacLean, P. D., 114
Madsen, R., 234
Maggiano, N. A., 163
Magnusson, J., 87
Mails, T. E., 7
Maimonides, M., 8
Main, M., 148
Major, B., 215

Malchior, L. A., 198
Mallozzi, J., 48
Mann, J., 51
Mansbridge, J., 286
Manteufal, L., 41, 111
Manucia, G. K., 69
Marcus, P., 60
Marine, S. K., 111
Marks, E. L., 181
Markus, H. R., 274, 275, 285
Martichuski, D. K., 224
Martin, G. B., 114
Marwell, G., 86, 172
Maslach, C., 241
Maszk, P., 119
Mathews, K. E., 30
Mathy, R. M., 135
Matthews, K. A., 118
Matthews, L. L., 82
May-Plumlee, T., 143
Mayer, J. D., 30
Mayseless, O., 196, 211
McAllister, H. A., 146
McCall, G. J., 155
McCarthy, P. M., 79
McClearn, G. E., 93
McClintock, C. G., 226
McConahay, J. B., 203
McDermott, V., 48
McDougall, W., 12, 13
McGillis, D., 214
McGovern, L. P., 45, 46
McGuire, A. M., 17, 18, 188
McGuire, M. T., 111
McKusick, L., 204
McLaughlin, C., 30
McLaughlin, F. J., 104
McManus, J. A., 204
McMaster, M. R., 80
McMillen, D. L., 30
McMullen, P. A., 189, 191, 206, 209
McNally, S., 135
McQueen, L. R., 224
McTavish, J., 224
Mechanic, D., 190
Medvene, L. J., 185, 208, 209, 284
Meindl, J. R., 287
Melamed, B. G., 188
Meltzoff, A. N., 95
Messe, L. A., 164
Messick, D., 220, 228, 239
Meter, K., 171
Mezei, L., 49
Midlarsky, E., 46, 59, 155, 174, 181, 235, 281, 278, 285
Mikolay, D., 163
Milgram, S., 30
Miller, D. T., 100
Miller, J., 136, 141, 266
Miller, N., 69, 287

Miller, P., 71, 113, 118, 119, 135, 140, 176
Miller, W. R., 196
Miller-Tutzauer, C., 192
Mills, J., 124, 187
Mineka, S., 120
Mintz, L. B., 194
Moghaddam, F. M., 111, 241, 275
Monson, T. C., 180
Monto, M. A., 41
Moore, B. S., 142, 147, 149, 152
Moore, C., 231
Moore, J., 105
Moore, L., 249
Moos, R., 188
Morgan, C. J., 105
Moriarty, T., 38
Morris, D., 91
Morris, S. C., III, 199
Morris, W. N., 245
Morse, S. J., 241
Moss, M. K., 62
Mueller, C. W., 73
Munekata, H., 137
Murchison, C. A., 13
Murphy, B., 119
Murray, J. P., 146
Murrell, S. A., 246
Myers, D., 18

Nadler, A., 20, 186, 188, 193, 196, 199–201, 207,
    211, 215, 216, 285
Neal, C., 134
Neale, M. C., 118
Neighbors, H. W., 195
Nelson, M., 200
Nelson, P., 205
Nelson-LeGall, S., 193, 203
Nestmann, F., 246, 247
Neuringer-Benefiel, H. E., 179
Newcomb, M. D., 41
Newman, R. S., 195, 207
Nias, D. K. B., 118
Nida, S. A., 33
Ninomiya, K., 137
Nisbett, R. E., 60, 168–170
Norris, F. H., 245, 246
Nuttin, J., 226

O'Boyle, C., 119
O'Quin, K., 45
Oakes, P. J., 286
Oden, A., 179
Ohmman, A., 120
Oleson, K. C., 75, 78, 82, 113
Oliner, P. M., 70, 148, 171–178
Oliner, S. P., 70, 178, 171–178
Omoto, A. M., 42, 248, 249
Orbell, J. M., 225
Orenstein, L., 248
Ortiz, A., 4
Osborne, J. G., 98, 149

Ostrove, N. M., 205
Otten, C. A., 38, 163, 177, 181

Packel, E. W., 107
Paduano, A., 153
Page, R. A., 62
Park, J. Y., 139
Parks, C. D., 220, 222
Partlow, M. E. P., 143
Paskal, V., 119–121
Pasternack, J., 135
Pate, S., 245
Paulhus, D. L., 79
Pavlov, I. P., 119
Pearce, J. L., 60
Pearce, P. L., 16, 18
Pecjak, V., 139
Peekna, H. M., 81
Pegg, I., 50
Penner, L. A., 38, 48, 163, 177–179, 181, 282
Pennington, D., 139
Peri, N., 196
Perry, R. P., 87
Piaget, J., 138, 139
Pierotti, R., 104
Pietromonaco, P., 169
Piliavin, I. M., 16, 29, 46, 52, 54
Piliavin, J. A., 15, 16, 29, 42, 46, 52–55, 59, 60, 70,
    71, 123, 144, 148, 154, 155, 159–164, 171, 175,
    191, 193, 234, 236, 239
Plato, 10, 11
Platt, J., 228
Plomin, R., 93
Pomazal, R. S., 163
Pomper, S., 200
Porter, R. H., 106, 107
Powell, A. L., 80
Preston, M., 154
Pruitt, D. G., 85, 222
Pryor, J. B., 204

Quarantelli, E. L., 245

Rabow, J., 41
Radke-Yarrow, M., 116, 137, 139
Radley, A., 232
Rahim, A. R. A., 139
Raven, B. H., 20
Raviv, A. M., 131, 135, 140, 199
Ray, M. L., 153
Reddy, R. D., 46, 59, 60, 84, 171, 233
Redler, E., 141, 150
Reed, A. J., 223
Reeder, G. D., 204
Regan, D. T., 65, 86
Regier, D. A., 204
Reicher, S. D., 286
Reinhart, M. A., 198
Rholes, W. S., 140
Riad, J. K., 273
Richardson, J. J., 231

Ridley, M., 98, 100
Robinson, J. L., 118
Rodell, P., 193
Rodin, J., 52, 54, 195
Rokeach, M., 49
Romer, D., 180
Rosen, S., 199, 278
Rosenhan, D. L., 30, 47, 148, 174, 274, 287
Rosenman, R. H., 118
Ross, L., 60, 169, 170
Roth, K., 134
Rothstein, S. I., 104
Rousseau, J. -J., 11
Rubin, J. Z., 20
Ruble, D. N., 140
Ruggiero, M., 161
Rushton, J. P., 104, 106, 118, 142, 143, 146, 149,
    152, 168, 177, 179, 249
Russell, D. W., 189
Russell, R. J. H., 106
Rutte, C. G., 228

Saas-Kortsaak, P., 150
Sachs, D., 50
Sagi, A., 71, 114
Salovey, P., 30, 47, 65, 69
Saltz, E., 32
Sample, B., 242, 243
Sample, H., 242, 243
Samuelson, C. D., 228
Sanders, D. Y., 30
Sanders, P. S., 38
Sarason, B. R., 195
Sarason, I. G., 195
Saunders, L. C., 193
Savin-Williams, R. C., 171
Schachter, S., 64
Schaerfl, L. M., 224
Schaller, M., 38, 67, 75, 79, 81, 118
Schindler, O., 173
Schlenker, B. R., 107
Schmidt, G., 64
Schmitt, D. R., 86
Schnedler, R., 50
Schoenrade, P. A., 153
Schroeder, D. A., 42, 81–83, 223–225
Schulberg, H. C., 205
Schwab, M., 223
Schwartz, M., 47
Schwartz, S. H., 38, 55, 84, 88, 89, 215
Searcy, E., 211
Segal, N. L., 94, 107, 111, 112
Seipel, M., 241
Selman, R. L., 140
Settle, T., 100
Shaffer, D. R., 145
Shaklee, H., 224
Shalker, T. E., 47
Shapiro, S., 204
Shea, C., 135
Shell, R., 135, 195, 216, 217

Sherman, P. W., 107, 109
Shinotsuka, H., 226
Shotland, R. L., 31, 40, 165, 166
Sibicky, M. E., 81, 82, 206
Siebenalar, J. B., 99
Sills, D. L., 60
Simmel, G., 237
Simmons, J. L., 155
Simmons, R. G., 111
Simmons, R. L., 111
Simner, M. L., 114
Simoni, J. M., 205
Simpson, J. A., 222
Simutis, Z. M., 149, 150
Singer, J. E., 64
Sinisi, C. S., 193
Skinner, B. F., 83
Skinner, E. A., 204
Slavin, R. E., 203
Slingsby, J. K., 81
Sliwa, C., 243
Small, S., 171
Smith, C. L., 143
Smith, G. L., 193, 194
Smith, K. D., 47, 80
Smith, M. B., 50
Smith, P., 107, 119
Smith, R. E., 36
Smith, T. W., 238
Smythe, L., 36
Snyder, M., 42, 60, 180, 248, 249, 280, 286
Sobel, D., 206
Sober, E., 19, 122, 123
Socrates, 10
Solomon, G. S., 30
Sopolsky, H. M., 60
Sorenson, S. B., 165
Sparkman, P., 245
Sparling, S., 65
Speer, A. L., 119, 178
Sprafkin, J., 146
Sprecher, S., 214
Sprengelmeyer, P., 80
Sroufe, L. A., 94, 148
Staub, E., 34, 39, 62, 149, 177, 274, 278, 280, 285
Steblay, N. M., 29, 39, 154, 237
Stech, F., 226
Steele, C., 215
Stein, A. H., 147
Stein, D. D., 50
Steinberg, J., 66
Steinmetz, S. K., 165
Sterling, B., 73
Stollack, G. E., 164
Stone, A. W., 181
Stotland, E., 47, 80
Strain-Clark, C., 46
Straus, M. A., 165
Straw, M., 165
Stryker, S., 155
Suh, K., 119

Sullivan, D. K., 223
Sullivan, W. M., 234
Sunaday, E., 30
Susman, E. J., 147
Swaim, G. W., 198
Swidler, A., 234
Swinyard, W. R., 153
Switzer, G., 178

Tajfel, H., 286
Takeuchi, D. T., 195
Tanner, J., 98
Taormina, R. J., 239–241
Taylor, D. M., 111, 275
Taylor, R. J., 195
Taylor, S. E., 208
Taylor, S. P., 46
Teachman, G., 143
Teger, A., 30
Terkel, S., 251
Tesser, A., 199
Tessler, R. C., 215
Thom, B., 191, 193
Thomas, G. C., 153
Thompson, R. A., 114
Thorndike, E. L., 62
Tice, D. M., 38
Tice, T., 85
Tietjan, A., 137
Tiffany, M., 203
Tiger, L., 91
Ting, J-C., 239
Tipton, S. M., 234
Tischler, G. L., 204
Tobin, S. S., 195
Toda, M., 226
Todd, R. M., 81
Toi, M., 77
Tremain, M., 50
Trivers, R. L., 104, 109
Troyer, D., 178
Tucker, L., 48
Turner, J. C., 286
Turner, R. H., 155

Unger, L., 233
Unger, R. K., 159–164, 193

Van de Kragt, A. J. C., 225
Van Run, G. J., 226
Vanderplas, M., 45
Varney, L. L., 79
Vaughan, K. B., 71
Veroff, J. B., 195
Vincent, J. E., 67
Vine, I., 107, 109
Von Korff, M., 204

Wagner, E., 116
Wagner, F., 194
Walker, I., 47
Wallston, B. S., 188

Walster, E., 85, 86, 214
Walster, G. W., 85, 86
Walton, M. D., 50, 54
Warren, P. E., 47
Waugh, G., 38, 163
Webley, P., 187
Weeks, J. L., 179
Wegner, D. M., 50
Weiner, B., 64, 65, 87, 190
Weisbrod, B., 229
Weiss, H. M., 196–198, 200
Weitzman, M. S., 236
Wells, P. A., 106
Welte, J., 192
West, S. G., 50
Weston, D. R., 148
Wetherell, M. S., 286
Whitcher-Alagna, S., 215
White, J. W., 165
Whiting, B. B., 141, 149
Whiting, J. J. M., 141, 149
Whitney, G., 50
Wicklund, R. A., 89
Wilcox, B. L., 186
Wilke, H., 220, 228, 239
Will, C., 271
Williams, M., 65
Williamson, G., 67
Wills, T. A., 184, 185, 189, 196–200, 204–208
Wilson, D. S., 100
Wilson, D. W., 33, 46
Wilson, J. P., 34, 181
Windle, M., 192
Winstead, B. A., 188, 194
Wispe, L. G., 18, 50
Wolcott, I. H., 205
Wolfe, T., 237
Wong, P., 190
Wood, E. E., 89
Wood, W., 194
Woolcott, M., 85
Worchel, S., 222
Word, L. E., 34, 41, 73
Worman, B., 245
Wright, R., 181
Wright, S. C., 111, 275

Yakimovich, D., 32
Yankeelov, P. A., 194
Yinon, Y., 67
Younger, J., 273
Yousif, Y. H., 29
Yunovitz, R., 199

Zahn-Waxler, C., 116, 118, 137, 139
Zaidman, B., 203
Zajonc, R. B., 258, 260
Zeldin, R. S., 171
Zeliony, R. D., 189
Zemke, P. E., 228
Zillman, D., 73
Zimbardo, P. G., 198

Subject Index

❖

Academic problems, seeking help for, 202–203, 208
Acquisition processes, 265
Adult socialization, 152–155
Affective empathy, 64–70, 139–140
Affective models, 258–265, 269–271, 275
African Americans, 4, 50–52, 87, 96, 172, 174, 195, 235
Age differences:
  in help seeking, 195
  in helping, 39, 126–156, 235
Aggression, 91
AIDS, 46, 61, 87, 204, 242, 249
Alcoholism, 96, 191–192, 200, 209
Almsgiving, 8
Altruism, 13
  definition, 18–20, 92
  genetic factors, 92–124, 272–277
  See also Empathy-altruism model
Altruistic genes, 105–106
Altruistic motivation, 18–19, 74–78, 265, 275
Altruistic personality type, 171–176, 179
Ambiguous situations, 34–35
Androgynous gender roles, 163
Animal research, 94–109, 122
Antisocial behavior, 15
Arousal: cost-reward model, 53–55, 70–74, 83, 144, 161, 164, 191–192, 222
Asian-Americans, 97
Attachment theory, 147–148
Attention, 29–31, 267
Attraction, 48
Attributions, 64–65, 71–74, 87, 140–141, 150–153, 169–171, 214–215
Aversive racism, 50–52

Behavioral genetics, 92–94, 111, 273–274
Behaviorism, 83
Bible stories, 7
Biological factors, 92–124, 259–261, 272–277
Blacks (see African Americans)
Blood donors, 60, 148, 152–155, 233–234

Brain mechanisms, 113–114, 259, 273
Bureau of Labor Statistics, 59
Bystander effect, 35
Bystander inhibition, 35–36
Bystander intervention, Latané-Darley decision model, 13–14, 21, 28–41, 52–58, 189, 222–224

Carnegie Hero Commission, 160–161
Census Bureau, 59
Charitable activities, 59, 171, 229–249
Cheating, 107–109
Children, development of altruism in, 126–156
Children's television programming, 146–147
Civil rights activists, 148, 172, 174
Classical conditioning, 119
Codependency, 282–283
Cognitive empathy, 139–140
Cognitive learning models, 130–132, 138–142, 152, 258, 265–271, 275
Cognitive reinterpretation, 54
Collective helping, 219–251, 284–286
Collectivist cultures, 49, 87–88
Communal relationships, 186–189
Communication, 120–121, 124, 149–151, 223–225, 260, 272
  See also Spontaneous communication
Community activism, 242–247
Cooperation, definition of, 20–21
Cooperative helping, 203
Cost-reward analyses, 42–58, 160–161, 164, 199, 210, 222–223, 268, 282–283
  See also Arousal: cost-reward model
Crisis hotlines, 199
Cross-cultural studies, 49, 87–88, 92, 94, 111, 131, 134, 137, 141, 148–149, 159, 171–172, 225–227, 238–242, 265–266, 274–276
Cross-racial helping, 49–52
Cross-species studies, 94–109, 122–123
Cultural diversity, 141–142
Cultural factors (see Cross-cultural studies)

331

Darwinian theory, 95, 98, 100, 105
Date rape, 166
Decision-making models:
    in help giving, 28–41, 53–58, 222–228, 268–269
    in help seeking, 189–191, 209–210
Demographic variables, 158–166, 193–196, 232–237
Developmental issues, 126–156
Diffusion of responsibility, 36–38, 51, 54
Disaster relief, 243–246
Discipline, parental, 144–145, 174
Dispositional empathy, 176
Distress cues, 31–32
Domestic violence, 164–166
Donor characteristics, 60–61, 171, 229–251

Educational level, 233–234
Ego-centrality, 200
Egoistic motivation, 18, 74–80, 265, 275
Emergency situation, 31–32, 54
Emotional consequences (see cost-reward analyses)
Emotional social support, 188
Emotions, 12, 64–70, 113, 263, 267–268
    See also Moods
Empathic arousal, 64, 70
Empathic concern, 18, 74–83, 263
Empathic joy, 80–81
Empathy, 18, 113–114, 119–120, 176–178, 260
    heritability of, 114–119, 272–273
Empathy-altruism model, 74–83
Empathy-specific punishment, 78–80
Empathy-specific reward, 80–81
Environmental stressors, 29–31
Equity theory, 86–87, 213–214, 262–263
Ethnic differences, 195–196, 234–235
Evolutionary altruism, 122, 263
Evolutionary theory, 95, 98, 100, 105
Exchange relationships, 187, 207
Executive help seeking, 203
Extensivity, 175, 177

Facial expressions, 95, 121
Fairness, 86–87, 213–214, 262–263
Family socialization, 107, 111, 262
    See also Parent-child interaction
Feelings (see Emotions)
Field research, 187
First-aid training, 41
Foot-in-the-door technique, 153–154
Foreign aid, 238–242
Functional analysis technique, 248–249
Fundamental attribution error, 169

Gay community, 242
Gay Men's Health Crisis, 242
Gender:
    definition of, 161–162
    (See Sex differences)
Gender roles, 161–164, 193–195
Genetic factors, 92–124, 259–261, 272–277

Give-some dilemmas, 221, 225, 228
Golden rule, 104
Good Samaritan parable, 4–5, 15
Group helping, 184–218, 284–286
Group identity, 225
Group selection theory, 100–101, 105–106
Guardian Angels, 243
Guilt feelings, 65, 67–68, 263

Handbook of Social Psychology, 13, 14
Health-care issues, 41, 188–189, 203–205, 283
Hedonism, 78, 81, 83, 114, 135
Help-seeking behaviors, 184–218, 257
Help-seeking paradox, 208
Helping behaviors, definition of, 16–18
Helping professions, 162, 177, 195, 206
Help providers, characteristics of, 47–52
Help recipients, characteristics of, 75, 184–218
Heritability, definition of, 96, 117
Heroism, 1, 73, 161–163, 175, 178, 243
Hinduism, 8
Hispanics, 195, 226, 235, 284
Holocaust, 96, 172–174, 249
Homosexual community, 242
Hormonal factors, 95
Human Genome Project, 93, 272–273
Humanitarianism, 60–61

Image-reparation hypothesis, 66
Inclusive fitness, 100
Indians (see Native Americans)
Indirect intervention, 54, 57
Individual differences, 158, 276
Individualist cultures, 49, 87
Infant studies, 71, 95, 106–107
    of empathy, 114–120
Informal helping, 16, 17, 246–247
Informational social influence, 32
Innate behaviors, 91–124
Instincts, 12
Institutional helping, 284
Instrumental (operant) conditioning, 62, 142
Instrumental help seeking, 203
Instrumental social support, 188
Interactionism (person-situation), 180–183
Intergroup actions, 50
Internalization of norms, 129–130
International helping, 238–242
Interpersonal attraction, 48
Islam, 8
Isolation, 105–106

Jews in Nazi Germany, 69, 96, 148, 171–174, 249, 262
Job-related helping, 247
Judeo-Christian traditions, 8
Just-world hypothesis, 86–87

Kin selection theory, 101–104, 260–261
Kitty Genovese incident, 13–14, 21, 25–28, 36–37, 43, 55–58, 157, 160, 165, 270

Law of effect, 62, 83
Learned helpfulness, 62–63
Learned helplessness, 203
Limbic system, 114, 259
Love withdrawal, 144

Male-female differences (*see* Sex differences)
Marital problems, seeking help for, 205
Market sector, 229
Maturational changes, 126–156, 262, 267
Medical care issues, 41, 188–189, 203–205, 283
Minimal contributing sets, 225
Misattribution paradigm, 72–73
Modeling, 145–148
Moods, 30–31, 47, 48, 65–70, 81–83, 211, 267
    See also Emotions
Moral behavior, 10–12, 25–26, 60, 133, 134, 174, 262
Moral dilemmas, 133
Moral exhortation, 149–150
Moral reasoning, 132–137
Mothers Against Drunk Driving, 243
Motivation, 59–90, 264–265, 277–279

Native Americans, 4–7
Natural disasters, 243–246
Nature-nurture issues (*see* Genetic factors)
Nazis, 69, 96, 171–174
Negative reinforcement (*see* Reinforcement)
Negative-state relief model, 67–70, 74, 81–84, 129
Neurological mechanisms, 113–114, 259, 273
Norm of reciprocity, 85–86, 104–105
Norms, 38–39, 84–89, 129, 267

Objective self-awareness, 89
Observational learning (modeling), 145–148
Operant conditioning, 62, 142
Other-oriented empathy, 177–179, 181

Parent-child interaction, 12, 119–120, 142–149, 174, 276
Parental discipline, 144–145, 174
Parental self-sacrifice, 103
Payoff-matrix analysis, 223
Peer tutoring, 213
Personal norms, 84–89, 267
Personal responsibility, 36–38, 51, 54, 89, 175, 177
Personality variables:
    definition of, 158–159
    in help giving, 167–183, 195–198
    in help seeking, 225–227
    See also interactionism
Physiological mechanisms, 113–114, 259, 273
Pleasure principle, 83
Pluralistic ignorance, 33
Positive reinforcement (*see* Reinforcement)
Postconventional morality, 134
Power assertion, 145
Preaching, 149
Preconventional morality, 133
Presocialization stage, 129–130

Private sector, 229
Prosocial behavior:
    cultural perspectives, 4–7
    definition of, 15–16
    personality traits and, 167–183
    philosophical perspectives, 10–12
    religious perspectives, 7–10
    scientific study of, 12–14
    sex differences in, 159–166
Prosocial moral reasoning, 134–137
Prosocial motivation, 59
Prosocial personality type, 171–172
Psychoanalytic theory, 83
Psychological problems, seeking help for, 205–206
Public goods (give-some) dilemmas, 221, 225, 228
Public sector, 229
Punishment, 63, 78–80, 131, 143–145

Racial differences:
    in help seeking, 195–196
    in helping, 50–52, 234–235
Racial prejudice, 50–52, 96
Rape, 165–166
Reactance theory, 214
Reciprocal altruism, 85–86, 105–109, 260–263
Reginald Denny incident, 26, 35, 50, 58
Reinforcement, 42–47, 62, 80–81, 142–145
Religious beliefs, 4–10, 169, 236
Resource management (take-some) dilemmas, 221, 228
Rewards, 42–47, 61, 80–81, 142–145, 281
    See also Cost-reward analyses
Role identity, 153–155
Rural-urban differences, 29, 39, 237–238

Sadness, 81–83
Self-consequences, 215–216
Self-deception (cheating), 107–109
Self-efficacy, 175, 178–179
Self-esteem, 196–198, 213–217, 241
Self-help groups, 200, 208
Self-image, 79, 153–155, 203, 208, 211, 263
Self-interest, 10–11, 25–26, 60, 83, 181, 286
Self-sacrifice, 18, 103, 111
Senior Gleaners, 242
Sex differences:
    in help seeking, 164–166, 193–195
    in helping, 88, 159–166, 235
Sex stereotypes, 98, 160–164
Sexual assaults, 165–166
Shyness, 198
Similarity factor:
    in help giving, 36, 48–49, 106–107, 225–226
    in help seeking, 200, 207–208
Situational variables:
    in help giving, 20, 29–34, 73, 167, 170–171, 177–178, 180–183, 239, 262, 267
    in help m seeking, 191, 198–206
    See also Interactionism

Skinnerian behaviorism, 83
Social activism, 231–251
Social comparison theory, 36, 208–209
Social cues, 107
Social Darwinism, 95
Social dilemmas, 21, 219–228
Social influence hypothesis, 33–34
Socialization:
   in adulthood, 153–155
   in childhood, 129–132, 142–152, 174, 267
Socialization model, 129–130
Social learning, 63, 142–152
Social norms, 38–39, 84–88, 129, 267
Social responsibility, 87–88, 177
Social roles, 155
Social support, 188–189, 193–195, 200, 246
Social traps, 221
Socioeconomic status, 233
Sociopathy, 182
Spontaneous communication, 120–121, 260, 272
Spontaneous helping, 13, 17, 222, 226, 232
Step-level public goods dilemmas, 225
Stimulus overload, 30–31, 38–39
Strangers (*see* Similarity factor)
Structural solutions, 227–228
Substance abuse, 96, 192

Sunshine Foundation, 243
Support groups, 200, 209
Survival of the fittest, 95, 98, 100

Take-some dilemmas, 221, 228
Talmudic writings, 8, 9
Taoism, 8
Television, impact on children, 146–147
Temperaments, 94, 119
Third sector, 232
Threat to self-esteem model, 213–217
Trait theories of personality, 167–171
Trustworthiness, 226
Twin studies, 111–112, 117–118, 263

Urban-rural differences, 29, 39, 237–238

Verbal communication, 149–151
Vernacular altruism, 123
Volunteerism, 59–61, 155, 171, 177, 229–251, 286

Women:
   physical violence against, 164–166
   See also Sex differences
World War II, 69, 148, 171–174